Acknowledgem ts

At the start this book was just an idea. but the idea l Dynan, the Parish Priest of Our Lady Star of the Sea since 2010. He reco vould be exactly one hundred years since the parish was set up in th ngst a year of celebrations to mark this happy event, what m in which was recorded the life of our parish over the e no book.

To begin with, I was able to look at an account of the . Mary Pollard, in a contributing chapter she provided for the book bouring but entirely independent parish of Our Lady and St. Joseph, Sta the first hundred years of that parish. Whilst this book is obviously larger chapter, it maintains the same structure as Mary's work, and I am deeply indebted to her.

The problem we faced was that much of the story of Our Lady Star of the Sea in Tilbury reached back further than the memories and lives of even our most venerable parishioners, and it involved people who are no longer with us. The solution was Father Stewart Foster, the Diocesan Archivist who has single-handedly organised the records of all of the parishes in the Brentwood Diocese. When we turned to him, he readily agreed to allow us access to the Tilbury records, held in the archive at Brentwood Cathedral. More than this, he organised each file in advance for me, so that the relevant material was easily accessed on each visit. The details acquired in the archives form the larger part of our book.

For the early history of the area I made use of a number of local authors, and the details of these writers and their works will be found in the bibliography at the end of the book. I am indebted to Thurrock Reference Library who allowed us to make use of some of their photographs and sketches of the early days of Tilbury. Similarly, *The Thurrock Gazette* permitted us to use a few of their articles within the book. Some material on the Apostleship of the Sea was taken from the AoS website, with their kind agreement. In each case, all of these references are acknowledged within the body of the text.

Fortunately, there are many parishioners with their own stories to tell, and these stories are found in the chapter entitled Parish Voices, where individual memories and some family photographs are found.

Our parish has an additional blessing, the Convent of the Sisters of Mercy. The Sisters helped to facilitate many of the interviews, provided material directly themselves and made use of their contacts to enable us to record the memories of some of the Sisters who were based in Tilbury in earlier years. Parish Secretary, Pauline Lacey, was also most helpful when parishioners were being interviewed. Thanks are also due to Jonathan Dynan (Jay) for the many beautiful photographs he took of the Church.

I am indebted to my wife, Felicity, for her gentle support and understanding whilst the book was being written. Writing is essentially a solitary occupation. In addition, both Felicity and Father Paul worked as proof readers to locate and correct the many mistakes which peppered the first draft.

My kind and sincere thanks to all of those named above, and for allowing me to take the credit for what was essentially an exercise in teamwork.

KSR : 2018

The Parish of Our Lady
Star of the Sea.
Tilbury & ESSEX 1918-2018

Published by
Dynan Publishing

KEVIN REDMOND
with a foreword by
Fr. PAUL DYNAN.

front cover: Church of Our Lady Star of the Sea, Tilbury

back cover: Icon of Our Lady Star of the Sea

ISBN 978-0-9573479-1-5

Table of Contents

Foreword

This book has been published in the lead up to the celebration of the Centenary of the Parish of Our Lady Star of the Sea, Tilbury in 2018.

After Bishop Thomas McMahon appointed me as Parish Priest to care for Stanford-le-Hope and Tilbury parishes, I moved into the parish in October 2010. A short while later, I contacted Fr Stewart Foster, Diocesan Archivist for Brentwood Diocese, to ascertain the official dates of the parish, and he informed me that Tilbury Parish had been established on 2nd August 1918. The history books inform us that the Parish of Our Lady Star of the Sea can trace its roots back to the late 19th century in the era of the very Rev. Canon Keens, who had been asked to take pastoral care of the people of Tilbury. In May 1887 the first stones were laid to begin the building of the church-chapel dedicated to Our Lady Star of the Sea. Indeed, the parish marked this fact by holding Golden Jubilee celebrations on 18th October 1937. The incumbent, Fr Patrick O'Donnell, arranged a number of events, including luncheon aboard *SS Strathard*.

The earliest recorded days and events were when Tilbury was part of the Westminster Diocese. However, in 1917 the Diocese of Brentwood was formed and on 2nd August 1918 the Parish of Our Lady Star of the Sea as we know it today was officially recognised. Fr Michael Hannan was noted as its first Parish Priest. In the light of these facts, on 2nd August 2018 the parish will celebrate its centenary.

With this in mind, a programme of events was planned throughout the year by which we could celebrate the centenary in 2018. One strand of this planning was the compilation of a history of the parish to coincide with the planned liturgical and social events. This book was always intended to be a companion to the book previously written by Kevin Redmond to celebrate the centenary of Stanford-le-Hope Parish in 2013. I would like to thank Kevin, who has worked tirelessly to gather together historical material from the Diocesan archives, parishioners and numerous other sources to compile what has proved to be a wonderful record of our parish history.

Fr Paul Dynan BA, STB, MA, FIBMS
Parish Priest, Tilbury

Chapter One : A History of Tilbury

Some local historians assert that there was little human habitation of Tilbury before the construction of the docks that give the modern town its significance. The area, however, was certainly inhabited for many hundreds, even thousands of years before this. The oldest known resident of what is now Tilbury was discovered in 1883 during the excavations for the building of the docks. His skeleton was found thirty feet below the surface, and his remains were exhibited at the British Museum, where the leading archaeologist, Sir Richard Owen, estimated that he came from the Paleolithic or Early Stone Age. Later studies suggested that 'Tilbury Man' was rather more recent, and that he lived in the early Neolithic era. Even this later date suggests an age for the skeleton of over 8,000 years.

It is believed that during the Roman invasion of Britain in AD 43, a sizeable group of Britons was chased into East Anglia, fording the River Thames at East Tilbury. There were clearly Roman settlements established in the area, for remains of Roman ovens and pottery, dotted along the river bank, have been found, and burial groups of that time have been excavated at Chadwell St. Mary. The dock construction also unearthed a Roman tombstone at Tilbury, with the inscription "Demetrius to Heraclia his wife (set up the stone at the expense of her own estate) as a memorial to her".

The area has links with St. Cedd, who was born in the early part of the seventh century. Educated with his three brothers at the monastery of Lindisfarne on the Northumbrian Coast, he was sent to do missionary work in Essex. He obtained a large number of converts among the East Saxons, and was ordained as Cedd, Bishop of the East Saxons. He was given two sites as bases for his episcopal duties in Essex, one on the southern bank of what is now the Blackwater, and one at Tilaburg, now Tilbury. That these two sites were on river banks was no accident; in the days when roads were relatively few and often poorly maintained, river transport was a much more efficient way to travel. A monastery was built at Tilbury but it did not survive, and both East and West Tilbury lay claim to the site.

The exploits of Bishop Cedd were recorded in the Venerable Bede's *Ecclesiastical History of the English Nation*. In an entry dated A.D. 653 he writes:

> Cedd, having received the Episcopal dignity (as Bishop of Essex), returned to his province and pursuing the work he had begun with more ample authority built churches in several places, ordaining priests and deacons to assist him in the work of faith and the ministry of baptising, especially in the city which, in the language of the Saxons, is called Ithancestir (Bradwell on Sea), as also that which is named Tilaburg …. on the bank of the Thames, where gathering a flock of servants of Christ, he taught them to observe the discipline of regular life, as far as those rude people were then capable. (my underlining)

The existence of St. Cedd's well, where tradition holds that Cedd baptised his first convert in Essex, has suggested to some that this gave rise to the name of Chadwell, although in the language of the Saxons, Old English, this name would be translated simply as 'cold well'. To confuse things further, Cedd had a brother called Chad who was also active in the area, spreading the message of Christianity. Whichever option is preferred, Chadwell's name is rooted in Saxon history.

In the Domesday Book, Tilbury is referred to as 'Tiliberia' (Tilla's fortified place) after the head of a Saxon clan involved in the Anglo-Saxon conquest of Britain (A.D. 450 – 600). It was noted in the Domesday Book as a good place for grazing sheep! The land in and around Chadwell was recorded as belonging to the Bishop of London, Grime the Sheriff, Hubert de Port and William the Conqueror's half-brother, Bishop Odo of Bayeux. The latter was given so much land in England after the Conquest that he became the second most powerful man in the kingdom – until he was arrested and imprisoned for planning a military attack on Rome. The Domesday Book recorded that there were four manors in Chadwell, Chadwell itself, Ingleby, Longhouse and Biggin.

During the reign of Henry VIII, the development of primitive canons made it possible to attack sea-borne invaders before they came to land. Accordingly, a line of coastal sea forts was built to defend the country, two being built in Essex, at Harwich and Tilbury. Although the bulwarks at Harwich were eroded away by the North Sea, the fort at Tilbury remains largely intact, with later additions in the seventeenth and eighteenth century. Prior to these defences, the protection of London was left to the lighting of beacons to warn people of an approaching invasion and to allow precious time to organise an army. On the Essex side of the Thames, these beacons were at Shoeburyness, Fobbing, Tilbury and Horndon on the Hill. This scheme had been set up in 1377, with instructions laid down for those who scoured the coast and manned the beacons. The watchmen

> who for the time being shall be at the same beacons … as soon as they can espy any vessels of the enemy coming with sails or oars, toward said river … make besides by horn and by cry that they can make to warn the countries around to come in their force to the said river and each to succour the other to withstand their enemies.

Two blockhouses were built, at East and West Tilbury, with the latter being used as the base for the larger fort constructed in the following two centuries. Strange details survive of these constructions. We know that 150,000 bricks were used to build just one of the blockhouses which, together with 200 tons of chalk, presumably for the foundations, and a large amount of timber added up to £131.13.4d. The wages of the workmen amounted to £80. It had a garrison of nine, and a small range of artillery pieces, including a demi-culverin (capable of firing an eight pound cannonball 1,800 feet), one or two sakers (four pound cannonball over a distance of one and a half miles) and two smaller guns. Captain Francis Grant was paid one shilling a day, his deputy eight pence, whilst the porter, two soldiers and four gunners were each paid sixpence. (*Ministry of Works Official Guide Book*) It will be seen that the difference between the pay of the Captain and the rest of the men was comparatively small, but it was not exactly a good rate of pay for anyone at the fort. Some of the gunners supplemented their pay by working as, for example, boat-builders or inn-keepers.

These defences were the backdrop for one of the most iconic events in British history. In 1588, the imminent arrival of the Spanish Armada put the future of the nation in peril. Angered by English support for the Protestant faction in the Netherlands which was ruled by Catholic Spain, and annoyed by English adventurers who attacked and plundered Spanish shipping, Philip II of Spain amassed a huge armada of fighting ships which were to collect an army of some 30,000 troops from the Spanish Netherlands and invade England.

Unfortunately, in the early years of Elizabeth I's reign, she had relied on her diplomatic skills to deal with the perceived threats from France and Spain. As a consequence, England's sea defences had deteriorated from the time of her father, Henry VIII. When the Earl of Leicester came to Tilbury shortly before the Armada set sail, he found the fort in a sorry state, with rotting gun platforms. Emergency repairs were begun, but Elizabeth was so alarmed by the inadequate fortifications at Tilbury that she stationed an army of over twenty thousand men there, to defend against a possible landing force.

Deciding to put on a brave face and appear undaunted by the very real threat of an invasion, Elizabeth I rode out to review one of her armies marshalled at Tilbury under the Earl of Leicester. As memorable as the date 1066, or the signing of the Magna Carta, the queen's address to her troops from horseback still stirs the heart:

> My loving people, we have been persuaded by some that are careful of our safety, to take heed how we commit ourselves to armed multitudes for fear of treachery. But I assure you, I do not desire to live to distrust my faithful and loving people. Let tyrants fear. I have always so behaved myself, that, under God, I have placed my chiefest strength and safeguard in the loyal hearts and goodwill of my subjects; and therefore I am come amongst you, as you see, at this time, not for my recreation and disport, but being resolved, in the midst and heat of battle, to lay down for my God, and for my kingdom, and for my people, my honour and my blood, even in the dust. I know that I have the body of a weak and feeble woman, but I have the heart and stomach of a king, and of a king of England too, and think foul scorn that Parma or Spain, or any prince of Europe should dare to invade the borders of my realm; to which rather than any dishonour shall grow by me, I myself will take up arms; I myself will be your general, judge and rewarder of every one of your virtues in the field. I know, already for your forwardness you have deserved rewards and crowns; and we do assure you, in the word of a prince, they shall be duly paid you.

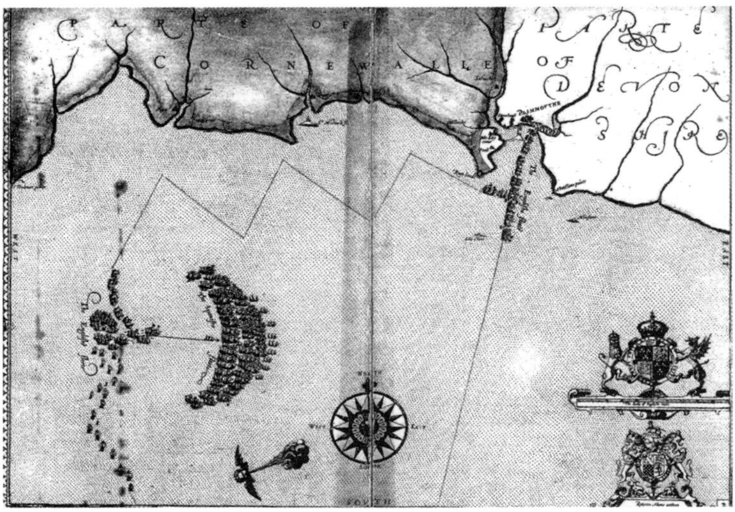

Old Sketch of Disposition of Spanish and English Navies 1588
(Reproduced by courtesy of Thurrock Library : ref. Tilbury,158)

Elizabeth commanded that a pontoon of ships be created across the Thames, from Tilbury to Gravesend, so that the Armada could not reach London easily. As we all know, the Spanish forces did not make landfall and the Armada was dispersed on the east coast of Britain and the west coast of Ireland. The English army was disbanded and went home grumbling, as they had not been paid, an early indication of 'the word of a prince'.

Tilbury fort was strengthened in 1670, after Dutch sailing ships made raids up the Thames and the Medway in 1667 during the second Anglo-Dutch War, set fire to the English fleet docked at Chatham and towed away two English warships as booty, including *The Royal Charles*, the fleet's flagship. A further storey was added to the blockhouse and a large guardhouse was built. In the eighteenth century the fire power of the fort increased steadily. In 1715, there were 48 demi-cannon, which could fire a 32 pound round about 500 metres, and by 1800 there were 70 such cannon. This impressive armament was not used however, the fort operating as a transit camp and as a prison for Scottish soldiers captured at Culloden in 1745. The English forces at that massacre were led by the Duke of Cumberland, whose nickname was 'The Butcher', so we may assume that the prisoners were fortunate to have survived the battle.

The Ministry of Works official Guide Book (1960) describes Tilbury Fort as

> The best preserved and in many ways the finest surviving example of late-seventeenth-century engineering in England. Its only rival is the Citadel at Portsmouth, which, while preserving much of its original character internally, retains virtually nothing of the complicated outworks – moats, ravelin (fortified island in a moat) and covered-way – which survive at Tilbury. The fort was designed by Sir Bernard de Gomme (1620-85), Charles II's Chief Engineer and Surveyor General of the Ordnance, and was comparable in scale and complexity with contemporary continental fortifications. The only major reconstruction, which occurred in the late 1860s, has left the overall plan substantially unaltered.

In the eighteenth century, the fort at Gravesend, New Tavern Fort, became the headquarters of the defence force. It seems that the senior officers preferred the amenities and facilities offered by the nearby town, so they chose to live there rather than in the more impressive Tilbury Fort. By this time, Gravesend had enjoyed four centuries of prosperity, as the chief port of London. Tilbury, by contrast, was largely marshland and facilities were limited. Even fresh water was in short supply, and rainwater had to be collected in cisterns to provide adequate sanitation at the fort. For a large part of the eighteenth and nineteenth century, Tilbury Fort was used to provide basic training to army recruits before they moved on to better accommodation on the Isle of Wight. The security at the fort was more to keep people in than people out, as the doors and gates were locked to stop the inmates from deserting.

Wind Against Tide by Clarkson Stanfield R.A., 1849
with Tilbury Fort in the background
(Reproduced by courtesy of Thurrock Library, ref. Tilbury, 129 a)

Despite, or maybe because of, its impressive appearance, Tilbury Fort has never been involved in serious military action. The anti-aircraft guns sited there did manage to shoot down a Zeppelin in the First World War, but it was the scene for only one other conflict, a cricket match in November 1776. The *Ministry of Works Guide* picks up the story:

> The match was a county match between Kent and Essex; feeling ran high and a fight broke out. Thereupon the Kentish men ran to the Guardroom, and, seizing a gun, killed one of the Essex men. There were only four soldiers on duty and they were unable to restrain the cricketers, who armed themselves with guns. An elderly invalid was bayoneted and the sergeant, who was commanding the fort in the absence of the officer, was shot dead trying to quell them. At this point the players panicked; the Essex men ran off over the drawbridge and the Kentish men retreated across the river.

A later resident in Tilbury was the writer Daniel Defoe, the author of *Robinson Crusoe* and the no less compelling *A Journal of the Plague Year*. In 1696 he managed a brick and tile company in Tilbury, living in nearby Chadwell. Originally the secretary to the company, he bought the concern outright, hoping to make money by providing a cheaper alternative to the largely Dutch tiles and bricks that dominated the market.

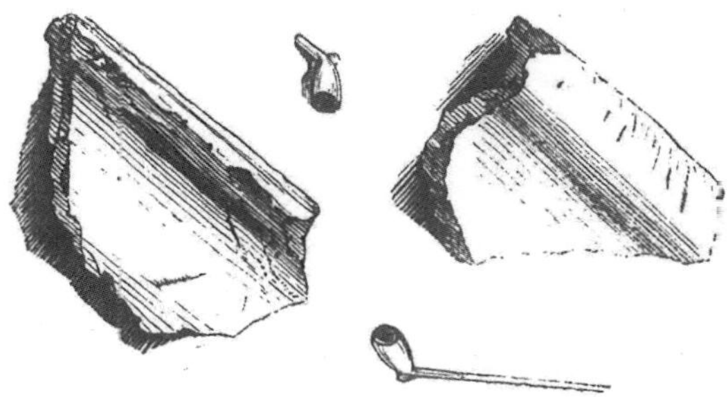

PANTILES AND PIPES RECENTLY FOUND ON SITE OF DEFOE'S TILE WORKS AT TILBURY.

(Reproduced by courtesy of Thurrock Library, ref. Tilbury 5a)

He proved to be a better writer than businessman. It is believed that he subsidised the company from his income as a commissioner for glass duty, collecting taxes on the sale of glass bottles. The company flourished initially, employing up to a hundred families and making a profit of about six hundred pounds a year. Unfortunately, he was not good at selling his products, although they were reputed to be of good quality. The goods stockpiled and Defoe was unable to pay his suppliers. Not for the first time in his life, nor the last, Defoe was taken to court for failing to pay his bills. The business foundered and Defoe gave up the Tilbury enterprise.

In his fascinating *Tour Through the Whole Island of Great Britain*, written some thirty years after his work in Tilbury, Defoe describes the area in some detail:

> This side of the county (Essex) is rather richer in land, than in inhabitants, occasioned chiefly in the unhealthiness of the air, for these low marsh grounds, which, with all the south-side of the county, have been saved out of the River Thames, and out of the sea, where the river is wide enough to be called so, begin here or rather begin at West-Ham, by Stratford, and continue to extend themselves. From hence eastward, growing wider and wider, till we come beyond Tilbury, when the flat country lyes six, seven, or eight miles broad, and is justly said to be both unhealthy, and unpleasant.
>
> However the lands are rich, and, as is observable, it is very good farming in the marshes, because the landlords get good penny-worths, for it being a place that every body cannot live those that venture it will have encouragement, and indeed it is but reasonable that they should.

Defoe wrote that the men in these marsh lands often had as many as 'a dozen and a half wives', and gave the explanation of one of the men living there. The men

> being bred in the marshes themselves and seasoned to the place, did pretty well with it, but they always went up into the hilly country, or, so to speak their language, into the 'uplands' for a wife, that when they took their lasses out of the wholesome and fresh air they were healthy, fresh and clear, and well, but when they came out of their native air into the marshes among the fogs and damps, there they presently changed their complexion, got an ague or two, and seldom held it above half a year, or a year at the most. And then, we go to the uplands and fetch another.

During his time at Tilbury, a warrant was issued for Defoe's arrest and a reward was posted for what was a considerable sum of money in those days. He was wanted for issuing a seditious pamphlet and a description was given, in the hope that he would be identified. This is the man whom the people of Tilbury would have seen:

> A middle-sized spare man about forty years of age, of brown complexion and dark brown coloured hair, but wears a wig; a hooked nose, a sharp chin, grey eyes, a large mole near his mouth; was born in London and is now owner of the brick and pantile works near Tilbury Fort, Essex. Whoever shall discover the said Daniel Defoe to one of his Majesty's principal Secretaries of State, etc., shall have a reward of fifty pounds.

For all the encouragement that Defoe offered its inhabitants, the population did not increase with the same rapidity as in many areas in South East England, so that by 1850 the population in the Tilbury area was sparse indeed.

There was, of course, the ferry, which could take passengers to the more developed south bank of the river, where Gravesend was in its heyday. In 1799, the authorised payment for the ferry fare was set at two pence (slightly less than a penny in modern currency). The reader is invited to check what the fare on the ferry is today!

The arrival of a railway line in 1854 could be seen as the first indication that there was to be a more secure future for people living in the Tilbury area, particularly as the line was called the London, Tilbury and Southend Railway. However, as Dr. Edwin Course suggested, in his wonderfully illustrated *Tilbury Loop*, a more apt name would have been the London, Gravesend and Southend Railway, as passengers alighted at Tilbury with the sole purpose of catching the steamer across the river to Gravesend, where there had been a thriving community since the thirteenth century.

Tilbury Ferry "S.S. Mimie" : built 1927
(Reproduced by courtesy of Thurrock Library, ref. Tilbury, 122)

At Tilbury, the major construction at the time was a landing stage built to enable the rail passengers to cross the Thames to Gravesend, which had become a favourite summer resort for Londoners. The ferry to Gravesend was owned by the railway company and their boat was used only by the rail passengers.

Mary Pollard summed up the situation rather well in her contribution to *The Parish of Our Lady and St. Joseph* :

> Tilbury itself was of little importance 130 years ago. There was Tilbury Fort, the World's End Inn, a railway station near the ferry and railway cottages and settlements in East and West Tilbury, but the area that we today call Tilbury was just flat, badly-drained marshland.

Apart from a few cottages clustered around The World's End public house, the first real houses in what was to become Tilbury were built by the railway company. Two rows of cottages for railway workers were constructed north of the railway line, but there was soon the prospect that even this small development was too optimistic, for there was news of a proposed new direct railway line from London to Southend via Upminster, which would bypass Tilbury entirely. And then something happened which was to change the fortunes of Tilbury at a stroke. In 1880, the East and West India Dock Company proposed a bold initiative to relieve the pressure of congestion at the London docks. They decided to build dock facilities some twenty-five miles downstream at Tilbury. Large ships would no longer be obliged to anchor near Gravesend waiting for the tide to provide sufficient water to enter the London docks. Freight could be unloaded onto the rail system at Tilbury and be transported directly to London, saving twelve to twenty-four hours in journey times and creating a considerable saving for shipping companies.

In July 1882 an Act of Parliament gave the necessary authority for the dock construction to start and the mammoth project began. It was to employ up to 6,000 men, most travelling by rail from Barking and by ferry from Gravesend. Three gigantic docks were built on a seventy-five acre site, each dock leading from a central basin. Initial problems included the discovery that the subsoil was unsound and the foundation piles had to be driven deeper to find firm ground. The engineering company required more money for this work but was replaced with some acrimony. The site soon developed a poor safety record, with injuries and deaths consistently greater than for the whole neighbouring town of Grays. Yet despite disputes over low wages, difficulties created when casual workers were laid off because of weather conditions, and bouts of

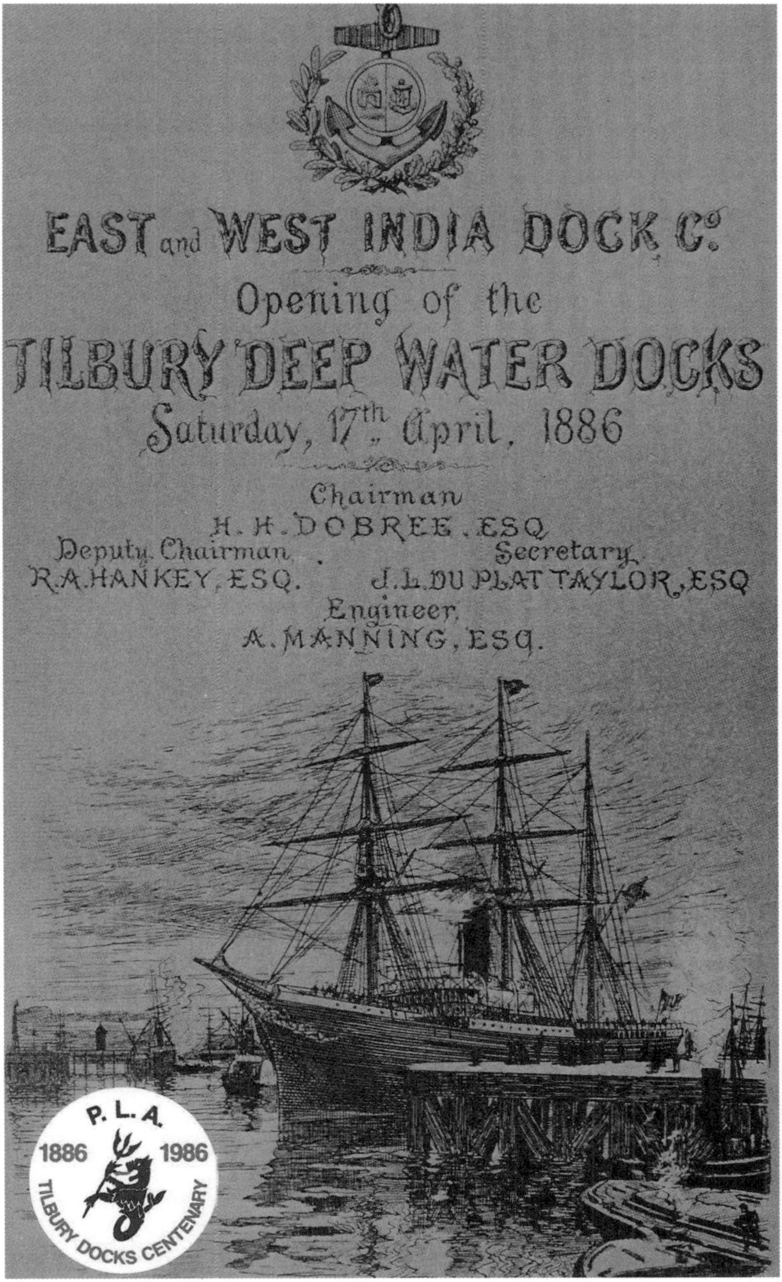
EAST and WEST INDIA DOCK Co.
Opening of the
TILBURY DEEP WATER DOCKS
Saturday, 17th April, 1886
Chairman
H. H. DOBREE, ESQ
Deputy Chairman
R.A.HANKEY, ESQ.
Secretary
J.L.DU PLAT TAYLOR, ESQ
Engineer
A. MANNING, ESQ.
P.L.A.
1886
1986
TILBURY DOCKS CENTENARY

drunkenness, the building work continued at a great pace. Two thousand cubic yards of concrete were laid each day, and all of it by hand. The dock was officially opened in April 1886.

Nineteenth Century Sketch of Tilbury Deep Water Docks
(Reproduced by courtesy of Thurrock Library, ref. Tilbury, 150)

The Dock owners began to invest in local housing, building what was called The Dwellings, and two roads in honour of the P. & O. Line, Peninsular Road and Orient Road. A very fine hotel, the Tilbury Hotel was also constructed at this time, and it would occupy a fine site overlooking the Thames, where it proved to be a landmark for returning sailors, until it was destroyed by bombing in the Second World War.

It would be reasonable to assert that the enormous success of Tilbury Docks was to make the future of Tibury secure. Housing, roads, infrastructure and the development of community followed as a direct consequence. A clear picture of what life was like in the area surrounding the early docks is provided by Edward Duffin, in an article printed in the *Thurrock Gazette*, on August 10th, 1962. This article is included here with the *Gazette*'s permission.

> Looking back to the time I first saw Tilbury Dock – in 1898 when a lad of thirteen, in the employ of a shipping company – and viewing it now, I am amazed at the great change that has taken place in just a lifetime. From 1898 until the early 1900s I only saw the dock occasionally, for my employer's ships did not use the dock then, but landed their passengers in

the river, the ferry boats bringing them to the pontoon and a special train conveying them from Tilbury Station to London.

The Tilbury Hotel
(Reproduced by courtesy of Thurrock Library, ref. Tilbury, 54)

From the latter period the company's newer ships commenced to berth regularly in the Western (quay) and I took part in the daily life of the dock. Even then, although only a little over twenty miles from the City, it was isolated, for transport was confined to a few horse-drawn vehicles, the trade of the dock being dependent on the London, Tilbury and Southend Railway and the lighterage companies. The marshes between Tilbury and London were almost bare, the extensive growth of factories coming much later.

Our offices bordered a large stretch of waste land which was part of the dock property. This was unused and deserted except occasionally by our cricket team and those dock employees who happened to be interested in the abundant wildlife. On sunny days, one of the quay foremen, with a cleft stick, caught venomous adders there, which he sold to a London shop.

The work of the dock, then under the control of the London and India Docks Joint Committee, was carried out with little mechanical assistance. Trucks were hand pushed along quays that were none too smooth and across badly-worn boards in the sheds. The pay was comparatively poor and 'pay-offs' frequent, yet the dockies seemed to keep cheerful. I have seen more than one fierce quarrel between a couple of the men end in a glorious scrap. Dan, the boss stevedore, a doughty fighter, hard-fisted but soft-hearted, would make sure that the fight was kept clean. When the disputants had hurt themselves so much as to forget what the quarrel was about, work was resumed in an atmosphere of good humour.

In the early days, the ships brought from New York large cargoes of flour in sacks and they were known as the 'flour boats'. The men poured out of the dock looking more like bakers than dockies. Later, grain came loose in the holds, was sucked out and 'blown' by elevators then poured into barges for conveyance to the London mills. At such times it snowed grain dust!

These ships had spacious 'tween decks, and although there were first class passengers in the luxurious superstructure, in the deck below several hundred head of cattle were imported each week. When the passengers had disembarked, the cattle were transferred to a small steamer and taken to Deptford for slaughtering. Progress in refrigeration eliminated this trade. A contractor cleared the deck of the well-manured peat litter, which filled a few barges and gave us a hefty farmyard odour.

The 'tween decks were also used for the transport of bloodstock and fine British breeding stock of all kinds. Famous racehorses travelled in these ships. Their names soon flew round as they were escorted along the quay and the men had many a jest on the way these noble animals had let them down or given them an extra couple of pints.

Elephants sometimes gave us some fun, especially when an over-cautious one, after testing the special brow, imagined it was not strong enough and had to be 'slung'. Their tricks and manoeuvres to avoid this operation beat any circus act.

At the end of the Western quay, which was the extent of the dock then, was a shelving beach where we lounged after dinner. In this bay the Lascars from the P. and O. ships dredged for shrimps. These Lascars on one of their religious festival days danced until sundown outside the P. and O. offices, oblivious of the heat and without food or drink. It was a sight to see the hefty Indian wrestlers from these ships when they practised their art on the field, their oiled, dark-skinned bodies glistening in the sun like bronze.

Ships were coal-fuelled. Barges brought coal alongside. It was shovelled into baskets, hauled up and pulled through a small 'tween deck opening, pushed along temporary rails and emptied down small hatches into the bunkers. Firing in ships was a hot, strenuous, poorly-paid job, but the firemen seemed to keep cheerful. Some of them formed a drum and fife band and merrily played themselves down to the ship on sailing days.

> Well, I have nostalgic memories of my invigorating early morning walks from Grays to Tilbury Docks through unspoiled country and across the open marsh – especially in the spring and early summer, when the larks sang overhead, flocks of plovers wheeled around, and I caught glimpses of stoats, rabbits and other interesting wild creatures. The unpolluted ditches were then gay with wild irises; a field would sometimes be adorned with a rich carpet of tinted clover and the air perfumed with the scent of flowering 'horse' beans.
>
> Now, the song of birds has given way to the roar of lorries, buses and motorbikes. Exhaust fumes fill the air. Except for rats, the animals have gone. The fields are plastered over with houses and shops. In the dock, ships with beautiful lines have been superseded by huge vessels of utilitarian ugliness.
>
> Change, of course, is inevitable, but at what expense? It seems to me that the great philosopher, Emerson, in his essay on the laws of compensation, hit on the truth when he wrote "For everything we gain, we lose an equivalent."

In the nineteen thirties, the entire world suffered from the effects of the Great Depression. Beginning with the economic crash in America in 1929, the resulting loss of confidence affected world trade and caused a slump in manufacturing. Working class people were disproportionately affected. Work became scarce at Tilbury Docks, the mainstay of the local economy, and the overwhelmingly blue collar workers in Tilbury saw a reduction in their income, causing real destitution for the area. In his excellent book *Thurrock in the Thirties* (2005), Terry Carney reported that in 1931 the Tilbury Distress Committee found that 900 families, a quarter of Tilbury's population, were 'on the verge of starvation.' In some homes there was nothing but bread to eat and malnourished children fell asleep at school. When the local Salvation Army organised a Pease Pudding Supper at half a penny a head, 150 people turned up. A Salvation Army Captain reported :

> The guests brought their own cups and other receptacles, and when they had finished, the platters were so clean that it was difficult to detect that they had been used.

Carney added that even the good news from East Tilbury that a new shoe factory was to be built there caused its own problems, as jobless men flooded into the area seeking work. Unfortunately, the actual jobs were slower to materialise and Tilbury found itself with more unemployed men desperate for work.

The derivation of Tilbury road names was investigated by the Tilbury Riverside Project in 2013. They were able to show how early, Victorian roads were named after British statesmen, Melbourne, Russell, Landsdown, Sydney and cities of the British Empire such as Ottawa or Calcutta. In the Edwardian period, poets, novelists and composers were selected, as in Kipling, Dickens, Handel and Elgar. Later, there were references to local councillors, including Brennan and Feenan, the latter bringing electricity to Tilbury in September 1927. For those of you who wish to know more on this subject, there is an excellent DVD available (free!) from the local library. Produced by Peter Benson for the Tilbury Riverside Project, it is entitled *Tilbury : The Story Behind The Roads* and most of the words of the project are spoken by local residents.

During the Second World War, many houses in Tilbury were destroyed, including the East Block of The Dwellings, and the Tilbury Hotel proved to be an easy target for German bombers following the Thames to London. Later in the war, Tilbury Riverside Railway Station received a direct hit from a V2 rocket. The town played a major role in the preparations for the invasion of Northern France in 1944. Not only was it an embarkation point for thousands of soldiers and their vehicles, it was also a headquarters for the building of the Mulberry harbours that enabled the allies to disembark the huge volume of soldiers and equipment needed to sustain Operation Overlord.

After the war, Tilbury continued its expansion. Road links were improved and many new homes built in the nineteen sixties and seventies. During the nineteen sixties, at a time when the Port of London Authority was closing down London based docks, Tilbury saw massive expansion, with the construction of a fourth branch dock, running almost a mile in length from the main dock. By the nineteen eighties, Tilbury had become the only enclosed dock still run by the Port of London Authority.

The steam-powered ferries across the Thames were in service from 1883 right through to the modern age, when diesel power took over. The names of the early steam ferries recall a previous, illustrious time in the story of Tilbury, when it played a part in the defeat of the Spanish Armada: *Queen Elizabeth, Earl of Leicester, Sir Walter Raleigh*. In his excellent book on the Tilbury – Gravesend ferries, *The Five Minute Crossing*, John Ormston wrote of the typical experience of post-war passengers taking the ferry from Tilbury to Gravesend.

On all the ferries it was possible for passengers, by looking through the engine room grill, to watch the engineers and stokers attending to the boiler, fires, steam engines and other machinery, and also to hear the sound of shovel on steel, the hiss of escaping steam, the ringing of the engine room telegraph and to smell the special aroma of oil and steam. On the occasional journey, the sound of operatic singing came from below, as the engineer or stoker gave a powerful rendering of an aria.

Tilbury Ferry "M.V. Catherine", built 1960
(Reproduced by courtesy of Thurrock Library, ref. Tilbury 119

On a typical journey, the passengers arrived at Tilbury Riverside by train, passed through the ticket barrier at the end of the platform, and entered the large, lofty booking hall. Passing through the booking hall they followed the signs to the ferry and Gravesend and another ticket barrier, and then proceeded down the link bridge to the floating landing stage where a ferry awaited, for the ferries always connected with the trains. Usually, the pierman was in position to let go the mooring ropes once all the passengers had boarded via the gangway which was slightly inclined. The captain and helmsman made their way to the bridge and the deckhands positioned themselves at fore and aft of the vessel.

On the signal being given, the gangway was withdrawn to the landing stage and the door closed. The mooring ropes were let go and at the same time the telegraph from the bridge rang instructions to the engine room. The engines burst into life and the vessel headed out into the river. The captain gave his instructions quietly to the helmsman and the "five minute crossing" had commenced.

The passengers could now choose between the two lounges – fore or aft – stand in the companionway watching the action in the engine room below, lean on the gunwales or, best of all, climb the stairs to the top deck from where the whole expanse of Gravesend Reach could be seen. There were ships of every description, moving or anchored, tugs swinging at their moorings downstream, cranes and the superstructure of ships in Tilbury Docks, the busyness of the Pilots' launch changing the River and Estuary Pilots, or the Port Health Officials swinging up a Jacob's ladder on the side of a ship to give her a clean bill of health. As the ferry approached Gravesend, the bawleys (small sailing vessels) could be seen at their moorings between Town and Royal Terrace Piers with their nets hanging from the rigging.

The captain kept a watch for shipping proceeding up and down the fairway in order not to impede their progress, giving way to sail, for there were always sailing barges to be considered, and threaded a course to the Town Pier.

Once across, the ferry was brought alongside the pontoon, the telegraphs again rang and the deckhands threw the mooring ropes to the pierman on the pontoon. The vessel was secured, the door rolled back and the gangway swung from the pontoon to the ferry to bridge the slight gap.

The passengers now queued to file off the ship and to cross by means of another gangway from the pontoon to a landing on the Town Pier, where they then ascended the steps and made their way to the ticket barrier, surrendering their ticket to the collector stationed there. A few more steps and the passengers were at the bottom of Gravesend High Street. To the left was the Three Daws Public House, to the right a couple of shops, Pier Hotel and West Street. Before them was the narrow High Street with its small shops, each with a signboard hanging outside reminding the traveller of a medieval town. The time from arriving at Tilbury Riverside to being in Gravesend High Street was ten minutes.

In more recent years, Tilbury has grown steadily. With its good rail link to the City, and some comparatively cheap housing, it has been a magnet for those who work in London. When St. Chad's School merged with Torells School to form the new Gateway Academy on the outskirts of Tilbury, the original school site was used for the construction of 128 new homes in the town. Most of the homes are rental properties, in response to a need for local low-cost housing and the completion date for the development was given as September 2017.

Despite recent competition from the London Gateway development downstream near Stanford-le-Hope, Tilbury Docks continues to flourish and remains the principal port for London.

Chapter Two : The Early Days of Tilbury Parish

As the docks were built, the construction company began to build houses for its workers. A block of tenements, known as The Dwelling, was constructed and Tilbury began to grow. During a visit to the area, Cardinal Manning saw the potential for development, judging that Tilbury could come to rival the seaport of Liverpool. He bought a few acres of land there in 1885, and earmarked them for a church, a presbytery and a school. This was recorded in the directory of 1886, the first record of what was to become the Tilbury Mission. By 1888, the directory recorded that a church had been built in Dock Road, although the 'church' was no more than a part of a room in the newly built school. The listing for 1888 reads

> Tilbury, Our Lady Star of the Sea, served from Grays. Sundays, Holidays, Mass : 10.30 a.m. Confessions before Mass.

The Tilbury Mission was served, as the listing reveals, from the Parish of St. Thomas of Canterbury, Grays. The parish in Tilbury was created in 1887, when a priest from Grays, Canon Keens, was asked to care for the people of Tilbury. He was to be responsible for the building of the school and the 'church' there, and was to set up the Mission, as *The Universe* reported on 17th September 1887 :

> in view of the establishment of the vast line of docks which must inevitably lead to the transformation of this portion of the desolate Essex shore into a busy mart of commerce and centre of industry, and the expansion of the faith here.

On Saturday 28th May the following year, *The Tablet* reported that

> The first stone of the new school – chapel of Our Lady Star of the Sea, by special permission of the Cardinal Archbishop, was laid on Tuesday by the Very Rev. Canon Keens, assisted by the Very Rev. Canon Bamber and the Rev. James Gilligan, the Rev. Joseph O'Sullivan being the master of ceremonies.

Canon Keens marked the occasion with an address designed to illustrate how much Christian education had done and would continue to do by contrast with purely secular education. Referring in particular to the work of St. Mark in the area of Alexandria in Egypt, who brought a spiritual dimension to schools already rich in secular resources, Canon Keens asserted

> What St. Mark did for Christian education in the first century of the Catholic Church, we, the children of that same Church, are doing now in the nineteenth century.

Canon Keens : Founder and First Parish Priest of Tilbury Parish

The recently opened Tilbury Docks had indeed resulted in an increase in the population of Tilbury. Whilst the docks were being built, there was temporary accommodation for some of the workers, but most were obliged to travel into the area on a daily basis. Once the docks were open, there was a large influx of workers, many of them Catholic, and more permanent arrangements had to be made. In the ten years between 1881 and 1891, homes for two hundred people were built, but these were on badly drained land and subsidence was all too common. The housing was considered to be of poor quality, and the new arrivals were certainly very poor indeed. The Tilbury Mission set out to provide educational and spiritual support for the many Catholics amongst the newcomers, with the school opening its doors to Catholics and non-Catholics alike.

In the building of the school, Canon Keens was helped by a wealthy Australian convert, Ada Mary Auguste Stephenson, who was later known as 'Sister Mary'. The school was for two hundred and fifty children and was dedicated to 'Our Lady Star of the Sea'. It had five classrooms, and was opened by no less a personage than Cardinal Manning, on September 8th 1887. For some people, this date marks the founding of the parish. The school cost £1,300, and was much the largest building in a parish composed of just a few streets of small houses. A chapel was created by screening off part of one of the classrooms. The school was also to double from time to time as a presbytery in the early days until this was built some thirteen years later. Space must have been at a premium in those early days!

It was recognised from the start that there would be severe financial difficulties for the mission. *The Tablet* of May 28th, 1887 commented on this:

> The congregation is an extremely poor one, consisting chiefly of the labouring classes, so that Canon Keens, unless assisted by many outside of the new mission, cannot hope to carry on his work at Tilbury with the success which all desire.

The school chapel continued to be served from Grays, and the first priest-in-charge of the Tilbury Parish was Father Joseph Upton, who had resigned as Rector of Grays in July 1901 in order to become Tilbury's first resident priest. As there was no presbytery, Father Upton lived in the school. The Westminster Diocesan Council for Temporal Administration approved the building of a presbytery at Tilbury, with the proviso that the cost should not exceed £750. Records are not clear on the precise date of the building of the presbytery, although 1901 and 1902 are mentioned. If 1901 is correct, that must have been a very quick build – or a very small presbytery.

The teachers in the little Tilbury school were provided by Sisters from the La Sainte Union Convent in Grays. This Order was founded in Northern France after the French revolution. What began as a desire to deepen spiritual understanding amongst a small group of needleworkers led to an organisation that has spread across the world, founding schools in Europe, South America, Africa and the West Indies.

The Grays Convent archive records the history of the La Sainte Union in the areas of Grays and Tilbury.

> It was in response to an urgent appeal from Cardinal Vaughan, Archbishop of Westminster, that the first Sisters of La Sainte Union came to Grays in 1899. The Diocese of Brentwood had not yet come

into being and Grays and Tilbury were under the jurisdiction of Westminster. Fr. Joseph Upton was Parish Priest of the joint parishes of Grays and Tilbury. For a long time the Cardinal had been looking for 'a good, zealous community of nuns' who would teach in the two parish schools. Writing to the Superior General of La Sainte Union in 1898 he said, 'There is no mission in or near London that offers such a future for the salvation of souls as Grays does.'

Writing at greater length and from first hand experience of the area, Fr. Upton was even more emphatic. 'This part of Essex is given over almost entirely to Dissenters and there is real danger that the children will grow up without real knowledge or love of the Faith; the people of both Grays and Tilbury are poor and there is little social life in the area to attract secular teachers.' So his request was for a sufficient number of Sisters to completely staff the Grays school (160 pupils) and the Tilbury School (200 pupils).

La Sainte Union, in 1899, was still a comparatively young Congregation, having been founded in France only in 1826. The first house in England, in Bath, was founded in 1858. There were a limited number of English speaking Sisters, so staffing two schools must have been a daunting prospect. However, nine brave souls arrived in time for the start of the new school year, four to teach in Tilbury and three in Grays. Fr. Upton had found them a suitable house to serve as a convent; this was 42-44 Orsett Road.

A preliminary visit to the school at Tilbury by the Provincial, Mother Theona, seemed to have caused quite a sensation among the children. They had never seen a nun before, so their parents were told they had nurses to visit them. The families needed much help, both materially and spiritually. Gifts of clothing and food for the children were always very welcome. The journey to and from the school in Tilbury was very tiring for the Sisters who often walked the two or three miles because they could not afford the train fare. In 1902, the two parishes separated. The Sisters of Mercy were able to carry on the good work in Tilbury, while La Sainte Union Sisters concentrated on work in Grays.

On October 29, 1899, La Sainte Union opened a fee-paying school, known as the Convent Day School. The school initially grew slowly. It opened with only three pupils, and by the end of the year there were still only nine. The survival of the school was to remain in doubt until the 1930s. Both boys and girls were accepted for many years. However, soon after the day school had opened, the Sisters were looking for a site on which the school could expand. They chose land in College Avenue and by March, 1906, the building was ready for occupation and the Sisters moved out of their convent in Orsett Road.

After new classrooms and an assembly hall were built in 1934, the convent day school grew quite rapidly and it earned an excellent reputation. Part of the 1930s building was destroyed in the Second

World War, but was later rebuilt and extended. Voluntary Aided status followed in 1969 and soon afterwards Grays Convent School became one of the first Catholic comprehensive schools in the southern part of Essex.

In 1989 the Sisters moved out of the Convent to enable further expansion of the Convent School. A computer suite and music and art blocks were established. The Sisters now live in a house that was built in 1872 and has been known as 'The Dell' (when owned by Alfred Russell Wallace) and the 'Wylie's' (Mr. Wylie was a vet). Today it is known as 'LSU Convent'. Wallace worked closely with Darwin; together they produced 'The Origin of Species'.

The work of the LSU Sisters continues. Ministries continue in Teaching, Nursing, Chaplaincy in hospitals, schools and prisons, Amnesty Spiritual Direction, Facilitation, Pastoral, Refugees, Adult Literacy and many more. Many Sisters work abroad in Argentina, Cameroon, Haiti and Tanzania.

By early 1902, however, a very significant conflict occurred in Tilbury between the Superior of the Sisters and the Parish Priest. This is all the more strange in the light of Father Upton's comments recorded in January 1902 :

Since the Sisters have been here the state of the Mission has completely changed for the better. The reports of H.M. Inspector have steadily improved. The attendance of the children has also steadily improved. We have not a single Catholic child attending any school but our own. The attendance at Holy Mass and the reception of the Sacraments has increased 300%. The Sisters have now the esteem and respect of every class in the docks.

Yet Father Upton goes on to suggest that his work in establishing the mission was being damaged by the attitude of the Reverend Mother, who had, in his words 'steadily set herself in opposition to my ideas of carrying on the work.' The arrival of the Sisters on Sunday afternoons to give catechism was interrupted by the Mother Superior, and the Sisters' presence at weekday Masses was suspended, resulting in their later arrival at school. Father Upton commented

The Schools open at 9. If the children arrive and find their teachers not present it has a bad effect.

He had made 'appeal after appeal' but to little or no effect. Father Upton came to the conclusion that a personal element was at work and that matters might improve if another priest were to be appointed in his place. He also suggested that because of the current conflict the work of the

Sisters in both Grays and Tilbury should be separated. This finally happened in 1905.

In October 1904, a new priest was appointed to Tilbury. A Belgian by birth, Father Van Meenan was a young priest of the Diocese of Westminster. He had the additional responsibility of saying Mass at Corringham and at Vange, and he travelled across these distances on a bicycle. It is fortunate that he had age on his side.

Father Van Meenan came to the Tilbury mission at an early point in what was to prove a lifetime of distinguished service to the area of South Essex. He clearly thought that he was destined to come to Tilbury, as he recorded in a reminiscence many years later.

> The Church of Our Lady of the Sea, Tilbury, is an answer to prayer. In the year 1903 I was Curate to Father Donlevy at Mile End, when two priests from Scotland called in on their way to Lourdes. At the suggestion of Father Donlevy, who said I needed a rest, I joined these Holy men to Lourdes. At the Grotto I made my request – I wished to build two churches, one in honour of the Sacred Heart of Jesus and the other in honour of Our Blessed Lady – I prayed to our Lady for help.
>
> Time passed and I was appointed to Tilbury, and there was no church. Cardinal Manning, much interested in Dockland, had visited Tilbury with Canon Keens of Grays, and His Eminence purchased a fine big site for future developments, anticipating that Tilbury would be a second Liverpool. On the fringe of that site Canon Keens built a school chapel, a handsome and substantial building which was opened by His Eminence The Cardinal Archbishop of Westminster, on September 28th, 1887. It was dedicated to "Our Lady Star of the Sea", and was capable of accommodating about 350 children.
>
> The School Chapel was served from Grays. My predecessor at Tilbury, Joseph Upton, had been Rector of Grays, but he resigned to come to Tilbury and was the first resident priest. He had no presbytery and made his home in the school. Canon Keens built many churches – he built Grays, Maiden Lane, The Holy Redeemer, Chelsea, etc. In these good works he was assisted by a rich lady, a convert to the Catholic Faith, who dedicated her fortune to the Holy Church and took the name of Sister Mary. Shortly after my appointment to Tilbury, Canon Keens died. We were still talking of building a church, when a dock labourer said "Why not build a church in memory of Canon Keens? Sister Mary might help!" Sister Mary was pleased with the idea. Bishop Fenton was consulted and took the matter in his hands. He laid the foundation stone on 21st June, 1906. The Architect was R.L. Curtis, who had built the churches at Silvertown and Custom House.

Father Jules Van Meenan

Jules Joseph Meenan was born in Bruges, Belgium in January 1877. He was raised and educated in Bruges, where his studies for the priesthood began at the Grand Seminaire, Bruges. However, in August 1897 he transferred to the seminary of the Missionaries of Africa (White Fathers) at Binson, Chatillon-sur-Narne, near Rheims. His intention was to seek ordination as a missionary priest.

In June 1898 he was incardinated as a student for the Archdiocese of Carthage, Algeria and in August 1898 he became a novice in the White Fathers, beginning his studies at their seminary in Carthage. He obtained good results and was commended for his piety and conduct, the rector considering him to have 'a real vocation to the priesthood'.

Having expressed a wish to work in England, he left the White Fathers and came to the attention of Father (later Archbishop) Edward Myers, who arranged for him to be accepted as a student at the central seminary, Oscott. He began his course there in September 1901 and was incardinated into the Diocese of Birmingham, although he was adopted the following year by the Archdiocese of Westminster. This movement across Europe must have caused some language problems for the young man. In 1901, he wrote to the Rector of Oscott, stating:

> I found it very hard to talk Flemish and French. The people is laughing at me for I am speaking with the English accent. But I am not sorry therefore.

Father Van Meenan was ordained priest at Oscott in June 1902 by Bishop Ilsley of Birmingham and in August of that year he was appointed as assistant priest at Mile End. He soon displayed his musical skills with the parish choir, which later led to his appointment as Diocesan Choirmaster.

In October 1902 he was appointed to take charge of the new mission at Tilbury, where he built the church and presbytery. He also celebrated Mass at Corringham and Vange. He visited his extensive territory by bicycle which, together with his pipe and snuff, became a 'trademark' for his priestly work in South Essex. Bishop Wall later described him as the 'apostle' of the area.

After his time in Tilbury, Father Van Meenan was to work in Southend, Romford, Barking and finally Hornchurch, where he was to remain for thirty years. In January 1928 he was appointed as a Canon of Brentwood Cathedral.

In June 1962 a special booklet was produced to honour the occasion of his Diamond Jubilee. This is just a short extract from the booklet.

> January the 18th 1877 probably passed unnoticed in the history of Belgium, and its effect on the people of England appeared, no doubt, equally unimportant.
>
> Nevertheless on that day was born a boy destined to bridge the natural differences in the way of life of the two countries, and in due time to become himself a spiritual bridge to countless souls on their journey to God.
>
> Jules Van Meenan was that boy, none other than our Right Reverend Monsignor Provost Van Meenan, whose Diamond Jubilee in the Priesthood we now commemorate with our thanks, congratulations and prayers that God may continue to shower his blessings on him for many years in this life, and for all eternity.
>
> Young Jules spent his early years among his family in Bruges, a medieval city redolent of the Faith. Its Cathedral of St. Sauveur, the great church of Notre Dame and the Chapelle du Saint-Sang (Shrine of the true relic of the Holy Blood) were, to him, ever present prayers in stone. In his day even the wonderful Carillon set high in the belfry of the Town Hall (Hotel de Ville) played an ancient hymn but now it plays modern airs only.
>
> As we leave his old world city, we might reflect that its former name was BRUGGE, signifying the bridge or place of bridges.
>
> To leave your old home is always sad; sad for him who goes, and for those left behind, unless there is a great ambition, a great challenge, such as that in the heart of our young Jules. He intended to study for the Priesthood, for he knew then what he has known and preached over the years: "We must have Priests."

At an early age he was on his way to England to study at Oscott College. Years of hard work under austere conditions in a strange country was a formidable prospect, but he accepted this in the full understanding that it was all for the Honour and Glory of God.

While there, he worked with many who eventually became notable Priests up and down the country, and with at least one who served as a link with his boyhood – Count Van Den Steen, a nobleman from his own city.

On the feast of SS Peter and Paul, June 29th 1902, he was ordained priest by Archbishop Isley at Oscott College, Birmingham, to work in the Archdiocese of Westminster.

Father Van Meenan was first appointed Assistant Priest in the Mile End Road Parish of the Guardian Angels. The church was new, opened but a year before, and our young priest was fresh from the seminary – two fine gems in the old setting of the Mile End Road.

The Mile End Road! What a change from quiet Bruges and serene Oscott! The wide, cobbled main road, the horse trams now giving way to the electric tram-car, the great brewers' drays with their magnificent horses, the teeming thousands intent on buying and selling, must have made the assault on Father Van Meenan's eyes, ears and nose well nigh overpowering.

Missionaries (and such was our young priest) are generally understood to receive a modicum of training in the tongue and habits of those they are to work among. Here however the circumstances were different and the new curate went into the jungle of the East End of London very slightly equipped for the battle with the Cockney tongue.

Come with me to the door of one of the little houses in the warren of small streets breaking off the main road. It is a few days before Christmas in 1902 and mother is all agog with her preparations for the holy festival as she opens the door to a sharp "rat-tat". On the step is a tall young man in black, wearing a clerical hat of the period (imagine a very shallow Bowler with a wider brim).

"Come in Father, welcome to our home!" Soon he was at ease watching the puddings coming out of the "copper". The steam subsides and all are hoping for a "taster", but first to our visitor: "Have a piece of Christmas pudding Father?" Armed only with his native courtesy and his French vowels he replies "Thank you – no, but I would like a mince pie." (Oh! These English Einz and Eees!)

He soon acquired a working knowledge of the local language which was an uneasy basis for the variety of accents he was to meet in the next half century all along the North Bank of the Thames.

He was soon at home too in his priestly progress, for in 1903 he assisted H.E. Cardinal Vaughan at the opening of Westminster Cathedral, then a magnificent brisk shell waiting to receive its rare and costly linings. Of the many present on that day he is one of the few privileged to see with earthly eyes the partial realisation of this wonderful conception of the great Cardinal whose Requiem was so soon to follow.

It was not long before Father Van Meenan's love for, and knowledge of, music was manifested. He took in hand the training of the Choir, first to the Glory of God but also to the pleasure of all the parishioners of the Guardian Angels' Church. Well not quite all; there was the exceptional case of Mr "X", an Irishman with a great heart in a great frame enclosing a great voice coming through a great head. He could sing, so he would sing in the choir. But there was a snag! Father Van Meenan insisted on training, and practices for his choristers. Most of these had to be in the evenings – and Mr "X" was a master baker. 60 years ago all bakers worked at night and he was no exception; he had therefore neither training nor practice. So when he joined his great voice to the carefully prepared programme of the choir there was pandemonium. This was too much for our young Master of the Music who felt constrained to tell the master baker "I am the Captain of the Ship." Mr "X" retired broken in heart and in voice and there was peace (and harmony) once more in the loft of the House of God.

There was peace and work in plenty for Father Van Meenan for the few years he was to remain in London, but in 1905 he was sent to Tilbury by Francis Bourne, the fourth Archbishop of Westminster, later to be created Cardinal. This great priest, saintly of visage and princely of bearing, was concerned with conditions on the North bank of the Thames. True, there had been a church at Tilbury since soon after the docks had been opened in 1886, but our new and very young parish priest was sent there to build something more in keeping with the times and with its unique situation – the Gateway to the Eastern half of the World.

He had spent his boyhood in the lowlands and now he came back to them. The site was almost level with the river, and the problems arising were only overcome by recourse to the most modern building methods of the period.

60 foot long piles had to be driven through the marsh before a sound bottom could be found which naturally increased the cost of the building in money and in time. In fact, quite half of the cash was spent below the ground before a brick had been laid above. It was nearly three years before the solid pinnacles of the Church of Our Lady Star of the Sea opposed the waving pinnacles of the masts of the ocean going ships and the tall cranes of the docks.

Whilst we think of Father Van Meenan's efforts as for the people of Essex, let us remember the countless thousands of all races and all colours who gazed upon this church as their first or last solace in their journeyings across the globe.

Almighty God alone then knew what we all know now – that this was the start of a great pattern of church – and school – building seldom matched in modern times and excelled only by the few in the past.

At the time of his retirement in 1963, he had served as a priest for sixty-one years, all but four of which had been spent in South Essex. Accordingly, Bishop Beck paid him this tribute:

He was a true founding father not only of the Diocese of Brentwood but also of Catholic life in Essex and East London in the period immediately before the erection of the new see in 1917. His devotion to parish visiting, to the care of the sick, and to the confessional was legendary. Likewise, with bicycle and dog, he ventured each Sunday afternoon to take the outdoor collection for the Catholic schools, and is still remembered for this by the older parishioners.

In 1905, the Sisters of Mercy came to the parish. Their primary task was to take over the teaching of the school's children, replacing the La Sainte Union Sisters from Grays Convent. They initially agreed a one year contract with the parish, and they paid the sum of £50. From little acorns mighty oaks do grow.

In the Diocese of Westminster Triennial Return of 1905, Father Van Meenan was asked whether the diocesan collections were always made at the church. He replied

No. The people are too poor to give anything to these collections.

Fr. Van Meenan summarised his judgement of the Tilbury congregation at the end of the 1905 Triennial Return.

The people come from the lowest class in the East End of London. They came here to labour in the docks. The labour is casual and when they earn money they spend it in Public houses. Consequently they are very poor – they incur debts and never think of paying them off. Those who cannot get work in the Dock go away to sea; they are hopeless. The intellect of this people has never been developed. They are most ignorant of their Religion and duties They scarce know their prayers and the priest must dwell continually on the essential points of the Christian life. Those who went their Easter duties this Lent had not been for ten to forty years. The priest must gain the hearts of this people by constant visiting – speak to their senses by Processions and outward show and give them a great idea of the Church.

Canon Van Meenan

> Nearly every one who did not make his Easter Confession told me the reason that kept him back and keeps him back from Church : a good many are not married or live in sin – others are freemasons etc. I see the possibility of making this a good mission in less than 3 years.

The extent of the poverty he encountered might be judged by a subsequent Triennial return of 1911. A collection for the African Missions had raised eight pence, and the Ecclesiastical Education Fund had received eleven pence. The year 1912 saw these two charities receiving eight pence and ten pence respectively, and subsequent returns revealed a similar picture: the congregation was desperately poor.

Initially, Father Van Meenan had the additional responsibility of looking after the Catholic community at Corringham, but shortly after his arrival he asked to relinquish this task, believing that the 50 Catholics living there could be better served from elsewhere. One of the parishioners, however, a Mr. Curtis, paid the interest on the parish debt on condition that a monthly Mass was celebrated in Corringham. A grant of ten shillings a week was made by the diocese towards the saying of Mass at Corringham for a period of three months (*Westminster Diocesan Council Minutes*) and Franciscan Conventuals were considered as a solution. Temporary arrangements were organised for most of 1906, until Grays took over responsibility for Corringham in November of that year.

During 1906, a very important event in the history of the Tilbury parish occurred. On 21st June the foundation stone of a church was laid. Father Van Meenan took responsibility for its construction. There was an immediate problem with the foundations as the ground was marshy, and so forty ferro-concrete piles had to be driven into the ground to a depth of sixty feet and joined together to form a raft strong enough to support the church building. The church was in the Early English style, with a vaulted roof, pointed arches and a spire. It was built in yellow brick with red dressings, had a solid wood block floor and a balcony to the interior. Funding was supplied one again by Ada Stephenson.

High in the gable end of the church, overlooking the docks, was placed a statue of Our Lady, a copy of the statue of Notre Dame de la Guarde near Marseilles, so that she could 'watch over all those who go down to the sea in ships'. The church was opened on Ascension Day, 9th May 1907. Inside the church are memorial tablets to Canon Keens, founder of the Tilbury Mission and to Ada Stephenson, the church's benefactress. A donation towards the cost of furnishings also came from Canon Keens's legacy, where the balance of his estate of £358.1.9d was to be used to pay for a site at Rainham, the remainder going to furnish the church at Tilbury. (*Westminster Diocesan Council Minutes 15th November 1906*)

In 1908, when Father Mulcahy was in residence, there were two Masses on Sunday at 8.00 a.m. and 10.30 a.m. Weekday Masses were at 8.00 a.m. A group of boys from the school was formed into a choir and taught by the Sisters to sing in church. About 70 children attended catechetical instruction at 3.00 p.m. on Sundays. The average congregation at Sunday Mass in May 1908 comprised fifty-four men, fifty-eight women and one hundred and eighty children. The parish school contained one hundred and sixty-five children, and in the religious examination that year the Sisters managed to achieve the grade 'excellent' in every area.

The all-important ferro-concrete piles being driven in for the foundations of the Church of our Lady Star of the Sea, 1906.
(In the background, you can just see Father Van Meenan watching.)

Yet the extreme poverty persisted, with the congregation barely able to provide sufficient funds to keep the parish viable. On 21st May 1909, Father Mulcahy asked the diocese for financial assistance. He had managed to gather in one hundred pounds from various sources, but stated that he was not receiving any financial support from the convent. In July, the Reverend Mother offered a sum of £26 per year 'for a weekly Mass and honorarium to confessor'.

Despite the poverty, the congregation did what they could to support the parish. In 1911 a new Parish Priest was appointed, Father Jerome Deady. The Parish Bazaar in 1911 raised £259-15-3d, a magnificent achievement for the time. Yet the same year Father Deady summarised the repairs on the presbytery as "Trying to keep the rain out". The school building also needed attention. The exterior was in need of protective paint, repairs to the roof were urgently needed and a wooden club room for the children was decaying badly. The priest concluded with the depressing comment : 'the drains are also bad'.

Father Jerome Deady

Jerome (Jeremiah) Joseph Deady was born at Kanturk, Co. Cork in April 1879. He was the son of Jeremiah Deady, a grocer and baker. In the 1911 Irish Census, Mr Deady was living with his second wife Kate, who was thirty years his junior. Jerome Deady had one brother and three sisters. He was educated at St. Colman's College, Fermoy, and St. John's College, Waterford, where he was accepted as a student for the Archdiocese of Westminster. In June 1902, he was ordained priest by Bishop Sheehan at St. John's College, Waterford.

Father Deady was appointed as an assistant priest at Commercial Road, London in 1902. As a life-long teetotaller he was active in promoting the League of the Cross. At the end of 1910 he was appointed as a curate at Canning Town. On 23rd February 1911 he was appointed to take charge of the Mission at Tilbury. In September 1917 Bishop Ward appointed him as Parish Priest of Canning Town. Father Deady retired in April 1936, suffering from ill health, and he died in September 1937.

When Bishop Butt visited the parish in December 1912, the population of Tilbury had grown to 6,000. It was estimated that there were some 520 Catholics, of whom 108 men, 116 women and 199 children came to Mass. This was a substantial increase in the number of adults who now attended Mass regularly. At the end of 1913, the Sisters of Mercy increased the annual sum they gave to the Tilbury priest to £36. The parish had a debt of £1,220, with interest payable at 3 and 1/8%. Asked for his judgement of the religious condition of his congregation, Father Deady replied :

> There is a Mission every Lent for the people. More than half the people made their Easter Duty last year. The vast proportion of the people are good too but their poverty prevents their attendance at Mass. I consider they do their best to support the Church.

In 1917 Tilbury Parish moved from the Archdiocese of Westminster to the newly formed Diocese of Brentwood. The 1917/18 Visitation Return for the new diocese estimated the Catholic population at 330 adults and 170 children. Of these, 100 adults and 90 children attended Mass. About 20 adults and 40 children received Holy Communion. Each day, the church was open from the 8.00 a.m. Mass until nightfall. Confirmation was recorded to have taken place on 7th December 1917.

The parish first became a parish in the Diocese of Brentwood on August 2nd 1918, just before the end of the First World War. It had a debt of £1,100, carried over from its earlier days in the Archdiocese of Westminster. The first Parish Priest, Father Hannan, wrote in the 1917/18 Visitation Return

> Owing to the slackness of dock-labour, consequent on the war, and the absence of those Catholic sailors, who in pre-war days were a great source of income, the Mission is at present suffering a very considerable financial loss.

Father Michael Hannan

Michael Joseph Hannan was born in Craglea, Killaloe, Co. Clare, where he was baptised on 3rd September 1877. He was one of four children (one twin brother and a younger brother and sister) born to Cornelius Hannan, a farmer, and his wife Mary (nee Roughan) of Craglea, Killaloe, both of whom were natives of Co. Clare. He was educated at Ennis College and in 1898 began his training for the priesthood at All Hallows College, Dublin, for the Archdiocese of Westminster. His ordination for the priesthood was on 24th June 1904 at All Hallows College, Dublin.

In 1904, Father Hannan was appointed as assistant priest at Millwall and in 1906 he became assistant priest at Tottenham. In July 1907 he became assistant priest at Bow. In 1910, he was appointed as chaplain to St. Anthony's house, Feltham, but in October the following year he had to go on sick leave. In 1912 he became assistant priest at Colchester. By July 1913 he was assistant priest at Silvertown.

In July 1914, Father Hannan was offered the opportunity to lead the mission at Shoeburyness, but he was advised by his doctors that the work would be too much for him. He was appointed as Parish Priest in Tilbury in September 1917, where he continued until October 1921, when a further breakdown in his health made it necessary for him to resign his position. He held no further priestly office, and from 1921 to 1924 his address was listed as 'c/o Bishop's House, Brentwood'. He later lived in the Orsett Union Workhouse, on account of a further deterioration in his health. His successor at Tilbury, Father Patrick O'Donnell, recalled seeing him leaning on the fence outside the Tilbury church. Father O'Donnell attended him at the Orsett Workhouse.

Father Hannan died on 25th July 1927. The details of his death and burial are somewhat sketchy owing to the circumstances surrounding the breakdown in his health, but it is believed that he was buried on 29th July 1927, when his occupation was listed as 'builder's watchman'.

Chapter Three : Father Patrick O'Donnell

When Father Hannan resigned as Parish Priest of Tilbury, due to his ill health, Father Patrick O'Donnell was asked to report for weekend duty at Tilbury. He was appointed as Parish Priest on 10th January 1922, and stayed on for the next thirty-one years.

Father Patrick O'Donnell

Patrick O'Donnell was born at Killiney, Castlegregory, Co. Kerry, on 24th February 1891. He was one of twelve children (of whom nine survived) born to Michael O'Donnell, a farmer, and his wife Mary (nee McKenna) both of whom were natives of Co. Kerry. He was baptised at Castlegregory on 28th February 1891, when his godfather was his maternal uncle, Father Patrick McKenna (later Canon) of St. Mary Moorfields and subsequently Westcliff-on-Sea. Two of Patrick O'Donnell's own nephews would be ordained to the priesthood.

He was educated by the Irish Christian Brothers at Tralee and St. Brendan's College, Killarney, where he was sponsored by his uncle, Father McKenna. As a boy he suffered from a speech impediment, and his consultant advised him to climb the mountains of Kerry and shout aloud to the Atlantic Ocean. This he did, and his impediment was cured. Indeed, for the rest of his long life he was famed for his powerful voice. Through his uncle he was accepted as a student for the Archdiocese of Westminster and he began his studies for the priesthood at St. Edmund's College, Ware, in September 1909. He was selected by Bishop Ward as a student for the Diocese of Brentwood, at which time he was the Senior Divine (April – December 1917).

Patrick O'Donnell was ordained priest by Bishop Ward on 16th December 1917, at St. Edmund's College, Ware. On the first day of 1918 he arrived in Canning Town, where he had been appointed as an assistant priest. As a boy he had read the *Sexton Blake* detective stories and had been fascinated by the description of murderers depositing their victims' corpses over the Iron Bridge at Canning Town. He had wondered what sort of place Canning Town was, but little did he guess that he was to spend a total of thirty-two years of his life there. When he arrived in Canning Town, the country was gripped by a Spanish 'Flu epidemic and he went to work anointing the dying; in one week alone he 'closed the eyes' of fifty parishioners.

In November 1921, while hearing confessions in St. Margaret's Church, he was interrupted by Father John Pettit, secretary to Bishop Doubleday (and a future Bishop of Menevia) with a message that he was to report for weekend duty at Tilbury, where Father Michael Hannan had had to resign owing to ill health. He was to remain at Tilbury for thirty-one years. Throughout his ministry at Tilbury, which included the era of the Great Depression, and living through the severe bombing of the Second World War, Father O'Donnell had a special care for seafarers and their families. He did much to secure the provision of Mass aboard the liners sailing from the port and, via an arrangement with the shipping companies, vessels were supplied with altar requisites. Among the Goan seafarers employed by the P. and O. Line he became a living legend. Tilbury and Canning Town were very much centres for seafarers and Father O'Donnell was instrumental in establishing the work of the Apostleship of the Sea in the Diocese of Brentwood.

At Tilbury he was conscientious in his visits to parishioners and he was very involved in extending Catholic education in the area. He became a co-opted member of the local education committee, and from October 1934 he served as diocesan representative on the Essex Education Committee. In December 1951 he was appointed as an Honorary Canon of Brentwood and in November 1952 he became a Chapter Canon.

On 24th September 1952 Canon O'Donnell was appointed as Parish Priest at Canning Town, taking charge the following month. He retired in March 1977 and celebrated his ninetieth birthday on 24th February 1981. He died a week later at St. Margaret's Convent, Canning Town, on March 4th 1981.

In May 1923 Father O'Donnell wrote to Bishop Doubleday to suggest changes to the northern parish boundary. The current boundary, although straight and well defined, ran straight through what was to become the heart of the village which now was officially known as 'Tilbury North Ward', rather than Chadwell. This had been the main residential area at the time of the building of the docks. If the boundary remained the same, then the 'Tilbury North Ward' would be in the Grays or Stanford-le-Hope Parish. Father O'Donnell wanted Chadwell St. Mary to remain in his parish. This appears to have been recognised, because the 1925 Visitation Returns state the civil and ecclesiastical names of the parish as Chadwell St. Mary, Tilbury.

The population of the area was now 10,000 and the Catholic population included 326 adults, of whom 200 attended Mass, and 286 children, of whom 90 attended Mass. At this time about 45 adults and 40 children received Holy Communion. It was also stated that the ships in the docks were visited every Saturday and Tilbury Hospital visited occasionally. *(Visitation return to Diocese of Brentwood 1925)* Father O'Donnell frequently visited the homes of his parishioners.

Guilds which met in the parish in 1926 included the Children of the Angels, the Children of Mary, the Apostleship of Prayer and the St. Vincent de Paul Society. The debt on the parish was now down to £750. *(Visitation Return 1926)*

An early photograph of Dock Road, Tilbury
(Reproduced by courtesy of Thurrock Library, ref. Tilbury, 17)

There were quite a number of letters between Father O'Donnell and the diocese. One dated 19th October 1927 stated that Bishop Doubleday would be coming to the parish on 4th December 1927 and that the Mass would include a special sermon on the life of St. Francis Xavier. This would suggest that the Goanese seafarers were already featuring largely in the life of the parish. Father O'Donnell said that the church had recently been internally redecorated by the parishioners and electric light had been installed. He added

> The Sanctuary and 4 side altars have been decorated in a simple and I hope, tasteful manner by the Benedict Arts and Crafts Company and the rest of the Church is being completed plainly in 3 or 4 colours. Also, our beautiful altar has been cleaned and renovated and four statues have been renewed. The chess-board design in paint has been removed from the sanctuary floor thus revealing a fine wooden block floor. The total cost will be about £300 and though we started with only a few pounds about 2/3 is already paid from ordinary income – less £20 contributed by the Children of Mary from a play.

He also implies in this letter that there was criticism about this work in some quarters as the school was very much in need of repair and refurbishment, and concerns had been raised about spending scarce resources on the church. Father O'Donnell explained in a letter to the diocese that

> the money contributed week after week would hardly have been given for the school extension as it has largely come from McAlpine workers and from seamen.

In the meantime, the school was set to expand, with an extension to house an additional one hundred and fifty pupils. Shortage of classroom space had already led to the use of the McAlpine Club as a 'temporary' classroom, whilst in the main school 200 children were accommodated in rooms designed for just 140.

The reorganisation of St. Mary's School was also predominantly due to the efforts of Father O'Donnell. The new school was finally built in 1929. Father O'Donnell was required to obtain special permission from Rome to increase the mortgage to cover school building costs. This parish debt had decreased to £750, but £4,000 was needed for the new school. For a while the original mortgage document could not be located, with the solicitors plaintively asking Bishop Doubleday 'I suppose your Lordship is quite sure that it is not in your strong room'. Rome gave the required permission, although the sum to be borrowed was reduced to £3,600, and the school was built. Father O'Donnell agreed to the terms of the loan, which were that the rate of interest was to be 4% per annum, and that the capital was to be repaid at the rate of £100 per year. Father O'Donnell wrote to the diocese

> I accept these conditions and will carry them out as far as is humanly possible, while I am Parish Priest here.

Father O'Donnell's continued interest and work in the sphere of education resulted in St. Mary's becoming the first Catholic voluntary secondary school in Essex. Although predominantly a poor area, the parish continued to grow. This was partly due to the generosity of the Goanese seafarers, many of whom felt the parish was their parish too, contributing both pastorally and financially to its development.

Father O'Donnell spent many Saturday afternoons in the docks talking with the seafarers, and amongst the Goanese seafarers he became quite a legend. In his letters to the diocese there are requests for portable altars, which were clearly to be placed in various ships where the seafarers requested them. At least one shipping company, the P. & O. Line, began to provide these for their crew and, sometimes, the passengers, but Father O'Donnell willingly took on the responsibility for these altars and always visited the ships and their crew when they docked at Tilbury.

At the end of 1928, in a letter to the diocese where he suggested the theme of a sermon to be delivered by Bishop Doubleday, Father O'Donnell recommended a reference to vocations. He added

> It is an amazing fact that this parish has never produced a Priest or a Nun in its 40 years existence! But happily one of our girls left yesterday for the Franciscan Missionaries of Mary.

A report made on 10th February 1930 stated that £16-16-0d had been spent the previous year on a bus to bring parishioners from Chadwell to Mass in Tilbury. The following month, Father O'Donnell received a nasty surprise. He was informed that since 1917, tax had been deducted from the mortgage interest on the parish buildings, but that the mission had not had any taxable income, so there was no tax that could be deducted. The consequence was a tax bill of £86 . 16. 0d. Father O'Donnell appears to have been overwhelmed. He replied at the beginning of April 1930:

> Your letter of the 24th of March has come to me as a great surprise …. I cannot understand how this tax has been allowed to accumulate over such a long period of years. The amount is so staggering and the matter so important that I think you ought to refer it to the Diocesan Authorities and especially to the Trustees of the Gillow Fund.

The reference to the Gillow Fund was well made. John Gillow was a wealthy benefactor who left money when he died in 1894 to establish, promote, support or service the Catholic religion in a number of areas of

England, including Essex. The money usually found its way to parishes that were experiencing severe financial difficulties. When one considers the poverty in the Tilbury area, it might seem surprising that it was not already in receipt of such support. Father O'Donnell had his own views on this, as he made clear in a letter to Bishop Doubleday the same month that he received the tax bill.

21st April 1930

Income Tax
My Lord Bishop,

I much appreciate your personal letter and am very grateful for the grant of £41 from the Gillow Trust towards the income tax on our debt.

Now. my Lord, I am seriously suggesting that during the present difficult years Tilbury should be reinstated upon this Fund.

In the first place, I know that Tilbury lost benefit because of the misleading impression gained by Bishop Ward when he came here on Visitation in 1918. Without going into detailed reference to the past, let me say that he found a house that was richly furnished and he naturally went away with the idea that the Parish was prosperous and promptly cut off the Gillow allowance.

At the time the offertory collection was about £2 per week and all the house fittings with the exception of a desk, bookcase and ancient bed were the property of the Parish Priest as I found to my cost when I came here.

In the second place, Tilbury had three good years 1926 – 8, but now we are relatively much worse off than say in 1922. Our obligations have surely outstripped our means. This past quarter the Sunday offertory averaged only £4 . 5. 0d per week, and if I include £100 per annum off our capital debt, our weekly debt charges come to a little over £5.

The only other source of normal income is the O.W.C., which averages about the same as the church collection and will meet only a half of the usual expenses of the Parish. Actually, there is a deficit of £71 on last quarter's working.

There is a dreadful slump in employment here and I beg you, my Lord to consider putting Tilbury back upon the Gillow Fund, until such time as our resources improve and our burdens become lighter.

I remain,
Yours respectfully,
P. O'Donnell

The repayment record of the original parish loan certainly bears this out.

Between 1906 and 1925, capital repayments had been made every few years, with sums averaging £150. In the ten years between 1925 and 1935, however, no payments were made at all.

Although he had previously stated that he did not want a curate, Father O'Donnell was very pleased when, in 1932, Rev. Francis Brennan, from the Diocese of Kilmore, Ireland, became the first assistant priest to arrive and help with the work in the parish. Our Parish Priest hoped that Father Brennan would put new life into the parish. One of the issues that needed addressing was the plight of the parishioners living at Chadwell St. Mary. There were some seventy Catholics living there, a distance of over two miles from the Parish Church. About thirty of them hired a private motor coach each Sunday to take them to the early Mass, whilst others walked or cycled over for the later Mass. Father O'Donnell suggested that they could hire a room there in a club or a school, to say Mass each week in the area 'which was the centre of the Faith in the old days.' A more permanent solution was out of the question, as the parish was struggling to pay its bills and simply could not afford to buy land or build a Mass Centre.

20,000 people lived in Tilbury in 1933 with a Catholic population of about 1,400. The population had more than doubled but the parish income had hardly increased. Father O'Donnell wrote in that year

> The newcomers are of the very poor, with a few outstanding exceptions, and of necessity they are more of a burden than a help.
>
> The coming of a curate has taken from me part of the source which I have had to use to supplement ordinary parish income – namely half the Christmas and Easter Offerings, stole fees and Mass offerings. This means about £60 a year. It also means a new burden of say £100 per annum – this is curate's salary, keep, extra lighting, heating etc.

A letter from Father O'Donnell in March 1933 recorded that the collections averaged £3-9-8d but expenses continued to be greater than income. In 1933, the Sunday Mass attendance was approximately 600 - 700 people each week and by 1935 Mass was celebrated at 8 a.m. and 10-30 a.m. in Tilbury with additional Masses at Chadwell at 8-30 a.m., and at East Tilbury at 9-45 a.m. There was also a weekly class for children who attended non-Catholic schools. The debt on the church stood at £750 and on the school at £2,800.

Every three years the exterior woodwork and iron work of the church was repainted. The parish certainly made good use of voluntary help, as Father O'Donnell made clear in his report on the five years ended 31st December 1934.

> Re. Schools: most of the expenditure was on the playground surfacing and fencing. Certain men of the Parish gave their labour freely and thereby there was a saving of about £150 to the School's Fund. All have merited the special thanks of the Bishop (Doubleday).
>
> All the Parish property was repainted exteriorly during the summer 1934. Much of the paint was given gratis by Councillor J.J. Sullivan, Southend, and the remainder at a reduced price.
>
> The whole work was done, in their spare time, by certain men and boys of the Parish. Here there was a saving of well over £100 to the Parish Funds. All deserve the Special Commendation of the Bishop.

In February 1936, Father O'Donnell began to make preparations for the golden jubilee of the parish, which he dated from the opening of Tilbury School and the little chapel it contained. He suggested to the diocese that they might wish to become involved :

> In the unlikely contingency that you may feel overburdened with your wealth at any time before October 1937, you might choose to unload a little of it upon us. I am writing this last bit more in play than in earnest – it just struck (me) that you might like to have a hand in the work.

He wrote an open appeal to the parishioners and friends of the parish. In its zeal and enthusiasm in what must have been difficult times, the depth of the Great Depression, it is a salutary example of hope in adversity. Accordingly, I include the full text of the appeal.

The Catholic Church, Tilbury Docks
GOLDEN JUBILEE

OCTOBER
1887

OCTOBER
1937

PLEASE HELP TO FREE IT FOR EVER FROM
ALL EARTHLY BONDS

An Appeal to the Parishioners and other Friends

THE BIRTHDAY
Our Parish was founded in October, 1887, by the Very Rev. CANON KEENS, who was a devoted and much loved priest and a famous Church and School Builder in his day. God rest his soul. Here is an account of the beginnings in his own simple words : "In the early autumn of 1886, having obtained a site in Grays, I began the Church and School of St. Thomas of Canterbury. But I was not allowed to 'graze' long. Another field, two miles away, wanted turning up. This was at Tilbury, where a great immigration of Catholic workers had taken place, in connection with the new Docks. A site of nearly two acres was secured and a School for 200 children was built, a portion of one of the classrooms being screened off for a Chapel. This was opened in October 1887."

THE GOLDEN JUBILEE
Hence our Parish will have been established 50 years on October, 1937, and it behoves us to celebrate the event in a worthy manner.

THE CELEBRATIONS

Please God, there will be a rousing Mission in preparation, a Solemn High Mass of Thanksgiving in the presence of the Bishop (Doubleday), a Solemn Requiem for the Parish Priests and old Parishioners who have gone to their reward; no doubt a Parochial Dinner and Social and of course a Treat for the Children.

THE PROBLEM

But before the great day comes, there is a special work to be done, for which I invite the enthusiastic support of every soul in the Parish and of many generous friends who dwell outside our boundaries. This is the work that awaits our generosity: there is still the remains of an old debt upon the Parish. It originated as a loan of £2600 in the time of Canon Keens and it now stands at £750. We must do all in our power to clear this away before October, 1937, so that on the Jubilee Day we may be able to rejoice that our beautiful Church is free forever for the Worship of God.

THE SOLUTION

At a meeting of the Parishioners, held in the School on February 9th, the following resolution was accepted: That every adult Parishioner aim at contributing £1 to the Golden Jubilee Fund during the next twenty months. It is fully realised that, while many can manage this amount, some cannot do so owing to their small means and some others, urged on by generous impulse, may well exceed it. The Children will be given an opportunity of contributing their pennies and they will gladly do so.

THE METHOD

It is left to the good-will of each adult to decide how and when he/she will provide his/her gift. Some may choose to send their donation direct to the Parish Priest in a lump sum or by instalments, while others may prefer to have a collector call on them weekly or monthly. You are earnestly requested to make known your wishes on the enclosed form and return it to the presbytery as soon as possible.

OUR BISHOP

When our Bishop (Doubleday) became aware of our project he sent me a most encouraging letter, from which I quote: "I am delighted to hear that you and your Parishioners have decided to make a special effort to free the Church at Tilbury from debt before the Golden Jubilee in October 1937. The resolution which the Parishioners have made to contribute individually one pound towards this purpose is in keeping with all the generosity and meritorious labour that this genuinely Catholic congregation has shown in supporting religion during these long years …. I hope to be able to make a contribution to the Fund before the year is out …. I am glad to hear that you are putting the effort under the protection of Our Lady of Lourdes. It shall be remembered in my Masses during the Novena …. and I shall ask her to have a special care of her children at Tilbury, who are setting out on a year's voyage in an argosy to bring honour to her Son ….”

OUR LADY OF LOURDES
Let us place this holy work under the Patronage of our Lady of Lourdes on whose Feast Day it was launched and in whose honour we have already made a Novena of prayers. And let us continue our supplications to her during the months to come, that she might aid us in our long struggle and eventually crown with success our high endeavour to free for ever from all earthly bonds the House of God our Father and the Tabernacle of her Divine Son.

PATRICK O'DONNELL,
Parish Priest

The Feast of our Lady of Lourdes
11th February, 1936

The Golden Jubilee Celebration for the parish was held on Monday, 18th October 1937. Prior to the celebration, Father O'Donnell had asked the P. & O. Company if he could hire a ship for the reception after the Mass. The office staff laughed at this request but, because the P. & O. Company greatly appreciated the efforts made by Father O'Donnell for the welfare of the Goanese seafarers, they were delighted to entertain Bishop Doubleday and other guests to luncheon on the *S. S. Strathaird*, served by the Goanese.

A detailed account of this luncheon is to be found in the booklet created to mark the Consecration of the Church of Our Lady and St. Joseph, in June 1954.

> At the function on the Strathaird, the Chairman was the Staff Commander (Capt. D. Stuart), who, with Capt. Fulcher (Marine Superintendent) represented the P. & O. Shipping Company. Among those also present were the Bishop of Brentwood (Bishop Doubleday), Canons McKenna, Van Meenan, Cameron, Wilson, Fitzpatrick and J. Dacey (Brentwood), Senor Luiz de Castro (Portuguese Consul-General), Mr. J.H. Freeman (Chairman of the Thurrock Urban District Council), Mr. J.A. Brown (a

School Manager and member of the same Council), Mr. G.S. Tilbury (representing the Essex County Council), and others.

The Chairman extended a welcome on behalf of the Chairman and Directors of the P. & O. Company, and said that they were particularly honoured to have with them the Bishop of Brentwood. He felt sure the Bishop's presence would make a deep impression on the Goanese members of the crew. As they knew, the Company had employed Goanese for many years; he did not know exactly how many years, but he had served with them for thirty years, and he knew of no more trustworthy and loyal employees. No one knew them better, from every point of view, than Father O'Donnell. That invitation from the Chairman and Directors of the P. & O. Company was, he was sure, greatly due to Father O'Donnell's devoted attention to their welfare in every way for the past sixteen years. During that period the parish priest had given up much of his time and leisure on their behalf, spending something like two hours every Saturday afternoon with them. Father O'Donnell had also been greatly assisted by members of the Catholic Women's League, many of whom, he was glad to say, were present that day. Since 1932, Father O'Donnell had had the care of some twenty-two altars which had been provided in the P. & O. ships, and the Company were grateful to him and those who assisted him for their work in looking after these altars. He had said, "It's just part of my job as parish priest here," but everyone would agree he had done it very nobly. (Applause)

The Bishop of Brentwood thanked the Chairman for his remarks and the Company for their hospitality, and went on to remark that there was a strong connection between the P. & O. Company and their Catholic Church at Tilbury. That connection had come about because on the ships of the Company there were employed a number of Goanese seamen, who were Catholic, and who had interested themselves in the church at Tilbury and done so much to make it as excellent as it was today. He was extremely pleased to hear Captain Stuart express such a high opinion of the Goanese seamen. When the rumour went abroad, some time ago, that there was a great danger of their losing them, everyone who knew them from a Catholic point of view was extremely sorry. They felt something would be lacking, not only from Tilbury, but from all along the Thames shore, and other ports, such as Southampton and Liverpool, which were blessed by the presence of the Goanese seamen. These men were having a great influence on Catholic life, and it was a great pleasure to know that the connection was going to continue. One never heard the slightest word against their conduct when they were ashore, and they did everything possible to promote the work that was being done in the Catholic Church at Tilbury. They helped Father O'Donnell, and it was only right that the parish priest should be devoted to them. They helped him out of their meagre resources financially and kept the church going. Besides that, they had established an altar of their own, dedicated to St. Francis Xavier, in whose honour they held a special service every year. That was only one side of their goodness. He had been pleased to have some association with them. He remembered on one occasion, when he was holding a reception at their Tilbury Church, forty or fifty of the Goanese seamen formed a square around him, and two of them addressed him in English. They told him they looked upon him as a representative of their Holy Father the Pope, and that as such they were prepared to extend to him the allegiance and honour that was due to His Holiness. Afterwards, when lunch was served in the presbytery, two of the Goanese asked for the honour of waiting upon him. He was delighted to have their services.

Continuing, the Bishop said he proposed sending a telegram from that gathering to the P. & O. Company, expressing thanks for their generous hospitality, and offering felicitations on the Company's centenary. (Applause.)

Referring to the presence of Canon Van Meenan, a former parish priest at Tilbury, the Bishop recalled that when at Tilbury the Canon was told by the Goanese that they would like a statue of St. Francis Xavier in the church. Canon Van Meenan said, "I'll get you one." He bought a statue of St. Francis and was very disappointed when the Goanese, on returning from a voyage and seeing it in church, said, "That's not St. Francis." So they went off to India and returned with a statue of St. Francis – in black. (*See photograph in Chapter thirteen.*)

A further Tilbury story related by the Bishop had reference to another Parish Priest. An elderly lady who came to Tilbury to sail on a ship found that the vessel did not leave until the following day, and elected to stay at Tilbury for the night. She called on the priest to enquire where she could find lodging, and was so disgusted by the humble nature of the quarters in which he was living that she said, "I will give £1,000 to build a presbytery." He hoped that the present fine building was due to the action of a P. & O. Company passenger. (Laughter.)

He thanked the previous rectors for their benefactions to Tilbury, and particularly alluded to the present Parish Priest. Father O'Donnell, he said, had been a great supporter and provider of all the good things that were going on at Tilbury. When he came to Tilbury, Father O'Donnell was faced with an enormous debt on the church and school, but he had paid part of it off and had also brought the old school up-to-date and had built a new school. Obviously the best thing for a Bishop to do was to keep Father O'Donnell there as long as possible, and a good deal longer. (Laughter.) When Father O'Donnell had paid off the debt, given his last ounce of assistance to the Goanese seamen, and given as much attention as possible to the P. & O. Company, he (the Bishop) would think about moving him from Tilbury. Seriously, he was very grateful for the work Father O'Donnell had done, and would like them all to help him in clearing off the debt. He received a letter at the beginning of the year describing the effort made to raise £750, and later, when he was told that £350 had been collected by means of small subscriptions, he had said that he (the Bishop) would give £100.

Finally, the Bishop also expressed his thanks to the Sisters who had worked for so many years in the schools. (Applause.)

In the absence of the Portuguese Ambassador, Dr. Alberto Oliviera, a speech was made by the Consul-General of Portugal, Senor Luiz de Castro. On behalf of the Goanese, as natives of a Portuguese possession, he thanked Father O'Donnell for his care of them and wished every blessing on the church at Tilbury.

Rev. P. O'Donnell, Parish Priest, expressed his thanks to the P. & O. Company for their grand gesture of kindness and hospitality, and he praised the Catholicity of his Goanese flock. He stressed the difficulties of seamen who were without proper churches, schools or even a parish. He thanked the P. & O. Company for its courtesy towards priests. He also thanked Captain Stuart for his kind words in reference to the Goanese seamen. He expressed his gratitude to the P. & O. and other companies for providing altars and altar cases etc., which were much appreciated by Catholic priests, seamen and passengers. He also thanked the Catholic Women's League for caring for these altars.

The Chairman read a message received from Lord Craigmyle and the Directors of the P. & O. Company, in reply to the telegram sent from the luncheon earlier, reciprocating the good wishes expressed.

This lunch followed the Golden Jubilee Mass, which was celebrated by Bishop Doubleday, Canon Van Meenan, Father J. Mulcahy and Father Stonham, O.F.M., a native of the parish. Bishop Doubleday preached at the Mass, referring to the great educational leader, Cardinal Manning, who had opened the school, and praising the sacrifices made by both teachers and parishioners. He also paid tribute to the help received from the Educational Authorities. His Lordship added,

May we be more virile in putting our Catholicity into practice, so that God may give us strength and courage so that His Religion shall be put into the hearts of men.

The schoolchildren sang the Jubilee Mass under the direction of Sisters Borgia and Francis and they were assisted by a priests' choir under the direction of Canon Cameron.

In the evening a social was held in the junior school for 'parents and old folk' with the young people acting as hosts. Two days later the young people had their own celebration holding a dance and on the following Saturday the children 'had a treat'. The next evening the celebrations came to an end with an outdoor torchlight procession. Part of the purpose of the celebration was to reduce the debt on the parish that had originated as a loan of £2,600 and had been steadily reduced to a figure of £750 by the time of the appeal. At the Golden Jubilee the debt was all but eradicated. The parish was now free from debt, as had been hoped, and a valiant effort had been made.

During these celebrations, frequent references had been made to the Goanese seafarers who had become such a feature of life in the Tilbury Parish. But who exactly were these men? *The Thurrock Gazette* reported on the Jubilee celebrations and decided to find out more about the Goanese sailors. Here is the article which appeared in the October 23rd 1937 edition of the paper:

> There were one or two unique features about the celebrations which marked the golden jubilee of the Roman Catholic Church of Our Lady Star of the Sea, Tilbury Docks. The hospitality of the P. & O Steam Navigation Company in lending an ocean-going liner and providing an expensive luncheon for over one hundred people was something that will long be remembered by all those who took part. It gave the celebrations an air of distinction and importance which they could hardly have acquired otherwise, and enabled a notable anniversary to be observed in a fitting manner. But there was a definite reason for this gesture on the part of the shipping company. It was no mere generous whim which caused Lord Craigmyle and his directors to thus entertain the Tilbury Roman Catholics who took part. Definite indication was given during the proceedings that the welfare of the Goanese seamen, who form an important part of all P. & O. crews is a prominent consideration in the Company's policy, and it was made plain that the executive authority appreciated the efforts made by the local priest (Rev. P. O'Donnell) on behalf of these men. The Goanese are devout Roman Catholics, and it is probably no coincidence that they are also one of the most quiet and law-abiding bodies of merchant seamen to be found on English shores. They are a credit both to their faith and their profession, and, as was remarked during the proceedings on Monday, they are an example to other seamen, whatever their colour may be.
>
> The celebrations, therefore, were to a large extent dominated by this Goanese link between a famous shipping company and the Tilbury church. The fact that the jubilee was a memorable one in other respects was not lost sight of, however, and due credit was given to the various priests and their homeland supporters who have assisted in maintaining the community for half a century.
>
> GOANESE
>
> Passengers on P. & O. ships are always interested in the dark-skinned stewards and waiters who attend so quickly and quietly to their material wants. It is obvious to anyone that they are a race apart both from Europeans and the Lascars who undertake the more menial tasks on these vessels. Enquirers are informed that they are natives of Goa, a Portuguese possession in India, not far from Bombay. Their distinctive

racial characteristics are due to the fact that they are descended from a union between the original Portuguese conquerors of Goa and the Indian natives. Albuquerque, who captured Goa in 1510 and all but wiped out the Mahomedan inhabitants, encouraged his men to marry the native women, and in time there grew up a large Eurasian population.

Hard on the heels of the soldiers came the priests and the considerable progress in the conversion to the Roman Catholic faith was consolidated by St. Francis Xavier, when he arrived in 1542. In later years, following the appearance of the Dutch in Indian waters, the colony declined in importance and population. It now has about half a million inhabitants, and its area is 1,350 square miles. The Goanese have a great reverence for the memory of St. Francis Xavier, who was a highly successful Spanish missionary to the Indies.... One illuminating story about the Goanese concerns the remark of a woman who watched a number of them taking part in a Roman Catholic procession through the streets of Tilbury. "Well, that's the first time I knew there were black Irishmen!" she observed.

The day after the Golden Jubilee Mass, Father O'Donnell wrote to the diocese to assure Bishop Doubleday that none of the expenses of the celebrations had been taken from the Parish Jubilee Fund, but had been paid from a special fund raised by a parochial committee which had collected £25 for that purpose. Bishop Doubleday did indeed make a contribution to the Golden Jubilee Fund and his gift of £100 went some way to helping the parish break even.

The parishioners suffered a great deal during the Second World War and many of the children from the parish were evacuated to safer areas. A transit camp was also established in Tilbury and there were many Polish and Canadian soldiers passing through. During war time bombing, the church suffered only superficial damage. A high explosive bomb damaged the church roof and some of the leaded lights in September 1940, with Father O'Donnell attending to the former and leaving the latter to the end of the war. However, in September or October 1940 Father O'Donnell wrote that the church was now practically isolated from the people by a ring of 'time bombs'. He added that most of the parishioners would have to take a very roundabout route to church and was wondering what would happen the following Sunday. In the same air raid, the Grays parishioners had seen bombs falling within one hundred yards of their own church, 'but all is well.' Our redoubtable priest had found 'a much bigger Hall' to accommodate the Chadwell St. Mary parishioners for Sunday Mass, although the offertory from the three Sunday Masses in the parish came to just over two pounds. On 2nd November 1940 there was just one Mass at 8 a.m., followed by

Confessions and then Mass at 9 a.m. at Chadwell. Father O'Donnell also noted that all the Goanese seafarers had left for the duration of the war.

In November 1940, Father O'Donnell wrote to Bishop Doubleday, requesting permission to take down a stone pinnacle over the tabernacle. Weighing nearly half a ton, it had shifted slightly in a bomb blast, and another 'near-miss' could bring it crashing down. Fortunately, the Bishop agreed!

On January 8th, 1941, Father O'Donnell applied to Bishop Doubleday to request assistance from the Diocesan Distress Fund. He had unpaid bills and no money to pay them. The total liability was over £86. It is probable that the disruption in Tilbury caused by the war had led to a reduction in parish income. Father O'Donnell wrote Bishop Doubleday again a few days later.

> We had another 'close shave' last night, three H.E. bombs dropping nearby. Our only damage were some tiles off the Church roof which can be replaced for the cost of twenty to thirty shillings. I am wondering whether his Lordship desires me to make a claim for this small amount: my own feeling is that it would be cheaper in the long run to ignore it.

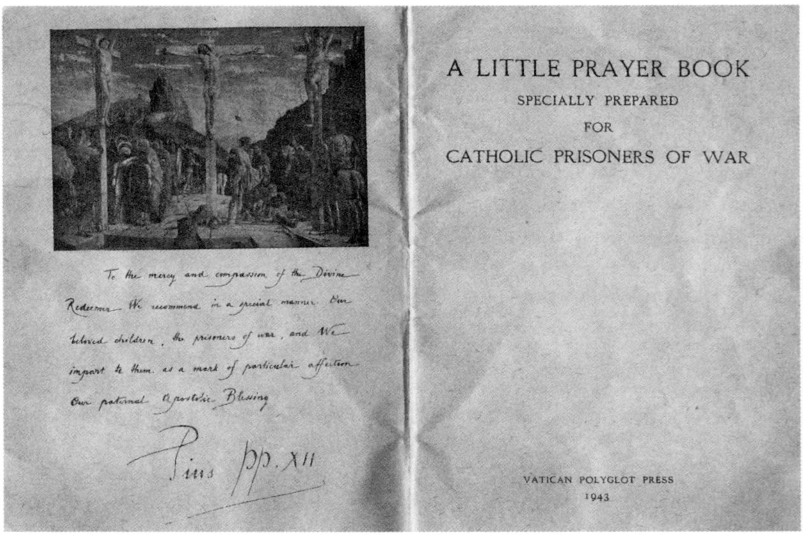

German Prisoners of War made use of this special Prayer Book sponsored by Pope Pius X11

By November 1944, Father O'Donnell estimated the cost of repairs to the church as a consequence of war damage at £125. When we consider that the London docks were targeted by the German airforce, the Church of Our Lady Star of the Sea escaped relatively unscathed. Tilbury docks avoided the massive damage inflicted on the docks closer to the centre of London. The only major building destroyed seems to have been the Tilbury Hotel, which had been a landmark for ships returning to the Thames and had been used by many military personnel preparing for D – Day.

At the end of the Second World War, Father O'Donnell was rather cautious about future expenditure in the parish until everything returned to normal. In April 1946 he estimated that £1,000 would be spent in the next five years, half of it on repairs to the church as a consequence of war damage and half on the building of a new army Hut (?). If Father O'Donnell's instinct was to cut back on expenditure, he was to receive a surprise in November 1949 when he received news from Bishop Doubleday about the inauguration of the Brentwood Schools Building Fund. The Bishop had made a contribution of £20,000 to start the ball rolling. The Parish of Our Lady Star of the Sea was required to make a contribution of £485 per year. The Co-adjutor Bishop of Brentwood, Bishop Beck, wrote:

> I fully realise what an immense burden this places upon the parish, but I have every confidence that your people will generously respond to this appeal for the well-being of our Catholic children throughout the diocese.

This could not have been an easy task for Father O'Donnell, but he responded positively. In January 1951 he wrote to Bishop Doubleday

> Despite the Arctic weather that evening, our Bazaar was fairly successful and I am able to send you our school quota for this year, plus £15 as a nest egg against the possible rigours of 1952!

The parish was obliged to find additional sources of funding to keep the finances afloat. A weekly football pool had been introduced, but Tilbury's assistant priest, Father Martin Kirwan, spotted what he regarded as a flaw in the system. He wrote to Bishop Beck on January 16th 1951, to express his concerns. Briefly, non-Catholics had been allowed to participate in the pool, contrary to the regulations of the Betting and Lotteries Act, 1934. Their presence had been disguised by listing their contributions under the name of an agent, always a Catholic. This seems to have become accepted by custom and practice, but Father Kirwan thought he saw a difficulty, as he explained to the Bishop.

> Now my problem is this: are we being fair to the Catholic Church in violating the civil law in this matter? Do you not think that the non-Catholic who sees us violating the civil law will think less of the Church and is there not the possibility that it might turn away possible converts? I can easily imagine the non-Catholic joining the pool and being very friendly but being a little surprised to see us Catholics doing something not in order. Would it not seem a pity, if not even worse, to lose even one possible Catholic simply because we gain extra money by admitting non-Catholics to the pool?

The Bishop's reply, dated the following day, was both pragmatic and reassuring, if a little short on detail:

> Dear Father Kirwan,
> I have read your letter attentively, and I am quite sure that you need not be anxious about the effect on non-Catholics which the arrangements in your parish, in connection with the football pool, may possibly have.
>
> With a blessing and all good wishes,
> Yours devotedly in Christ,
> Bishop of Tigia

Another connection between Tilbury and Stanford came to the fore around 1948 but was not settled until early 1950. The parish boundary was once again causing concern, but this time it was the East Tilbury boundary. The Bata Shoe Company was extending its housing and the existing parish boundary ran straight through the new housing estate. The factory was in Tilbury Parish and the new residential area predominantly in Stanford Parish. Father O'Donnell celebrated Mass in the Bata Estate Hotel each Sunday. Both he and Father Snell, Stanford's Parish Priest, felt that the whole of East Tilbury should be in one parish and as Father Snell could not provide a Mass there it was agreed that East Tilbury should be entirely in the Parish of Our Lady Star of the Sea, Tilbury. This was agreed by Bishop Beck. A further extension of the parish's work occurred in 1950, when approval was given for an early morning Mass to be celebrated at Tilbury Hospital on one weekday each week.

Councillor Feenan, a prominent member of the Catholic community, died in 1951. Aged 76, he was the oldest member of Thurrock Council. He had first been elected in 1915 as Labour candidate for the old Tilbury Urban Council, and he served there for fifteen years, becoming chairman.

On the amalgamation of council authority in 1936, he became a representative for Tilbury ward. He was returned unopposed in 1939 and was a member of Thurrock Council until his death. He served on all the committees of the Council, including the Redevelopment Committee which oversaw the further development of the dockside area, and was a manager of a number of local schools.

Councillor Feenan was born in Liverpool and came to Tilbury with his parents whilst still a child. He obtained his first job at a Grays printers and then went to sea. When he finished with the sea he looked for work on land. It is a mark of the harshness of those times that he was then not yet thirteen. He worked for a long time with the Atlantic Transport Line.

Father Walsh spoke at Councillor Feenan's funeral. 'Jack' Feenan, as he was affectionately known, was a Catholic by conviction and he remained true to his convictions to the end of his days.

> He kept the faith and now God has allowed him to receive his reward. We must thank God for giving him those precious gifts. He was more than a good citizen, he was an outstanding figure in the civic life of this area. It has been thought and sometimes said that it is very difficult, even impossible, for a loyal Catholic to be a good citizen. It is men like John Feenan who show how misconceived and unmerited is that notion.

Hugh Delargy, Member of Parliament for Thurrock, paid this tribute to Councillor Feenan.

> Everyone in Thurrock knew of Jack Feenan, but the people of Tilbury knew him best. He gave them a lifetime of service and he served them right to the end. It was Jack Feenan's achievement more than anyone else's that the appearance of Tilbury has changed. The broad Highway that bears his name and the new redevelopment scheme that is nearing completion are monuments to his memory.
>
> He was frank and forthright, sometimes truculent, but he was quite devoid of personal ambition. Although he was the senior on the Council in age and experience, he refused the biggest offices.
>
> I am personally indebted to him. From the moment I arrived in Thurrock, he gave me his help and advice and, above all, his friendship. But we were all his friends. We will all miss him.

In November 1951, Bishop Beck decided to honour Father O'Donnell.

> I feel that some recognition should be made of your persevering and patient work on the Essex Education Committee, and I should like to offer you an honorary canonry in the Diocese.

Canon O'Donnell informed Bishop Beck on 23rd April 1952 that the Council had promised an acre of land in Chadwell for the building of a church but that they had not yet fixed the price or the exact location. He was also seeking land in East Tilbury, but here, the Bata Shoe Company would not sell any land and he was seeking a site on the perimeter of their estate. Money remained a problem, as can be seen in a letter to Bishop Beck in April 1952.

> I have received both your letters on the remainder of the old mortgage on this parish and much regret I cannot see my way at present to pay off the whole amount. I am enclosing a cheque for £33 . 19 . 0d in settlement of interest and £30 off the capital.
>
> Since Christmas I have been spending rather heavily on necessary repairs and at the same time I am trying to put together a nest egg for the badly-needed decoration of the Church and for the purchase of land at Chadwell St. Mary and East Tilbury.

On 13th July 1952 Bishop Beck briefly visited the parish on his return from a Seafarers' Meeting and unveiled a statue of the Sacred Heart in the church grounds, erected by Goanese seafarers in memory of fallen comrades.

In September 1952 Canon O'Donnell became the Parish Priest of Canning Town, and his thirty-one years at Tilbury came to an end. He had steered the young parish through some difficult times, from the early days when its financial future seemed perilous through to the long years of the Great Depression and the rigours of the Second World War and its aftermath. He had encouraged a parish with few financial resources to offer what it had – the active participation of its people in the repair and refurbishment of its parish buildings and the steady growth of a strong, Catholic community. He played a major part in the construction of school buildings, and a greater role in the spiritual support he gave so unstintingly.

Chapter Four : Father John Byrne

The parishioners who welcomed Father O'Donnell in 1921 and saw him appointed as Parish Priest in 1922 would have had no idea that he would remain in the parish for over thirty years. Equally, when Father John Byrne arrived in September 1952, no-one would have realised that another era was about to begin. Their new Parish Priest was also to remain in Tilbury for over thirty years.

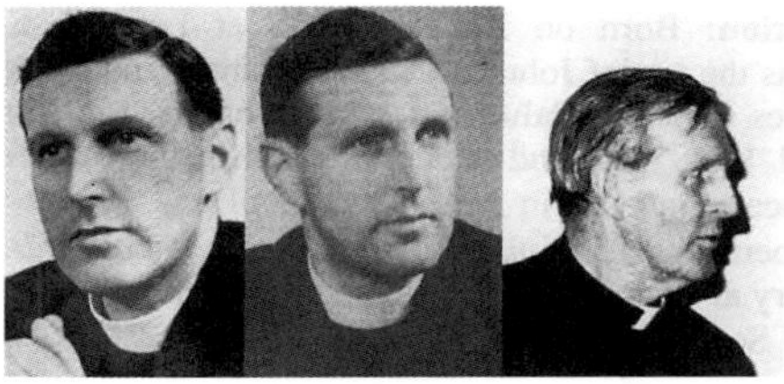

Father John Byrne

John Joseph Byrne was born on October 27th, 1902 at Bagenalstown, Co. Carlow. He was the eldest of five children (two brothers and two sisters) of Joseph Byrne, a baker and his wife Margaret (nee Fitzpatrick) of Royal Oak Road, Bagenalstown, both of whom were natives of Co. Carlow. He was baptised at Bagenalstown on November 2nd 1902 and confirmed on May 8th 1912. He was educated by the De La Salle brothers at St. Joseph's Academy, Bagenalstown, and in 1921 entered St. Patrick's College, Carlow as a student for the Diocese of Kildare and Leighlin.

He applied for incardination into the Diocese of Brentwood, which was granted on September 30th, 1925 and on June 12th 1927 he was ordained priest at St. Patrick's College by Bishop Cullen of Kildare and Leighlin.

Father Byrne entered the Diocese of Brentwood on 26 July 1927, where he was appointed as assistant priest at Leigh-on-Sea. Two months later, on 27 September 1927, he was appointed as an assistant priest at Canning Town. In 1932 Father Byrne was appointed as assistant priest at Brentwood Cathedral where, on 4th May 1933, he was appointed as priest-in charge *pro tem*, following the death of Canon Norris. Later in 1933 he was appointed as assistant priest at Chingford.

Father Byrne became the Parish Priest of Witham on July 1st 1939. He became a much respected figure in the town, known for his gentle manner and pastoral zeal, especially among the families of his widely scattered parish, and he grew particularly attached to the countryside.

On September 21st 1952 Father Byrne was appointed as Parish Priest of Tilbury, where he took charge on October 10th. Although the move from a rural setting to a busy port was unsettling at first, Father Byrne came to love his dockside parish, and its people him. Apart from an annual holiday in Ireland and a pilgrimage to Lourdes, Father Byrne ministered tirelessly at Tilbury. His contribution to the life of the diocese was recognised when, on April 5th 1977, Bishop Casey appointed him as an Honorary Canon of Brentwood, two months before his Golden Jubilee. This gesture greatly touched him and was much appreciated by the parishioners of Tilbury.

Canon Byrne died in Orsett Hospital on December 30th 1982. His Requiem Mass was celebrated by Bishop McMahon at Tilbury on January 7th 1983 and his burial took place in the cemetery at Chadwell St. Mary.

One of Father Byrne's first tasks was to confirm the boundaries of his parish. In a letter to the diocese, he provided the detail.

> I enclose our Parish boundaries.
> <u>Tilbury and Grays</u>
> Lighthouse at Tilbury Ness, thence by straight line to where Dock Road leaves the railway; North along the Dock Road to the Rookeries and by path past the Rookeries to the Chadwell Road, just east of the Cemetery. Across the road and by Russell's path to the Chadwell-Baker Street Road, just west of point 96.
> <u>Tilbury and Stanford-le-Hope</u>
> Thence to point 96 on the Brentwood-Tilbury Road; across this road and by path to point 85 on the Chadwell-Muckingford Road. East along this road to the George Inn at Muckingford, then by direct road through East Tilbury, Coalhouse Fort to the River Thames' County Boundary. By the River Thames to the Lighthouse at Tilbury Ness.

The very first document I encountered in the research for this book was the Boundary Commission statement on Tilbury. It seems to date from a simpler time.

> Thurrock Wharf as crow flies to Dock Road, along the road by Cemetery, along Chadwell Road, to George Inn, thence by Main Road, to East Tilbury, and Jetty, thence by river to Thurrock Wharf.

The year after Father Byrne's arrival in Tilbury, a national crisis occurred. On the night of Saturday 31st January, a combination of high tides, low pressure and a heavy storm caused a severe rise in the water level of the North Sea. The coastlines of Eastern Scotland and England, of Belgium and the Netherlands were inundated and sea levels were recorded at over 18 feet above normal. In the Netherlands, there were almost two thousand deaths. In Britain the death toll on land was over three hundred, with the media concentrating on Canvey Island, where 58 people drowned in their homes or died from exposure.

At Tilbury two major breaches of the sea wall occurred, one near to Tilbury Fort and a second, more serious breach, in the marshes to the east. At just after one o'clock in the morning of February 1st, the seawater began to flood into Tilbury. What happened next was recorded in an excellent book, *The 1953 Essex Flood Disaster*, written by Patricia Rennoldson Smith.

> Within minutes the whole of Tilbury, to the bottom of the hill at Chadwell St. Mary was flooded and water was halfway up the second storey of most houses. Residents Angela and Jim Rowland were woken at 3.00 a.m. by a neighbour warning them that water was coming across the fields: floodwater from the east, where it was least expected. The police and local volunteers began running through the streets, shouting and blowing whistles to wake people. Once upstairs, with whatever they could grab for comfort to take with them, people were trapped, unable even to flush their toilets as the sanitary services had failed. The Rowland family were rescued late on 1 February by servicemen wading through waist-high water level to reach them. They were taken to an emergency centre at Chadwell St. Mary School. The whole town was evacuated, most returning home by the end of February. There was one fatality in Tilbury; a 79 year old lady died alone in her home.......
>
> Police Inspector Northover of Tilbury, in his report, praised the efforts of the services, hospital staff and volunteers, especially Scouts, Cubs and Brownies. He also commented that 'The courage and cheerfulness of the people of Tilbury in the face of widespread disaster was really wonderful'.

There was no damage to the church, school, convent or presbytery. However, the flooding was extensive as the above account shows, but Tilbury received little media attention. The primary focus was on Canvey Island. The diocese was aware of the situation and distributed grants from the Catholic relief funds that had been set up internationally to help the flood victims, as a letter from Bishop Beck reveals:

February 26, 1953.

My dear Father Byrne,

I am sorry that I have not been able to get over to Tilbury to see you since the floods, but I hope that things in the parish are gradually getting back to normal. As you probably know, we have received a number of generous subscriptions and donations towards the cost of flood relief, among them a cheque for £800 from the Apostolic Delegate in the name of the Holy Father. I have great pleasure in enclosing herewith a cheque for £200 which I am allocating to Tilbury from the Holy Father's donation. It is to be used at your discretion to help the victims of the floods, both non-Catholic and Catholic. I would suggest that you write to the Apostolic Delegate, asking him to transmit the thanks of the parish to the Holy Father. Should you require any further assistance, please do not hesitate to let me know. I hope to be able to come over to Tilbury during the course of the week after next.

We have received a number of very touching messages of sympathy from school children in France, and I shall be grateful if you can arrange for a reply to be sent to the enclosed letters from some of the school children at Tilbury. I know that replies to these letters will be much appreciated in France.

With a blessing, and all good wishes,

Yours devotedly in Christ,

Bishop of Brentwood

Father Byrne replied almost immediately, on February 28th.

My Lord Bishop,

I am most grateful to you for your kind letter enclosing £200 from the Holy Father for Tilbury Flood victims and I thank you on my own behalf and on behalf of the people.

The salt water has caused heavy loss in many homes, especially in the case of ground-floor flats, bungalows and pre-fabs. There is however a good organisation working to investigate all losses. I am on the committee and we meet every evening. It is now known that over 7,000 people were evacuated from flooded houses in Tilbury and a total of 2,500 homes were flooded out of a total of 2,750. Less than 4 Catholic homes escaped having the flood in. 33 streets had over 2 feet of water. 22 streets had under 2 feet of water. The local police (officer) Inspector revealed this at one of the meetings, adding that Tilbury was next after Canvey Island for numbers evacuated and homes flooded.

The Headmistress of the Primary School drew my attention to the fact that all the local schools received help, gifts etc. from other schools in various places but ours did not receive any, due possibly to the fact that Tilbury received little notice in the Catholic Press.

If any Catholic Schools make an offer of help for Catholic School children in flood areas, I know you will think of Tilbury.

I am very pleased to know you will visit us soon, and I would be glad if you came to us for lunch on the day of your visit.

With many thanks for the generous help you have sent us,

Yours very gratefully in Domino

John J. Byrne

A month after the floods a £500 donation was received from the Canadian Hierarchy and the Bishop of Luxemburg. The following year, January 1954, Bishop Beck sent another cheque for a very precise amount for Flood Relief, as Father Byrne's response reveals.

15th Jan 1954

My Lord Bishop,

I am most grateful to you indeed for the cheque for £55. 19. 6d which you so kindly sent me for Flood Relief donations.

I am glad to say the Tilbury people have made a remarkable recovery from the Flood disaster, and many homes look bright and cheerful again, but in a number of cases where the water reached up to 4 feet and more the walls have become wet, spoiling the wall-paper and paint and these people will receive no further help from the Lord Mayor's Fund. Then there were people who claimed very little and who now need some help.

With renewed thanks and best wishes to Your Lordship
Yours very obediently,
Respectfully in Domino
John J. Byrne

But whilst attention was focused on the crisis caused by the extensive flooding of Tilbury, ordinary life had to go on. The population of Tilbury was growing, and with it the number of Catholics. The primary school could no longer accommodate all of its pupils and an extra classroom was needed. Father Byrne wrote to Bishop Beck to request permission to proceed with the building. Wishing to improve the interior of the parish church, he had enlisted the support of an old friend of the parish, as this letter shows:

May Procession

17th September 1953

My Lord Bishop,

I enclose information which will show the urgent need of an additional classroom in our Primary School.

1. Two reports from Sister Bernadette showing the position as on 24 July (the end of the school year) and what the position is at present (the start of the new school year).
2. A report obtained by Councillor Feenan, school manager, from the Council offices, regarding the future development of Tilbury.
3. The Education Authority has notified Sister Bernadette that she may have an additional teacher 1953-1954 but there is no class-room or school space available.
4. We now have 40 children from Chadwell in the Primary School. The Catholic families there are growing in numbers and show a good percentage of families with young children. On Wednesday, for example, I discovered 7 families with a total of 17 children.

When I visited you in July you very kindly assured me we could have an additional classroom. The land is available. May I ask could we proceed in the near future with arrangements for it to be erected at an early date.

I wrote to Canon Van Meenan about having windows in the Sanctuary of our Church. He stated that there was no reason whatever why these windows should not be put in and also said they would make a great improvement. Even when the sun is shining brightly in the nave, the sunshine never comes on the altar or on the immediate vicinity. The windows would brighten up the whole Sanctuary.

Would your Lordship grant me permission to proceed with this work giving more light to our Sanctuary at a cost of £85.

Begging your Lordship's Blessing on us
Your obedient servant
John J Byrne

The Consecration of the Church of Our Lady Star of the Sea took place on 8th June 1954, by Right Rev. George Andrew Beck, Bishop of Brentwood. A special booklet was produced for this momentous event. Although the Consecration took place in June, the Consecration Feast Day was to be celebrated annually on 14th May. By this time, the population of Tilbury was estimated at 20,000, of whom over 2,000 were Catholic, including 1,550 adults and 750 children (Brentwood Visitation Form 1954).

Bishop George Beck summarised the history and progress of the Parish of Our Lady Star of the Sea in a foreword he wrote to the special booklet created to mark the Consecration. It might serve as a useful summary of what you have read so far in this book.

The history of the parish of our Lady Star of the Sea at Tilbury is typical of the growth of the Catholic Church in and around London in the later years of the nineteenth century, and in our own days. Slowly at first, but with gathering momentum, the Church is coming back again to Essex, from which it was almost completely driven in the penal days after the Reformation.

The story of Tilbury parish is one in which a number of important names figure prominently. It was through the zeal of Father Keens, better known as Canon Keens, a great church builder, generously supported by a wealthy benefactress, that the foundations were laid at Tilbury, and it is significant that the Catholic school was the first building to be erected. It is proper that the names of Canon Keens and Sister Mary should be commemorated on the memorial tablets in the church.

Canon Van Meenan, a worthy successor of Canon Keens, carried the work a stage further with the building of the present church – thanks again to the generosity of Sister Mary. No reference to the parish could fail to note the sterling work of consolidation achieved by Canon O'Donnell, through whose efforts the school was re-organised, thus giving us the first Catholic voluntary secondary school in Essex. Catholic sailors from all over the world will pay tribute to Canon O'Donnell's work for the crews of ships docking at Tilbury, and particularly for his care in the provision of altars and Mass equipment.

The beautiful cover of the souvenir booklet issued to mark the Consecration of Our Lady Star of the Sea : June 1954

The devoted work of the Sisters of Mercy must not be overlooked. It has been of permanent value, particularly to the youngest members of the parish.

The seal of the Church's approval on all this work will be the formal consecration of the church for which Father Byrne has now so happily provided.

George Andrew Beck: Bishop of Brentwood

Apart from these outstanding names, there is a living history of the parish in its day-to-day life – a history of the ordinary parishioners, the Catholic people of Tilbury and its neighbourhood. For them the church is a centre of religious life – where they assist at Mass and receive the Sacraments, where so many of them have been baptized and had their marriages blessed. It is the church to which so many former members of the parish have been brought after death, where the prayers of the liturgy have gone up for their eternal rest. All this work, prayer and activity will be remembered with joy and gratitude when the solemn consecration of the church takes place. The elaborate ritual leading up to the consecration of the altar with oil and fire in the midst of incense is a vivid reminder that this building is something more than bricks and mortar. It is a place of sacrifice, housing the altar of God, where day by day the Holy Mass, the Sacrifice of the New Testament, takes place. In the words of the liturgy, it is meant to be the House of God and the Gate of Heaven.

May the solemn consecration of the church of Our Lady Star of the Sea draw down God's blessing on all the members of the parish, and on all who come to worship within its walls.

GEORGE ANDREW,
Bishop of Brentwood

The Interior of the Church in 1954

In the same booklet, Father Byrne was to add his own thoughts on the Consecration.

"This is the House of God and
the Gate of Heaven"

(Genesis *xxviii,* 17)

The Consecration of a church is one of the most picturesque and most inspiring ceremonies in the Catholic Ritual. By Consecration our church of Our Lady Star of the Sea will be dedicated in perpetuity to Almighty God. Year by year, the anniversary of the Consecration will be celebrated as a great Feast Day; and the twelve candles under the Consecration Crosses will be lit and will burn throughout the octave. The Consecration of our church will thus be a memorable event and another great landmark in the History of the Parish.

If this were just an ordinary year we would not have invited our Bishop to come to us so soon for the Consecration of the church, we would have waited until 1956, the Golden Jubilee of the Church. But this Marian Year (8th December, 1953, to 8th December, 1954) is a very special year for all of us, and particularly for this Parish of Our Lady, for it is a Year of Joy and Thanksgiving for the Proclamation of the Dogma of Our Blessed Lady's Immaculate Conception, a most appropriate year, therefore, in which to have this church of Our Lady Consecrated. How grateful then we must be to Almighty God that our church has been preserved from destruction during the war, and especially from one particularly near miss one Sunday morning during the celebration of Holy Mass. How grateful we must be also, that the Church, Convent, Schools and Presbytery were all undamaged by the disastrous flood waters which inundated nearly all Tilbury on that awful Sunday morning of 1st February, 1953, when so many hundreds of houses were flooded and thousands of men, women and children had to be evacuated inland.

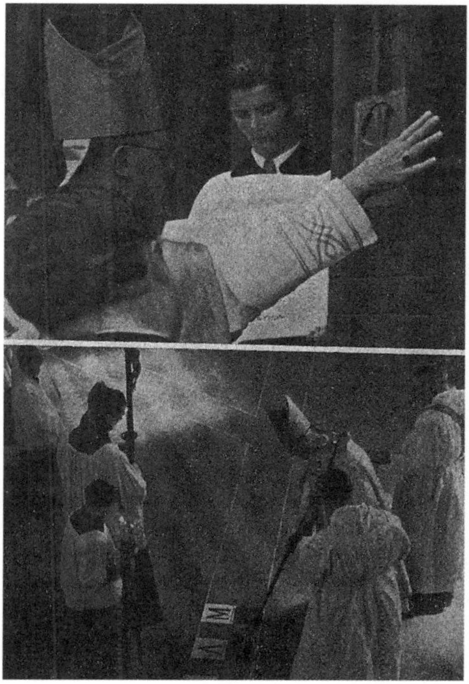

Scenes from the Consecration of the Parish Church of Our Lady Star of the Sea, Tilbury, 8th June 1954

We owe a big debt of gratitude to Very Rev. Canon Van Meenan for having undertaken and built for us this beautiful and lasting memorial to the Glory of God. We must remember, too, in our Masses and Prayers, all those early pioneers of this parish – those priests and people, who have lived and struggled and made such heroic sacrifices throughout the past sixty-seven years. We are now enjoying the fruits of their prayers and generous self-sacrifices. May their devotion and fidelity be a great inspiration to us all for the future, to pray and work for the Honour and Glory of God and the salvation of souls.

Very Rev. Canon O'Donnell, who laboured here for thirty-one long years, found a beautiful church on his arrival; his work lay in other spheres, particularly in the educational sphere. We owe him a debt of gratitude for his work for Tilbury Catholic Schools. Overcoming many difficulties he was instrumental under God for the erection of the present Junior School in 1929 and the Secondary Modern School in 1947; and what a big debt of gratitude we owe to the Mercy Convent Sisters for their long years of untiring work for the schools and Parish since they first came to Tilbury in 1905. We thank also the Headmaster and the Headmistress, and all their staff for carrying out their noble work so faithfully, and also all who have laboured in this parish for God and His Church.

On the doors of the Tabernacle are written these words "Dominus Dei et Porta Coeli" (House of God and Gate of Heaven). May these significant words inspire all to pay due honour to Our Divine Lord truly present in the Tabernacle, to receive Him frequently in Holy Communion, and to visit Him frequently in His Church, where He dwells Sacramentally amongst us.

In conclusion, may we in this parish of Our Lady Star of the Sea be deeply influenced by the words of the Holy Father, addressed to us for our guidance in this year of Our Lady.

"Let us all gather around the Altar of the Virgin Mother of God .... and let them offer not only the flowers of the field and of the garden, not only their suppliant prayers, but also the resolution to lead a more holy life in the conviction that nothing is more acceptable to the Divine Redeemer, nothing more welcome to His Mother."

(Encyclical Letter of Pope Pius XII)

(FULGENS CORONA)

" In Thy Name is this House begun, in Thy Name may it be completed, and may Thy Blessing long preserve it from all harm." (Consecration Prayers)

23rd April 1954 JOHN J. BYRNE

During the celebrations at the Consecration, many references were made to the Sisters of Mercy and the major contribution they had made to the parish. At the time of the Consecration, they had served in the parish for almost fifty years, but by the time that you read this book it will have been well over one hundred and ten years.

The Lady Chapel at the Time of the Consecration

The special booklet created for the Consecration included detail on their history and their boundless charity.

THE COMING OF THE CONGREGATION OF THE MERCY SISTERS TO TILBURY

The Congregation of the Sisters of Mercy was founded in Dublin in 1831 by Reverend Mother Catherine McAuley, for "the relief of the suffering and the instruction of the ignorant." During the 120 years of its existence, the Congregation has spread to an extraordinary degree, and the Sisters in their black habits and veils, white coifs and guimps, are now to be found all over the English-speaking world.

The Sisters first came to Tilbury nearly fifty years ago. The "parish" at that time consisted of a few streets of small houses and a school building in Dock Road ("the Old School"), which was used as a Mass Centre on Sundays and as a schoolroom on weekdays. The Parish Priest, Canon Van Meenan, at that time was anxious to obtain the help of a Community of Nuns, who would teach in the Schools and also undertake the visitation of the Catholic families in the district, and was able to arrange with the

Reverend Mother Superior of the Sisters of Mercy, Tavistock Square, London, to send some of the sisters to open a new Convent in Tilbury.

So, in January 1905, the Sisters, who are bound by their Religious Vows to devote their lives to the "service of the poor, sick and ignorant," took a house in Dock Road (the present Trevor Villas) and began their work of teaching the children and visiting the small Catholic population in their homes. Later on, the adjoining house was also acquired and, in 1909, the present Convent in Malta Road was built.

An early photograph of the Sisters of Mercy Convent, Malta Road

The Tilbury Community continued to flourish as a "branch house," dependent on the "Mother House" in Tavistock Square until 1923, when that part of the Archdiocese of Westminster which was in the County of Essex was formed into a new Diocese of Brentwood. The Tilbury Convent of Mercy then became an independent house in the new Diocese.

At the outbreak of war in 1939 the Sisters were evacuated with the school children to Holt in Norfolk, and the Convent had to be closed for a few months. However, in January 1940, some of the Sisters returned to re-open part of the School for those children who still remained in Tilbury. Shortly before the fall of France, in 1940, a second evacuation took place, and the Sisters accompanied the children to Wiltshire. The Convent withstood the heavy bombing, which levelled so many of the Tilbury houses, although walls and ceilings were cracked, for, like the Church, it was constructed on reinforced ferro-concrete piles.

On the Feast of our Lady of Mount Carmel, July 1952, a branch house was opened at Thorpe Bay, as a Guest House for ladies. Here, at "The Haven," a happy home in a Catholic atmosphere is offered to elderly ladies who need to find quiet and rest, with care and sympathy, in their declining years. Ladies are also received for short holidays. A year later, in May 1953, the house adjoining "The Haven" was also obtained as a Rest house for Sisters. Plans are also being made for a second branch Convent to be opened at Chadwell St. Mary, as soon as practicable, to serve the needs of the Church and Parish, which will develop there when the Council's new Housing Estate is built.

The Branch House in Burgess Road, Thorpe Bay

Sister Therese Connolly was appointed as the first Superior of the Branch House in Thorpe Bay. It proved to very popular for both Sisters and other ladies until it closed in December 1963.

Brentwood Diocesan Pilgrimage to Lourdes, May 1956

In 1956, the Diocesan Pilgrimage to Lourdes included a good number of the parishioners from Our Lady Star of the Sea, as this fine photograph reveals. Do you recognise any of the participants?

Canon O'Donnell with members of the Tilbury Parish, on the Lourdes Pilgrimage, May 1956

At the beginning of 1957 Father Byrne asked Bishop Wall for permission to celebrate an evening Mass every Sunday, because many of the men in the parish were unable to attend Mass on Sunday as they had to report for work in the docks in the morning. He also added that this too would benefit the Goanese seafarers as many of them also had to work on Sunday mornings. At the time of writing the letter there were three P. & O. ships in the port, with a total of 500 Goanese on board. Permission was given by Bishop Wall on 11th January 1957, and on 3rd February 156 people attended the evening Mass, with 25 receiving Holy Communion. These were mainly dock workers, seafarers, nurses and people from Chadwell, of whom about 40% formerly attended morning Mass. To begin with, the arrangement was agreed as a temporary measure. However, in June 1957, Father Byrne asked for a more permanent arrangement, based on the numbers of people who were now attending the Sunday evening Mass, 140 people being the average attendance. The diocese agreed with this request, and renewed the permission for the Sunday evening Mass indefinitely.

A beautiful interior photograph of Our Lady Star of the Sea

The Brentwood Visitation Form dated 29th June 1958 stated that every family in Tilbury was visited each month and families in Chadwell and East Tilbury visited every four months by the two priests. The Sisters taught in the schools, cleaned the sanctuary weekly and prepared the altar for Mass. Two confraternities existed in the parish, those of the Blessed Sacrament and Christian Doctrine. The Visitation Form stated

> When the boys leave school they join the Squires. There is a youth club for 11+ boys. ... To encourage conversion the laity are encouraged to bring Non-Catholics for instruction.

The church was open from 6-45 a.m. to 9 p.m. Nor was the parish in debt; in fact there was a credit of £1,327. 1. 7d. There was, however, no shortage of deserving causes for this surplus. The main concern was the need to extend and improve the two St. Mary's schools which the parish maintained. Although the total costs of the extensions were estimated at over £24,000, the Ministry of Education would pay 75% of the bill, leaving the parish to find over six thousand pounds.

In 1961, it was reported that 350 families were visited each month and there were lots of new families moving to Chadwell. The Sisters were noted as visiting the sick when asked to do so. Confraternities were now the Pages and Knights of the Blessed Sacrament, looked after by the Sisters. After leaving school, both boys and girls were asked to join the Young Christian Workers.

Father Byrne's first Double Wedding : 22nd October 1960
Noel Fields and Kay O'Toole; Dave Robinson and Sheila O'Toole

The Church of Our Lady Star Of The Sea, 1963

Three years later there were still many new families moving to Chadwell and 58 children from there travelled by coach to St. Mary's School. The Catholic children from East Tilbury travelled to St. Joseph's School in Stanford-le-Hope. Two youngsters from the parish were mentioned as interested in becoming priests.

A Tilbury Skyline that Illustrates the Significance of the Docks

The parish continued to be beset with financial difficulties. In February 1965, Father Byrne wrote to the diocese requesting help.

> Very Rev and Dear Canon,
>
> I enclose £781 towards the Schools Quota.
>
> As things are in this Parish, this amount is particularly heavy. We have to maintain a Secondary as well as a Primary School. The recent improvements to existing toilets as shown on enclosed list indicate the heavy expenditure involved. The total cost to us on whole project is also shown, £6,072 . 18 . 3d.
>
> Another Primary Class Room is urgently required, cost approx £5,000.
>
> The weekly Envelope Collection for Chadwell Church Building Fund comes to approx £13. The result is a small offertory collection of about £3. The Fund now is £4,500 . 8 . 0d. The East Tilbury Fund Collection, also by Envelope, brings in £5 . 10 . 0d per week. The Fund Total is now £1221. 10. 10. The two funds now amount to £5721. 18. 0d. So the burden of paying the Schools Quota rests almost completely on the Tilbury Congregation; 1st Mass attendance 58 last Sunday; 2nd Mass 147, many children; Evening Mass 165.

I feel justified in appealing to you to let us off this year, 1965 and reduce our Quota to £350 per annum for the subsequent years. We are too heavily assessed.

Yours gratefully,
John J. Byrne

It must be acknowledged that with the Chadwell and East Tilbury congregations focused on fund-raising for new buildings almost to the exclusion of all else, Father Byrne had a point. The only real parish income was indeed from the congregation at the Church of Our Lady Star of the Sea. However, if Father Byrne was hoping for some relief, he was soon to be disappointed. A few days later, he received his reply.

Dear Reverend Father,

Thank you for your letter of the 12th February enclosing your Schools Quota. I do appreciate the burdens which you have to face but I cannot hold out any hope for a reduction in the Quota, and in no case can it be remitted. School building which has been undertaken has been done so on the assumption that the Parishes will meet the Quota fixed, unless this happens certain projects will have to be brought to a standstill.

With every kind wish.

A Mission was held in the parish in May 1966.

By 1968 the Sisters' role in the parish now included instructing converts and visiting the sick at home and in hospital. St. Joseph's Church Hall in Chadwell had opened in March 1968 and Mass was now celebrated there, and occasionally on a weekday in Tilbury Hospital.

A Mission was given in the parish by the Redemptorist Fathers between 21st September and 5th October 1969.

In 1971 the parish had a debt of £4,247-13-10d on St. Joseph's Church Hall. By 1973 a Parish Council existed and a youth club which met once each week. In 1975, Father Byrne made an attempt to obtain a pension for his housekeeper, but the diocese advised him that the maximum age for entering such a pension scheme was 55 years. Unfortunately, the lady was 56 and so nothing could be done.

The parish boundaries were once again altered in 1975 when the Parish of St. Joseph, Chadwell St. Mary was formally created. East Tilbury was then finally transferred to the Parish of Our Lady and St. Joseph,

Stanford-le-Hope, and Tilbury no longer had a need for an assistant priest. The new boundaries effectively cut the number of Catholics in the Tilbury Parish by half.

In April, 1977, just two months before his Golden Jubilee, Father Byrne was appointed as an Honorary Canon of Brentwood.

> The installation of the three new Canons at Brentwood Cathedral was a most impressive ceremony. Canon Petry said it was inspiring to see so many supporters and "Fans" present. His Lordship the Bishop remarked that it was most gratifying to see such a big crowd on what was after all a working day, and it showed how pleased parishioners were about the honour conferred on their Parish Priests. In a short homily, the Bishop thanked Canon J. Byrne for his devoted service of fifty years to the Diocese and congratulated him on his coming Golden Jubilee on the 18th June at which his Lordship would be Chief Celebrant at the Concelebrated Mass.
>
> Just before 11.00 a.m. the Canons-elect took their places in the middle front bench. Then the Canons went in procession to the door of the Cathedral where they met the Bishop (Casey) and escorted him to the altar while the hymn "Come Holy Ghost" was sung.
>
> When they were all in their places the Secretary of the Chapter read the documents of appointment which gave details of the special work done by the Canons-elect. Then the Canons-elect were brought to the altar by their sponsors, to kneel before the Bishop and make profession of their faith before being vested by the Bishop in rochet and mozzetta. The sponsors then took the new Canons to their places in the stalls and they all proceeded to the sacristy to prepare for Mass. (From the parish newsletter, May 1977)

In 1982 Pope John Paul II visited Britain. Many members of the parish, religious and laity, travelled to the various open air celebrations and Masses to mark the Holy Father's arrival, including a huge gathering at Wembley Stadium .

Wembley 1982 : Sr. M. Emmanuel Walsh, Mrs. Eileen Edmunds, Sr. Margaret M. Kelly

Wembley 1982: Mrs Eileen Edmunds, Sr. Margaret M. Kelly, Sr. M. Carmel McHenry

An Unusual Procession for Wembley Stadium

Chapter Five : Into the Modern Era

Having had just two Parish Priests in sixty-two years, things changed with the death of Canon Byrne in 1983. He was replaced for the next two years by Father Donal Donegan. Father Donegan realised that the presbytery was in urgent need of refurbishment and he accepted a quotation from Greenan Contractors, who have had a long and distinguished record of service in the building and repairing of Catholic churches and schools.

The Presbytery at Tilbury

The total bill was in the region of twenty thousand pounds, but Father Donegan omitted to request permission from the diocese to proceed until the work was done. It appears that the first time that Brentwood Diocese knew of the work was when Father Donegan requested a bridging loan of eighteen thousand pounds for the repairs, as this letter to a locally based firm of architects shows:

7th March 1983

Dear Mr. Ash,

Tilbury Presbytery

I have now been in contact with Father Donegan at Tilbury regarding the Finance Board request that you supervise the repair and renovation work at Tilbury. It seems that we have been presented with a fait accompli, since Father Donegan has informed me that the work is due to be completed this week!

However, we would still like you to have a look at the work and verify to the best of your ability in the circumstances the various bills. So far Greenan, the contractor, has received no payment.

If you are able to agree the cost etc., the bills should be sent to this office. I am enclosing the only documentary information we have been able to obtain. This is a specification which was extracted from the builder by Canon Petry.

Father Donegan's address is 96, Dock Road, Tilbury ….. At the moment however, I believe Father Donegan is staying at Anchor House next door…..Father Donegan can be contacted through the Chaplain, Father Greatorex.

Thanking you for your help in this matter.

Yours sincerely,

Rev. Brian Drea
Financial Secretary

Father Donegan intended to pay off the bridging loan by selling off the presbytery at Chadwell St. Mary, after the closure of this short-lived parish. He was distressed by the criticism that he had rushed ahead with the refurbishment of the Tilbury presbytery, by-passing the normal diocesan bureaucracy, and he defended his actions in a letter to Father Drea, dated March 11th, 1983.

Dear Fr Drea,

As Secretary of the Finance Committee I write in reply to your letter of the 7th as Parish Priest of Tilbury.

I can understand your concern about my quick action in re-doing the presbytery. Of course, I know this is a diocesan property as was Harlow and every other parish in the diocese and that procedures for spending more than £1,000 need the approval of the Finance Committee but, I believe, my case was an exception to the rule, in as much, as I had three weeks from my appointment to Tilbury to prepare a house full of furniture and all the Canon's belongings to get my own furniture in.

In the words of a parishioner, the Chief Officer of Health for Thurrock, the house was unfit for human habitation. How Canon lived in it baffles me! The housekeeper's apartments were locked shut for two years – it was a hovel. I, or none of you reverend gentlemen, would have lived here without endangering your health. No heating in the upper part of the house and damp musty walls. Thus my quick action.

Mr. Greenan sent you a budget estimate of the work needed to be done, a very good and honest Catholic. He is not taking his own personal profit to save the diocese and the parish from further expenses and now you want to spend extra parish money checking on him.

I inherited a debt of £39,000 in Harlow which, with hard work and the loss of my most precious possession, my health, I cleared. No-one offered then to pay my bills, I did ask your help and was refused. Why the change? This too was diocesan property. I am perfectly well able to pay my own bills thank you and to deal with the Parish money.

The money from Chadwell is Parish money, as I understand it, and you are the Trustees. I am the Steward of the Trustees but you make me out to be a crooked, unreliable and untrustworthy Steward. Well Gentlemen, if you so wish find another Steward. My mother will be glad to have me near her in the last years of her life. Either you trust me or you do not.

Faithfully yours

D.P. Donegan.

Father Donegan wrote to Bishop Thomas, apologising for his 'bad temper and bad manners' but standing by the details of the letter sent to Father Drea. He added that the sale of the presbytery in Chadwell had been at well below market value because it too had been poorly maintained. Father Donegan concluded this letter with the following comment:

> I left Harlow presbytery fit for a gentleman to live in without any help from the finance board, and am now treated as a fool by them in Tilbury. Diocesan policy or not this is no way to treat a fellow worker in the vineyards of the Lord. It smells of a great hypocrisy.

Meanwhile, there was pressing need for further building repairs in the parish. Most of the tiles on the church roof were badly cracked and leaking water onto the supporting rafters and the general internal decoration of the church. The central heating system in the church was inefficient and outdated. Warming the building for Sunday services took two days, at a cost of about £40, and succeeded in raising the temperature a mere 10 degrees Fahrenheit. The Parish Hall had an asbestos roof, broken window and door frames, no damp course and male-only toilets. Whilst members of the parish were willing to assist, their success was limited to repairing and overhauling the central heating system. The other issues would cost a substantial sum of money.

A View of our Parish Church from the Garden of the Convent

Father Donegan's ill health meant that he was replaced in 1985 by Father John Duckett. Father John was instrumental in the reordering of the church but there was a great deal of opposition from many members of the community who wanted the style of the sanctuary to remain the same. The Second Vatican Council closed in 1965, but the church still had a temporary altar placed in front of the old ornate plaster altarpiece. This reordering of the church would include the removal of the original altar, and the proposal caused considerable upset for many members of the congregation. Three letters addressed to Bishop Thomas NcMahon in 1987 summarised the objections.

Your Lordship,

I wish to register my total disgust at plans to dismantle and replace the altar of the church of Our Lady, Star of the Sea, Tilbury. Apart from the fact that it is a beautiful altar, are you right to ransack the church as we are led to believe that the altar was a gift to the catholic Community of Tilbury from Goanese seamen. If the altar is unsafe I suggest it could be made safe at far less cost.

I feel that the church is being hypocritical when there are countless thousands of people suffering in under-privileged parts of the world.

The people of Grays have still not seen the accounts for a similar project completed 12 months ago. I would be rather interested to see the accounts for the alterations at Grays. When Fr. B. O'Brien was here, the accounts were regularly published in our bulletin.

I await your reply with interest.

The Church Sanctuary before Vatican II changes

The New Altar

My Dear Lord Bishop

I am appalled at the removal of the Altars in our churches. First of all, Grays, St. Thomas Of Canterbury, where I was brought up. I dread to think what our dear departed relatives must think, all the hours they worked in the church. I remember my dear father R.I.P. spent hours carving altar rails to match the existing centre partition.

The Priest wanted them extended across Our Lady and St. Joseph's Altars and now all that has been removed. For what I wonder!!

The latest one I hear about is our Lady Star of the Sea at Tilbury with a most beautiful Altar, which I understand is to be removed and I dread to think of the cost.

Maybe on this All Saints Day, many of the babes baptized and placed on the Altar by Father Patrick O'Donnell will be in Heaven now praying that this destruction will cease.

Is it any wonder with all this happening in our Catholic Churches that there are so many leaving the Church and also criticizing us Catholics.

I remain, yours sincerely,

To His Lordship,
Bishop McMahon (Brentwood)

Dear Sir,

It is with great sorrow I must write to you to protest that in spite of the fact of objections from numerous people I hear the work of disposing of the lovely Altar in Tilbury Church is about to start in January. Reading in *The Universe* I see that millions of people are dying of starvation and we are asked to help by giving money to buy food for them.

In Tilbury I hear that the Parish is about to borrow £30,000 or more to destroy something of great devotional value to quite a few Catholics. I find it quite incongruous and almost inconceivable that the Church should ride roughshod over the wishes of the Parishioners and others who have a sentimental attachment for Tilbury Church.

Enclosed please find a stamped addressed envelope. I would be grateful if you will send me your observations on this matter.

Bishop Thomas was obliged to implement the changes required by Vatican II. He had to carry out the necessary alterations and equally to respond sympathetically to the expressed concerns of those who felt the changes both arbitrary and unnecessary. This is a difficult balance to achieve. His reply to the last letter serves to illustrate the diplomacy and sensitivity that a good Bishop needs.

Thank you for your letter and for sharing your views with me about the re-ordering of the church at Tilbury.

May I first say that I am sorry that you find the proposed changes distressing. The reason for moving the altar is because of the changes in the celebration of our liturgy since Vatican II and a priest no longer celebrates Mass with his back to the people. A free standing altar is required and because it is not possible to have two altars the old altar has to be removed.

You mention the starving millions, and I very much agree that we must do everything possible to help provide for the needy. When I visit each parish, I urge the priest and the parish council to have a consistent link with a parish or project in the Third World and I am greatly encouraged by the fact that so many parishes throughout the diocese are endeavouring to commit themselves in this way. Money spent to help our communities to celebrate the liturgy in the right way thereby encourages in a marvellous way all of us to live out the Gospel more authentically in every way, including concern for our less well privileged brethren.

I have found that where liturgical renewal at all levels is approached with calmness step by step all but very few people come to appreciate the reasons behind them and no dramatic effects or unduly heavy financial burdens are placed on the resources of a parish. I hope that this would be the case in Tilbury, which has a very good tradition of liturgical high standards and pastoral concern.

With my blessing,

Yours sincerely,

Despite the detailed response from Bishop McMahon, the recipient was not satisfied, as can be seen in her reply.

To His Lordship Bishop of Brentwood.

Dear Sir,

Thank you for replying to my letter regarding the Church at Tilbury. Actually I knew when I wrote to you that there was very little chance of you changing your mind. After seeing the alterations at Brentwood Cathedral and Grays Church I could see you intended to alter as many Churches as you could to your own specification.

May I say with respect in reply to your comment about Vatican II that it also gave us to understand that the Churches belonged to the people not the priests or Bishops therefore they should have some say about any changes that are made.

Tilbury Church may not meet with your aesthetic taste, but we are simple people who like their Churches to look like Churches not like barns or someone's front room. I also do not see why the existing altar cannot be left as a reredos and the Tabernacle placed in one of the niches that are there at the side. As it is, lots of Catholic people are sorely displeased and scandalised at the highhanded attitude to which they have been subjected. I myself liken it to the dissolution of the Monasteries in the time of Henry VIII.

I beg one request, that I be allowed to photograph the altar before it is confined to the scrapheap, so that future generations will see what a Catholic Church looked like in the days it had some followers.

Yours respectfully,

The Bishop replied that no permission was needed from him to photograph the church, although it might be courteous to ask the Parish Priest. He reminded the writer that he was not personally responsible for the re-ordering of the church, and that it had nothing to do with a matter of taste. He suggested that a conversation with the Parish Priest might help to clarify the reasons for the changes.

But a fourth parishioner decided to take matters further. She wrote to Father Donnelly, at Cathedral House, but first of all she organised a petition and went to the local press. An article appeared in *The Thurrock Gazette* (below).

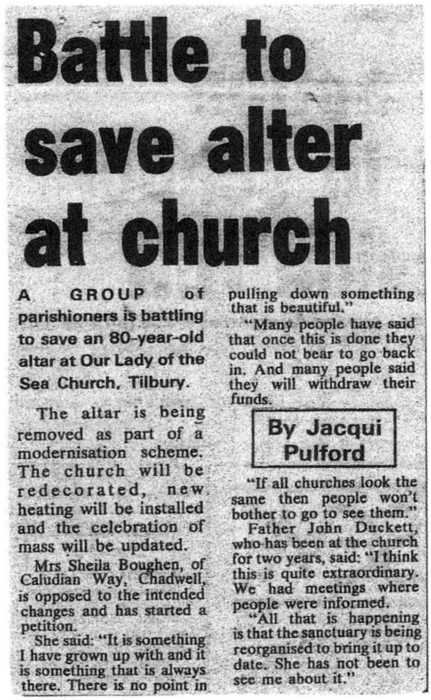

Battle to save alter at church

A GROUP of parishioners is battling to save an 80-year-old altar at Our Lady of the Sea Church, Tilbury.

The altar is being removed as part of a modernisation scheme. The church will be redecorated, new heating will be installed and the celebration of mass will be updated.

Mrs Sheila Boughen, of Caludian Way, Chadwell, is opposed to the intended changes and has started a petition.

She said: "It is something I have grown up with and it is something that is always there. There is no point in pulling down something that is beautiful."

"Many people have said that once this is done they could not bear to go back in. And many people said they will withdraw their funds.

By Jacqui Pulford

"If all churches look the same then people won't bother to go to see them."

Father John Duckett, who has been at the church for two years, said: "I think this is quite extraordinary. We had meetings where people were informed.

"All that is happening is that the sanctuary is being reorganised to bring it up to date. She has not been to see me about it."

Article in the Thurrock Gazette
(Spot the mistake?)

Mrs. Boughen wrote:

Dear Reverend Mgr. Donnelly,

Could you please give me some of your time on behalf of the people of Tilbury concerning the changes that are to be made to the Altar at our Church, Our Lady Star of the Sea.

I heard of the news last Monday and I was so unhappy that anyone could think of pulling down the Tribute that the people of Tilbury gave to Our Lord 80 years ago. I just had to put pen to paper, so I wrote to our local newspaper, just saying how I felt, and that I had got the news from a local lady who had a petition against what was planned to happen. Well since then so much has happened, "that was just last Friday."

I feel that I would be letting the people down if I can't do more for them, I can't trust the priest at Tilbury, I'm not getting anywhere with him and I have tried. I am at my wits' end trying to do the right thing for them. I shan't sleep easy till it feels right again. My heart is so heavy because I know how the people feel for their church.

I have had lots of phone calls, and I try to reassure them, but when I come off the phone I say "Please God, help me."

Do please give me your time, I am begging of you. God Bless You for now,
Yours Sincerely,
Sheila Boughen

Mgr. Donnelly wrote back as soon as he could.

Dear Mrs. Boughen,

Thank you for your recent letter which I have just received. I regret that it has not been possible to respond to it earlier as I have been away, and I am afraid that I am just about to go away for a month, and so it will not be possible for me to see you.

I have taken careful note of what you have said in your letter, and note that you have organised a group which is referred to in the press cutting from the paper that you sent me. With all due respect, I think that was an unusual thing to do. Practising and church-going Catholics do not usually go to the secular press about matters which are very much concerned with sacred and official concerns.

The whole question of the re-ordering of your Parish Church has not yet been finalised, and will be considered by the Bishop's Commission for Liturgy before any recommendation is officially made to the Bishop himself.

I am sure that you will now have come to know from the time that Fr. Duckett has been your Parish priest what a very caring, pastoral and spiritual man he is. Sunday by Sunday you will have listened to his preaching, and also on other occasions, to his discussing the whole range of liturgical renewal in the Church. It is only in this way, of course, that we can come to understand what the Church is asking us to do as a pilgrim people, and how to accept changes which sometimes appear to be difficult to accept. But the most important thing always for us – especially in the Catholic Church – is to work for and encourage and preserve the unity of the parish community, particularly in union with the Parish Priest.

Yours sincerely,

Meanwhile, the Parish Priest, Fr. Duckett, had his own plans for the re-ordering of the church. In November 1986, Father Duckett had written to Mgr. Donnelly, indicating that he had 'certain proposals for making a few alterations to the Church here in Tilbury." The following May, he provided more details of these 'few alterations'.

> First of all, concerning the Sanctuary. This is what is proposed:
>
> a) To move the present Altar forward to where the Altar rails are at present.
>
> b) To remove the Altar rails altogether
>
> Therefore this leaves the Tabernacle, Reredos, Font, Lectern and Chair in their present position.
>
> In addition to the above, the porch area is to be reorganised and a Reconciliation Room constructed in the side chapel. All this is evident from the plans, a copy of which you already have.
>
> Though you may feel that the Tabernacle should be moved to the side and install a new altar and ambo and remove the reredos which houses the Tabernacle, my feelings are that it would be very difficult to explain to the people why this should be done. For most of the people who use the Church, its attraction as a Church is focused upon the present Altar and the Reredos.
>
> I have already had several indications that the people are disturbed about the fact that all the side altars are to be removed and in fact one parishioner was thinking of getting up a petition about it, to send to the Bishop.
>
> I want to go ahead with these proposed alterations, but I honestly feel that they can only be done as I have explained. Maybe later on, more could be done for the Sanctuary.
>
> Perhaps if you were to come to Tilbury and take a look yourself it might make things a little clearer.
>
> If the Liturgy Commission does not go along with these ideas, then I would like to know if I can go ahead with the other alterations, i.e. decoration of Church, installation of new heating system, construction of Reconciliation Room and the reorganisation of the porch area.
>
> I would appreciate a reply on this matter as soon as possible as we have accepted the lowest tender of the three Building Contractors who estimated for the work.

Within the fortnight Mgr. Donnelly did indeed visit the church. There was to be a new Altar, Ambo and Tabernacle plinth, and the material for all of these was to be stone. The reredos was removed completely.

Father Duckett was replaced by Father Bob Hamill who completed the re-ordering of the church. Father Bob also encouraged and supported social events in the parish and established a social committee that did a great deal, especially for the sick and housebound. Their weekly Lenten lunches, the monthly lunches for the Senior Citizens Club and the regular outings to Aylesford and beyond were looked forward to by many of the older members of the parish.

Fr. Bob Hamill's three dogs receive a warm welcome from the Sisters
L. to R.: Sr. M. Camilla Hunt (Wanstead), Sister M. Columba Keena (Local Superior), Sr. M Camillus Walsh (on holiday from Kenyan Mission) and Fr. J. O'Hanlon
(not forgetting Ragna, Bodea and Laika!)

In 1983 St. Joseph's Chadwell had ceased to be a parish in its own right and parish boundaries were once again redrawn. This was to cause problems in its own right, as the Chadwell parishioners had to adjust to their loss of identity, reverting to the Tilbury Parish once again. This dilemma was recognised by Father Bob Hamill. In his Visitation Return Form of 1990, he commented:

> Chadwell are still upset over closing down as a Parish. I have managed to help them realise that it is a right decision but it will take time. Have to be so careful that they don't think they are 2nd class. But we do get on well and that's important

Father Bob made a really good job of developing the Tilbury Parish, as Bishop Thomas acknowledged in March 1988.

> I am extremely grateful to you, Bob, for the wonderful way in which you are building up the parish and I know that your people also greatly appreciate all your hard work on their behalf.

There was more praise from Bishop Thomas after his Pastoral Visit to the parish in January 1990.

> Thank you very much indeed for an extremely enjoyable Pastoral visit. It was a lovely day and I was delighted with all that I saw and heard.
>
> There is a wonderful spirit in the parish, which I know owes much to your inspiration and leadership. You are such a fountain of life and give yourself so generously, which, of course, your people also appreciate. So many of them told me of the great affection in which you are held and said they hoped you were not being moved! You have built the parish up in a marvellous way and it is a great tribute to you, personally that so much is happening and the parish is really alive.
>
> The re-ordering of the Church has been beautifully done and I am looking forward to the dedication of the altar on September 7th. It would be lovely if the chair was ready by September (made of the same stone and wood) but I do realise that it would add to the debt but I know you have it in mind to do.
>
> I enjoyed my visit to the Convent and was sorry to have missed some of the Sisters. It was very thoughtful of them to give me such a nice present. I was also glad to have the opportunity to visit Stella Maris and look forward to visiting the docks in the not too distant future.
>
> The Confirmation was a real celebration and please do pass on my thanks to all those involved, the catechists, musicians, etc. and indeed all your people and tell them how much I enjoyed my visit. My special thanks to your Parish Council for the wonderful way in which they are contributing to the life of the parish which I know you also appreciate.
>
> Finally, Bob, thank you for all your hard work and commitment in caring for the mentally handicapped. You are a tremendous inspiration and example to all of us. I greatly value and appreciate the many ways in which you serve the diocese, the deanery and the parish and I am tremendously indebted to you. Your people are indeed blessed to have such a caring pastor.

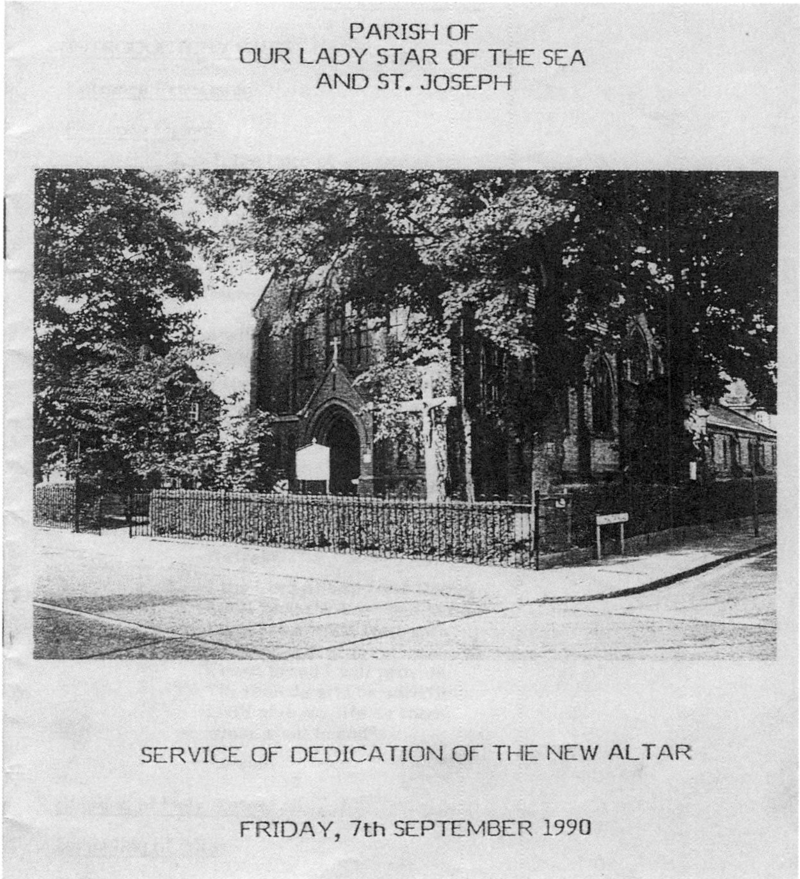

Cover of the Booklet prepared for the Dedication of the New Altar, September 1990

Father Bob revealed the generosity of the Tilbury parishioners, when he reported that the magnificent sum of £1075 had been raised in 1990 for the famine crisis in Ethiopia. Whilst Bishop Thomas made a point of thanking the many priests who served the diocese well, he was sometimes on the receiving end of thanks himself.

Such a letter was written in October 1993 by a lady who attended the Confirmation Mass in Tilbury, where Bishop Thomas spoke. Here is part of the letter:

Dear Bishop Thomas,

I feel compelled to write to you today on two counts. Firstly, to say how much my sister and I enjoyed the Confirmation Mass last night at Our Lady Star of the Sea Church in Tilbury. Our Parish is at St. Thomas of Canterbury in Grays, and the reason we attended the Mass was because someone in Tilbury had asked for it to be said for our mother who sadly died in June this year.

Your interesting sermon touched a deep point within me, I found your talk very enlightening and positive. I watched you closely when each child came up to you to be confirmed and noted the kindness you showed by chatting to them in turn, making them feel at ease.

My second point is to express the very caring nature of yours when you a) came up to my sister and greeted her with the sign of peace; b) you made a point of going to her to give her communion saving any difficulty on her part in approaching the altar and c) the beautiful way you conversed with her when we were getting in the 'Popemobile' taxi, talking to her in a very natural way – which sadly many people do not do as she is so very disabled. Your special blessing, you made time to stop and give her, made her feel very happy and I appreciated these kind gestures very much indeed.

Father Bob Hamill was replaced by Father Paul Bhanji in 1994. Although the re-ordering of the church had been completed some years before, Father Banji wished to make changes to return the Tabernacle to a central point in the church.

He had participated in the drawing up of a petition to this end, as he indicated in his letter to Mgr. Donnelly, dated 2nd October 1995.

Dear David,

I am writing to you as Chairman of the Liturgy Commission on the matter of repositioning the tabernacle in our Church here in Tilbury.

Please find enclosed a copy of the petition from the priest and people of the Parish of Our Lady, Star of the Sea, Tilbury to move the tabernacle from its present obscure position to a central, prominent and pre-eminent one.

I hope that we will hear from you soon as I intend to act on this by the end of October, sooner if we hear from you.

I have sent a copy to the Bishop for his information.

I look forward to hearing from you.

The heading of the petition read as follows:

> We, the undersigned, understand that according to GIRM n.276 and HCWEOM n.9 the place for the reservation of the Eucharist should be "prominent" and "pre-eminent". This is not the case in our church at the present moment. We therefore desire and intend, in line with local custom, to move the tabernacle from its present position to the centre of the back wall of the sanctuary, so that our worship of Jesus present in the Blessed Sacrament may be enhanced and Jesus may be seen to be the centre of our lives.

The petition was signed by 185 people, including the Parish Priest. The reply from Mgr. Donnelly came four days later. It was hardly the encouragement that Father Banji might have anticipated.

> Dear Paul,
>
> Thank you for your letter of 2nd October enclosing the photograph and copy of the petition. I have considered them most carefully and I am deeply concerned over a number of points. These points arise from the typed part of the petition which sets out your reasons for the present application.
>
> Two church documents are relied upon in the petition: *General Instruction of the Roman Missal* (G.I.R.M.) and *Holy Communion and Worship of the Eucharist Outside Mass* (H.C.W.E.O.M.) both issued by the Congregation for Divine Worship and therefore expressing the Church's official teaching. Furthermore, two specific paragraphs from these documents are cited in the petition: no. 276 of G.I.R.M. and no. 9 of H.C.W.E.O.M. These two paragraphs are, in reality, completely contrary to what is stated in the petition, for they both stress that, where possible, the Blessed Sacrament should be reserved in a separate chapel or area. This is exactly the present situation at Tilbury. These paragraphs are in fact expressing the teaching that there is to be a balance between the place of celebration and the place of reservation. This is expressed as follows in the book *The Parish Church*, issued by the Bishops' Conference to state the norms for re-ordering:
>
> Reservation is dependent upon the celebration from which it derives, the Eucharistic liturgy of the Mass. To have both celebration and reservation in one place diminishes the significance of each" (para 97).
>
> This principle – that the space for reserving the Blessed Sacrament should be separate from the space for celebrating Mass – is the true meaning of both paragraphs. It is worrying that this was not the meaning ascribed to them by your Parish petition.
>
> More worrying, however, is the misuse of the words "pre-eminent" and "prominent". In your petition, these two words have been wrenched

from their context and given a completely misleading meaning. When para. 9 of H.C.W.E.O.M. is looked at as a whole, it is clear that the document is saying that a "pre-eminent" position is best achieved precisely when there *is* a separate chapel or space for reservation. Equally, when one looks at the whole of para. 276 of G.I.R.M. it is plain that the "prominent" place is to be in some part of the church *other* than the sanctuary. (This is particularly obvious from the context and wording of the Latin original, which I have consulted on this point.) The documents never equate "prominent" or "pre-eminent" with the word "central" and such an equation imposes a completely erroneous interpretation on them.

The petition claimed the right to decide the positioning of the tabernacle by "local custom". This is very surprising and completely ill-founded. I assume that the phrase is taken from G.I.R.M. para. 276 "*legitimas locorum consuetudines*". In law, a custom is something which exists now and is exercised now; it is not something which existed years ago or which it is hoped to revive in the future. In addition, I am authoritatively advised that, in Canon Law, a legitimate local custom can only be created by a body such as a diocese or religious order. It cannot be created by a parish.

This brings us to the question : "Which is the legitimate authority in this matter?" I would refer you to the Directory on the Pastoral Ministry of Bishops (*Ecclesiae imago*) issued by the Congregation of Bishops in 1973 where it is stated that one of the duties of a diocesan bishop is to "make sure that the construction and placement of the tabernacle meet liturgical norms" (para 90(9)). This is a specific application of the overriding liturgical authority of a bishop defined by the Decree of the Second Vatican Council *Sacrosanctum Concilium* (art. 22(1)). In this Diocese, the Bishop exercises his authority in consultation with the Diocesan Commission for Liturgy and it is the Bishop's rule that any change to liturgical space or objects can only be effected after consultation with the Liturgical Commission and with the permission of the Bishop.

I wish my conclusion to be as clear as possible. An approved and appropriate re-ordering of the church at Tilbury was carried out some eight years ago by Father Bob Hamill after proper consultation. That re-ordering followed the liturgical norms of the Church and created a separate space for the tabernacle. The petition you have presented gives no valid reason in theology, canon law or liturgical theory and practice to justify the change. Consequently, permission is refused to allow the tabernacle to be moved from its present position.

I feel that it is a great shame that, due to a petition which was based on incorrect information, false expectations will have been raised in your parish. If I can give help by giving further explanations or background information, please let me know as my desire is to assist in this matter. In the meantime, perhaps you would be kind enough to confirm in

> writing (1) receipt of this letter and (2) an assurance that no action will be taken to move the tabernacle. No doubt you will wish to let the parish know the position over the next couple of weekends, so perhaps I could hear from you by 17th October. Since you sent a copy of your letter to the Bishop, it may be helpful for you to know that I have sent him a copy of this letter.
>
> With good wishes,
> Yours sincerely,
>
> Chairman, Liturgical Commission

In the following year Father David Clemens was appointed as Parish Priest. In 1996, Father Clemens stated his view of the charitable, Tilbury parishioners in his Visitation Return:

> The people are down-to earth, practical and generous, when they believe they have good cause to be.

The issue of the Chadwell parishioners now reunited with the Tilbury Parish had not been resolved as effectively as Father Hamill had once hoped. Father David commented in the same Visitation Form, 1996:

> There is still a certain feeling among some (a minority) that Chadwell doesn't belong to Tilbury.

Father David sought help from Bishop Thomas to emphasise that Tilbury and Chadwell were indeed 'one, single parish – the people of God.' Father David was trying to bridge the gap by organising more parish social events at Chadwell, which had proved to be quite successful.

Father David was again to pay tribute to his parishioners in the 1999 Visitation Return Form. Asked whether the parish was involved in projects to help the Third World, his reply was emphatic:

> Yes! In quite a substantial way. Our Parish Care group have helped to build a convent/school in Uganda, as well as a children's home in Poland – to name but two. A project is always on the go.

Five priests had now served the parish in just twelve years, and when Father David left in 2000 the parish would be served by four more Parish Priests in the coming ten years – Father Peter Connor, Father James McShane, Father John Meehan and now Father Paul Dynan.

On Mother's Day, 18th March 2007, a beautiful framed icon of Our Lady Star of the Sea, which had been created by Gwen Perkins, was unveiled.

Father Paul arrived as our Parish Priest in October 2010. He took on a considerable responsibility, as at the same time Father Paul was appointed as Parish Priest for Stanford-le-Hope. This means that his week is characterised by a continuous movement between the two parishes as he involves himself fully in the life and pastoral work of both parishes.

Yet this was not the first time that Fr. Paul had stepped across the threshold of the presbytery in Dock Road. Almost nineteen years earlier to the day, he had been asked by a Maltese priest, Fr. John Azzopardi, a Discalced Carmelite, to help him to visit a friend in Tilbury. Fr. John was supplying in the Parish of Our Lady Immaculate, Chelmsford, Fr. Paul's home parish. Fr. John had a Maltese friend, Fr. Herman Mizzi, a fellow Carmelite, who was supplying for Fr. Bob Hamill in Tilbury. One evening, Fr. Paul, although simply Paul Dynan in those days, drove Fr. John over to Tilbury, and parked around the corner from the church. As they walked back to Dock Road, they noticed the apt name of the road in which they had parked : Malta Road. This brought a customary smile and chuckle from Fr. John.

A photograph of this visit survives. Standing at the doorway of the presbytery is Fr. John and Fr. Paul, as yet unaware of the direction his life would take in the future. Those of you who have seen the famous photograph of Harold Wilson as a boy standing on the steps of 10 Downing Street may see a similarity.

The following account of Father Paul appeared in the Brentwood Diocesan Directory, 2005.

> His career was spent exclusively working in the National Health Service. At the age of twenty-three he qualified as a Fellow of the Institute of Biomedical Sciences, specialising in Medical Microbiology and Haematology. He moved into the field of Blood Transfusion and was for many years Chief Biomedical Scientist in a busy district pathology department.
>
> In the early days of his working life he met Connie, a nurse working at the time at the same East London hospital. They married at the church of Our Lady of Compassion and had three children, Michael, Claire and Jonathan. Following Connie's untimely death through cancer in 1988, Paul committed himself to family, parish and career. He has been a member of the Knights of St. Columba since 1982 and has held a number of offices. When the children reached adulthood he broached the subject with them of possibly leaving the hospital service and applying to Bishop Thomas to train for the priesthood.
>
> Father Paul studied at Allen Hall in Chelsea, the seminary of the Westminster Diocese, and gained the degree of Sacrae Theologiae Baccalaureum from the University of Louvain.
>
> His Diaconate year was spent in the newly formed Basildon Team Ministry working alongside Father Julian Wiener, Father Peter Fitch and Sister Clare Kane, OSU. The Team Ministry, whilst demanding at times, was a period of great joy and he made numerous new friends. He holds himself very fortunate to have had so many and such varied student placements during his time as a seminarian and deeply appreciates the love, help and kindness shown to him during his years as a student for the priesthood. He believes that such preparation has been invaluable in equipping him for the path ahead. Father Paul has been appointed to serve in the parish of St. James the Less and St. Helen in Colchester.

But of course a priest must spend a lot of time preparing for his ministry. One important stage is the Diaconate year that occurs in the year before ordination as a priest. Here, Father Paul reflects on what that year was like for him. This article appeared in the Summer 2004 edition of *The Parishioner*, the magazine for the Parish of Our Lady Immaculate, London Road, where Father Paul was ordained in July of that year.

Appointment
It was a pleasant afternoon on Wednesday, 25th June 2003 when I took the bus from Chelmsford to Stock for an appointment with Bishop Thomas McMahon. It was just a few weeks prior to my ordination to the Diaconate and, as one does, for some days I had been reflecting upon which of the parishes that I might be sent to for my year's placement.

Some possibilities were slightly more obvious than others. For instance, parishes which often in the past had a deacon working there for their pre-priestly ordination year – others were parishes where deacons had been working until recently and had now created a vacancy by their recent ordination to the priesthood. I had a list, one might even say a league table, of seven and I felt fairly certain that wherever Bishop Thomas was about to send me was one of those I had in the back of my mind.

After a bit of a chat, Bishop Thomas told me that there were plans to set up a "Team Ministry" in Basildon and informed me that he wanted me to go there as a deacon, to work alongside Father Julian Wiener and Father Peter Fitch, who was newly ordained. We would share the Priests' House at St. Basil's and some sisters from the Brentwood Ursuline Order would be resident in the presbytery at The Holy Trinity Church.

All I could think of at the time was "Basildon – that's not on my list!"

Having said that, I was truly pleased and excited about my placement and felt that it would indeed be an honour to be part of this pioneering ministry and to work with those that the Bishop had mentioned. I could not wait to get to Basildon and meet the parishioners and their families or visit the schools or hospitals, but protocol demanded that I waited until October the 1st before going to the parish.

It was not until some weeks after my meeting with Bishop Thomas that I was to meet the fourth member of the Basildon Team as we were to become known – the charming Sister Clare Kane.

For those who (as I was on the 25th June) are unfamiliar with the area, the district covered by the Team Ministry includes the Parishes of St. Basil the Great, at the Vange/Pitsea end of the town, The Most Holy Trinity near the town centre, the Parish of St. Therese of Lisieux in Laindon, four schools (one at secondary level) a large teaching hospital and a hospice.

Not too busy
Life at first was fairly gentle. Moving in, getting to know the area and finding out where things were and who was responsible for what. However, that is of course for all three parishes. It was what you might describe as a steep learning curve. Trying to remember the

many names is one of the hardest tasks. Particularly when half a dozen people are introduced at any one of the parishes at the same moment, it takes a little time to assimilate who's who. But I did try – honestly. I tried very hard to emulate Father Brian O'Higgins who is renowned and admired by all for his almost photographic memory to remember who is who and even who their second-cousin-twice-removed is. I know how much people appreciated this.

During Mass for the first two weekends we each had to get up and say a little about ourselves and "our journey on the way to Basildon". I recall stating that I was very pleased to be in Basildon and that during my year I was looking forward to getting to know those parishioners better. When I mentioned that Father Brian O'Shea was my parish priest back home in Chelmsford my ratings soared, especially in St. Basil's Parish, as he is still to this day warmly remembered for his time spent caring for the people in this parish.

One good thing about being the first of such team ministries is that there is no "model" to follow – no accepted method of working, and so, under Father Julian's guiding hand we planned and organised who would be doing what. On the other hand, not having a "tried and tested" method to follow meant that we had to learn by trial and error about things and had to be flexible enough to allow for adjustment if things required to be modified. Having said that, the year during which I was due to be working with the Team had been designated as a year of discernment during which no major decisions were to be made. Being the deacon in this new type of team ministry was to prove a unique and rewarding experience for me.

Getting busier

Within weeks of our arrival we received a pastoral visit from the Bishop, and a group of ten young people received the Sacrament of Confirmation. A number of steering groups were established from each of the three distinct communities and these met in January. In fact a round of meetings began, culminating in May in the gathering of the three steering groups under one roof.

I learnt what it meant to be available to minister to the bereaved and conduct funerals, as well as to officiate at baptisms and weddings. It was a delight to begin the visits to schools. I was assigned the delightful task of visiting St. Anne Line Infants School where I have spent many a happy morning, with the children and the staff, in classrooms, assemblies and even in the playground. Children love to sing and I dusted off my aging twelve-string guitar and in the classrooms we always included one or two songs which hopefully fitted in with what they were currently studying – albeit that the links were sometimes a little tenuous. At Christmas I received a new guitar and this contributed to us making better music in the spring term!

Life within the team

Among the happiest memories of my year as part of the Basildon Team Ministry will be the tremendous mutual support given by the team members. There was a real level of concern and humour which helped us through some difficult and stressful times. This goes for the "extended team", those who are in a close daily working relationship with the Team and provide help and assistance for the Team to function. These are a veritable army of people who work quietly and efficiently at what they do. They are the backbone of any enterprise and truly the ones who make things happen. I make unreserved thanks to these people for enabling me to carry out my role within the team ministry.

Parishioners too have been superb in this. Without fear of exaggeration, I would say that in the order of 98 per cent have worked in collaboration and encouraged the Team in their efforts at every turn. Those who sadly have appeared to work deliberately against the Team were, I am pleased to say, a very small minority, but even these we had hope to bring on board and help them to understand that the concept of team ministry is new for everybody – particularly those who have been given the mantle to make it work.

Looking back

As the time approaches for me to leave Basildon, I wish to put on record how much I appreciate the way that the good citizens of Basildon, including Vange, Pitsea, Laindon and Langdon Hills, took me into their hearts and their homes. I have been incredibly privileged to spend so much time in their company, to share both the highs and the lows, to visit the Isle of Wight with a year six group from St. Anne Line School, to minister to the bereaved, to officiate at baptisms and weddings and to be present at so many social occasions.

A great joy for me has been sharing at the heart of the spiritual life of the parish. Being so much involved in liturgical activity as I have been has meant that I have been able to feel completely involved with the growth and life of all that happens in a spiritual context. For instance, sacramental preparation, whether it be baptism, confirmation or marriage, and not forgetting the RCIA group of 2003-2004 drawn from all three parishes in the Basildon Team Ministry area, with whom we all shared so much.

When I first stood in the pulpit to say how happy I was to be in Basildon I mentioned too that it was only for a short time. As I write, that time now sadly draws to a close. My chief regrets are that I had hoped to spend more time visiting people at home and in the schools, but the realities of parish life soon taught me how much I could plan for and how much I had to respond to the urgent needs of others.

There are a small number of things I would have done differently in my time as Deacon Paul in the Basildon Team Ministry, but not too many. The sense of camaraderie within the Team has helped me immensely and not a day went past when laughter did not ring out in the house. I have felt it a huge privilege to be a part of the setting up of the first Team Ministry and a bit of me is sad that I will not be around to continue the work so earnestly begun. Like others I will have to watch from the sidelines as things develop, but look forward to being invited back from time to time for any big events within the Team.

All I can say is, thank you Basildon, my time with you was quite *fantastic*.

Postscript
As I pen these few words it is early June, and at the end of this month I will once again be invited to make the journey to see Bishop Thomas to see where my first appointment will be. I do not know where he will send me as an assistant priest. I try not to think about it too much. I would probably be as wrong as I was last time if I were to try. All I do know is that I will be delighted to take up the ministry to which he will assign me, to be with God's people where they are, as I did last October when I walked through the door at Basildon.

A text that has helped me to remain focused during my years of priestly formation is a quotation from the prophet Jeremiah which Pope John Paul II has written about on a number of occasions.

I will give you shepherds after my own heart and these shall feed you on knowledge and discretion. Jer. 3:15

The Lord, who promises to be with us until the end of time, tells us that he will send pastors to tend his flock who will ensure that his Word and his Love will reach past the end of time.

Deo Gratias

In 2013, the year of the centenary of one of his parishes, Our Lady and St. Joseph, Stanford-le-Hope, Father Paul was diagnosed with cancer. He continued with his responsibilities in both parishes right until the time he entered hospital for the first of what were to be six operations. During his recovery, Father Paul indicated that he wished to continue to serve as Parish Priest for both Tilbury and Stanford-le-Hope. Always eager to show an equal loyalty to each of the parishes, he would never wish to be obliged to choose one of these parishes above the other. In the meantime Tilbury Parish has been supported by the work of supply priests, many of whom have made a valuable contribution to the life of the parish. But no-one has made a bigger contribution, in more ways than one, than our Ugandan visitor, Father David. Many will remember the first time that they saw Father Paul and Father David standing

together at the altar, and no-one can forget Father Paul's comment : 'Well, that's the long and the short of it'. It is worth noting that Father David is six foot seven inches tall.

The parish continues to respond to those in need across the world. During what became known as the refugee crisis in Europe, which began as early as 2004 and continued throughout the 2010s, in 2015 alone more than a million migrants and refugees crossed into Europe, sparking a crisis as many countries tried to cope with the influx and creating division within the European Union over who would accommodate and resettle those seeking asylum. Although some migrants travelled overland, notably via Turkey or Albania, the vast majority attempted to travel by sea. The majority were refugees from Syria fleeing the civil war during the Assad regime but on October 11th 2013 a boat carrying migrants from Libya to Italy sank near the coast of the island of Lampedusa in the Mediterranean Sea. An emergency response from the Italian coastguard resulted in the rescue of 155 survivors whilst a figure of more than 360 deaths by drowning was later reported.

A carpenter on Lampedusa Island who made his living by making wooden furniture met survivors of the disaster and was moved to do something positive. He therefore collected fragments of the wrecked fishing boat that the migrants had travelled on and had washed ashore, and he made the pieces of the wreckage into rudimentary crosses as a reflection of their salvation from the sea and hope for the future. One cross was given to Pope Francis who carried it at a memorial service for those who had perished and another was given to the British Museum.

In September 2016 Fr Paul Dynan obtained one such Lampedusa Cross and it was kept in the Church of Our Lady Star of the Sea, Tilbury over the weekend of 10th/11th September before being taken to the Parish of Our Lady and St. Joseph, Stanford-le-Hope.

The Lampedusa Cross : St. Mary's Pupils and Fr. Paul

When Fr. Paul took the cross into St. Mary's School in Tilbury on the afternoon of Friday 9th October, Mrs. Jones, Headteacher at the school, arranged for an impromptu assembly where the whole school were shown the cross and told of its significance, and prayers were said for all the migrants, concluding with a blessing for the children, their families and the staff. This was repeated on Monday 12th October 2016, when Mr. Spencer Bragg, Headteacher of St Joseph's School in Stanford-le-Hope, convened a similar assembly. The presence of the cross in the parishes was used as a focus to collect £450 to support the work of Aid to the Church in Need.

Bishop Alan's first Visitation to Our Lady Star of the Sea, Tilbury

As we approached the start of the Centenary Year for the Parish, the pattern of services continued as usual. One of the last celebrations of 2017 occurred on 26th December, St. Stephen's Day. On the Feast Day of the Patron Saint of altar servers a special Mass was held to acknowledge the work which the parish's altar servers had carried out during the year. New altar servers who had completed a year were enrolled in the Guild of St. Stephen and given a medal to mark the occasion.

Father Paul and his Altar Servers : December 2017

Chapter Six : St. Mary's Primary School

The first Catholic school in Tilbury, which was opened on 17th October 1887, began as an 'all-age' school with just sixteen pupils. Poverty was a major problem from the start. On opening day the school equipment consisted of four dozen slates, one box of pencils, six dozen exercise books, three and a half dozen copy books, three and a half dozen Longmans new readers, a box of chalk, a gross of holders and a box of nibs. There was one teacher, the Headmistress Miss Nora Sullivan, who was a member of the Congregation of La Sainte Union des Sacres Couers de Jesu et Marie (a French Order from Douai) who was based in Grays. She would walk to the school each day. The sixteen children, all taught by her, were 'classified' on the first day as follows - three standard V, two Standard III, four Standard I and seven Infants. Part of the school was used as a chapel.

By 1888, forty-eight children attended the school. The school logbook indicates the sad story of the school conditions and poverty of the area. On 16th January 1888, Father Doyle visited and heard the children of Standard I read – he found them very backward! On 16th March 1888, Standard III were examined in Arithmetic – one child failed and the rest had three or four sums right. On 23rd March 1888 the Board Officer (a man to be feared!) visited the school for the first time. The attendance that day was low 'on account of the dirty state of the roads owing to the bad weather'. By July, many of the children were absent because they had gone 'pea-picking' but there were sixty children on roll at this time.

In May 1889, nearly one hundred children were 'at school', officially on the registers, but many were often absent. Absences were caused by illnesses such as 'the blight', Typhoid Fever, Scarlet Fever and Diphtheria, pea picking or hop picking depending on whether it was July or September, poor weather conditions and the sheer poverty of the people resulting in a lack of shoes and clothing.

In August 1889, cement paths were laid down in the playground 'to prevent the children getting wet feet'. In January 1890, the School Attendance Officer said that he could not compel parents to send their children to school on account of the mud – there were no roads or footpaths built across the marshes. On 1st May 1891 the school log book records – 'The first drawing lesson given today'. However, a far more notable event took place in September of that year as parents no longer had to pay to send their children to the Catholic school. It was now free and there were three teachers employed.

As time passed conditions in the town did not appear to improve. A note on the state of the school buildings on 28th September 1893 included the comment 'the playgrounds and offices are defiled by cattle' and on 4th June 1894, 'twenty nine windows found broken this morning in the school'. In September 1894 four children were admitted to Standard I - the big school - not knowing their letters and an extract from H.M. Inspectors' Report of 12th June 1895, a time of payment by results for teachers, stated

> Nor are the children so zealous in their work as they should be and hence the full Grant under Art. 101(b) of the Code has been barely earned.

In April 1896 the school was closed for a month because of Scarlet Fever in the district. All however was not gloom. On 10th July 1894 a half holiday was given on account of the visit of the Duke of York to Grays and another holiday on 15th January 1896 for a treat in the parish.

The first major change to the school came in 1897 when, after an examination on 12th April, the Infant Class was changed into an Infant Department, which was placed under the charge of Miss Margaret Sullivan. The Infant Department consisted of two rooms on the south side of the building. Tilbury continued to expand so much that by June 1898 the Managers were told that the accommodation was insufficient for the average attendance. The school's official name was now Tilbury Dock Road R.C. School.

The population in the area was always fluctuating and children came and went. Times were hard, work often difficult to find and many families needed much help. After a tea party on 11th January 1901, a New Year's gift was given to each child 'consisting mainly of clothing'. There were now 183 children on roll. In March 1901 the school was visited by Cardinal Vaughan.

On 1st October 1903, in accordance with the new Act of Parliament, the school was reorganised by the County Council. There were now 260 pupils on roll with the Infants school providing accommodation for seventy-seven children. The remainder of the school was known as the Thurrock Tilbury RC (Mixed School).

In 1905 Canon Van Meenan, the Parish Priest, became Manager of the schools and on 9th January 1905, at his request the Sisters of Mercy took charge of the schools, replacing La Sainte Union Nuns from Grays. Miss Bridget O'Connor was the new Headmistress. In August 1905 there were 285 children on roll and on 24th August the children had their photographs taken 'amid some excitement'. There was then a staff of eight, all of them Religious. On 9th May 1907 the school ceased to be used as a chapel as the new church had been opened. The children were given a holiday to mark the occasion.

In the coming years many people left Tilbury as they were unable to find work. In 1908 it was recorded that the 'poverty of the children is so great that many have to remain away while their mothers are out working'.

By 1911, there were 150 Catholic and 85 non-Catholic children on the school roll. 90% of the children attended Mass and 60% Catechism Classes. *(4th Triennial Visitation Report 1914)*

The outbreak of war in 1914 had little immediate effect on the school. However, Diphtheria and Whooping Cough did. In 1915 there was a new influx of children and a new teacher from Belgium, possibly escaping from the effects of the First World War. The Club room was refurbished to make a classroom for the 22 Belgian children. In July 1915 there was a Zeppelin raid and subsequent raids caused the children to be sent home. The school was closed for a variety of reasons, due to a lack of coal to keep the fire burning, for the children to see a pantomime and because of an epidemic of influenza.

Tilbury grew rapidly between 1919 and 1924 and the number of children grew too, with the accommodation problem becoming acute. In 1922 there were 61 Catholic boys, 55 Catholic girls and 44 Catholic infants attending the schools. 30 boys, 33 girls and 37 non-Catholic children also attended. *(1925 Visitation return to Diocese of Brentwood)*

In 1926 Sister Aloysius Leonard became the Junior Head Teacher and every child left the school able to read and write. Sister Aloysius also taught the girls needlework, knitting and craftwork. Concerts were put on for parents and the Sisters took an interest in the home life of the pupils. By 1927 there were 320 children on roll, and the shortage of accommodation was acute. This was eased in 1927 when a temporary wooden building was placed at the disposal of the Managers of the school by the McAlpine Company, who had originally provided the building for the use of their workers enlarging the Docks. Before this, the Infant Department had accommodation for only 62 children but there were 120 on roll!

By July 1928, Father O'Donnell summarised the range of accommodation at the primary school and the number of pupils in attendance. Although the Board of Education had approved the school buildings as sufficient to house 206 pupils, there were 340 on roll. An expansion of the school was required, not least because the Urban Council had erected 1,600 houses in the area and planned to build another 300. An application to Rome was made for Church approval. Father O'Donnell was given permission to build additional classroom space and offices, at a cost of just under £4,000, and a 4% loan was arranged. Our Parish Priest was in no doubt about the pressing need.

> The matter is of extreme urgency, particularly as at the moment there are 45 children in a hut which is entirely unsuitable for use during the winter and 300 other children are packed into rooms which have accommodation for under 200.

In December 1928 the school was closed for two days as the school rooms were being prepared for a bazaar, the proceeds of which were to be used to pay off part of the debt on the new school building. This was opened on the Feast of Our Lady of Lourdes, 1929, when 141 children were transferred from the old Infant school. The official opening took place on 19th March 1929. Lord Eustace Percy, President of the Board of Education, officiated and the Bishop of Brentwood was also present. There were four classrooms in the Junior School. Sister Borgia Colahan became Headmistress of the Senior School and Sister Angela Colahan was appointed as the Infant Headteacher.

Tilbury remained a very poor area but the number of children in the school continued to increase. However, on one day in November 1929 only 96 out of 187 were present – there was an outbreak of Diphtheria in the area. In January 1930 the Dock Police began to provide about 30 of the poorer children with hot milk. In 1931 the Dock Police provided some of the children with boots, and in 1932 a Relief Committee was formed to try and relieve some of this poverty. Free school meals were provided for up to 60 children. According to the school's log book, 'the teachers wait on the children and the caretaker assisted by the senior children, has kindly undertaken to do the washing up'.

Between 1929 and 1934 most of the £383-1-8d spent on repairs to the school was on playground surfacing and fencing. Men from the parish volunteered to carry out the work, saving about £150.

By May 1932 there were nearly 200 children on roll between the ages of eight and fourteen. There were four classes and a four year age range in most, with plans for 100 extra places approved by the L.E.A. Father O'Donnell asked the diocese for permission to borrow about £1,000 and stated that the old McAlpine Hut had been removed so that the new extension to the school, three new classrooms, could be constructed there. Although approval was given by the diocese, the Board of Education had other ideas. After delaying the authority to proceed, and conducting what the Parish Priest called 'an exhaustive enquiry', they then insisted on a three month breathing space. The Board finally came to the conclusion that the site was unsuitable for further building work, as a one sentence letter dated March 15th, 1934 indicates.

> With reference to the Authority's letter of the 21st ult., I am directed to state that the Board have given further consideration to the question of the suitability and adequacy of the site of the school for the proposed extension, and have come to the conclusion that the site is already recognised for a greater number of pupils than good practice would allow upon it, and having regard to the importance of free space around the school and especially for sufficient unbroken spaces to permit of those activities forming part of the Physical Education of the pupils which are described in the Board's recently published Syllabus of Physical Training, the Board do not feel that they should be justified in agreeing to the proposed extension unless the Managers can extend the site or secure other additional playing space.

Notable events for the children during the thirties included a tree planting ceremony, when six children from the top class planted a tree each; a netball court being marked out for the first time; the football team winning the local Cup Final match; a visit to Grays Regal Cinema to see the film 'Twenty Five Years a King' and a visit to the Docks to see the destroyers, 'The Crusader' and 'The Cygnet' and the Submarines, L21 and L53.

The result of a school medical examination in 1935 was that the doctor

> expressed appreciation of the general cleanliness and good manners of the children but found many of them were under nourished and quite a large number ill clad and ill shod.

In September 1936, the Infants School was renamed Tilbury R.C. Infants School and from February 1937 the Junior School was known as The Thurrock, Tilbury R.C. (Mixed) School. On 18th October 1937, the staff and children of both schools took part in the celebration of the Golden Jubilee of the parish and schools. The title 'St. Mary's R.C. Primary School' was conferred on the school to mark the occasion.

The imminent outbreak of war in the summer of 1939 caused major changes to the normal school routine. In July, registration forms for an evacuation scheme were distributed and on 2nd September 1939 the Sisters and many of the children were evacuated to Holt in Norfolk. The school log book makes the first reference to the impending Evacuation in an entry dated 5th July 1939. Evacuation Registration Forms were distributed to the families, and the parents of 90 children completed them. School teaching staff were recalled from their holidays to supervise the registration of the evacuees. On September 2nd 1939, the day before the outbreak of the Second World War, the St. Mary's Evacuation Party of 112 persons was shepherded to the Tilbury Riverside Landing Stage en route to an 'unknown destination'. It was composed of unaccompanied pupils, mothers with children of pre-school age and the teaching staff, all under the leadership of the Head Teacher, Sister M. Angela Colahan. Here is an account of the experiences of the evacuees.

> As we sailed towards the mouth of the River Thames, there was both excitement and tension – tears from unaccompanied children trying to cope with gas masks, carrier bags of basic rations, suitcases, purses and items of clothing; babies wailing; young male teachers from the Council Schools discussing their 'Call-Up' options, and even fear of an enemy submarine or mine attack. After much speculation about our destination, and hours of sailing, our boat berthed at Yarmouth Dock, where the evacuees were met by Evacuation Officers, and taken to a local Centre; here we received a snack meal. Then St. Mary's Party were told that Yarmouth was not be their permanent 'billet', but that for one or two nights we would be accommodated at the St. Louis Convent School towards which we were put 'on the road' again. On arrival, the Sisters and Party were welcomed. Parents and children were conducted to the School's Assembly Hall, where large smelly soya sacks were strewn on the floor to provide sleeping accommodation. As the Hall was not yet adequately blacked-out, electric light could not be used, so bedding-down had to be early. The Sisters were taken to the Convent for the night, again with the warning not to turn on lights.
>
> After a meal from their rations, the Sisters went to make sure that all was well with the Party. To their dismay and annoyance, they found that a few fathers had come privately (despite all the secrecy), and taken their wives to a local Pub, some even leaving screaming babies to the teachers, who were pacing the corridor trying to soothe the crying

children. When peace was somewhat restored, the Sisters went to bed, but later, the air raid alarm hooter wailed. They fumbled in the dark for clothing, put on gas masks and struggled through unlighted passages to the Hall. One Sister had not put on her veil and, until she spoke, was not recognised by the frightened children. 'Sister', one cried, 'we fought (thought) you was a lady!' All procedures for an air raid alert were put into practice; then the 'All Clear' sounded, and efforts were resumed to get a few hours sleep.

On Sunday 3rd September, the Staff conveyed the Party to the Catholic Church, and after Mass, because it was warm and dry, all went to the beach. There, the announcement came through the radio that war had been declared. There were various reactions to the news: some (parents and teachers) were shocked and worried, the school children excitedly asked questions about their families left in Tilbury which was a prime target for bombing, and we all speculated about our next war-time destination.

Next morning, 4th September, our evacuation party was required to assemble in the grounds of the Parish Church (a graveyard), with all their trappings, including an extra carrier bag of rations for each evacuee – even for unaccompanied Infants, who staggered under the weight of luggage. After hours of waiting, sitting on tombstones, we were packed into buses and taken to the Norfolk village of Holt – always referred to afterwards as 'HOLE', by the frustrated and bored mothers. Holt was about nine miles from Cromer, and noted for its famous Public School – 'The Gresham' – around which life in the village revolved. Here were gathered officials, the Billeting Officer, the local Schools' Representatives and the householders who were prepared to accept families (mother+children) or unaccompanied school-age boys/girls, into their homes. The village's ethos was rural, Church of England and largely Conservative, and very different from the urban Dockland, working-class outlook of the evacuees. The Sisters and other teachers were distributed among the village homes, where they received varying degrees of hospitality. For the first few days, the Staff tried to locate the evacuees in their billets, consulted with the foster-parents, listened to their tales of woe, comforted the lonely children and sent messages to their families back home in Tilbury.

There was not even one Catholic resident in the village and the nearest Catholic Church was at Cromer – quite inaccessible under the circumstances. On the first Sunday, Sr. M. Angela Colahan gathered the Party together in what seemed to be an ordinary empty field. A Service of Prayers and Hymns was in progress when one of the Gresham School Staff protested, and asked the 'trespassers' to leave. The Priest at Cromer – Father Banham – heard of our plight and proved a Guardian Angel to us. He got in touch with a well-known Catholic Lady (of a County Family), who approached the Authorities for permission to use the village Shire Hall for Mass. She provided a portable Altar and all Mass requirements, and from them on we had a weekly celebration of the Sacrifice. Father Banham also appealed to the Cromer parishioners for food and clothing.

The question of school provision was the next hurdle. There was an Infant/Junior School and a Senior School, neither of which had spare accommodation, so 'half-day school' was the solution. St. Mary's was allocated a classroom in the Senior School for our pupils of all ages, and we shared Playground facilities with a large Tilbury Council School Party. For the rest of the day, the Staff had to provide outdoor activities, mostly in a local Playing Field. Fortunately, the weather was fine, so the children were kept occupied with Lessons (outdoor), Nature Walks and Physical Education.

There was no place for the Sisters to meet together to discuss their needs and the problems which inevitably arose. So, one day they went into a newly-built house which was 'For Sale' and open for inspection, and sat on the damp, dusty floor. To their dismay, the Estate Agent arrived with a prospective buyer, so, red-faced, they had to make their excuses and depart. Before Christmas, one of the Gresham School Staff was called for military service, so the Sisters rented his home on a temporary basis. At last, we had a home and a Prayer Room, not only for ourselves, but also for the children's welfare. Our Tilbury Parish Priest – Father O'Donnell – visited us, bringing gifts, and all were thrilled at his visit.

By this time, most of the mothers had returned to Tilbury, the secular Staff had also been recalled, and, despite all the inevitable tribulations - the evacuees were the scapegoats for any misdemeanour - we were settling down to some sort of acceptable routine. As numbers had fallen, our School Party was transferred to a classroom in the smaller Junior/Infants School for full-time education. This was a well-disciplined school, with high standards, and we enjoyed friendly relations with the Staff. However, a group of boys, evacuated from a Catholic School for Maladjusted Children (unaccompanied and suffering from Enuresis), were rejected by the fostering-parents and placed in a special Unit in the Holt area. Probably because of adverse experiences, they were badly behaved. Without any consultation with us, this group arrived at our host school to join our class, where thy proved to be disruptive, disobedient and unresponsive to kindness or advice. Imagine our consternation on our early arrival at school one morning, to find written in very large chalk-white letters, on the outside of the school wall: 'We are wet-beds'! Knowing how indignant the villagers would be, we got pails of water and brushes and, using elbow grease galore, we managed to erase the offensive inscription.

The Spring of 1940 was beautiful in Norfolk, and whenever possible we took our pupils on country walks to local beauty spots, e.g. Bluebell Woods. The Sisters and children now received many kindnesses and hospitable invitations from local personages, even from the C. of E. Army Chaplains. We had frequent visits from the down-to-earth soldiers, billeted next door, and their choice of language when they quarrelled, often amused us: 'You 'eard!' and 'I'll bash you in the clock', being samples of the milder expletives!

The 'phoney' war was coming to an end, and our situation near the N.E. Coast was now extremely vulnerable, so we were warned that a re-evacuation was being planned. Many of our original party had returned to Tilbury, and we now began to arrange for the termination of our Holt connections, to be ready for leaving on 2nd June 1940. Truly, there were tears at many of the partings, and a highly representative body of Holt inhabitants gave us a warm, friendly send-off, as our train set out on the long journey to Leek in Staffordshire.

On arrival, we had to spend hours with the billeting officials. The residents had already experienced or, (according to their reports) 'suffered' from a previous evacuation from Manchester, and were now not very enthusiastic fosterers. When the children were settled, the problem of accommodation for the Sisters seemed insoluble. The Sisters at the Loretto Convent were unable to offer long-term hospitality. It was now quite late and we had been a long time 'on the road', so the Superior rigged up sleeping arrangements in the Science Laboratory, and this would be ours for a few nights only. We tramped the streets throughout the next week, knocking at doors and receiving many rebuffs, such as 'I couldn't take you because of your Religion'. Finally a non-Catholic lady, very well-connected, offered us rooms on her top floor and attic. The Sisters were restricted to tip-toeing and 'No cooking smells'! Our hostess, though very domineering, showed us many kindnesses and introduced us to many 'top-drawer' relatives!

Leek, a silk mill-town, where refugee Huguenots had introduced silk manufacture from France, had a predominantly Protestant population. The tall, red-brick mills towered over the pavements, and they were now, in war time, making parachutes. Most girls and wives worked in the mills and this influenced the life-style of the town. Practically every night, the heavy German bombers passed over, as we were in the air route to Birmingham and Coventry. Often we had to crawl downstairs and shelter in the Basement.

There was a well-equipped Catholic Junior/Infants School and a fine Catholic Church with an old Church Hall, where, for a few weeks, we were allowed to teach our own group – to us a very happy arrangement. But the Authorities condemned this set-up, and transferred us to the School, where our children were integrated into the appropriate Classes, and we Sisters given full-time charge of two age-groups. It was amusing to hear our 'cockney' children trying to cope with the Staffordshire dialect. Two Sisters were recalled to accompany another evacuation party to Wiltshire. Then, a Teacher's house was advertised 'To Let', so we moved in and, once again, tried to make a home in a strange land.

Now and again, one or two war-disturbed children would arrive to join our party. Late one evening, a telephone message informed us that two

Junior boys would turn up for class in the morning. On our way to School, we met a large herd of wild-looking cattle coming along the street on the way to the open air Market Square. Fancy our disbelief when we saw two boys wearing Evacuation Labels, carrying long sticks and acting as 'drovers' – using their sticks and voices to speed the herd! These boys were, very reluctantly, rescued and then received a 'dressing-down'. One night we heard loud knocking at the back door. 'Knock 'ard, Siddy, knock 'ard', a boy's voice repeated. Two Junior boys had had 'words' with their foster-mother and had run off. So, once again, the Sisters had to act as peacemakers. Many extra duties were expected of them e.g. arranging treatment for small ailments, accompanying them to the Doctor/Dentist, providing and mending clothing, getting shoes repaired, keeping up communication between children and parents, celebrating birthdays, and in general pouring oil on (everyday) troubled waters.

When Sister M. Angela was recalled to organise the Wiltshire Evacuation, only two of us remained, so we had to leave our large house and seek accommodation yet again. An old English Catholic family offered us rooms and provided a mid-day meal. Our new address entailed a long walk eight times a day – to Church and School. In the Winter '41 – '42, the snow was feet deep for months; this added considerable difficulty to the supervision of our 'charges'. We had no heating in our bedrooms and, on many mornings we had to break the ice in our water jugs and scrape the frozen snow from our clothes. We provided Breakfast and Evening Meals under rationing and kitchen restrictions.

Several parents felt that their children would be safer in Wiltshire, so arrangements were made for them to travel to the raid-free town of Devizes. As our numbers decreased, only one Sister was left to maintain services to St. Mary's Group, whose members were now reasonably settled. How that Sister welcomed her eventual recall to Tilbury and her Community, can easily be imagined!

Much later, one of the evacuees, twelve year old Kathleen Hurdle, recalled

To us it was a great adventure. My brother and I were being evacuated. Each of us carrying a brown paper parcel, tied up with string, containing a change of clothing, we were taken to school at 9 a.m. There we boarded a coach which took us to Tilbury Riverside. Here we were shepherded along a gangway and found ourselves, to our delight, on a boat – a paddle steamer – which took us to Yarmouth. We were then taken to a school where we had to sleep on sacks filled with straw. We had a great time having pillow fights with them! The next day, Sunday, war was declared and that night the sirens sounded. On Monday morning we re-boarded coaches and travelled to a small village called Holt. We were taken to another school where all the local people were

> assembled. Here, we were 'sorted out' and allocated to the villagers in ones and twos. I was separated from my brother.

Meanwhile, back in Tilbury, St. Mary's School was closed on 4th September 1939, due to the danger of possible air raid. Father O'Donnell was aware, of course, of the status of the Evacuation Party in Holt, but he was less sure of the whereabouts of other families. As he wrote to Bishop Doubleday in mid-September 1939,

> Several other children and mothers have disappeared in twos and threes and I am gradually tracing them and referring them to the nearest Priest.

Later the same month, Father O'Donnell informed Bishop Doubleday that the evacuees in Holt were far from a Catholic church. The priest at Sherringham had arranged for Mass on Sundays in the Court House at Holt and a Lady Sanderson was trying to move the entire party to Walsingham, a transfer which came to nothing. The *Norwich Mercury* reported the Mass arrangements in Holt under the heading CATHOLIC SERVICE.

> For the first time since the Reformation, a Roman Catholic Service was held in Holt on Sunday, when Father Damian from Walsingham took Mass at the Shirehall for the Sisters and evacuees from Tilbury St. Mary's. The hall had been transformed on Saturday and the vestments used were brought from Walsingham.

Some of the evacuees began to return to Tilbury as early as October. The problem was that parents had been asked to contribute a little towards the cost of their children's keep in Norfolk, and some were not in a position to to do this. In October, the teachers who had returned from Holt began instruction in the Parish Church for those children who had not been evacuated and who wished to attend for one and a half hours, three times a week. In December, correspondence classes commenced for the older children and tutorial classes, for children under seven, were opened in private houses.

In January 1940, some of the Sisters returned to Tilbury and on 4th March the school re-opened, operating on a half time shift system for all children over seven. On 3rd June the children in Holt were transferred to Leek, Staffordshire and on 18th June forty three children left for Wiltshire, accompanied by Father O'Donnell, Sister Francis Boyden, Sister Margaret Mary Kelly and Miss Knott. On 20th June the school re-opened again with only five children present. In the course of the day teachers visited the children's homes to ask parents to send the children still in Tilbury to school but found many of them in the pea fields – life was going on as normal! On 1st July the school re-opened for full time instruction.

During this period, the Sisters moved to where the children were sent, whether to Norfolk or Staffordshire or Wiltshire, or even back to Tilbury. Their concern was the welfare of the children and their Parish Priest was no less concerned. Each proposed new evacuation was scanned anxiously, to determine that the children's social welfare, education and spiritual needs were properly addressed. It must have been a nightmare for those involved, for there were countless rumours about alternative destinations and each had to be examined carefully, even if it came to nothing. Whilst Father O'Donnell was concerned about the needs of all of his charges, Bishop Doubleday took a more pragmatic view. If evacuees were not properly catered for, the problem lay in their small numbers. Father O'Donnell should endeavour to persuade the 200 children still at Tilbury to join the evacuation programme, so that then proper arrangements could be made for a suitable school and church. Failing this, the Bishop did not think that the relatively small number of evacuees warranted his attention. As time passed some children began to return to their own families.

The evacuees had certainly splintered into smaller groups. By June 1940 there were 22 children in Leek, Staffordshire, with two teachers, and 43 children in Devizes, also with two teachers. When the older children in Leek were obliged to attend a Council run Senior School, all their parents insisted on their return home to Tilbury. By 1942, almost all of the children were back home in Tilbury, where there were 171 children, with only 27 children in either Leek or Devizes. At this time, the Headmistress of the Junior School, Mother M. Angela, became seriously ill and had to resign her position.

From 5th January 1942 the two schools resumed their normal independent existence. The school staff began fire watching duties two nights each week and on Saturdays and Sundays. On 1st September 1942 Sister Bernadette Roche became Headmistress. Throughout the rest of the war there were many bombing raids on Tilbury and a great part of the town was badly damaged. Fortunately, the school itself suffered little damage. The number on roll increased back to 250, with two extra classrooms once again needed.

As from 21st January 1949, St. Mary's Primary School was granted Aided Status. In October 1950, the school debt was at last paid off, with a donation from the Diocesan Building Fund. In 1952 there were over 200 pupils on roll and it was hoped that a new school would be built in

Chadwell St. Mary but the economic conditions of the time put an end to that idea. The school had to be closed yet again in February 1953, this time for a very different reason. The River Thames had breached its banks and there was extensive flooding. This led to a visit to Tilbury by Her Majesty the Queen on 13th February. She passed by the school and everyone was outside waiting to see her.

Staff of St. Mary's School circa 1954
Front Row: Sister M. Vincent, Sister M. Brendan, Sister M. Francis, Mr. P. Harty, Rev. John J. Byrne, Sister M. Bernadette, Sister M. Margaret, and Rev. W. Caffrey.
Back Row: Mr. P. Bolger, Miss S. O'Kane, Mr. K. Side, Mr. P. Rice, Mr. C. Fisher, Miss L. O'Kane, Mrs. A. Hughes, Miss C.N. O'Kane, and Mr. L. Fitzgerald.

By July 1953, there were five classrooms in the primary school, each scheduled to accommodate 40 children. In other words, the school could accommodate 200 children. The school roll was 244, and this meant that children could not move from one year to the next on an annual basis. The parents were very unhappy at the wide age-range that could occur in a single classroom, but with seven year groups accommodated in only five classrooms there was no immediate solution. The Parish Priest, Father Byrne, wrote to Bishop Beck to request at least one additional classroom and reminded the diocese that the school had no hall where all the pupils could gather together. The Essex Education Committee, however, stated that the school site was too crowded to allow further building, and came up with a temporary solution to make use of one of the classrooms in the senior school, which had not yet reached its full intake of older pupils.

In 1954 the state of the schools was described as fairly good but the offices and the children's toilets were said to be in a rather poor condition. To meet the increasing classroom needs of the primary school, the Essex Education Committee suggested in April 1955 the erection of two 'Spooner' classrooms, temporary structures to ease the overcrowding in the school. The school was also in need of a kitchen and dining room, and consideration was given to building a dining room with classrooms on top. Although temporary classrooms were provided, the other needs of the school were not addressed.

As from 1st January 1957, the official name of the school became 'Tilbury, St. Mary's R.C. Primary'. By 1961, the primary school which had been built in 1929 consisted of four classrooms and one extra class taught in a nearby Council school - Lansdowne. There were 190 children on roll. In November, 1961, her Majesty's Inspectors visited the school. Their report contrasts the very poor accommodation of the school building with the very fine educational work that was done by the teachers and pupils alike.

> The school has 186 children in five classes working in such poor physical conditions that the fine achievements which come from stimulating teaching are to be admired and commended. The thirty year old building consists solely of four classrooms, a quite inadequate cloakroom and two tiny rooms used for administrative purposes. The small playground and the poor outside water closets are shared with the senior pupils of the other school on the site. There is no hall, so lessons requiring movement are much restricted during the part of the year when the weather is bad; the teachers have no staffroom but a room in the presbytery has been set aside for their use; there are no toilet arrangements for the staff who must share those allotted to pupils. The Managers have put forward proposals to build some accommodation for teachers, a cloakroom and indoor water closets for the pupils; these are welcome improvements but the school also needs the use of a hall, more teaching space and better storage facilities. One infant class is housed in a re-conditioned, spare practical room on the site of a nearby school. this serves its purpose well and the Headmistress is careful to see that the children are not isolated from the main school. The dining room at the same school is used to capacity; three schools have their meals there and, although the service is very well organised, it follows that the hurried meal gives no time for social training. There is no cloakroom, or even pegs, for garments so the children take their meals dressed in outdoor clothes. The Managers have planned to build a scullery at the main school at some future date when financial provision is made for it, but, in fact, the whole problem of this school is linked with that of a secondary school on the site and the urgency of tackling this unfortunate situation quickly cannot be overstressed. It is against this unpromising

background that one finds the classrooms remarkably colourful with excellent displays of interesting material and work. Modern furniture, well-stocked bookshelves and a good selection of teaching equipment in measure counterbalance the shortcomings of the premises and the teachers have done remarkably well to make the work so vigorous and stimulating.

The school has enjoyed unusual stability in its staffing and this, coupled with the fact that all the teachers are skilful, experienced, qualified and dedicated people, has overcome many of the difficulties arising from conditions. The Headmistress, who has quietly and efficiently led the school for 20 years, keeps thoroughly up to date with teaching practices and, with her loyal five assistants, these are followed with considerable success. She and three members of staff are members of a religious teaching community.

The planning of the work, the conduct of the teaching and the general standards of attainment reached by the children win high praise. The school does not pattern its work as a series of separate subjects to be studied in isolation but rather seeks to give a wide body of knowledge, based as far as possible on practical experience and in the accumulation of this knowledge the children gain proficiency in the basic skills. From the earliest stage in the infants class to the older juniors the need to read, write, speak and calculate is presented to the children through the interesting practical work they are given. This is carefully planned to include all the subjects usually found in the curriculum of a primary school. Clearly this kind of work requires skilful organisation and meticulous planning to see that the correct books, apparatus and materials are available – and so they are. Progress in speech, reading, written English and mathematics is uniformly good. Points about the work and the achievement of the children which deserve special mention are

(a) The sound basis of practical work in arithmetic which has given the pupils a clear understanding of its function as well as its processes.

(b) The very wide range of reading and written English. This not only includes the whole breadth of the curriculum but results in these skills being exercised for pleasure, i.e. the monthly newspaper, edited by a group of older children, not only contains the usual short anecdotes and compositions but also records what new activities are to be seen in the various classes; an example of the interest shown by all the pupils in each other's work and typical of the sense of unity felt within the school.

(c) The introduction of science through the current broadcasts has inspired wider reading and discussion about the subject and a burst of experimentation both in school and at home.

(d) Despite the limitations of space some well finished examples of craftwork in many kinds of materials are to be found.

Unfortunately the girls have no games; this is an omission which should not be allowed to continue. They engage in dances round the furniture piled in the centre of a classroom.

> It would seem that with only 20 boys over 10 years of age it might be difficult to find a team for league football. Not only is there a smartly turned out team but the school has headed the league in two recent seasons. In addition to its own activities the school takes an active part in Church and parish affairs. The pupils are happily busy and show the confidence and satisfaction which comes from work well done.
>
> This account of the school and its work makes no allowance for the poor physical conditions; by any standards its achievements are highly commendable. The most urgent matter is to provide better facilities for the teachers and children.

More space was desperately needed and the first phase of the school extension was begun in April 1963. The hall and a new classroom, Junior Four, were completed first but by now there were 231 children on roll. In June 1966 a second classroom, which later became the nursery, was ready to use. This had been expedited by the intervention of the local M.P., Hugh Delargy, who wrote directly to the Department of Education and Science on behalf of the school, reversing an earlier refusal.

Even these additional classrooms did not alleviate the serious overcrowding at the primary school. Father Byrne wrote to the diocese requesting additional classrooms in February 1968. He wanted at least one demountable, temporary classroom, a request that the local education department had already rejected.

> There are no demountable classrooms surplus in this Division which could be made available for the use of the Roman Catholic Primary School.

The local authority suggested that the school purchase or lease a demountable classroom on its own initiative. The involvement of the local authority could only be via an Aided Schools Minor Works Programme, a process which inevitably involved delay. Whilst the diocese might be expected to be more forthcoming, there was no positive response, despite Father Byrne's reference to the building of a further 580 new homes in Tilbury, which could only add to the school roll.

St. Mary's Primary School was obliged to wait until the secondary school vacated their own prefabricated 'hutments' in August 1970, leaving this sub-standard accommodation for the use of the primary school. Two classrooms were created in one of the prefabs, for use in the Autumn term of 1970, but this went only part of the way towards improving the cramped accommodation at the school. This position was summarised in a report of the school's accommodation, drawn up by the School Managers just prior to the start of the Autumn Term, 1970.

> There will be eight classes at the start of the Autumn Term in 1970, and there are only six classrooms in the Primary School, so two extra classrooms will have to be provided for the start of the Autumn Term in September. This present year, 1969/70, one of the Infant classes is using part of the middle hut belonging to the Secondary School.
>
> As the Secondary School will be vacating the hutments at the end of this term, it would be most helpful if they could be maintained to accommodate Primary pupils. At present three classrooms in the Primary School have no water laid on, and the pupils have to use the few sinks in the corridor cloakroom for all cleaning of art and craft tools and for all hand washing. The Top Junior class is overcrowded, and all activity is very restricted. If this class could remove to one of the large rooms in the hutments – either the woodwork or the science rooms – they would then have space to develop the practical work on their many projects.
>
> There is water laid on in all the hutments. Both the middle and the woodwork sections have indoor toilets and cloakrooms, and these could be used by those Juniors who have at present no indoor toilets or cloakroom. The playground Boys' toilets are in a deplorable condition, and we feel that they should be demolished.
>
> If the Top Juniors could remove to one of the larger rooms in the hutments, the middle room of the Primary block could be converted into a Staff/Medical/all purposes room. At present the Head and School Assistant have to give up their small rooms for all medical inspections, and the first Infants' classroom has had to be divided to make a temporary Staff room. This means that the Admission Class, which should have generous accommodation, has not anything like sufficient floor space for their needs.
>
> The Managers kindly request that the hutments be taken over by the Primary School, and that the toilets and cloakrooms in the middle block be prepared for use of the classes using this hutment. A Staff Room could then be provided so that the Infants could have the piece of their room returned to their use.

The Thurrock Education Office agreed to the use of two of these hutments on a temporary basis, which somewhat eased the school's overcrowding, and the boys' toilets were refurbished after Father Byrne reported that they were in such a sorry state that the children were unwilling to use them at all.

In June 1971, the headmistress, Sister Bernadette invited the Headmaster of Saint Thomas More High School for Boys, Westcliff on Sea to visit St. Mary's School. It just so happened that Mr. McGregor was a member of the Diocesan Commission for Education. Mr. McGregor issued a report which he sent to the Commission's Secretary, Mr. L'Estrange, adding

> There may be very good financial reasons why so little has been done to improve the educational environment of the children attending this school.

Mr. McGregor thought that many improvements could be made without the spending of large sums of money, adding

> Sister Bernadette and Mother Superior assured me that they have tried all they knew to make people aware of their problems. They have sought my help, not in a spirit of criticism or recrimination but, because they felt that members of the Commission are in a position to bring their problems to the attention of others who may well be able to offer advice and tangible help.

The content of Mr. McGregor's report will come as no surprise. What is surprising is that so little had been done to improve conditions at the school despite repeated requests for help over many years.

<u>Report of Visit to St. Mary's, Tilbury</u>

<u>1. Classroom Accommodation</u>
There are 8 classrooms – only two of which are modern and two of which are in old hutments. 5 classrooms have no sinks or running water. 3 classrooms are separated by thin partitions and the noise is a mutual disturbance to all.

The top classroom is much too small for the kind of integrated day which Mr. Fitzgerald would like to operate. It is not insulated enough for noise, and like many other rooms has no sink or running water.

<u>Note</u> There is one hutment with 2 rooms standing empty. It was previously used by St. Mary's Secondary School. The rooms possess sinks and store cupboards. If painted outside and inside the hutments would provide a good base for the top Junior class.

The L.E.A. are permitting the use of one of the other hutments by boys from a neighbouring secondary school. <u>Could the Managers ask for the other to be used by St. Mary's? Perhaps the Diocese would be willing to pay the maintenance costs?</u>

> 2. Staff Accommodation
> There is no official staffroom. The room formerly used by the H.M. of the Secondary School is being used unofficially at present by the Staff. The Headmistress's office is very tiny, quite inadequate to receive visitors, and the storeroom for the entire school which adjoins her room is a converted broom cupboard.
>
> 3. Cloakroom and Lavatory Accommodation
> This is virtually non-existent. Such facilities as exist are very poor and the outside lavatories have no heating or washbasins.
>
> 4. Recreation Space
> Playground accommodation is very restricted. Playing field accommodation is nil. Some 5 years ago the Diocese gave (or sold?) land to the L.E.A. on which a new primary School has been built. The understanding was that alternative playing field accommodation would be provided by the Authority. Nothing has materialised. How can this be?
>
> 5. Administration
> (a) No representative of the L.E.A. attends Managers' meetings.
> (b) There is no Education Committee Councillor on the Board of Managers. Grievances do not get back to the Education Office. The Managers do not put pressure on them and when the H.M. writes, which she has done often, little action has been taken except in minor matters.
>
> Summary
> The surroundings in which the children and staff have to work are very sub-standard. I would suggest that the following points could be investigated with some success.
> 1) The need for the Managers to initiate action or give way to those who will.
> 2) The need for Managers' meetings to be attended by L.E.A. official.
> 3) The desperate need for playing field accommodation.
> 4) The use of the hutment to provide extra classroom accommodation.

In response to Mr. McGregor's report, Mr. L'Estrange picked up on the need to have L.E.A. representation at the Managers' meetings, but was less positive about the prospect of the diocese actually footing the bill for maintenance costs for one of the hutments.

> Apart, however, from the fact that the Diocese doesn't have any money for this sort of thing, don't you think it would be a mistake for us to accept in principle, even in an urgent case like this, that we should pay for maintenance other than external?

Despite all these difficulties, the school continued to flourish. But a sea change was apparent. The Head Teacher, Sister Bernadette, summarised the condition of her school in a report she issued in July 1972.

Report on Conditions and Accommodation

The School was built in 1887, and the Sisters of Mercy began their work of teaching in 1905. As far as I know the Parish has never received financial help from the Diocese. The Catholic Community in this Dock area is almost 100% working class, and part of Tilbury is now considered an E.P.A. (Educational Priority Area). There has nearly always been a struggle against poverty, poor conditions and unemployment, and many of the children are handicapped by some form of deprivation.

Until September, 1970, the Primary School shared the site with the Secondary Modern School, which was sited in the 1887 building, plus three Horsa huts put up in 1947 to last ten years. These huts are still on the site, and one is being used by two of our Primary classes, as there is no other accommodation for them. Another is being used as a Parish meeting room for Bingo, etc., and the third was taken over for woodwork by an overflow from a nearby County Secondary School. This School has had extensive new buildings just completed, so the hut has now been vacated.

There will be 300 children in the school during the Summer Term. These are accommodated in 8 classrooms, only two of which are modern. Five rooms have no sinks or running water laid on, three have no cloakrooms, (except improvised spaces) and hand-washing facilities are poor. In the playground there are very old outdoor lavatories without washbasins or heating. The playground, bordering on Dock Road, is insufficient for the children to move about freely. About seven years ago our playing field was handed over to the County to provide a site for a County Infants School. We have no kitchen, (meals are conveyed from a kitchen in Grays), no dining room, no medical room, no staffroom and no storeroom. The old building vacated by the Secondary School is providing temporary accommodation for the Staff. This building is now in a most dilapidated state, and the whole outside appearance of the School is depressing and unattractive. The Head Teacher's room is very small and badly placed, and the Secretary's room is also small and congested. There is no place to do any remedial teaching.

Bishop Casey visited the school in March, 1971, and he expressed great concern at the conditions under which we were working. He suggested that the Managers should approach the Diocesan Commission straightway with a view to getting a building programme. Mr. L'Estrange has also inspected the premises. The Divisional officer has recommended that the development should get under way, as I think that we are the only School in the Division not being brought up to standard.

There was by now a considerable groundswell in favour of a major rebuilding at the school, but this still needed to go through the usual bureaucratic hoops. Despite the recognised urgency, a letter from the Department of Education and Science, dated December 1972, turned down the development in the current year, but promised action in the years 1973-74. However, in January 1973, approval was given for the first phase of this 'remodelling' of the school at an estimated cost of £40,000, in the 1972-73 time scale. The only stipulation was that the project should begin before April 1st, 1973, which did not give the Managers much time to publish necessary public notices, seek building tenders, agree contracts and begin the construction of the new buildings. The cost of the enlargement was agreed at £48,200, with the Managers liable for a charge of £9,300 which was secured with a 30 year loan from the Department of Education and Science.

All schools face bureaucratic difficulties when contemplating new changes to school buildings. Briefly, major contracts are obliged to join a queue, with the demands for school rebuilding and/or school improvements far exceeding the sums of money set aside each year by local and national government. Even when the Local Education Authority and the Government concur, there is this quite inevitable delay. Catholic schools must also traverse the minefield of the Diocesan Commission, which ranks school improvements in the diocese and offers this shopping list to the necessary authorities, with the highest prioritised given some chance of action and the less prioritised having to await further delay. One solution is to break building work at any school into smaller stages, so that agreement can be reached more quickly, there being less outlay involved at any stage. This is what St. Mary's Primary School did, dividing the major work into two smaller stages. There is, of course, one problem with this approach. There is no guarantee that stage two of the work will be agreed once stage one has been completed. Any delay would also involve an increase in costs, and minor works programmes have their own upper limits on what can be spent. Some schools have seen the first phase of a building programme completed then suffered delay in the implementation of the later stage(s), resulting in later building being postponed or cancelled as this is now too costly.

On 3rd May 1973 the demolition of part of the old school began making way for a new Infant extension that opened the following year. Phase one was completed in record time. The primary school would now be able to accommodate up to 300 pupils. 1974 also saw the end of another era when Sister Bernadette retired as Head Teacher. She was replaced by Sister Agnes Williams. The second phase of rebuilding was also authorised and in September 1975, the school kitchen and new offices were opened. There were new toilets for both Staff and pupils, a proper office for the Head Teacher, and rooms for administration and medical inspections.

Father John Timmins and Sister Etheldreda of the Brentwood Religious Education Service visited the school in October, 1975, to evaluate its religious education They complimented the school on its work and made a few recommendations for improvements. Here is a digest of their report.

1) The Head Teacher is Sr. Agnes of the Wanstead Mercy Community.
2) There are eight teachers on the Staff, including three Sisters (Mercy) Two teachers are not Catholic.
3) There are 225 children on roll. Numbers are dropping. It is felt by the Head Teacher and the Parish Priest that the Nursery class at the local school could be partly responsible for this.
4) The Konstant syllabus forms the basis for R.E.work. There is quite an amount of good material available for the teachers to support and fill out the syllabus, but some of the scripture material leaves a lot to be desired.
5) Assemblies take varied forms, with the children taking part in preparation and presentation. The Infants have their own Assembly. The school is developing a musical tradition, with beneficial effects on the liturgy.
6) There are regular Masses for the Junior and top Infant children.
7) Efforts are made to help the parents to assist their children in preparation for First Communion and Confession.

> The school is in a very deprived area, with many of the children from unstable home backgrounds. The Infant school is now complete and in use. The teachers are very keen and anxious to help the children grow in faith, and on the whole appear to be doing good work. We have some reservations about how the biblical material is handled and presented. In some teachers there seemed to be a lack of awareness of what are now generally accepted approaches to interpretation of scripture and its application to teaching. We had hoped to return to the school and have a discussion with the staff about this area of their work, but we have not yet been able to do so. Perhaps it is something we can arrange in the near future.

In March 1979, a Parents' Association was formed and in the same month thieves stole lead from the roof of the Infant school, the kitchen and the hall – an on-going problem to this day!

Class 4 Photograph : 1979

Class 3 Photograph : 1979

Class 6 Photograph : 1981

Class 8 Photograph : 1981

Sister Agnes remained in post until 1981, when Sister Patricia Staunton took over the leadership of the school. One of Miss Staunton's first major tasks was to recommend Nursery provision for the school. After conducting extensive research, she wrote to Mr. Helvin, a member of the Diocesan Commission for Education, in July 1984.

Sister Patricia Staunton

Dear Mr. Helvin

Further to your visit to the School on 12th June, I send you the following information indicating the need for a Nursery Unit at St. Mary's School.

On our current waiting list we have forty-five children of three years and over. All of these children would be eligible for nursery education immediately.

> A survey of children attending school at present shows that 23.5% are receiving supplementary benefit. There is a similar percentage, though not the same families, under stress of broken homes.
>
> Social Services approach me from time to time requesting that particular children be admitted to school. A limited concession only can be made due to staffing and capitation restrictions.
>
> Children in the three County schools enjoy the benefits of nursery education and I have expressed my concern to the Education Officer (Schools) that comparable provision is not made at our School. His efforts on our behalf to Urban Aid have failed and the project will be re-submitted in August 1984.
>
> I would urge that the strongest plea be made on behalf of our children who live in this educational priority area.
>
> I thank you for your interest in this matter and I am hopeful that the situation will be resolved for the academic year 1985/86.

Sister Patricia enlisted the support of the local M.P., Dr. Oonagh McDonald. In response to her enquiries, the County Education Officer indicated that St. Mary's had narrowly missed out on nursery provision in the period 1984/85, being placed third in a priority list, with only the first two accepted by the Department of Education and Science. A future application would have to be balanced against any new priorities in future years, so acceptance could not be guaranteed. But Sister Patricia continued to apply the pressure. In August 1984, Mr. Squires, the Assistant to the Commission for Education's Executive Secretary, enquired of the local education office whether St. Mary's School was indeed the only school in Tilbury without a nursery unit. At the Department of Education and Science, Bob Dunn, who was responsible for all school matters in the Department, was obliged to field further enquiries from Dr. Oonagh McDonald and Sister Patricia's name was becoming known in higher circles. Even the Education Secretary, Keith Joseph, became involved.

With all this mounting pressure, it came as no surprise when, in May 1985, the nursery project received a grant under the Urban Aid scheme and by September 1985 the Nursery school was opened. There was provision for 20 children each morning and 20 children each afternoon.

In 1985, the Essex County Council issued guidance to parents on its schools. Its reference to St. Mary's Roman Catholic Primary School included a section on the curriculum followed in the school. Those brought up on the 'three Rs' might be impressed at the range of subjects offered.

The school has established a balanced programme of primary school subjects which is reviewed periodically and is adapted and planned in relation to the age and ability of the children.

These subjects include Religious Education, English, Mathematics, Social Studies, Science and Nature Study, Music, Art and Craft, Physical Education and Games.

Great importance is placed on English – oral and written. The basic skills of reading are systematically taught so that children may read with fluency and understanding. Children are encouraged to read for pleasure. They are encouraged to express themselves in writing descriptively, imaginatively and factually. A substantial collection of books is available for reading and reference. Children will be given the opportunity to purchase their own books periodically from the Bookshop.

The Mathematics programme has been constructed after consultation with the secondary schools. Much of the work is of a practical nature to help the children to acquire a knowledge of number combinations, order, pattern and concepts of space time estimations, the understanding of principles. The particular field trains a child to think logically.

Part of the programme for Social Studies, Science and Nature Study is of a formal nature to give children a format on which to build their own studies in topics of their own choice.

Much of the work in Art and Craft arises from topic work using a variety of materials.

The children are given opportunities to take part in group singing, to learn to play the recorder or tuned percussion instrument. Groups of Infants and Juniors take part in inter-school festivals.

The hall is well equipped with large apparatus and the Physical Education programme includes gymnastics, games, dance and movement. The school teams play competitively in the Thurrock School Netball and Football leagues. By arrangement with Thurrock Borough Council swimming lessons for Juniors are available at Blackshots Swimming Pool.

<u>Religious Education</u>

As a Catholic school we pay particular attention to Religious Education which gives the school its special ethos.

We follow the "Veritas" syllabus. We encourage the children to take an active part in assemblies and in the Parish liturgy. Children are prepared for the Sacraments at the appropriate time and are given the opportunities to receive them regularly during the primary school years.

Meetings are arranged to inform parents of the content of Instruction.

The school is organised in seven classes in accordance with their age. The class teacher is responsible for the preparation of the children's work. In accordance with County policy, children are not given formal homework. Parents are, however, encouraged to hear their children read in accordance with good educational practice.

Pupils with Special Educational Needs

Pupils with special educational needs are given help in small groups in the classroom. Extra tuition in reading skills is given by a peripatetic teacher who visits the school regularly. After consultation with parents, children experiencing difficulty over an appreciable length of time may be referred for further support.

Sex Education

It is regarded as a parental prerogative to impart the biological aspects of sex education to their children. The wider implications of mutual respect and good relationships is recognised at all levels.

The school's capacity for detailed planning will come as no surprise to those conversant with modern day schools, but it needs to be remembered that this commentary pre-dates the introduction of the National Curriculum in primary schools by some four years and yet it anticipates many of the features of the new plan when it came into being.

In October 1986 a decision was made to form a Parent Teacher Association and at the end of October 1986 an extensive programme of improvement commenced in the Junior school. The asbestos ceilings were removed and replaced by suspended ceilings. The hall and classrooms were re-wired and everywhere redecorated. In the following year, on 13th October 1987, the Centenary Mass for both the school and church was celebrated by Bishop Thomas McMahon.

Mass of Thanksgiving : Centenary of St. Mary's School

By 1989, the school was experiencing some difficulty in recruiting and retaining staff, a problem that was evident throughout Essex. A combination of low salaries and high housing costs had driven many in the profession to move to areas where housing was cheaper, and St. Mary's School was understaffed. The recently founded Parent Teachers Association was now playing a significant part in the life of the school, and its fund-raising activities were making it possible for the school to buy much needed equipment. The social events they organised also did much to foster good relations and understanding between parents, children and teachers.

Pupils of St. Mary's Primary School begin the second century of the school's story

The provision of facilities as basic as store rooms, however, still carried with it a bureaucratic minefield that the school was obliged to traverse, aligning the differing priorities of the Diocesan Education Commission, the Essex Education Committee and the Department for Education and Science, each anxious to place ultimate responsibility for buildings and maintenance on one of the other two. The school actually required two small store rooms, one to house tables and chairs and other school furniture, and one to keep the steadily growing computer facilities in a secure area. The store rooms had two things in common: they were remarkably easy and cheap to build and they both occasioned a snowstorm of paperwork as the bureaucrats fought their respective corners.

In 1990, a visiting team from the LEA expressed some concerns about the relative lack of differentiation in the planning of the curriculum, and in the scarcity of educational resources in the school. Sister Patricia leapt to the defence of her team. Acknowledging that national staff shortages meant that suitably trained primary school teachers were not always available, and that recruitment was often from those who had had secondary school experience or were professionals returning to teaching, Sister Patricia praised the efforts of her teachers.. She referred to the experience and expertise of her Staff which had enabled every child to access the curriculum. Programmes of work had been devised for mixed ability classes, programmes which showed awareness of 'varying levels of understanding', and allowed for due adaptation for those children with special educational needs. In a letter to the Education Officer for Schools, Sister Patricia asserted

> Contrary to the report, staff meetings are a focal point of the weekly routine. Through my own professional and up-to-date knowledge and regular practice, I have led the staff in discussions which enabled each member to contribute, through sampling or verbal accounts, to a clearer understanding of the systemic progression in the core subjects. I myself have expertise in every area of the primary curriculum. This open sharing has ensured that there is continuity throughout the school. Knowledge of pupils' ability, interest and aptitude is central to policy making.

Referring to the positive use of displays around the school, the overall good behaviour of well-motivated children and the discriminating purchase of educational resources, Sister Patricia concluded with the comment

> During the last year the children have made remarkable holistic progress.

The children took part in an impressive school production of *Joseph and his Technicolor Dreamcoat* in June 1991, and this was reported in *The Thurrock Gazette.*

> Children from a Tilbury primary school loved appearing in a musical so much they performed their own version of the show.
>
> The pupils of St. Mary's Primary school put on a performance of Joseph and his Technicolor Dreamcoat after some of the children took part in a production in Brentwood in April.
>
> Headteacher Sister Patricia Staunton said: "It was a wonderful musical experience for the children, and the parents, who filled the hall to capacity, also enjoyed themselves."

In March 1993, a group of pupils from St. Mary's Primary visited the House of Commons as part of a school project. They were greeted by their local Member of Parliament, Andrew Mackinlay who said

> I am delighted to host this visit. The children were very well behaved and they thoroughly enjoyed their tour of the Palace of Westminster. I look forward to seeing their project when it's completed.

The children outside the House of Commons with their M.P. Andrew Mackinlay

In 1993 Sister Patricia retired from the school and this brought to an end the daily role of the Sisters of Mercy in the life of St. Mary's, which had spanned over ninety years. Mrs. Anne Ennefer became the first lay Head Teacher in January 1994, and ten years later Mr. Jonathan Shields took over this role.

A Visit to St. Mary's Primary School, November 2017

As soon as I enter the building, I am aware of the fact that I am in a Catholic School. A beautiful tapestry of the Madonna and Child holds pride of place, there is an impressive School Mission Statement on display and a statue of the Virgin and Child looks down on the visitor. A television screen shows a loop of all the children in the school, one by one.

School Mission Statement

Respect Ourselves, Respect Others, Respect our School, Love God

St. Mary's is a Catholic School which endeavours to develop and support the individual needs and talents of all members of its community and enables them to learn and live through faith and education.

The school aims are:-

(a) To integrate each child's holistic development through a balanced and creative curriculum which sees God as the centre of the learning process.

(b) To ensure that we lead our children to a greater understanding of the Catholic Faith. Through worship and the development of spirituality and community life, we aim to enable the children to appreciate and respect themselves, their world and the beliefs and cultures of others.

(c) To provide a curriculum that will develop the full potential of each person and educate the whole child, in an environment which encourages growth in self-confidence and the acquisition of skills, attitudes and values.

(d) To acknowledge that we are commanded to love God, love one another and to respect ourselves and other people by encouraging the development of meaningful relationships in our school.

(e) To share our aims and beliefs with our children through the "St. Mary's Way".

(Note: St. Mary's Way is summed up in the words *Respect Ourselves, Respect Others, Respect our School, Love God* and this is on the school's paperwork and displayed throughout the school.)

I am greeted warmly by Mrs. Alison Bishop, School Secretary and Clerk to the Governors and my guide for the day. A past pupil of the school, Alison has been in post now for some nineteen years, so is well-placed to tell me about the day to day work of the school. Her father, too, was once a pupil at the school. As we enter the school itself, the main corridor is a blaze of colour from the impressive displays that seem to take up every wall. There is a magnificent collage representing Noah's Ark, created by the children under the direction of a professional company who visited the school over two days. I am told that there are quite a few of these dotted around the school, and so it proves. They are to include Jonah and the Whale, the Loaves and Fishes, and the Prodigal Son, each one a representation of a biblical scene. (Note: For a photograph of the Noah's Ark collage, please see the centre pages of this book.) I arrive just after Remembrance Day, and there is a quiet corner where there are poppies and references to those who lost their lives in times of war, with the heading *We Will Not Forget*.

In the multi-purpose Hall, there is a Year 2 class busy with a Dance Class, and on the back wall there are further collages : The Good Samaritan, Loaves and Fishes, The Prodigal Son. On one wall there is a display of the Inter-House Competition, which runs throughout the School Year. The four Houses are named after the U.K.'s four Patron Saints, St. George (Red), St. David (Yellow), St. Andrew (Blue), and St. Patrick (Green). Points are awarded for good work, behaviour and competitions such as Sports Day, when the children are encouraged to wear their House colours. I notice that there is a second teacher present in the Dance Class. Her job is to take special care of a nominated child who needs additional support in lessons.

Outside the Hall, I notice a display cabinet housing some of the awards which are presented to children during the course of the year. A silver cup is presented each Sports Day, when the winning team has the honour to have ribbons of their House colour tied to the Sports Trophy. Another award, the Sisters of Mercy Award, is given to two children in Year Six, one girl and one boy, for their dedication and commitment to the school. There is also a glass trophy, the Diocese of Brentwood Citizenship of the Year Award, which is presented by the Bishop at a special ceremony in Brentwood Cathedral each year. One child and their family will attend the ceremony, together with a senior teacher from the school.

We enter the School Library which is also utilised for interactive learning, making use of laptops that are stored in a huge lapsafe in the corner. Children with headphones are involved in one to one learning with teachers. Selected children follow lessons, usually in Mathematics, which are tailor-made to the ability of each child, with each pupil communicating on a microphone with their own teacher who will assist them with their learning. This is part of an intervention programme, designed to assist those children who need additional help. The library also operates as a traditional library, with classes coming in to borrow books as part of their timetable.

We see a Year 6 class, where the children have already made their choices for secondary school in September 2018. The deadline for applications was the end of October 2017. Parents have a lot of responsibility these days, guiding their children towards the right schools. Parents of younger children have until January 2018 for applications to St. Mary's School, which will have to be signed by Father Paul.

When the Sisters of Mercy created a beautiful embroidered tapestry to celebrate their 100 years in the Parish of Our Lady Star of the Sea in

2005, they donated it to the school and here it is. Represented in the tapestry are the church, the convent, the school, the docks, the power station and the band hall, all of the buildings in the immediate vicinity of the Sisters of Mercy Convent.

Mrs. Bishop is able to remember the school as it was when she was a pupil here. The overall dimensions of the main school building are the same, although some classrooms have been enlarged for bigger classes and bigger children. Three classrooms thus become two. In addition, classrooms which were once 'outside' are now incorporated in the main building. Wall recesses that could only have been windows in the past stand testimony to the changes that have occurred over the years. Many of the original classrooms would have been separated off by room dividers, a less than ideal solution to a general lack of space. I am reminded that the site also once housed St. Mary's Secondary School. There couldn't have been a lot of room for everyone!

In those days, most of the teachers in the primary school were Sisters of Mercy, but there are no Sisters working in the school today. The first lay headteacher was Mrs. Ennefer who became Head in 1994 on the retirement of Sister Patricia Staunton, the last Sister to be employed in the school. Since that time there have been three Heads, Jonathan Shields 2004, James Bradley 2013, and Maggie Jones 2014.

A room which was added to the original building houses the Computer Suite, which once contained one computer for each child before growing school numbers made this a more difficult target. Software updates for all of these computers is ever more expensive and time-consuming. Safety online is controlled by firewalls and through a borough wide protection scheme. Even the youngest children in the school's nursery section have access to computers, so three and four year olds are learning keyboard skills.

The wall displays continue to impress, with a representation of school trumpet players that seems to burst right out of the picture. I was informed that sometimes the school looks to professional photographers in the search for excellence. The School Chapel was recently opened and blessed by Father Paul Dynan. Schoolboy memories are revived at the sight of the cloakroom where the Year Six pupils hang their coats.

In the playground area there are two equipped cabins for small group or one to one learning. There are two main playgrounds, one for the infants and one for the juniors. Two gates in one corner lead to the convent and the presbytery, although it is a long time since the nuns used the gate to walk into the school where they worked, and Father Paul uses the main school entrance, leaving the presbytery gate locked for security reasons.

There are forty-three staff at the school, including cleaning staff and midday assistants. There are two hundred and twenty children attending full-time and twenty three in the nursery. When seven children join the nursery in January, after the term in which they have their third birthday, every class in the school will be full to capacity. There is a waiting list for every Year Group.

All classrooms have interactive whiteboards, one of the reasons that most staff meetings take place in a classroom so that these facilities can be used for presentations. Most of the staff meetings are run by the Headteacher, Mrs. Maggie Jones, although subject leaders will sometimes take the chair. There are meetings for Key Stage 1 and Key Stage 2 teachers twice each term.

The Opening and Blessing of the School Chapel by Father Paul Dynan with the School's Faith Council

In a new block the younger children in the school are accommodated. Door handles are placed strategically high so that no child can 'escape'. The nursery section is placed right next to the youngest children in the school, the Reception Class. It has its own outside area, well stocked with equipment and games for the children to enjoy. The places funded by the Government's nursery scheme, the children attend each day for the morning session.

There is a buzz of activity in the school's Reception class, with the children engaged in free play in two activity areas, and gaining access to an outdoor area in fine weather. We are almost mobbed by the enthusiastic children who are keen to show us what they are doing. The children are allowed to choose their activities, with each option having a particular focus. There is an impressive atmosphere of energy and concentration.

A more formal atmosphere is seen in the adjoining classroom for Year 1 pupils. All attention is directed to the teacher who is talking to them.

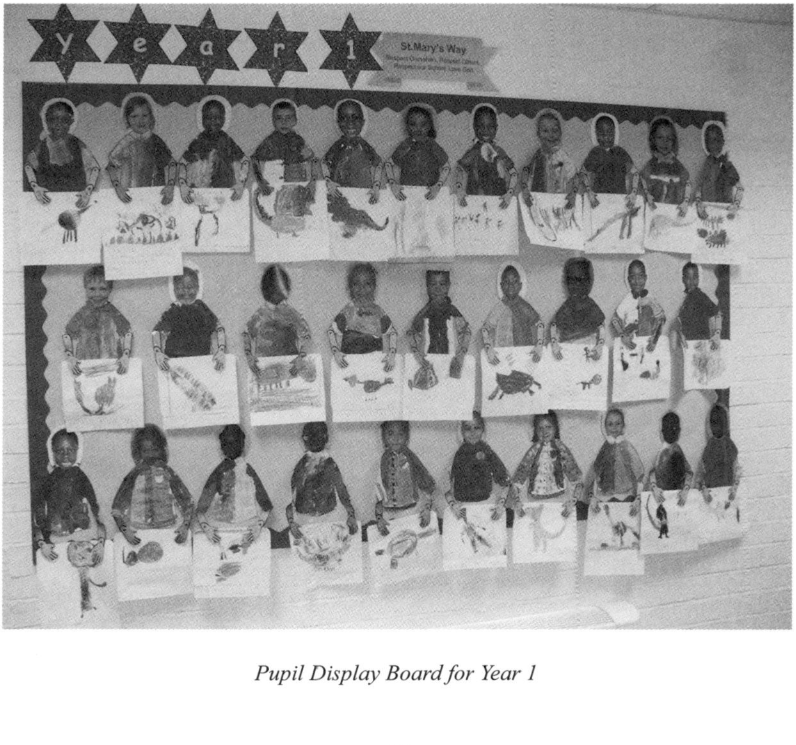

Pupil Display Board for Year 1

We now climb to the first floor of the building, added about six years ago, the increased space allowing cramped classrooms to be enlarged and the school library to have its own dedicated space. We see another intervention class, where particular children are given special attention, whether they need support to keep up with their peers or are identified by the teaching staff as gifted.

We enter a bustling school kitchen which starts each day at about 8.00 a.m., preparing fresh meals for the children. I am very tempted by today's curry and there are trays of delicious looking chocolate cake. Meals are eaten in the main school hall, which is also used for assembly (this morning on anti-bullying for Key Stage 2 children), for meetings, dance classes, breakfast club and after school clubs. Breakfast club welcomes children at 7.30 in the morning, when a breakfast is provided and the children play games until they go to class at 8.50 a.m. The after-school clubs run on three days a week. It follows that the hall is used from 7.30 in the morning through to 4.30. p.m. on almost every day.

There is a Dance Teacher who comes in one day a week, a Music Teacher who comes in two days a week and a P.E. Instructor who comes in two days a week. When they are teaching, St. Mary's School teachers are released for their Planning, Preparation and Assessment time.

Mrs. Bishop finally brings the comprehensive tour to an end by offering me a host of photographs which celebrate the life of St. Mary's School. Choosing just a few for the book is to prove very hard. As I leave the school, I reflect that when you pass the building, you have little understanding of the exciting and stimulating activities which are provided inside for all the children. This is a wonderful school.

Chapter Seven : St. Mary's Secondary School

Early in 1937, the Parish Priests of Tilbury, Grays and Stanford-le-Hope met together to discuss the possibility of creating a senior school for the three parishes. They appointed a sub-committee to see what sites were available for a joint senior school. Father Snell of Stanford-le-Hope, a Mr. Price from Grays and Councillor Feenan from Tilbury examined six sites and found one to be the most suitable. Bishop Doubleday was informed of the discussions and asked for his blessing and the three Parish Priests had ‘informal discussions’ with the Director of Education for the County.

The Director, John Sargent, wrote to Bishop Doubleday the following year about senior school accommodation for Catholics, particularly in the area of Grays and Tilbury. The managers of the Grays Catholic Primary School had submitted plans for an extension to their buildings, which held ‘280 odd children’ (?) and the Director, aware of a shortage of funds in the diocese, wished to know if the Bishop had plans for a senior school in the area.

Bishop Doubleday suggested that his Diocesan Schools Commission might meet with the Essex Education Committee to see what assistance could be provided with the purchase of a site, the construction of suitable buildings, the payment of teachers and the transport of children from one area to another. He had plans for a senior Roman Catholic school housing some 160 pupils, sited close to the border with Grays, so that children could travel to the school easily from both areas. Unfortunately, the Bishop had not been able to locate a suitable site for such a school, and did not wish to build one in a place too far from Grays, which might discourage students from that town from making the journey. As he stated to the Director of Education:

> It would be extremely disappointing and wasteful to build a modern Senior Elementary School and not be able to make full use of its accommodation.

In the following year, in the months leading up to the outbreak of the Second World War, Fr. O’Donnell wrote to Bishop Doubleday indicating that a site had been found on land owned by the St. Vincent de Paul Society, and plans had been drawn up for a senior school there. Unfortunately a rival claim had been made for a nursery school on the same site, and the Essex Education Committee was considering a Compulsory Purchase Order to acquire the land for the nursery school.

In November 1939, major building works were postponed due to the start of the war. The Board of Education, responsible for the provision of education in England and Wales, announced:

> The Board consider that the best course will be to review the whole position after the War when sympathetic consideration will be given to the possibility of legislation to meet cases which have failed to materialise for causes which are beyond the control of the promoters or the Authority.

At the end of the war, provision was at last to be made for a secondary school to serve older Catholic children in the three areas. The minimum school leaving age had been increased to 15, and an increase in numbers was anticipated. Temporary buildings were erected next to the primary school, saving money both on site purchase and building costs. But Father O'Donnell saw a problem.

> … from one point of view, it is unfortunate that Tilbury had to be chosen for this temporary scheme, for the truth is that to the rest of Thurrock, the name Tilbury is "mud". This arises from the history of our Town and I fancy that Fathers Snell and O'Brien will have difficulties with some of the parents about sending their children here.
>
> Your Lordship may be coming amongst us in the autumn for Confirmation and you might find it well to call together the parents of the three Parishes and address them on the new scheme – for I feel that if parents and Priests do not whole-heartedly support the temporary arrangement at Tilbury, we shall have great and increased difficulties in establishing later on a proper and worthy Secondary School for this area.

Be that as it may, a secondary modern school, St. Mary's, was opened on 9th September 1947, with a roll of 168. It was recognised as a voluntary aided school, which meant that all of its running costs were provided by the government. The children did indeed come from the Catholic primary schools in Tilbury, Stanford and Grays. There was a staff of five, the Headmaster and four assistants. The school itself included the old school building, together with three prefabricated huts, the H.O.R.S.A. huts. In these huts were a Woodwork room, a General Science room, a Domestic Science room and two classrooms.

There was, however, no main hall in the school for the daily religious assembly required under the 1944 Education Act. Father O'Donnell asked Bishop Doubleday for permission to make use of the church for this purpose. A nearby Club Hall was earmarked for Physical Training in the winter months. Bishop Doubleday duly agreed, subject to the provisos that the church would be utilised only for religious assemblies and that general school notices and other announcements would not be expected.

By 1955, there was a serious problem with overcrowding in the primary school and the prospect of a similar overcrowding in the growing secondary school. A request for an additional primary classroom had not been agreed by the Essex Education Committee. The new Parish Priest, Father Byrne, discussed the situation with the two head-teachers and arranged for two secondary school classrooms to be used as primary accommodation. However, the expectation of a growth in numbers at the secondary school meant that this could be only a temporary solution. This would be exacerbated by a Tilbury Rebuilding Scheme, expected to increase the Tilbury population by over 6,000, and the Council's plans to build 1,400 houses in Chadwell St. Mary.

There was cause for some optimism with the news received in October 1955 that land on Linford Road, Chadwell St. Mary had been allocated by Essex Education Committee for the building of a new Catholic Secondary School. The nine and a half acre site would at last give a little breathing space for those crowded together in the old school buildings. There would be two acres for the new school with most of the rest of the site reserved as school playing fields. What seemed like a minor issue, the extraction of gravel from the site before school building could start, was to become a major barrier to the building of the new school. By early 1956 the Area Planning Officer asked that the school be built on another part of the site to facilitate 'the proper and economic working of the gravel deposit. It was clear that the gravel workings were given a higher priority than the new school.

In January 1957, an entirely new site for the school was suggested by the Essex Education Committee. The Chadwell St. Mary's Hospital site had 38 acres surplus to the requirements of the Regional Hospital Board, and there would be ample room for the new school and its playing fields. Initially, the Catholic authorities were opposed to the change. They liked the site previously offered, and had already been offered land just across the road from the school site, where they would be able to build a church, convent and presbytery. The diocese was willing to accept the new proposals, but only if there could be land allocated for these buildings as well.

Agreement was reached in principle by April 1957, although once again all arrangements would have to await the extraction of minerals from the site. Father Byrne gave detailed advice on the siting of the new secondary school, church, convent and presbytery, linking this with good bus routes for pupils and parishioners.

The only remaining issue was the price of the land that was to be purchased for all of the new building. Thurrock Council had offered the previous site at one quarter of its market value, but the new land was offered at market value. The price was only £350 per acre, however, so there were at last no barriers to the start of this ambitious new scheme. A plot of 4.24 acres was earmarked for the school, the church, the presbytery and the convent. A further 7 acres was to be used as school playing fields, once the mineral workings were completed.

By 1960 the old secondary school was giving great cause for concern. The actual classrooms as well as toilets were reported to be in a very poor condition. The school roll had almost reached the 300 mark. Of these, 123 were children from Tilbury and 158 children were from other parishes. But the decoration and repair costs of the old buildings were borne by the Tilbury parishioners. There was a gentleman's agreement that adjoining parishes would make a contribution, and a levy of ten shillings per pupil was introduced, but Father Byrne admitted that this had been a failure and some parishes showed no indication that they would pay anything. Father Byrne asked the Diocesan Schools Commission to authorise a levy of £1 per pupil for those attending the senior school from other parishes.

The overriding concern, however, was for the transfer of the secondary school to the Chadwell St. Mary site. The Education Development Plan gave the move no particular priority, indicating that it should occur in the period 1961-65. The primary school site, meanwhile, was severely overcrowded and there was scarcely the space for 300 secondary school children. There was still no strong support for the secondary school in Tilbury, as the audit for 1960 shows. Grays sent 58 children, Aveley 71, Stanford 19, Laindon 6, Canvey 4 and Basildon 2. Many Catholic parents seemed to prefer to send their children to non-Catholic secondary schools.

Despite many letters to and from the various official bodies responsible for the development of the site at Chadwell St. Mary, little real progress was made. The Mercy Convent at Tilbury indicated that the Sisters did not require the acre of land set aside for them for an additional convent in Chadwell St. Mary, whilst the Catholics in Chadwell St. Mary stated a strong preference for a church rather than a church hall. The thorny question of gravel extraction on the site returned. The original school site had been selected so that gravel extraction could occur on other parts of the former hospital site. Now the Essex Education Committee saw merit in permitting gravel works on the school site as well. The promise of a levelled surface after the gravel had been extracted seemed to be more important than the inevitable delay in holding off any building until the excavations were completed. Once again, the parish would be obliged to wait.

Worse was to follow. The Essex Education Committee decided in October 1960 to relocate the position of the proposed Grays County Technical School so that gravel workings could continue in the richer deposits on the north of the site. This meant that the two proposed new schools would be crammed in next to each other, with a common entrance, whilst the gravel company enjoyed unrestricted access for its gravel extraction. Once again, commercial considerations were accorded a higher priority than the educational needs of children.

In June 1961, the parish received the news that the transfer of the Tilbury Secondary School to the Chadwell St. Mary site had not been included in the Building Programme for 1963-1965. The process for prioritising Catholic school buildings goes through two main stages. First is the list of buildings created by the diocese, with those needing most urgent attention at the top of the list. Secondly, the Essex Education Committee draws up its overall list of school buildings for a specified number of years. It draws from the diocesan list as well as from school building requests from non-Catholic schools. If the diocese does not place a building request right at the top of its own list, there is little prospect of success for that particular building project. In its wisdom, the diocese had not responded to the urgent appeals from Tilbury and other projects were placed above it.

The minutes of a School Governors' meeting held in October 1961, in the presence of two H.M.I (Her Majesty's Inspectors) and education officers, show that the need for a new school was most urgent. One of Her Majesty's Inspectors said of the secondary school:

> It must be obvious to you that the old building is not satisfactory.... The school started with three huts of the H.O.R.S.A. type for Science, Housecraft and Woodwork. (Note: These were temporary structures of precast concrete, usually with asbestos roofs and metal window frames, built as emergency measures to house the growing numbers of secondary age schoolchildren after the minimum school leaving age had been raised to 15.) There are five classrooms in the old building. .... There are

> many deficiencies – it is a poor setting for a Secondary School. The Primary School will eventually occupy the whole of this site.
>
> The lack of a Hall is a very serious handicap – there is no place for P.T. or any other activities. The Playground – I do not know what you would feel on a wet day, passing the high stack of coke (which always seems to be there), the old boiler house with its low smoking chimney, (one day the caretaker had the dustbins on fire), these are the things the children see every day. It is not a very bright outlook, but no doubt they get used to it. These are material problems. There is the outside and the inside to tidy up: we do not now build schools with high windows. Education facilities today are very good. Our children are given the best; but your school is very far behind.

The school was judged to lack suitable furniture for children and teachers, the playground toilets needed urgent attention, there were no display boards, an insufficient number of books, the absence of a proper school library, survey maps were needed, as was equipment for drawing and needlework. The Inspector concluded that the best option was for a new, purpose-built school, stating that this hope had been expressed when the secondary school was founded in 1947. An H.M.I. stated

> I have not heard when we can now expect it and the possibility of getting it I fear is still very far away.

A few days later, Father Byrne wrote to Canon Hurley of the Diocesan Schools Commission, pointing out the deficiencies in the secondary school building identified by the H.M.I. Foremost amongst these was the lack of a school hall, which could be solved temporarily by hiring a local hall for the use of both the primary and secondary schools, or more permanently by the building of a school hall on land next to the Palace Cinema. Of course, all these problems would be solved by a move to the Chadwell St. Mary site – the older pupils would have a properly built and equipped school and the younger pupils would benefit from having more space around their existing school. Yet this was not to be in the 1963-65 Building Programme, a fact that Father Byrne believed to be ‘very surprising, disappointing and disheartening to us’.

Father Byrne wrote again to Canon Hurley in February 1962, enclosing details of the H.M.I. Inspection Reports on St. Mary's Primary and Secondary schools. Referring to the many deficiencies identified in the secondary school buildings, he reported that the general view of the officials had been that the transfer to the new site “should receive top priority from the diocese”. Father Byrne went on to say

> You will appreciate what a shock you gave me last summer when you stated that we had not been recommended by you for inclusion in the Schools Building Programme….. Priority has been given to Aveley. The Reports show that the exclusion of Tilbury was a grave error. It may not be too late to remedy this mistake.

The demand for classrooms had reached a critical stage. One primary school classroom had been 'borrowed' from a neighbouring council school, who now wanted it back. The secondary school had grown to such an extent that two primary classrooms had been pressed into service, leaving just four classrooms for the primary school children. Father Byrne's policy had been never to refuse entry to a Catholic child, but he was now obliged to inform Father Johnson at Aveley that no more children from that area could be accepted in Tilbury. Even the anticipated expansion of the primary school, with much needed additional classroom space, was still awaiting diocesan permission.

Late in 1963, further news was received by the Governors of the secondary school. There was a proposal to create a new secondary school at Grays Convent, which would have major implications for the future of secondary education in Tilbury. Father Byrne asked Canon Hurley to attend a meeting of the Tilbury Governors to clarify the situation. It transpired that the secondary school in Grays would be a grammar school, so the majority of children in Tilbury and surrounding areas were still in need of a new Catholic secondary school.

In December 1964, Father Byrne received the news he had been awaiting for so long: the diocese had given top priority to the transfer of Tilbury St. Mary's Secondary School to Chadwell St. Mary and the Essex Education Committee had recommended this project. The time frame was 1967-68. The following November, however, the Brentwood Diocesan Schools Commission came up with a new plan. There was to be an eight form entry two tier comprehensive school. The junior component for children aged 11-14 would be established at the Grays Convent School, and the senior component for children aged 14-16 at the Chadwell St. Mary site. This was now scheduled for 1968.

Yet this was still some years ahead. To help with the cramped and inadequate accommodation in the existing site, Father Byrne proposed to lease West Africa House, a former Missions to Seamen establishment, for the use of the secondary school. Father Byrne listed its potential advantages:

> 1. Extra accommodation urgently required for pupils to prepare for the Secondary School Certificate.
> 2. To be used for Secondary School Meals, as there is no more room at Lansdowne Road School (Council school)
> 3. A P.T. and Games Room, very urgent.

In November 1966 came further news from the Diocesan Schools Commission.

> The proposals of the Commission that two Catholic comprehensive schools should be established as follows:
> (a) The existing Grays Convent Independent School for Girls to seek Aided status and to be enlarged as a Girls Comprehensive School for pupils aged 11 to 18.
> (b) A new Boys Comprehensive School for pupils aged 11 to 18 to be established in the premises of the Courts Secondary School, Aveley, which will become surplus to the requirements of the Authority when the scheme of comprehensive reorganisation is implemented.

After so many years of waiting, the Tilbury Parish was denied the opportunity of a new secondary school at Chadwell St. Mary. The old school would struggle on in the cramped accommodation it had occupied since 1947, until the new comprehensive reorganisation that occurred in Thurrock in the early 1970s. But what of the children and their parents? One letter, written in February 1968, will illustrate the dilemma that many families experienced. It was addressed to Father Hayes, who was based at the Bishop's House, South Woodford.

> I would like to take this opportunity to request that you bring to the notice of our Bishop this letter from one of the parents of his Lordship's Diocese.
>
> My five children, ages ranging from 6 years to 13 years, attend the St. Mary's Catholic Primary and Secondary School, Dock Road, Tilbury, and though I may say it myself, they are educationally very bright, my eldest boy especially, who is also a very proficient sportsman, particularly adept at football.
>
> But I do feel that it is time that there was something done regarding the space that is available to accommodate our children. They are in no way on a par with other schools, and I am afraid the environmental aspect is very adverse.
>
> I have approached the Secondary School Headmaster, Mr. Bolger, who was very understanding, but as he has said there is no solution in taking the children away from the school (as several parents have)! But to write and to back the teachers in their demand for the move sooner to the school at Courts.

I'm afraid I do not want to take my boy away, but if there seems no likelihood of improvement regarding school conditions in the near future, there will be no alternative.

Hoping for your favourable comments ....

Father Hayes did not feel he knew enough about the situation to make an informed reply, so he passed the letter to Canon Hurley, who responded.

Father Hayes has asked me to thank you for your letter and to reply.

As you know, the proposal of the Governors to move the girls from St. Mary's Secondary School to Grays Convent and the boys to Courts has been accepted by the Essex Education Committee, and is in the hands of the Department of Education and Science.

It is not likely, however, that this re-organisation will take effect until all the secondary schools in Thurrock "go" comprehensive, which I understand will be in 1971.

Once the secondary school is rehoused, the site at St. Mary's will be available for the development of St. Mary's Primary School to regulation standard.

In the meantime, the playground space will remain limited; but the provision of playing-fields, which is the responsibility of the Local Education Authority, should be the same, in proportion to its size, for St. Mary's as for any other primary or secondary school.

If these schools have no playing-fields of their own, they have the right to the use of county playing-fields which will be shared with other schools. It is for the Managers and Governors of St. Mary's to see that this is arranged, and I suggest that you enquire of them that this has been done.

In the early 1970s secondary education in Thurrock was reorganised and St. Mary's Secondary Modern School closed in July 1971. Most of the children from there transferred to either Grays Convent School, run by the Sisters of La Sainte Union who had taught at St. Mary's at the beginning of the twentieth century, or to St. Cedd's Secondary School in South Ockendon.

Photograph of a Second Year Class at St. Cedds School, 1979

Chapter Eight : The Sisters of Mercy

The Congregation of the Sisters of Mercy was founded in Dublin in 1831 by Catherine McAuley. Catherine McAuley was born in Dublin towards the end of the eighteenth century. Her family were wealthy tradespeople but Catherine saw the desperate poverty of working people at close hand, and she was moved by the dreadful conditions they had to endure, both at home and at work. Catherine's parents died when she was still young and she now had to look after her younger brother and sister. With little money surviving the death of her parents, Catherine found work as a companion to an elderly lady and her husband. The Callaghans were a Quaker family and they were suspicious of Catholics and their faith. Yet they were impressed by Catherine's steadfast determination to help the poor in whatever way she could. After Mrs. Callaghan and, shortly afterwards, Mr. Callaghan died, Catherine found herself the sole heir to a considerable fortune. Her employers had realised that Catherine could be trusted to put their money to good use.

Despite family objections, Catherine built a House of Mercy in a very fashionable part of Dublin. This took place before the Catholic Emancipation Act was passed, when Catholics still found it difficult to gain acceptance in society. There was some objection to the work that Catherine and her supporters began, partly because such charity had traditionally been performed by nuns in cloistered settings, and partly because some of the poor of Dublin were now near neighbours of the rich and privileged.

This first building encapsulated the aims of the new religious Congregation. It contained a school for the poor, an orphanage, a hostel and training centre for young women in service in the fashionable houses of Dublin, and accommodation for the ladies who carried out these charitable works. They were soon challenged by the cholera infested slums of Dublin, but their numbers grew with their determination. The ladies were originally volunteers but, as they began to realise that God was calling them to do this work, they founded a non-cloistered order, dedicated to works of mercy. Along with their vows of poverty, chastity and obedience, they added a fourth, to serve the sick, poor and ignorant.

In the remaining ten years of her life, Catherine opened twelve new convents dedicated to this work, ten in Ireland and two in England. When she died in 1841, there were already plans for convents in

Liverpool, Pittsburgh, and Newfoundland, indications of an international involvement that is still in place today.

Many years later, in December 2006, a newspaper article was written by David Lang to commemorate the 175th anniversary of the founding of the Sisters of Mercy. The story of Catherine McAuley was told in greater detail.

> On a cold winter's morning in the early 1820s a young woman carrying provisions for a destitute family stopped to comfort a young child who was sitting on the pavement, with an infant in her arms, crying bitterly. She learned that both the child's parents and elder siblings had died of typhoid and on that morning, following the removal of their bodies for a pauper's funeral, she and the baby had been evicted from their basement room by another desperately poor family.
>
> The woman was Catherine McAuley and it was experiences such as this that shaped her future and led to the establishment of a new Religious Congregation, the Sisters of Mercy.
>
> Catherine McAuley was born in Dublin in 1778. At this time, the Industrial Revolution was gathering momentum. This was a period of tremendous energy, creativity and discovery. But there was a darker side with the massive development of slum towns and widespread exploitation of workers, women and, particularly, children who were cheaper to employ.
>
> Catherine was appalled at the exploitation of workers and the terrible conditions which they and their families endured. She had experienced poverty and deprivation herself when both parents died and she and her younger brother and sister were left without means of support.
>
> At about the age of 20 Catherine went to live as a companion to an elderly, wealthy couple, Mr. And Mrs. Callaghan. They were Quakers and though very suspicious of all things 'Catholic' were very supportive of Catherine's ministry to the poor of Coolock where they lived. Indeed, it was from the servants in Coolock House that Catherine learned of the plight of young serving girls at risk from the advances of the men folk in the houses in which they worked. Catherine yearned to help such vulnerable women.
>
> When Mr. Callaghan died in 1822 he left his entire fortune to Catherine knowing it would be well used. This providential act made Catherine's dream possible. To the consternation of her rather worldly family she used it to build a 'House of Mercy' in Baggot Street – a very fashionable part of Dublin. Her plan was to bring the poor to the doorsteps of the rich. The building was ready for occupancy on the feast of Our Lady of Ransom, also known as Our Lady of Mercy. This was a providential coincidence giving the House and later the Congregation its name.

The large building comprised a school for the poor, an orphanage and a hostel and training centre for vulnerable young women who worked, or sought work, in the houses of the rich. The house was designed to provide living accommodation for Catherine and friends, acquaintances and ladies of society who felt drawn to helping the poor and who would, hopefully, volunteer their services.

Many likeminded women did in fact join her. They soon became involved in teaching in the poor schools and nursing the sick and the dying in their homes and hospitals during cholera and other epidemics. At first all the ladies worked as volunteers. Later it became clear that God was calling them to devote their whole lives to these works of mercy and to form a new type of religious congregation. This would be uncloistered but would give their work stability and permanence.

Consequently, Catherine and two companions Anna Maria Doyle and Elizabeth Harley entered the novitiate in the Presentation Convent, Dublin and on December 12th 1831 professed the vows of poverty, chastity and obedience which the Catholic Church required for members of a religious order. All futures professions would include a fourth vow to serve the poor, sick, and ignorant, thus expressing the nature and purpose of the Congregation or as the Sisters say "our charism".

The Congregation of the Sisters of Mercy was thus born. Catherine was 53 when she professed her vows. Her religious life was to be very short – ten prodigiously fruitful years. Under her Spirit-filled guidance the Congregation spread very rapidly. In those ten years she opened ten new convents in Ireland and two in England, Bermondsey, London in 1839 and Birmingham in 1841. Others including Liverpool, Newfoundland and Pittsburgh, America, were in the pipeline when she died in 1841.

People started calling them "The Walking Nuns". This was a derisive term at first. Real nuns did not leave their convents and walk the streets as Catherine's sisters did. Catherine's dictum "need is our cloister" was exemplified in action. The Sisters visited the sick and poor in their own homes and in the hospitals. They ran day and night schools for the poor, and, where possible, found shelter for the homeless and orphans. They sought in every way possible to improve the lot of women. Soon the congregation spread due to two factors: need and the restoration of the Catholic hierarchies in England and Wales and then that of Scotland.

Today in their 175th jubilee year Sisters of Mercy minister from 160 Convents of Mercy establishments throughout England, Scotland and Wales. Some of the houses have outreaches abroad in Kenya, Lebanon, Peru, Romania, South Africa and Ethiopia.

In recent years there has been a steady fall in the number of women who respond to a call to life-long commitment in Religious Congregations.

However, an interesting phenomenon is the development worldwide of the Mercy Associate Movement. Many thousands of men and women drink deeply from the wells of mercy spirituality and find inspiration in Catherine McAuley. They are engaged both with and alongside the sisters and frequently sustain the mercy presence in areas where sisters are no longer present.

A bronze sculpture of Mary Catherine McAuley

> The Youth Mercy Associate Movement which started in England is also spreading rapidly to other parts of the world. It is the sisters' policy to share the mercy charism with all co-workers and colleagues. Through them too Catherine McAuley's charism and ministry is continued in the world of today.

Her story is recorded in the annals held by the Sisters of Mercy at Tilbury. In turn, these are based on the annals of the Sisters of Mercy in Bermondsey, London, dated 1868. The full detail is given below, as this records the very start of an Institute that has spread itself across the world.

> Our Reverend Mother and Foundress, Mary Catherine McAuley, was born on the 29th September 1776-7. She received the Religious Habit in the Presentation Convent, George's Hill, on the 9th December 1830, made her Holy Profession on the 12th December 1831 and died on the 11th November 1841.
>
> She was in stature rather above middle height, well proportioned and erect, with a fair complexion and high colour. Her eyes were large and penetrating, of a very bright blue, with a most kind expression; her manner dignified and reserved, while tender and compassionate to the poor and maternally affectionate to the Sisters; her movements were quiet and her words few: her whole demeanour showing constant recollection of the presence of God.
>
> During the ten years of her Religious Life, fifty-one Sisters were admitted to Holy Profession by her, she and the two companions who were professed with her at George's Hill making the number amount to fifty-four. The names of those whose Vows were received by our revered Foundress are as follows:
>
> 1833: Sisters Mary Angela Teresa Dunne, Mary Francis Xavier Warde Mary Clare Moore, Mary Magdalen de Pazzi Delaney, Mary Joseph Teresa McAuley.
>
> 1834: Sisters Mary Magdalen Teresa Flynn, Mary Gertrude Jones, Mary Elizabeth Moore, Mary Agnes Marmion.
>
> 1835: Sisters M. Mechtildis Gaffney, Mary Jane Frances de Chantal McCann, Mary Genevieve Jarmy, Mary Joseph Warde, Mary Teresa of Jesus White.
>
> 1836: Sisters M. Cecilia Marmion, Mary Anne Agnes McAuley.
>
> 1837: Sisters M. Ursula Frayne, Mary Teresa White, Mary Rose Lube, Mary Aloysius Thorpe, Mary Monica Murphy, Mary Vincent Deasy.

1838: Sister M. Aloysius Scott.

1839: Sisters M. Francis de Sales White, Mary Angela Maher, M. Francis Marmion, Mary Francis Xavier O'Connell, Mary Anne Frances de Chantal Markey.

1840: Sisters M. Catherine Leahy, M. Gertrude Blake, M. Clare Augustine Moore, M. Anne Teresa O'Brien, M. Francis Boylan, M. Agnes O'Connor, M. Elizabeth Butler, M. Rose Lynch.

1841: Sisters M. Camillus Byrne, M. Aloysius Cowley, M. Vincent White, M. Justina Fleming, M. Francis Creedon, M. Augustine Horan.

(For Birmingham): Sisters M. Juliana Hardman, M. Francis Xavier Wood, M. Vincent Bond, M. Cecilia Edwards.

The Lay Sisters Professed by her were:

1836: Sister Martha Wallplate.

1837: Sisters Veronica Corrigan, Lucy Teresa Breen, Teresa Carton, Agatha Brennan.

The last Sister to receive the Holy Habit from the hands of our venerated Foundress was Sister M. Juliana Delaney, a younger sister of Mother M. de Pazzi Delaney, and the Silver Ring of Profession worn by our Foundress was bestowed on this Novice.

The Covents founded by our revered Foundress were:

First: Tullamore, whence branched forth the Convents in Kells, Londonderry, Drogheda, Clare, Trim and Commercial Road, East London.

Second: Charleville.

Third: Carlow, whose filiations are Nass, Westport, Tuam, Bilston in England, Pittsburgh (U.S.A.) and Auckland (N.Z.). This last colony passing through London was joined by one of the Chelsea Community, Sister Mary Bernard Dickson, who, from Auckland was sent to found the Convent at Wellington in the same island.
Sister M. Bernard was Professed in Bermondsey in 1850, and was one of those who remained in Chelsea when it ceased to be a Branch House.

Fourth: Cork, which sent the first foundation for England at Bermondsey, and again, four years later, to England at Sunderland; also Queenstown, Bantry, Templemore and a Branch hospital in Cork.

Fifth: Limerick, from which the Convents at Kinsale, Killarney, Mallow with the Branch Houses at Adare, Mount St. Vincent, the Limerick Workhouse, and Edinburgh and Glasgow in Scotland, were founded.

Sixth: Galway, which founded Castlebar and Clifton, with Branch Houses for the Magdalen Asylum and the Asylum for Widows and Orphans.

Seventh: Birr, which founded Fritruth and a Branch House at Nenagh.

Eighth: Birmingham, the Parent House of Nottingham, of St. Anne's, Birmingham, and Wolverhampton, Mary Vale.

Ninth: The Branch House at Kingstown, and

Tenth: The Branch House at Booterstown, both dependent on Baggot Street.

Before her death, our Foundress had promised Sisters for Newfoundland and Liverpool and they were sent to both places by her successor in Office. The Superioress appointed for Newfoundland was Mother M. Ursula Frayne, who afterwards founded the first Convent of our Institute in Australia at Perth, a second at Freemantle and a third at Melbourne. Mother M. de Sales White was sent to establish the Convent at Liverpool, where all the works of our Institute have been most fully carried out, and numerous Foundations and Branch Houses have filiated from it.

Twenty-five years had not elapsed from the death of the Foundress when her Institute numbered one hundred and fifty Houses, spread throughout the world. It is observed by a pious writer that the history of Religious Orders testifies to us that the Institutes which have lasted the longest are those from which their commencement spread rapidly; the same Divine Providence which watched over their foundation, watched also over their extension.

The convent in Macklin Street had been set up at the request of Father Skrimshire, who had approached the Bermondsey Community asking for Sisters to take responsibility for the schools in the area around Macklin Street and for the visiting of the poor and sick in the area.

The Convent in Macklin Street

Macklin Street, London

Bishop Butt gave his approval and three Sisters were assigned to the new Foundation, beginning their work in April 1892. Fr. Skrimshire provided a furnished house next to the school in Maiden Lane, described as "a street which was the headquarters of the London thieves." Gradually, through their patient and tireless work, the Sisters transformed the tone of the area, so that the schools and parish had a more positive outlook. Of course, the Sisters missed their convent in Bermondsey but, as the annals record, there were compensations:

> The Sisters' loneliness at leaving Bermondsey was mixed with joy when they were greeted by "a poor old flower-seller in Drury Lane, as she handed them a bunch of flowers with a 'God bless ye Sisters and it's welcome ye are'", and on other occasions with "Take this little bunch for the Chapel, Sister, for God's blessing…". The Lord blessed this particular 'Mustard Seed' in the challenges inevitably associated with all new beginnings, so much so that by the beginning of the new century the Community numbered fifteen whom the Superior playfully named her 'Fifteen Mysteries'. Pleas for help in Old Gate School, Lincoln's Inn (1900) and Mill Wall, Dockland, Parish and School (1904) received positive responses, as did Canon Van Meenan's appeal for a Community of Sisters in the developing town of Tilbury.

At the turn of the twentieth century, the Parish Priest in Tilbury, Canon Van Meenan, wanted the help of a resident Community of Religious Sisters who would teach in the school and undertake the visitation of the Catholic families in the area. He arranged with the Superior of the Sisters of Mercy in Macklin Street (known today as Tavistock Square), London to send some Sisters to open a new convent in Tilbury. On 8th January 1905 three Sisters, Teresa O'Connor, Camillus Ryan and Ethelburga Dwyer moved to a house in Dock Road, Tilbury, now named Trevor Villas. It was just opposite the school. They started work teaching the very next day, with Sister Teresa O'Connor appointed Headmistress.

The numbers of pupils attending school rose steadily in the next few months and by August 1905 there were 285 on roll. Absenteeism was rife, with children needed for pea picking on neighbouring farms and hop-picking in Kent, where the Gravesend ferry provided transport. This cheap child labour helped to supplement family incomes for, although the Docks were in full operation, employment was on the casual 'tally' system and daily work could not be guaranteed for the men.

Great excitement was shown at the school on 24th August 1905, when the pupils had their photographs taken! As the school grew, so did the number of Sisters needed to teach the increasing school population. The house adjoining the Sisters' house was purchased, and then in 1909 the convent that we all know and love was built on church land on Malta

Road. There were now seven Sisters in the Community, but sadly one young Sister, Sister Clare Joseph Phelan, had died in 1908.

As was the case with the building of the Church of Our Lady Star of the Sea, the ground on which the new building was to be erected was unstable, and huge ferro-concrete piles had to be driven deep into the earth to create a stable raft on which to build the convent. The bombs which fell on Tilbury in the Second World War did no damage to the convent and it emerged unscathed from the floods which did so much damage to Tilbury in 1953. Whilst the convent was completed in 1909, it took rather longer to furnish the new building. Some Sisters from Tavistock Square were interviewed in 1989, and recalled seeing Professed Sisters, assisted by Postulants or Novices, boarding trains at Liverpool Street en route for Tilbury, carrying items of furniture, crockery and even fruit to the new convent.

In 1914, an agreement was signed by the Parish Priest, the Reverend J.J. Deady and Sister Mary Catherine, the convent's Superioress. The curious wording survives.

Agreement

> The Reverend J.J. Deady, Church of Our Lady Star of the Sea, Tilbury Docks, agrees to provide the Sisters of the Convent of Mercy, Tilbury Docks, with Mass once a week.
>
> In consideration of the weekly Mass, the Reverend Mother Mary Catherine, Superior of the said Convent, agrees to pay to the Reverend J.J. Deady, the sum of £40 a year, to be paid quarterly, and to provide the priest with his breakfast, when he comes to say Mass.
>
> This agreement shall be binding on both parties, from the 1st of January 1914, and they shall be free to cancel it, by giving three months previous notice.

The Tilbury Community continued to flourish as a 'branch house' dependent on the 'mother house' in London. However, once the Diocese of Brentwood was formed in 1917, the Sisters in Tilbury were unsure which Bishop held authority over their convent. With the Mother House in the Diocese of Westminster and the Branch House in the new Diocese of Brentwood, there was some confusion. When the Mother House decided to close down the Tilbury Convent, withdraw the nuns to London and sell off the property there was consternation. The Sister-in-Charge of the Tilbury Convent favoured this policy, although most of the nuns wished to remain in Tilbury. Cardinal Bourne and Bishop Ward were at loggerheads, the former wishing to support the Mother House and the latter desperate for the Tilbury Convent to remain open. Arbitration was sought from Rome, where a temporary stay on any closure was issued. Unfortunately, the Sister-in-Charge at Tilbury did move out some of the nuns to Tavistock Square in London and sold the convent to the local Council. The Parish Priest and his Bishop were very concerned at the impact this would have on the work of the parish, and on the possible effect on other parishes who also had branch houses owing allegiance to the Diocese of Westminster. The closure of these convents would also damage the viability of other parishes.

A compromise was reached when it was finally agreed that the convent in Tilbury would become an Independent House as from 8th January 1923. Some of the nuns who had been 'transferred out' were reinstated, a new Sister-in-Charge was appointed, and the local Council agreed to cancel the purchase of the convent, returning it to the Sisters of Mercy. For a long time, the nuns lived in some privation, as the convent had been stripped of its furniture and effects prior to the 'sale' of the building.

There remained the problem of the outstanding debt on the convent. The Mother House in Westminster was to be compensated for the surrender of the convent to the new diocese and various sums were suggested. The Bishop of Brentwood, Bishop Doubleday, considered that the nuns at Tilbury should take over the £1000 debt on the convent, an arrangement that the nuns at Tilbury thought they could manage. But to their consternation a further £2500 was requested from the Mother house in Westminster. Sister Aloysius wrote to Bishop Doubleday in February 1921 to indicate their preparedness to pay the one thousand pounds requested, but added

> but that plus the £2500 would be quite out of the question as we could never cover such a debt…… there is great peace, but that dreadful £2500 always looms in the background.

The Reverend Mother at Tavistock Square had her own priorities, including the enlargement of their work in Twickenham, and the money from Tilbury would help to fund this expansion. She was most unwilling to accept the offer merely to shoulder the debt and asked her ecclesiastical superior in Harrow to negotiate on her behalf. A figure of two thousand pounds was suggested, to help the Sisters based at Tavistock Square with their work, although how the Sisters at Tilbury were to pay this amount was a matter of some concern.

Bishop Doubleday suggested his own compromise in July 1921:

> I take it that we are agreed that whatever the past history of the difficulty, the only practicable solution now is to establish the Tilbury Convent as a separate foundation. My predecessor took the view that when a separate foundation is made it should be handed over without encumbrances.
>
> Personally, I think it fair to the Mother-house that this daughter-house should bear the responsibility of the £1000 Mortgage upon it. I have been into the accounts and unless something unforeseen happens the sisters ought to be able to pay the interest upon it. But it would be unwise, especially if they are to make any progress, to put a bigger burden upon them; indeed I much doubt whether anyone would lend them a larger sum upon the property with the credit they can give.
>
> It might possibly help towards a solution if the Convent gave a promise that if the Convent were sold, say during the next 21 years, any balance remaining after the repayment of the mortgage should go to Tavistock Square.

Sister Aloysius Leonard was now the Superior and seven other Sisters formed the Community. All the Sisters were teaching in the school and they continued to carry out pastoral work. Tilbury remained a very poor area and there was much need across the parish. Sometimes the Sisters would visit families carrying bread and other foods hidden in the large sleeves of their habit! As well as teaching and visiting families in need, the Sisters always supported the annual Parish Bazaar. Altogether fourteen Sisters joined the Sisters of Mercy through entering the Order in Tilbury.

By 1932, the number of Sisters at the convent had increased to thirteen, under the leadership of Sister Angela. The Sisters were listed as Sister Patrick and Sister Anthony (Lay Sisters), Sister Marie (Postulant), Sister M. Francis (White Novice), Sister M. Margaret Mary and Sister M. Bernadette (Black Novices), Sisters M. Teresa, M. Gerard, M. Borgia and M. Alphonsus (Senior Sisters), Sister M. Joseph (Acting Novice Mistress), Sister M. Aloysius (Mother Assistant) and Sister M. Angela (Mother Superior).

Whilst the convent had weathered the precarious early years, it was far from stable and there were many difficulties, as a commentary from

Bishop Doubleday made clear in March 1938, in a letter to Monsignor Smith.

> <u>Convent of Mercy, Tilbury</u>
>
> I saw Sister X of this Convention the 19th of March last. Since the application was made to the Congregation for her dismissal she has tried hard to fall in with the regulations of Convent life, and I feel that an effort should be made to save her vocation if it is at all possible. She has been some sixteen or seventeen years in this convent which for the past 20 years has had a troubled and precarious existence. When the Brentwood Diocese was formed it depended on a Convent of Mercy in Westminster; after a struggle it was erected into an independent house in the Diocese of Brentwood. Never with more than 8 to 10 subjects it undertook the teaching in the parochial schools.
>
> Dissensions continually existed among the sisters. The first Superior, with whom I was acquainted, is now living by transfer in a Westminster House of Mercy; another sister has been transferred to a Convent in my Diocese. Both of these sisters seem to be doing well in their new surroundings.
>
> At present there are 10 sisters belonging to the Community; one of these, a lay-sister, slightly mental, is provided for in a home by the Mother-General of the Westminster Sisters of Mercy; there are only 8 choir sisters and one lay sister in residence.
>
> The house is very small and restricted for space; it is too closely associated with the parishioners and the Parish Church. The present Superior (now and often away ill) has been in office for nearly six years; another of the nuns is her sister. The present assistant, who rules the Community, is a young nun and inexperienced.
>
> I suggest that the Mother-General of Westminster Sisters of Mercy be put in charge of the Convent and report what is best to be done for its future. She knows Sister X, the nun now in difficulties, quite well; in fact she has a sister of Sister X at present under her jurisdiction. I recognise that Sister X is not altogether a satisfactory subject; she is nervous in the extreme and under the present strain may break down altogether; the other sisters in the house under the direction of the Superior are not making it easy for her to right herself; even if she were exclaustrated she is not likely to get a livelihood and the Convent at Tilbury is not able to provide for her.
>
> I shall be obliged if you will put these particulars before the Congregation.

At the outbreak of war in 1939 the Sisters were evacuated with the schoolchildren to Holt in Norfolk, and the Convent of Mercy had to be closed for a few months. However, in 1940, some of the Sisters returned to re-open part of the school for those children who still remained in Tilbury. Later that year a second evacuation took place, and Sisters Frances Boyden and Margaret Mary Kelly accompanied the children to Wiltshire. Throughout the war the convent suffered little more damage than cracked walls and ceilings.

Whilst most of the work done by the Sisters of Mercy related directly to the spiritual life of the parish and the education of its children, occasionally more mundane matters had to be handled as well. One such event was the purchase of a small plot of land adjoining the convent garden. Sister Angela wished to buy the land to extend the small garden and the Parish Priest, Father O'Donnell, was willing to sell the land. Easy enough, you might think. The sticking point was the price, as this letter to Bishop Doubleday, dated 1st December 1950, reveals.

> My Lord,
>
> Reverend Mother sent us over last evening to discuss the matter of the land with Fr. O'Donnell as she is still in bed with sciatica.
>
> I told Father I'd been to see your Lordship and that you had advised us to see him about the business as we had reached a stalemate with the two valuations. He pooh poohed the idea of the £4 valuation, suggested that Mr. Bannister did not know the details of the New Land Scheme and Regulations until I told him that Mr. Bannister had studied all that and that his correspondence had been forwarded to Messrs. Arnold Foulkes etc. He then added that Messrs. Witham & Co. knew their business and I said "Evidently Foulkes' firm did too, as the firm is acting for the Southwark Diocese."
>
> No amount of talk would make him alter his figure of £100 for the bit of land. He said he would not take it himself for £20 believing it to be worth £100 if it were offered to him! I told him we would willingly take it for £4 at which it was legally valued. He then asked me if we would like to get his Valuer (Mr. Porter) to value it again for us. I said "No" as I considered it would not be business to have the same Valuer for seller and purchaser. After this he said he would not touch the thing with a forty foot pole.
>
> "Well," I said, "I only came to you at your Lordship's suggestion."
>
> "Oh well," he said, "I might consider it."
>
> I asked him what he paid for the piece of land on the other side of the school, purchased some years back when the value of land had not deteriorated as at present in this area, since it has been condemned as

> unfit for housing purposes by the Land Commissioners. He admitted that it was about £100. Then I pointed out that that piece was on a main shopping road with 'bus facilities etc. and that the frontage and area were larger than the bit under discussion. That was airily waved aside.
>
> Then I gingerly referred to our work here for over 45 years, always for the Parish, the Schools, the Priests – never one thing for ourselves. He jumped at this and said not to bring anything else into the discussion – and did I want the land as a favour for past services. I replied, "I wanted no favours but we did want the plot at a just value, not £96 above it."
>
> I knew, after 30 years experience, it was no good going on, as no-one can reason with Father – he is always right and I knew he would hold out to the last for the £100. Eventually I said "The Bishop sent us to you. What is to be done now?" After a moment's hesitation he said "I'll consider it, but I must get time." So there the matter stands.

After a protracted round of negotiations, the land was finally sold by Father O'Donnell for the sum of £20 and normal service was resumed.

The seeds were sown of a new role in the life of the Sisters of Mercy based in Tilbury in May 1952, when Bishop Andrew Beck visited the Sisters to ask if they would consider opening a branch house in Thorpe Bay. This happened in July 1952 when 34 Burges Road, Thorpe Bay was opened, with Sister Therese Connolly appointed as the first Superior. A year later, in May 1953, the house next door was bought. It became a rest home and a house for holidays for both Sisters and other ladies. In October 1953, Sister Angela Colahan suffered a stroke and she subsequently retired in March 1955 and went to live in Thorpe Bay. The branch house eventually closed in December 1963.

In 1954, there were plans for a second branch convent to be opened at Chadwell St. Mary to serve the needs of the church and parish which was to develop there when the Council's new housing estate was built, but this never came to fruition.

On 7th April 1958 a statue of Our Lady and the Divine Child was erected over the front door of the convent.

Whilst outwardly life went on as usual, with the Sisters making a big contribution to the life and the work of the parish, the arrangements at the convent were not without problems. With a small group of Sisters, and a large responsibility to the schools and the parish, resources were often stretched to the limit. In 1960, the involvement of the Bishop of Brentwood, Bishop Wall, revealed some of the difficulties that the Sisters faced. Writing to a Monsignor, the Bishop outlined some of the areas of concern, indicating a partial solution but also uncovering something of a mystery.

> You may (or may not) know that ever since my first visitation of Tilbury Mercy Convent I have been much exercised by the condition of things there. My chief concern was for the novices. The novice mistress, an excellent religious, I am sure, is also the Headmistress of the school, with the result that she never sees the novices except in the evening, and not even then if there is an educational meeting. She is also something of an invalid. I may say that she herself was worried about this. If the Superior pays a visit to Thorpe Bay, the two novices would be left alone in the house. At that first visitation one novice during her second year at Thorpe Bay told me that she was frequently sent out on errands alone.
>
> I recently made another visitation there and found of course that matters had not improved. I found further that there had been no retreat given by a retreat Father for eight or nine years.
>
> I told Reverend Mother that this was all on my conscience and something would have to be done. We made a start on the noviciate question and suggested that she find some well-constituted house of the Mercy nuns which would be prepared to take the novices. She said that this had been tried before when novices were sent to Brentwood, but then they did not want to return (which was revealing). However, she now writes that the Bermondsey Sisters would be prepared to take future novices (not the two who are already in the noviciate), though there was obviously some reluctance to do so.
>
> Here now is the point of my writing. We feel that this will require an Indult from Rome. But in looking through the very ample correspondence over the years we found that in 1939 a decree from Rome amalgamated Tilbury with Westminster. There is a covering letter, probably typed by yourself, accompanying an English translation of the decree, in which, notifying the Super-General of the decree, you add that the Bishop before executing it wishes to interview her. Thereafter silence descends. Can you give me some idea of what happened? We suspect that Westminster was reluctant to take Tilbury on. But if I write to Rome for the Indult I am determined to put all the cards on the table.
>
> With my blessing,
>
> Bernard Patrick
>
> Bishop of Brentwood.

In the early 1960s a reorganisation of the Sisters of Mercy was being considered and in June 1961 the Sisters found themselves being urged by Bishop Wall to join the Westminster Amalgamation. In support of the move, the diocese prepared a historical account of the Tilbury Convent and gave an outline of the context in which it had worked.

Convent of Sisters of Mercy, Tilbury, Essex

The Sisters of Mercy are of Pontifical Right. They were founded in Dublin, Ireland in 1827 and since then have spread throughout the English-speaking world.

There were several houses of the Congregation founded in the Archdiocese of Westminster, all of them independent, and those houses had dependent or filial houses in the County of Essex which was part of the Archdiocese of Westminster.

When the Archdiocese of Westminster was divided in 1917 to form the new Diocese of Brentwood, these filial houses were in the new diocese, whereas their Mother-Houses were in the former Archdiocese of Westminster.

The new Codex Iuris Canonici had not been promulgated at the time and the first bishop of the new diocese, acting on the less precise notions current in England, still in some senses a missionary country, considered that these daughter houses or filial houses should be dependent no longer on the mother houses in the Archdiocese of Westminster, but should be cut off, as the diocese had been cut off, and should be independent, as the new diocese was independent.

Unfortunately, these daughter houses, being cut off from the mother-houses, were not united or federated in any way, for the mother-houses in Westminster had all been independent of one another. Yet they were cut off with little resources and no novices or postulants, and very often with no experienced Sisters to govern the Community.

Some of them survived this drastic operation, but many were closed down within a short time, and were sold. Of those that survived, two were later re-united to the Westminster Union, one Community has survived and thrived, the other – Tilbury Convent of Mercy – has never done well, as the following chronicle shows:-

April 19, 1919
The Mother Superior of the Mother-House decided to withdraw the Sisters and to sell the Convent. The Bishop appealed to the Holy See and the sale was forbidden "pendente recursu". There were in fact at that time only 6 Sisters in the Convent and none of them was a Choir Nun, they were all lay Sisters.

December 1920
The new Bishop of Brentwood came to an agreement that the Tilbury Convent should be a separate Community, but that £2500 should be paid to the Mother-House for the buildings.

1920 – 21
There was much dissension in the new Community, some wishing to return to the Mother-House, some refusing to obey the sister in charge. There were two blood-relatives there and the accusation was made that these two were the main agents in the break-away.

1923
There were 6 professed Sisters, one choir Novice and one lay Novice; they were making their Novitiate in another House of the Congregation (Brentwood).

1925
There were 6 professed Sisters, 2 novices and one postulant.

1929
There were 7 choir Sisters, 2 lay Sisters and 1 novice. In the election of Superior, which went to four scrutinies, the voting was 4 to 2.

1930 - 34
Three of the original Community now asked to be transferred from Tilbury to other communities.

1934
There were 8 Choir Sisters and 2 lay Sisters.

1935
In the election of 1935 there were 7 vocals; two voting papers were left blank, one was cast for Sister Borgia and 4 for Sister Angela.

1938
Another member of the original Community was transferred.

1938
The S.C. de Religiosis (Prot.N.2531/37) gave permission for the Tilbury Community to be re-united with the (newly-formed) Westminster Union of Sisters of Mercy. For some reason this decree was never executed; it seems that the Westminster Union did not want to have the Tilbury Community because of the difficulties involved – there had been considerable trouble at the re-uniting of another of the daughter houses that had been cut off in 1917.

1956
There were 6 choir Sisters, 1 lay Sister and 2 novices. The Mistress of Novices was also Headmistress in the School.

1958

There were 10 choir Sisters and two lay Sisters, also 2 novices.

1960

There were 11 choir Sisters, 2 lay Sisters and 2 novices. The Superior was proposing to send the novices to another Community as she could not provide the facilities for training them properly.

1961

Another election is due in May. The present Superior will have done two terms. None other is suited to govern the Community.

If the Westminster Union was not keen to accept the Tilbury Community in 1938, there was no great enthusiasm in 1961, as a letter to Bishop Wall from the Mother Superior of the Tilbury Convent, Sister Margaret Mary, reveals.

My Lord,

I feel that I should write to let you know that we went to see Reverend Mother General at Harewood Avenue, on 20th July. I told her of Your Lordship's visit and the result of the voting. She asked me to send her definite information, in writing, regarding the Community, so that she could put the position before her Council. I will forward this to her as soon as possible.

Mother General's First Assistant was present at the interview and we got the impression that they were not over-anxious to accept us into the Amalgamation. If Your Lordship would be so kind as to use your influence in our favour, we feel that it would be a great help to us.

Trusting that you will forgive me for troubling you and asking your Lordship's blessing,

Yours very respectfully in J.C.

Sister Margaret Mary

In November 1961, the Tilbury Community joined the Westminster Union, after an Indult was received from Rome, authorising the move. Yet the transfer did not result in much improvement in the life of the Sisters at the Tilbury Convent. By May, 1964, just over two years after the transfer, the Mother General in Harewood Avenue, London wrote to Bishop Wall. The election of a new Superior for the Tilbury Community had revealed a considerable rift among the Sisters.

My Lord,

Very Reverend and Dear Father,

As the Superior of Tilbury completes her three year term of Office on May 16th, we had a Council meeting here this afternoon. Mother Vicaress held the usual Visitation and the customary Consultative Chapter previous to an Appointment, at Tilbury Convent on Ascension Thursday May 7th. Of the seven Sisters in the Community there, six voted for "a Sister from another Community".

Since then I have received letters from Sr. M. Brendan and Sr. M. Assumpta asking permission to transfer to Brentwood. Both Sisters are on the Teaching Staff of the Tilbury Schools and it would be impossible for us to replace them. Another Sister, Sr. M Catherine, who qualified at the Hospital of St. John and St. Elizabeth and then asked to be allowed to continue with what she was trained for, after a period of nine months nursing there asked to return to Tilbury. Now, she, too is anxious to join the Brentwood Community as her younger sister has already been transferred there.

It seems illogical that those Sisters who voted for a new Superior from another Convent should ask for a transfer on the following day. We had hoped to put a new Superior in Tilbury but as it is now obvious that the majority of the Sisters have no desire to remain in the Westminster Amalgamation it would be unjust to expose any of our Sisters to such insincerity and instability.

As three of the Community have already been admitted to the Covent at Brentwood and four others, including two of the Teaching Sisters, are awaiting admission, the Council Mothers respectfully suggest, with your Lordship's approval, that the Convent of Tilbury revert to being an independent House in the Diocese of Brentwood. If any of the Sisters wishes to remain in Westminster we could admit her to one of our Houses but we could not be responsible for the Convent in Tilbury.

Begging your Lordship's blessing,
I have the honour to be,
Your Lordship's devoted and obedient child in J.

Sister M. Benignus
Mother General

Clearly, the move to the Westminster Amalgamation had not proved too successful for the Sisters in Tilbury, and Westminster seemed equally keen for the link to be broken.

At first sight, this appeared to be a catastrophic turn of events, as Bishop Wall indicated in a reply to the Mother General.

> I note your decision that the Westminster Federation can no longer be responsible for the Tilbury Convent.
>
> Though I can understand the reasons for your decision I do regret it. It would appear that the community at Tilbury is doomed.
>
> My greater regret is that the educational and other work the Sisters of Mercy have carried on for so long is jeopardised.
>
> With my blessing,
> Yours sincerely,
>
> Bishop of Brentwood

However, a solution was found that would save the Tilbury Convent and relieve the Westminster Amalgamation of its responsibility. It was proposed by the Vicar General for Religious, and he outlined his plan to the Mother General in Westminster, in a letter dated September 14th, 1964.

> As I explained to you by telephone this morning, I have been acting for the Bishop in trying to arrange for the Wanstead Community to step in and help Tilbury. This was because the Bishop understood you to say that it would be better if Tilbury left the Union and reverted to independent status in the diocese.
>
> I had in fact got tentative agreement on both sides (Wanstead and Tilburury) for this proposition, when I heard from Tilbury that you were going to send a new Superior there. I thought that I had better telephone you at once to discover if you would agree to a new proposition.
>
> My suggestion is that Tilbury revert to Brentwood diocese; we shall then unite it to the Wanstead Community, and thus you will be relieved of all responsibility for it and obligations to it. I myself am confident that the new proposal can be made to work – I sincerely hope and pray that it will, for there seems no other solution. I have just spoken to the Bishop confirming his agreement to the proposal and I shall inform Wanstead and Tilbury that we proceed as planned.
>
> I am writing this letter so you may have a chance to discuss the affair with your Counsellors and also have a record for the Archive. I should appreciate it if you would let me have a note to confirm that I have your approval. You may leave it to us to prepare the necessary letters for Rome and to obtain any indults that may be required.

We are not unconscious of the worry and trouble this has caused you and we are very grateful for your assistance in a very difficult situation.

Conveying his Lordship's good wishes and blessing
Yours sincerely in Christ
Vicar General for Religious

Unfortunately, Rome refused to separate Tilbury from the Westminster Amalgamation as it had only recently agreed to it joining them. But within two years an indult was forthcoming from Rome, and Tilbury returned to the Diocese of Brentwood, when it was united with the Sisters of Mercy in Wanstead as a branch house. Soon after this happened, on 9th February 1966, some Sisters were sent from Wanstead to join the small Community in Tilbury.

The next change for the Sisters came in May 1969, when the Federation of the Sisters of Mercy was formed, with the Sisters in Tilbury joining this Federation. The Tilbury Convent now entered calmer waters. An extent of the change in its fortunes can be seen from a report on the Canonical Visitation of the Sisters of Mercy, by Fr. Philip Keys, O.F.M., dated 12th May 1973.

SPIRITUAL LIFE
Everything necessary for growth in the spiritual is provided and the members of the community obviously take advantage of the help provided.
One is struck by the truly wonderful atmosphere of prayer and devotion.

COMMUNITY RELATIONSHIPS
There is an excellent spirit of unity and co-operation among the members of this community. This is evident from the spirit of peace and serenity that pervades this Convent. Much of this is due to the leadership of the good Sister-in-charge, Sister Dominic, of whom all spoke highly.

APOSTOLIC SPIRIT
The spirit of dedication of these Sisters is evident in their work and one can see that they draw their strength from their spirit of prayer and devotion.

CHAPEL, SACRISTY AND CONFESSIONAL
These are all in splendid condition and a credit to those to whom their care is entrusted.

From 1973, there was the recognition that it might be good if the Sisters of Mercy across the country joined together. This finally happened in April 1983, when many Communities, including Tilbury, voted to become part of the Institute of Our Lady of Mercy.

Many changes in personnel began to occur as Sisters moved across the country. Sister Carmel, who had taught at St. Mary's School for many years and established a much needed Youth Club in the parish, moved to South Yorkshire and Sister Agnes, the former Head Teacher of St. Mary's, went to Frinton. Sister Emmanuel headed for King's Lynn, Sister Annunciata to Charlton and Sister Patricia, on her retirement as Head Teacher, went to Wanstead. Over time, in their places came Sisters Dominic Gollogley, Imelda Keena, Anne Waugh, Mary Keogh, Concepta Guidera, Rita Lynch, Teresa Croston, Stanislaus Culligan, Veronica Walker, Paula Cleary, Christine Mather and Deborah Stokes.

In January 2005, we saw the centenary of the arrival of the Sisters of Mercy in Tilbury. A special parish celebration was held in St. Joseph's Hall, Chadwell St. Mary in May, when a video of the life of Catherine McAuley was shown on a big screen and everyone enjoyed a buffet meal. To mark the centenary, the Sisters arranged for the East side windows of the Parish Church to be restored.

A beautiful altar frontal created by Sister Veronica to mark the occasion

The Beautiful Wall Plaque of Our Lady Star of the Sea
Donated to Tilbury Parish by John L'Estrange

Stations of the Cross

A View of the Parish Church from the Choir Gallery

School Nativity Play

Noah's Ark : Collage Created by Schoolchildren

The 75th Birthday Celebration for Mrs. Agnes Agharese Amu

Sister Christine with her brother James on the Day of her Golden Jubilee

A Parish Pilgrimage to the Holy Land 2013

Cover of the Booklet produced to commemorate the Centenary of the Sisters of Mercy's Arrival in Tilbury 1905 - 2005

The Outside View of the Restoration of the Windows

With the closure of the Convent of Mercy in Stanford-le-Hope in 2005, Sister Monica Cremin moved to Tilbury, although she continued to work in the Parish of Our Lady and St. Joseph, Stanford-le-Hope, yet another connection between the two parishes.

And so we move forward into the Millennium and a new century. Are the needs still the same? Is there so much dire poverty as the first Sisters experienced when they arrived in Tilbury? Hopefully not so, but there are many kinds of poverty that need to be met: the poverty of loneliness, the isolation of the refugee, the hunger for that special human touch. Catherine McAuley knew that the patient hearing of sorrows and worries would always be a ministry that the Sisters of Mercy could be engaged in. Therefore the work continues to this day: involvement in schools, work with refugees, visiting those in their own homes or in hospitals and sheltered accommodation nearby and still actively supporting the Parish in their ministries as Readers and Minister of Holy Communions. One hundred years of faithful service to the people in Tilbury and the surrounding area; such is the legacy of the Sisters of Mercy today.

(*Extract from the Centenary Booklet, issued to mark 100 Years of Service to our Parish by the Sisters of Mercy)*

The Community in Tilbury in 2005
Back Row: Srs. Monica Cremin, Paula Cleary, Teresa Croston
Front Row: Srs. Dominic Gollogley, Veronica Walker, Stanislaus Culligan

In the early 21st century a new role began with the development in Tilbury of the Mercy Associates, a group of lay parishioners, sensitive to the charism of the Sisters of Mercy, who now support their work across the parish. At the time of writing they are led by Sister Teresa Croston.

In 2014, the Golden Jubilee of Sister Christine Mather was celebrated in a Mass of Thanksgiving.

Mass
Of Thanksgiving
For the
GOLDEN JUBILEE

OF
SISTER CHRISTINE MATHER.

The Sisters no longer teach in the school, although they work there in a voluntary capacity. They continue to visit parishioners in their own homes, in hospital or in sheltered accommodation, work with refugees and seafarers and support the parish in any way they can. Today the work of the Sisters of Mercy in the Parish of Our Lady Star of the Sea continues, as does the legacy of all they have done for the people of Tilbury.

Chapter Nine : The Parish of St. Joseph, Chadwell St. Mary

The history of the Catholic Church in Chadwell dates back over 900 years, but the existence of a post-Reformation Catholic parish in its own right has a much shorter time span.

The needs of the people of Chadwell St. Mary were first mentioned in 1923, when Father O'Donnell suggested changes to Tilbury Parish's northern boundary. He wrote

> Chadwell is the most important place in this neighbourhood and is rapidly growing, as a sort of residential district.

He stated that there were fifty houses there already and rafts had been laid for 200 more. He went on to write, 'A year ago there were no Catholics there. Today there are at least twenty'. His final comments in this letter were

> Everything points to the fact that Chadwell St. Mary will need development from the Catholic point of view in the not-distant future but if the three parishes of Grays, Tilbury and Stanford-le-Hope meet right in the heart of it, there is a chance that it will become a sort of no-man's land and be neglected. *(Letter to Bishop Doubleday dated 24th May 1923)*

Later in 1932 Father O'Donnell wrote that his foremost problem is 'what to do with Chadwell St. Mary' where there were about seventy Catholics. About thirty of these attended the early Mass in Tilbury travelling by private motor coach, and a few others walked or cycled to the later Mass. He went on to write that he

> would like to bring back the Mass to Chadwell, which was the centre of the faith in the old days, for all this area.

He debated whether a room could be hired in a club or the local Council school. He added

> The provision of a building of our own or even the buying of a plot of land is out of the question with the school burden so heavy upon us. *(Letter to diocese dated 12th October 1932)*

Mass was offered in Chadwell St. Mary for the first time since the Reformation in January 1933, under the papal sign of the Cross Keys. The licensee of that public house offered the Catholics of the area the use of his hall, which was soon filled to overflowing. Father O'Donnell wrote to Bishop Doubleday in January 1933 to give him the news.

> My Lord Bishop,
>
> Following on your permission I have made arrangements for Mass at Chadwell St. Mary. I first applied for the use of a room in the Council School, but this was refused by 6 votes to 5 after an interesting debate.
>
> I am not now sorry because I have got something more suitable, namely a small new Hall attached to the Cross Keys Inn. It stands out in a nice garden and has a separate entrance – well lighted and centrally heated and only a nominal charge of one shilling per week rent. Seating accommodation for 40 is supplied.
>
> The first Mass was said on 1st January with a congregation of 37 and 43 last Sunday. We hope to have a model congregation there in the near future. Known Catholics of all ages number 68.
>
> The sisters and parishioners are very keen and helpful about it and after one appeal provided articles for the altar costing about £17.
>
> The manager and his wife are most courteous and interested and were surprised to hear that the Mass and the 'Cross Keys' were old acquaintances!

Chadwell St. Mary thus became a Mass Centre served from Tilbury, from 1933 to 1975. As the congregation grew to over seventy, it was eventually necessary to move to a larger hall, the Working Men's Club across the road, where the rent charged was ten shillings per week. This remained the Mass Centre in Chadwell for many years.

In the early 1950s the Sisters of Mercy considered opening a convent here, a branch house from Tilbury, but this never materialized. In 1952, Thurrock Urban District Council promised an acre of land for use as a church site but they did not locate the exact site. At the end of 1953, the Chadwell Hall Building Fund had begun, and by 1965 £4,000 had been donated.

By the 1960s, with the building of three large Council estates and a private estate, Chadwell had a nine hundred strong Catholic community and Father John Byrne decided that the people of Chadwell should have a Mass Centre of their own. At this time, a Ladies Guild was started under the leadership of Annie Hill and meetings were held weekly in members' homes. One of the chief objectives of the Guild was to raise money for the building of a church hall as well as giving an opportunity for new parishioners moving to the area to get to know one another. The Ladies Guild used the hall at the Working Men's Club for jumble sales and dances in order to raise funds.

As the membership of this Guild increased, the members began to meet in the new village hall in Waterson Road and Christmas Bazaars as well as jumble sales were then held there. Canon Byrne attended the meetings regularly and supported the Guild in every way. Tote tickets were also sold to raise more money for the building fund.

In February 1964, Father Byrne wrote from Tilbury to the diocese to report the pressing need for a proper Mass Centre in Chadwell St. Mary, whether this be a church hall or a church.

> Very Reverend and Dear Canon,
>
> The Catholic population of Chadwell St. Mary at the present time is 365, approximately.
>
> Families are being housed there every week, some of them moving from rooms, flats and old houses in the Tilbury area. The houses they were moved from are being demolished. They will be replaced eventually so we may recover our numbers as the new houses are rebuilt.
>
> Many of the young couples married in our Church in the last 5 years will continue to move to Chadwell which will cause a depletion in the number of our parishioners this year and next; at present we have 650 Catholics in Tilbury.
>
> The population (Catholic) in Chadwell could very well be 1,200 by the end of 1965.
>
> Rt. Rev. Monsignor Wilson advised me about 2 years ago to build a Church for at least 300 people. Mr. Bingham Towner, the approved architect, estimated in 1962 that the Church we have planned would cost £28,000, approx.

Referring to a Building Fund of three and a half thousand pounds, a new Covenant Scheme scheduled to bring in £330 per year, a war damage grant from Silvertown of £1,400 and a weekly collection of some £10 towards the cost of the new building, Father Byrne believed that they were in a good financial state to raise a loan for the building, subject to diocesan approval.

Eventually, Thurrock Council set aside a one acre site in Defoe Parade for the building of a Catholic Church, hall and presbytery. The Building Fund was largely swallowed up in the cost of this land, but Father Byrne was undaunted, believing that the income from Chadwell St. Mary, about £1,400 per year, would be sufficient to support a loan for any building.

Only the church hall ever came to fruition, a cedar wood building on a concrete base, built between 1967 and 1968. The hall was designed by Henry Bingham Towner, from Uckfield Sussex and the contractor, who was later to become a parishioner, was Michael J. Greenan. The hall cost £21,000 to build and could seat 250 people. A loan of £6,000 was agreed with the Westminster Bank, but Father Byrne's request for a grant from the diocese was turned down, as money was needed to help communities in new towns being established in Essex.

As money was in limited supply, another parishioner, Arthur Matthews, made a wooden altar for the hall. The Lady Chapel to the left of the stage, which later became the Blessed Sacrament Chapel, had a small altar, a gift from the Sisters of Mercy.

The church hall was officially opened on 17th March 1968, with a Mass celebrated at 10.00 a.m. on the thirty inch high stage. Initially Mass was celebrated here twice on Sundays, at 10.00 a.m. and 4-30 p.m. and also on Tuesday evenings at 7-30 p.m. The hall was now used by the Ladies Guild for their meetings, for Bingo on Sunday nights (beginning on 6th October 1968) and for social events, including a dance held on 27th September 1968 which raised £173-3-0d for the Building Fund. Des Pearson was the chief organiser of this event, with the Ladies Guild providing the refreshments and Father Pat Heekin, the Port Chaplain, supplying the bar. On 2nd October there was a Beetle Drive which raised £4-13-0d and on Wednesday, 30th October a Halloween Social. For many years there was also an annual pilgrimage to Aylesford, organised by Winefride Pollard, to celebrate the Feast of the Forty Martyrs of England and Wales.

As a new presbytery had not been built, a small semi-detached house was purchased to house the Parish Priest, even though one had not yet been appointed. 18 Cedar Road, Chadwell St. Mary, was a three bedroomed, centrally heated house with a small garden. The purchase of the property was in the hands of Father Byrne at Tilbury, but it took some time to complete the transaction, as a letter to Bishop Wall from Father Byrne's assistant priest, Albert Fitzgerald indicates.

Dear Lord Bishop,

I write on behalf of practically all the practising Catholics of Chadwell St. Mary. As you know, they are, by design, totally unorganised, and so inacapable of speaking for themselves collectively.

Since April, when Mr. Harvey made it common knowledge that he was selling his house to "to Fr. Byrne for the new parish priest of Chadwell", I have been asked daily how are things moving and almost always I have to say not at all. They are getting very frustrated and it is inclined to rub off on me.

Chadwell was as big ten years ago as it is to-day. It could fruitfully have become a parish then. If you knew all the reasons why they want to be an independent unit you would have a lot of sympathy for them. It might suffice to repeat what I said in the car a year ago – "It is very desirable."

The other point I made in the car was that Fr. Byrne could be very slow. This could easily be my greatest under-statement. The people were also disposed for slowness but they are describing the progress so far as incredible, even by Fr. Byrne's standards. What disedifies them most is that there is no machinery to make up for what is wanting.

The people here are fairly intelligent and those who have been involved in house buying say that the whole business should have taken a maximum of three months. Twelve months have gone by and the job is still not done. If I had kept quiet – which is my normal role - I doubt if anything at all would have been done.

The house was vacated in June. Until I rang you in October nothing happened. After I rang, the exterior of the house was painted, and the electricity, water and gas have been restored. Now another mini-eternity of non-activity is under way. The daily questions continue, so I have decided to write.

The house was left equipped with a cooker, fridge, washing machine and a bed – and carpets. A few more basic items are required to make it suitable for habitation. This could take up to 24 hours – if one were to engage one of the slower firms. It could take a hundred years if no firm is contacted.

I see in the Diocesan Newsletter that you have a lot of heavy commitments; I also suspect that you have a diocese full of problems of various sizes.... You can't give a lot of attention, in person, to each. You will appreciate that I am sitting on top of this one and know all aspects of it intimately. I would like you then, to see me as your assistant in this particular matter. If Fr. Byrne did not wish to retain the whole business to himself this channel would not be necessary.

So, the suggestion I make is done with full respect for you and, I'm sure, the best solution for all. My suggestion – appoint a priest to Chadwell immediately and instruct him to see Fr. Byrne with a view to making the house suitable for entry. From my position here this seems by far the best procedure.

Hoping you think so too, yours obediently,

Albert Fitzgerald.

Not for the first time in Catholic history, a young assistant priest is frustrated by the rather sedate progress of his more experienced superior. Whether this letter helped to unjam the works or whether there were other factors in play, within four months of the letter Chadwell St. Mary had its own priest. On 18th March 1975, Father Donald Mills became the first and only Parish Priest of St. Joseph's, Chadwell St. Mary.

The new parish received a gift of one thousand pounds, donated by Canon M. J. Mckenna of Becontree. Father Mills was very pleased with the donation, and to be back among the people of Chadwell St. Mary. From 1962 to 1969, he had been assistant priest at Tilbury, and so he knew the area and many of the people very well.

One of his first tasks was to take over the financial responsibilities of the new parish. He agreed with Fr. Byrne to pay half of the National Catholic Fund assessment which had been levied on Tilbury Parish, as many of his new congregation had previously been part of Tilbury Parish. Thus began a detailed concern that Fr. Mills showed in the correct administration of his parish's finances. The main debt on the parish related to the money that was borrowed to buy his house, effectively the presbytery.

A letter dated September 1975, six months after his appointment, was the first of many such letters to the diocese, relating to his financial obligations.

Dear Father Drea,

I am writing about the quota for the Diocesan Development Fund to be paid by this parish. Father Byrne has kindly offered to pay our share for the first six months of the Chadwell Parish. It would appear that we should start paying ourselves in the Oct.- Dec. quarter.

Father Byrne and I have agreed that the Mass attendance of the original Tilbury Parish has been split roughly 50/50 between the new parishes of Chadwell and Tilbury and we should be agreeable to accept half shares in the original Tilbury quota. This however, takes no account of the minor adjustments with the Grays and Stanford parishes. Please let me know what you think.

Could I also remind you of a request I made about a month ago for the precise figure of the loan outstanding to the Duffy Account from this parish and the manner in which you would like the interest to be paid.

The diocese confirmed that Fr. Mills had an outstanding debt of just over seven and a half thousand pounds on the purchase of his house in Chadwell St. Mary, together with interest free loans from the Parish of Tilbury (£1,000) and East Tilbury (£1,170). Faced with a total indebtedness of about ten thousand pounds, Fr. Mill set about repaying the money. A series of parish boundaries was redrawn at this time and the Woodside estate in Grays, together with Orsett and Bulphan, became part of the new parish. As well as daily Mass at St. Joseph's, Mass was now also celebrated at Orsett Hospital. Before long, the new parish had its own Youth Club, another sign of the growing confidence of this fledgling community.

Of course, there were other considerations for the new Parish Priest. One such was the timing of the Sunday Masses. Fr. Mills wrote to the diocese to explain the situation, in October 1975.

Dear Chris,

I am writing to ask permission to change the times of the Sunday Masses in this parish. The times at present are:

Orsett Hospital	9.00 a.m.
St. Joseph's	10.00 a.m. and 4.30 p.m.

The first two Masses are too close together for my comfort and the afternoon Mass is poorly attended. It is not possible to change the time of the Hospital Mass. I have conducted a poll, with the following result.

10.00 a.m.	2
10.15 a.m.	20
10.30 a.m.	15
4.30 p.m.	13
6.00 p.m.	27

All the Mass-goers had an opportunity to vote and probably about half the families expressed a preference – so I think we have a fair sample.

I would like, therefore, to change the times to:

Orsett Hospital	9.00 a.m.
St. Joseph's	10.15 a.m. and 6.00 p.m.

With effect from 4th January 1976.

It had clearly been difficult for Fr. Mills to take two Masses at 9.00 and 10.00 a.m. in two different areas, but it is noteworthy that he asked for the views of his parishioners before recommending these new times. This was just the start of a close relationship which Fr. Mills and his parishioners enjoyed.

The diocese was not as yet aware of the extent of the financial acumen that Fr. Mills possessed, but a significant pointer to this was seen in a letter he wrote to Father Brian Drea, the Diocesan Financial Secretary, in March 1976. This was just one year since his appointment in Chadwell St. Mary. It was clear that he had a good understanding of the financial situation. Reading this letter, I am sure that like me you will be glad it wasn't addressed to you.

18 Cedar Road,
Chadwell St. Mary,
Grays,
Essex.
RM16 4SX

10th March 1976

Dear Father Drea,

Thank you for sending me the statements of the various debts of this parish. I have however some queries.

During your absence in September Miss O'Sullivan, at the request of Canon Grady, sent me the details of the financial obligations of the parish (Letter dated 30th Sept. 1975). This stated that the expenditure on the house here was £11,827.49, which was provided by :

Duffy Fund Loan	£8,856.02
Loan from Tilbury	£1,000
Loan from East Tilbury	£1,170

"plus a small amount from the diocese which I can't verify at the moment."
It seems to me that this loan from the General Diocesan Fund must be £801.47 – not £1,801.47 as you state. I am not aware of any further £1,000 involved.

Our total payments to you re the Duffy Fund Loan in 1975 were £2,150.46 -- £1637.96 in June and £512.50 in December. On both occasions my instructions were that the payment was to pay the interest for 6 months and the remainder was to go to reduce the capital. You state that the interest for the year was £566.61, leaving £1,583.85 to reduce the capital. It would seem to me that the amount outstanding at the beginning of the year should be £7,272.17 – not £7,371.45 as you state.

I would be grateful if you would elucidate these points.

Yours sincerely,
Donald F. Mills

Father Mills's arithmetic is impeccable (I checked!) and Father Drea was obliged to acknowledge the accuracy of the calculations made by the new Parish Priest of Chadwell St. Mary and to correct the errors made by the diocese.

On the first day of 1977, Fr. Mills wrote to Canon Grady asking that the building of a new presbytery next to the church hall be placed on the diocesan list of planned buildings, so that it could be afforded some kind of priority. Several 'able parishioners' had sketched out a plan for the presbytery, and the bulk of the money required would come from the sale of the house in Cedar Road, where Fr. Mills lived. A church was also being considered, although Fr. Mills, who described himself as 'a complete innocent about money matters' (!) thought that the latter would have to wait for a few years, while the parish grew.

When he did not receive a reply to his request, Fr. Mills wrote again at the end of February to Father Drea.

Dear Father Drea,

Parish Development Budget

In reply to your letter of 4th February, I have already written to Canon Grady early in the new year about our proposed building programme. Possibly my letter may have gone astray as I have had no acknowledgement of it. I will repeat what it contained.

My parish council and I would like to build a presbytery by the Church Hall at the site in Defoe Parade. With two very knowledgeable parishioners I have sketched out a rough plan for this.

The work would be done in two stages. The first stage would provide accommodation for one priest and include a large room which could be used for weekday Masses and for meetings. A second stage would provide accommodation for a second priest and a housekeeper.

We feel that there would be great advantages in this project. In a new parish it is not easy to convince all the parishioners of the identity of the parish with an independent life of its own. If some development is seen to be going on it could well help in this respect. More concrete benefits are the availability of the meeting room and the hope that if the priest were living by the Hall vandalism would be reduced.

The cost of the first stage of the presbytery would probably not exceed £16,000. With the sale of the house at 18 Cedar Road, our debts would be increased by £3,000 - £4,000. This should be within our borrowing capability.

I know very little about financial matters but I presume that this could be financed by borrowing from the bank.

Incidentally, my parish council and I have been wondering whether we could not benefit from the 'centralized Banking' arrangement of the Diocese. Whereas many parishes have paid 4% interest, in 1976 we have been required to pay 7% on our Duffy Fund Loan. Granted that 4% may not be possible in subsequent years, we would probably benefit if this transfer of indebtedness could be made.

Many of our parishioners would like to set about immediately with the building of a Church, seeing this as essential if the parish is really to come to life. While it would seem to me that this is out of the question having regard to our Mass attendance and income, I would welcome advice about its feasibility, if only to be able to give informed answers to the enthusiasts!

There is the feeling that this parish was set up with considerable disadvantages, having no Church or school and with an income greatly dependent on bingo, and some of us wonder whether we may not reasonably expect some help from the Diocese as, for example, by some relaxation of our quota for the Diocesan Development Fund.

Yours sincerely,

Donald F. Mills

P.S. I think I left out in my financial returns the V.A.T. paid in 1976. This was £110.58

Of course, our own awareness of what was to finally happen to this new parish makes the attempt to build both a church and a presbytery quite poignant, but Fr. Mills did not need to wait long before the first stage of the presbytery building was rejected by the Diocesan Finance Board, as being 'inadequate for the future needs of the parish.' He had not been sufficiently ambitious in his plans, and the Finance Board recommended the expenditure of a further three to four thousand pounds so that a housekeeper's bedroom, sitting room and bathroom could be provided, together with a waiting room and interview room for parishioners. For Fr. Mills, this was quite a blow. He had deliberately broken the building down into two stages, so that the parish was not saddled with too great a debt at the outset, but now he was being told to build the presbytery in one go, and therefore to increase the debt the parish would have to carry. Other costs were already becoming a feature of parish life, including the repairs to St. Joseph's Church Hall, damage caused not by normal wear and tear but by targeted vandalism. This included many broken windows, damaged panels on the side of the hall, and the replacement of wooden boundary fencing by wire fencing. This cost many hundreds of pounds, but damage had to be repaired promptly or vandalism could easily escalate.

Fr. Mills responded to the diocesan refusal, and its recommendation to be more ambitious in his proposals for the presbytery, in a letter dated 23rd February, 1978.

> Dear Father Drea,
>
> Thank you for your letter of 13th December 1977 concerning the new presbytery at Chadwell St. Mary. I must apologize for the delay in my reply.
>
> My Parish Council has discussed the matter again in the light of the views of the Finance Board. They consider that very few priests now have a resident housekeeper and even fewer will do so in the future. They are strongly opposed to spending more than is absolutely necessary at the present moment on a presbytery in view of the general feeling among parishioners that a start should be made on building a church as soon as possible. I concur in these views.
>
> Perhaps I could remind you that our original proposal put to you in a letter dated 22nd February 1977 was for a two-stage programme and we rather presumed that general approval had already been given for us to proceed with the first stage. We have obtained planning permission for this and are making inquiries among local builders about the cost of such a building. This plan allows for adequate footings for the completion of the second stage, if this is considered necessary at some time in the future.
>
> The Parish Council would be happy to send a representative to explain their views more fully to the Finance Board if you think that this is desirable.
> Yours sincerely,
>
> Donald F. Mills

But within a month the Finance Board reiterated its refusal to allow the project to go forward, restating its earlier objections and not commenting on the points made by Fr. Mills. It stated that it did not wish to dim the enthusiasm of the Parish Council in any way, and promised to keep the matter 'under active review'. Yet there was to be no new building.

The Parish of Chadwell St. Mary responded to the diocesan request for details of the Mass attendance during the Lenten season of 1978. It revealed a healthy and stable community, even though the Orsett Hospital congregation was on the small size on the Saturday evening.

	Orsett 8.30 p.m. (Sat)	Orsett 9.00 a.m.	Chadwell 10.15a.m.	Chadwell 6.00 p.m.	
1st Sunday of Lent	8	25	110	48	191
2nd Sunday of Lent	14	26	89	68	197
3rd Sunday of Lent	16	32	102	58	208
4th Sunday of Lent	12	38	128	28	206

A notable date in the parish history was Sunday, 3rd June 1979, when the Annual Civic Service was held in the church hall at 11.30 a.m. A parishioner, Patrick Bolger, had been installed as Mayor and his Chaplain was Rev. Donald Mills.

Fr. Mills continued with his efforts to reduce the indebtedness of the parish, and by July 1981 it was down to £2,500. In the meantime, it was abundantly clear that money needed to be spent on 18, Cedar Road, where Fr. Mills lived, and on the refurbishment of St. Joseph's Church Hall. A Report on Parish Property, compiled on 19th May 1982 by Clerk of Works A.J. Matthews, revealed a very long list of urgent repairs needed on the two buildings. In focusing his energies on reducing parish debt, Fr. Mills had been prepared to live in some deprivation. These are the repairs needed on his house in Cedar Road, taken from the report.

- Front fence and posts have rotted. I would suggest a brick wall. Rear fence and side gate need repairs and treating with creosote.
- Porch post rotted – needs repairs.
- Overhanging timber over front window needs to be taken down and replaced by a facia board.

- All cedar cladding needs treating.
- All woodwork and metalwork needs re-priming, two undercoats and one finish coat.
- All defective and loose putties need making good and painting.
- All gutters front and rear and garage need cleaning out; and all drains need rodding out.
- Bird grill needed over chimney stack.
- Front and rear gardens need attention and paths need cleaning up.
- Felt to garage needs checking.
- A gardener is badly needed to maintain front and rear gardens.

The outside of the house was clearly rather run-down. But the report on the interior revealed a similar neglect.

- Heating Installation – All internal domestic low pressure hot water heating system needs to be removed for reasons of safety and replaced. New equipment should be installed by a C.O.R.G.I. registered heating engineer; the present system is a D.I.Y. makeshift and cannot be covered by the Gas Board for maintenance.
- Roof Insulation – Recommend installation of 80mm thick fibre glass insulation quilt with 150 mm laps.
- Bedroom One – Ceiling, walls, doors, frames, windows and skirting boards, all need decorating.
- Bedroom Two – As for Bedroom One.
- Bedroom Three – As for Bedroom One.
- Bathroom and W.C. – As above.
- Linen Cupboard - As above.
- Landing, Staircase and Hall – As above.
- Kitchen – Decoration as above. Wall and floor cupboards need attention. Cooker needs replacing. Washing machine needs checking and servicing.
- Cloaks – Decoration as above.
- Store – Decoration as above.
- Lobby to Garage – Decoration as above.
- All electric wiring to power points, switches and light pendants in every room needs to be thoroughly checked.

This is an extensive list of renovation and repair. Yet it was not the end of the parish's difficulties, for the church hall was also in need of attention.

- Fencing – Chain-link, timber ranch and close boarded fences need renewing, as does side gate.
- Entrance and Car Park Area – needs making good to tarmac. All gully gratings to be fitted. All manholes to be lifted, cleaned out and rodded.
- Grass Area needs cleaning up and garden maintained.
- Cedar cladding needs treating to one uniform colour.
- Glass to external windows needs renewing.
- Window glass where broken needs to be renewed.
- External door to kitchen – renew lock and handles. Make good fanlight above frame.
- Emergency Exit Doors – check door gear operation. Emergency lights not working. Cover to one light missing.
- Door frames to chapel and sacristy – in need of renewal due to damage by vandals.
- Gap to floor duct – in need of refitting to make good.
- Fire extinguishers – in need of inspection and servicing.
- Kitchen – in need of decorating. Cupboard doors need renewing.
- Club Room – in need of decoration.
- Entrance Lobby – in need of decoration. Damage to floor to be made good. Renew floor tiles.
- Male/Female Toilets – in need of decoration. Walls to be made good. New vents for windows to be fitted. Water heater in need of servicing.
- Cloakrooms – in need of decoration.
- Central-heating system – in need of complete bleed-through and service to boiler and pumps.

This is indeed a daunting list, and one which would have taken many years to address. But the parish was not to have many years to respond, for just a year later the parish lost its independent status and was incorporated once again into the Parish of Our Lady Star of the Sea, Tilbury.

In June 1982, Bishop Thomas visited the Parish of St. Joseph, Chadwell St. Mary. He discussed various issues with the Parish Priest, the Parish Council and parishioners. The Chadwell St. Mary Parish Council wrote to the Bishop of Brentwood after his visit. From the tone of the letter, it would seem that everything was going well in this newly established parish, and the Parish Council responded to suggestions made by the Bishop and outlined their hopes for future development.

My Dear Lord Bishop,

RE : THE PARISH OF ST. JOSEPH, CHADWELL ST. MARY

We, the members of the Parish Council, wish to thank you for visiting our Parish, and take this opportunity to confirm the following points discussed at the meeting in the presbytery on the 23rd June, 1982.

Renewal Groups

As you are aware, we have five groups at present; it is our intention to consolidate these groups over the next six months before extending this important aspect of Parish Life.

Visiting Generally

As you kindly pointed out, it is also important not to forget the sick, elderly and under-privileged people, less fortunate than ourselves.

CAFOD

We, in our Parish, are fortunate to have Mr. Terry Nuttall, the CAFOD representative. He manages to keep us on our toes with regard to this very important cause. With Terry's enthusiasm and the support of the Parish we hope to grow from strength to strength.

Masses within the Deanery

With regard to monthly Inter-Parish Masses, on the 24th June 1982 this subject was discussed with the Dean of Brentwood, Father P. Cavanagh. He is in favour of this proposal and intends to discuss it with all the Parish Priests in the Deanery towards the end of the Summer.

Proposed Presbytery

The Parish feel strongly about having a presbytery sited adjacent to the Church Hall. We realise the heavy responsibility of this for such a small Parish but, when all is said and done, it is only a small cross to bear.

We would respectfully suggest, that within the next six months we will submit to you our proposed drawings, specifications and costing for this project.

Christian Unity

As the Holy Father pointed out on His visit to our country, "We, as Christians, have the Love of God. We must share this Love with others."

We, in our Parish, intend to break down some of the barriers that exist and make a commitment to Christian unity.

Lord Bishop, we are sure that apart from the points mentioned there are numerous others which have not been stated; we beg your forgiveness.

We intend to heed the advice you have given us.

We, in the Diocese of Brentwood, are fortunate to have what no other Diocese in England has: Bishop Thomas McMahon.

Yours sincerely,

For and on behalf of Chadwell Parish Council,

Michael Greenan
Chairman of the Parish Council.

Within the year, the Parish of St. Joseph's, Chadwell St. Mary was closed down, Father Mills remaining in post until the parish was once again incorporated into its mother parish, that of Our Lady Star of the Sea Tilbury, in 1983. At the same time, the Woodside estate reverted back to St. Thomas's Parish, Grays.

18 Cedar Road was sold for £24,950 and the contents, including carpets, cooker, washing machine and fitted cupboards were sold for a further £3,050. The money was transferred to the Parish of Our Lady Star of the Sea, where Fr. Donegan had designated the funds to repair and refurbish the presbytery, which was in a sorry state and scarcely fit for human habitation. This caused a degree of disquiet among some of the Chadwell parishioners, as the following letter indicates.

Dear Canon Grady,

May we introduce ourselves as loyal parishioners of St. Joseph's, Chadwell St. Mary, now amalgamated with Our Lady Star of the Sea, Tilbury, Parish Priest Father Donegan.

May I point out that the money from our Chadwell presbytery had to restore the presbytery at Tilbury, because it was in such a poor state.

My husband and I would like to suggest that all Church property should be inspected annually for maintenance. We are mostly working class people here, therefore our money should be put to good use.

We are pleased that Father Donegan has now got a decent place to live in, but had the property been kept in good repair there would have been no need to have spent out so much money.

We understand that the Tilbury Church roof now needs extensive repairs, possibly costing thousands. This we feel could have been minimised by continual inspection. Our hearts go out to Father Donegan coming to this Parish and having to put this right.

Isn't it possible, Canon, for the richer Parishes of the Diocese to help us out with big expenses?

We remain,
Yours faithfully,
Mr. and Mrs. Matthews

Within the week, Canon Grady had penned a reply.

Dear Mr. and Mrs Matthews,

Thank you for your letter received this week. I do appreciate your interest and concern.

The parish priest, according to Canon Law is "the administrator of the goods of the parish" and "is to perform his duties with the diligence of a good householder". (Canon 1284.1) "In each parish there is to be a finance committee to help the parish priest in the administration of the goods of the parish". (Canon 537)

The Diocese asks the parish priest to appoint a competent layman who will advise on the care and upkeep of the parish buildings. When the Bishop makes his visitation of the parish every two years he demands an account of what has been and needs to be done. But the parish priest as the administrator is the one to put these needs into effect.

Some parish priests are better administrators than others – and some can delegate – others cannot. Some are hamstrung by shortage of money. Others have the ability to raise that which is required.

The Diocese has no money of its own and has to rely on the individual parishes helping themselves. Some parish priests do go to richer parishes for help but I have no power or authority to make this happen – but I am glad to say that it does happen occasionally.

I do hope this answers your letter.
Yours sincerely,
Canon Grady.

With the closure of the Parish of Chadwell St. Mary, the parishioners were to say goodbye to their Parish Priest, the much loved Father Mills. Many were very upset about this as he had made a real and lasting impression on the lives of his parishioners. Typical of the sense of loss they all felt is this letter from one of the parishioners, asking Bishop Thomas to reconsider his decision.

Your Lordship,

Please forgive the liberty I take in writing to you, but I, and all Chadwell and Orsett parishioners are deeply upset that we are to lose our Parish Priest, Father Mills.

Whilst appreciating the shortage of priests, may I earnestly and humbly beg and pray of you to reconsider your decision to remove him? Father Mills has worked so long and hard and is so dearly loved and respected by us all that we are desolate at the thought of losing him.

I am sure that the new priest, Father Donegan, will also be a good and kindly man, but with all due respect I don't think anyone will ever replace the affection we all feel for Father Mills.

I myself have knelt before the Altar and prayed that a miracle may happen and that we may be allowed to keep him – but the Blessed Lord can only grant that miracle through you, your Lordship. Won't you please reconsider and let us keep Father Mills? He has worked so long and tirelessly for St. Joseph's that it will never be the same without him.

I shall continue to pray most earnestly that you may find it in your heart to reconsider your decision. May God bless you.

Yours very respectfully,

Ann. M. Leggett (Mrs.)

Ever courteous, Bishop Thomas replied in person to Mrs. Leggett, but he was unable to help with the miracle for which she had prayed.

Thank you for writing to me. I do understand how sorry you are to lose Father Mills and I am aware of the great affection in which he is held by the parishioners. I too share your high regard for him and am very grateful to him for the wonderful work he has done.

During the past month, two parish priests resigned for health reasons and Canon Byrne died. You will I am sure appreciate that faced with this situation I was forced to move priests.

I know that Father Mills would like you to welcome your new Parish Priest and to give him all the help and support that you can, especially now that the parishes of Chadwell-St-Mary and Tilbury will be in his care.

Assuring you of my concern to do what is best for each parish and asking a remembrance in your prayers.

With all good wishes,
Yours sincerely,
Thomas McMahon
Bishop of Brentwood

Even though the parish had ceased to be independent, it still had a thriving and dynamic community. In 1982, St. Mary's Youth Club, under the leadership of Sister Carmel McEnerny, began to meet at St. Joseph's and they continued to meet there for the next twenty years. For most of this time it was organised by Pauline Lacey and Mary Pollard, with numerous other helpers. The hall continued to be used for Mass each Sunday and for a Saturday morning Mass. It was also the centre of many of the parish's social events, with jumble sales, beetle drives, dances and quiz nights regular features, and later the weekly meetings of the Senior Citizens' Club and the annual bazaar. The hall also hosted many private functions. The hall had a superbly well equipped kitchen and this was used extensively by the Care Committee to provide monthly lunches for the Senior Citizens' Group as well as weekly Lenten Lunches. The Chief Cooks, Diane Connelly and Pauline Lacey, ably assisted by a small band of faithful and hard working colleagues, also organised outings to Aylesford, London and elsewhere, an annual Mass for the Sick, followed by lunch, and wonderful Christmas Lunches for the elderly and housebound.

There were, inevitably, many regrets that Chadwell no longer had its own, designated Parish Priest, and some parishioners believed that the amalgamation with Tilbury resulted in less frequent and direct contact with their priest. In January 1983 one of the parishioners, Mrs.

Connelly, wrote to Bishop Thomas to outline what she saw to be the new situation in Chadwell St. Mary.

> My Dear Lord Bishop,
>
> I am writing to let you know how upset I and many others are, with regard to our Parish. We fail to see the need for five Lay Ministers of the Eucharist.
>
> The housebound, elderly and the sick look forward to a visit from the Priest and to receive Holy Communion. No Lay Minister will ever be able to take his place. Furthermore, four out of five chosen are in full-time employment and therefore weekday visits are out of the question.
>
> The Parish Council did not feel they were able to employ a person for the position of 'caretaker', without consultation with the new Parish Priest; but at the same time they chose five people for this extremely important job. When something as important as this involves all the Parish, how can a small minority speak for the majority. Would a ballot not have solved the problem?
>
> The Tilbury nuns would, I am sure, be willing to assist the Priest when the occasion arose. They would be more acceptable to the people, as they too have given their lives to Christ.
>
> I feel very sad about my religion and wonder where it is all going to end. Will there come a time in the near future when we will be told that a Communion Service performed by a Lay Minister will fulfil the Sunday obligation? I am afraid when that day comes, I feel it is time to give up all that I have been brought up to believe in from the time I was old enough to understand.
>
> A group of us made a protest on the same subject to Bishop Casey a few years ago, and we feel as strongly now as we did then.
>
> I hope you will be able to reflect on this subject and in your wisdom find a solution.
>
> Yours sincerely,
> Diane Connelly (Mrs.)

St. Joseph's Church Hall remained licensed for weddings. In 1984, the General Register Office in London wrote to the Brentwood Diocese enquiring who was now the 'responsible authorised person' for the church hall. If there were no acknowledged priest in attendance, the marriage registers at St. Joseph's would need to be closed and all future weddings there would be attended and registered by a Registrar from the

Thurrock Register Office. Fortunately, the decision had already been made by the Parish Priest in Tilbury, as the diocese was able to confirm.

St. Joseph's Church Hall, Defoe Parade

> With regard to the above-named church, the person responsible is now the Rev. Donal Donegan, who is also Parish Priest at Tilbury, and resides at 96 Dock Road, Tilbury. I have been in touch with him, and I understand he wishes to continue to have St. Joseph's Church Hall as a place of marriages, and that he will be contacting you with a view to being also the Authorised Person there, as well as at the main church in Tilbury.

In 1993, on 17th March, the Silver Jubilee of the opening of the church hall, a joint social was held with the parishioners of St. Michael's, East Ham and on 28th March a Silver Jubilee Mass was concelebrated by Bishop Thomas McMahon.

For the next seventeen years, Sunday Mass was celebrated at St. Joseph's Church Hall. And then, on the weekend of 7th/8th August 2010, the following statement from Bishop Thomas was read out at Mass.

> My dear people,
>
> As you will be aware, over recent years our Diocese and its people have faced a number of important changes and developments in terms of pastoral ministry and parish life. These were set out in our Diocesan Vision Document 'Put Out into the Deep', which was published in 2005. Equally our Vision Document contains the principles which direct the process of making pastoral provision for the future. The process is ongoing. As a good example, there was very recently a consultation in the deaneries on the Rationalisation of Mass Times and a consequent reduction in the number of parish Masses. The Diocesan Committee for Planning and Development is currently working on its implementation.
>
> An important principle of Pastoral Planning is for parishes increasingly to share resources, including priestly availability, and this is now happening in several places in the Diocese. You will be aware of course that this is about to happen here following the announcement that from the beginning of October Fr Paul Dynan will be responsible for the pastoral care of both this Parish and of Stanford-le-Hope. I know that Fr Paul will bring the highest standard of dedication and commitment to your communities, but the Committee for Planning and I are also conscious that despite these qualities it simply would not be possible for him to meet the current weekend Mass Schedule of 3 Masses in your Parish and 3 Masses in Stanford.

As a result I have to announce to you that as from the first weekend of October, Mass will no longer be celebrated at Chadwell St Mary or at Stanford's Mass Centre at Linford. Furthermore since this Parish has a Saturday evening Mass and a Sunday morning Mass at 11, a rearrangement of Mass times will clearly be necessary. Each Parish will however continue to have 2 Sunday Obligation Masses. The details of this will be worked on during the coming weeks to enable the new arrangement to take effect also from the 1st weekend in October. A similar statement is being read out today in Stanford.

I am aware that the prospect of change can be challenging and that living with change is not always easy. I would like to take this opportunity of expressing my deep gratitude to those who have cared for and supported your Mass Centre over the years. I would wish to assure you that the present step has been taken to give your communities the best pastoral provision available in the circumstances. And so I invite you to continue and to develop the marvellous spirit of your Parish community and I am sure that Fr Paul can count on a warm welcome and your whole-hearted support.

+ Thomas, Bishop of Brentwood

Sadly for the people of Chadwell, the last Mass was celebrated at St. Joseph's at 9.00 a.m. on Sunday, 29th September 2010, and after that the church hall remained empty.

Bishop Thomas McMahon consulted the Council of Priests in June 2011 to consider what was to be done. A briefing paper was provided by the Vicar General Mgr. David Manson, which summarised the brief history of the parish and its church hall.

<u>Council of Priests – St. Joseph Chadwell St Mary</u>

The Bishop wishes to consult the Council of Priests on the following two matters:

1. the formal suppression of the Parish of St Joseph, Chadwell St. Mary
2. the closure of the church building at Chadwell St. Mary (this probably leading to its demolition and the sale of the land).

<u>The Canonical Background</u>

Canon 515/2 prescribes as follows; the diocesan Bishop alone can establish, suppress or alter parishes. He is not to establish, suppress or notably alter them unless he has consulted the council of priests.

Canon 1222 prescribes as follows:

1222/1 If a church cannot in any way be used for divine worship and there is no possibility of its being restored, the diocesan Bishop may allow it to be used for some secular but not unbecoming purpose.
1222/2 Where other grave reasons suggest that a particular church should no longer be used for divine worship, the diocesan Bishop may allow it to be used for a secular but not unbecoming purpose. Before doing so, he must consult the council of priests; he must also have the consent of those who could lawfully claim rights over the church, and be sure that the good of souls would not be harmed by the transfer.

The History
In the document which accompanies this briefing paper, Fr. Stewart Foster has kindly set out the history of St. Joseph, Chadwell St Mary as recorded on various documents. As always, I am deeply grateful to him for his invaluable assistance. (Note: the history has not been included here as the same material has already been covered in this book.)

The Parish
As will be seen, Chadwell St Mary started as a Mass Centre served from Tilbury. In March 1975, it was erected as a Parish in its own right and Fr. Donald Mills was the Parish Priest. When he left in 1983, St. Joseph's reverted to its role as the Mass Centre for Tilbury and it was assumed that the Parish of Chadwell St Mary ceased to exist. However, no formal document is in existence to confirm this. The decree of erection of the Parish is in the Chancery but there is no decree of suppression.

The Bishop now wishes to establish the situation which everyone assumed to be the case for the last 28 years and formally to suppress the Parish.

The Building
It will be seen from the History that St. Joseph's was built as a Hall. It is a timber framed lightweight structure erected sometime between the mid 1960s and early 1970s. In the Quinquennial Inspection of 2009 (undertaken by Mr David Fairman) it was noted that the building was constructed as a temporary structure and would have had a 'design life' of about 20 years. Even at the time of that inspection the building was not in a good state of repair. Immediate repairs to make the building and car park safe were estimated in the region of £60,000.

Mr Fairman also noted that the infill structure of the building's framework was significantly decayed and within 10 years would require major replacement costing (at prices then) some £100,000. Although no formal report was commissioned, it was also estimated that considerable work would be required to the electrics. (Clearly, the cost of the material upkeep of Chadwell St Mary falls on Tilbury Parish. In the same quinquennial it was noted that repair costs to Our Lady Star of the Sea (for the roof, gutters and external walls) over the period of the following 5 years would be in the order of £254,000 and to the presbytery for the same period (for internal damp/rot, roof, walls and windows) would be some £98,000.)

The Pastoral Situation

In October 2010, Fr Paul Dynan was appointed to the Parishes of Tilbury and Stanford-le-Hope. A part of the preparation for this, it was announced in both Parishes that Sunday Mass would no longer be celebrated at Tilbury's Mass Centre of St Joseph or in Stanford's Mass Centre at Linford (held in the Methodist Church). Mass at St. Joseph was at 9 o'clock on Sunday morning and there was a Holy Day of Obligation Vigil Mass at 7.00 p.m.

An average of 40 people used to attend the Sunday Mass (although, understandably, in the months leading to the end of Mass there that figure diminished to 20). Of those who used to be regular parishioners at Chadwell St Mary, the majority now attends Mass at Tilbury and a minibus is hired by the Parish for those without public transport. A few now go to Stanford. Fr. Dynan estimates that there has been no general drifting away from attendance at Mass as a result of the cessation of Mass at St. Joseph's.

There was no weekday Mass; there had been no weddings there for a long time and baptisms were rare.

Soon after Mass ceased to be celebrated at St. Joseph's, the books, vestments and some of the moveable fittings were removed for safe keeping because the threat of vandalism remains uppermost in the minds of Fr. Dynan and his parishioners.

Without prejudice to the views of the Council of Priests, Mr. Tom King has been in negotiation with the local authority to gauge their view on a possible closure and sale, especially given the restrictive covenant affecting the property. The Authority seems quite willing to consider this, but municipal inertia sets in from time to time and we are currently experiencing one of those relapses.

Consultation

Fr. Dynan has consulted at local level and although among the people at Chadwell St Mary there was inevitably initial disappointment at the ending of Mass and the physical closure of the building, there is now general acceptance that due to the clergy situation and the material state of the building there is no long-term future for St. Joseph's. The matter has also been discussed at the Deanery Conference.

There is no other person who could claim rights over the church (canon 1222/2).

In these circumstances the formal closure of St. Joseph's had a sad inevitability about it. Yet the parishioners who had enjoyed the use of St. Joseph's Hall for so many years were understandably upset. Typical of their response was this open letter written at the time of the announcement that the Hall was to close. There was also a proposal at the time to link the parishes of Tilbury and Grays. There was a great deal of uncertainty about the future.

OUR LADY STAR OF THE SEA, TILBURY AND
ST. JOSEPH'S, CHADWELL ST. MARY

Yet again, another bolt from the blue for our Parish. We are definitely the poor relations of the Diocese. We have had six priests in 20 years and we feel we have been treated very badly, making the parishioners feel dispirited. In fact, if you take away the Mass Centre in Chadwell St. Mary many of the elder parishioners, those who worked hard to get St. Joseph's built, will be unable to get to Mass at all.

There is no transport from Chadwell to Tilbury or Grays during the evening. There is only a long walk to the station for Tilbury parishioners and a trip to Grays and then another long walk to the Church in Grays. St. Thomas's is already overcrowded so how would they accommodate more parishioners; Chafford Hundred is still growing.

Our parish is part of the Thames Gateway which is growing fast and we are at the central peninsular of this Gateway. If our Mass Centre is taken away and only two priests serve such a large area, Tilbury and Chadwell will be isolated. If the link should go ahead, as Grays has six Sunday Masses at the moment, could we not have one Mass in Chadwell, one in Tilbury and four in Grays, sharing all the Mass Centres.

This decision was no doubt put forward by Deanery priests, who I might add are no longer in our Deanery, suggesting that Tilbury and Chadwell should be linked with Grays. If this is the case, why have we not heard about this before, why now? There have also been derogatory remarks from other priests about the area, but ask any one of those who have served here about the warmth of the people, the support they give and the distinct character they have.

Surely we could keep our Mass Centre in Chadwell and a compromise be made to keep it going with one Mass as it will rip the social heart out of our parish if it goes. We need to maintain a presence in Chadwell and in Tilbury, not least because of the ageing population, our school and our Sisters of Mercy.

We would like to know exactly what it would mean if St. Joseph's were to close; would we have two priests in Grays or one in Grays and one in Tilbury? Would there be only one Mass in Tilbury and maybe one in Chadwell (if we keep St. Joseph's)? We really haven't been told anything, just that the Centre could well close. Surely we are entitled to some facts before a final decision is made.

The decision was made to close St. Joseph’s Hall as a Mass Centre and it began to fall into increasing disrepair. Fortunately, the Parish of Our Lady Star of the Sea retained its independent status, and the link with Grays did not materialise. In 2015, our Parish Priest, Father Paul Dynan, formally sold the St. Joseph’s Hall site for development, the money from the sale reverting to the Parish of Our Lady Star of the Sea. What was once St. Joseph's Hall is now a large building containing many independent retirement flats with communal areas and access to medical and social services, although the name of St. Joseph has been retained.

Chapter Ten : The Parish of Our Lady and St. Joseph, Stanford-le-Hope

A book was published in 2013 to mark the centenary of the Stanford-le-Hope Parish. Entitled *The Parish of Our Lady and St. Joseph*, the book included a chapter on the Parish of Tilbury, written by Mary Pollard. This was partly an acknowledgement of a neighbouring parish and partly a recognition that Fr. Paul Dynan is the Parish Priest for both parishes. Whatever the reasons for the additional chapter, it proved to be an excellent starting point for the creation of this book, and I do appreciate the considerable work which Mary Pollard completed. Now that there is a book about our Tilbury Parish, it seems only right to include a balancing chapter on Stanford-le-Hope. This is no more than a digest of the original book, compressed to a few pages.

It would be well to remember that at the start of the 20th century many people in this country were suspicious of the Catholic faith. The anti-Catholic clauses of the 1689 Bill of Rights and the 1701 Act of Settlement were still in force, and even after the Catholic Emancipation Act of 1829 there was some reserve and caution towards Catholicism from many in the professional classes, and downright hostility among some working class communities. The early priests in the Stanford-le-Hope Parish were occasionally abused and had stones thrown at them simply because they were identifiably Catholic.

The area of Stanford-le-Hope was then catastrophically poor. When the first priest set up a fund to build a church, he was able to state that we were the "Poorest mission in the archdiocese of Westminster". But then what does poor actually mean? The Rowntree Foundation reported on the conditions faced by working class people at the start of the twentieth century :

> A family living upon the wages paid for unskilled labour must never spend a penny on railway fare or omnibus. They must never go into the country unless they walk. They must never purchase a halfpenny newspaper or spend a penny to buy a ticket for a popular concert. They must write no letters to absent children for they cannot afford to pay the postage. The children must have no pocket money for dolls, marbles or sweets. The father must smoke no tobacco and must drink no beer. The mother must never buy any pretty clothes. Should a child fall ill, it must be attended by the parish doctor; should it die, it must be buried by the parish. Finally, the wage earner must never be absent from his work for a single day.

Post-Reformation Catholicism in our area began about 1903, when a few families joined together to build a church. They were given a plot of land by Messrs Kynoch, who had built an explosives factory in 1898 on the marshes below Fobbing. Why out in the wilds, you might wonder? Strangely enough, no-one wanted an explosives factory anywhere near **them**. The Kynochs brought 80 workers down from Birmingham, and many of them were Irish Catholics. Whilst a church was being built, the Parish Priest from Barking, the Rev Dean Clemens, would ride over once a month on horseback to say Mass, hear Confessions and conduct Baptisms at the house of a parishioner, riding back to Barking the following day. The little church continued in operation until 1921 when it was sold to the Essex Education Committee for conversion to a school. Part of the old church is still clearly visible at Corringham Primary School, in Herd Lane, Corringham.

Father Charles Carless

Our first full-time priest was appointed in 1910. The first little church was dedicated to St. Francis de Sales, and the priest's name was Father Charles Carless. He proved to be quite a character. On a winter's evening, Christmas Eve, a few years after the start of the twentieth century, he was to say Mass in a dilapidated barn, with snow flurries coming through the roof. After that service, the first public Mass said in Stanford-le-Hope since the Reformation, Father Carless slept on a heap of straw in a corner of the old barn.

A church was needed, and Father Carless set about the task with unusual zeal. Pictures appeared in the Catholic newspaper, *The Universe,* showing the priest on the roof of the barn, making it watertight with thatch.

In his appeal for funds for a new church, Father Carless discovered an unexpected talent for poetry. Here is an example, which appeared in *The Catholic Times*.

The Barn Mass Centre and School of St. Mary circa 1909

We're getting impatient at Stanford-le-Hope
For our present old barn's quite unable to cope
With the needs of this parish which grows every day
And it does seem a pity to send folks away.

The sum we are asking is not very great
But until it is ours we must certainly wait
If every kind reader would send us a shilling
The church we'd soon be completing and filling.

Six hundred and sixty gold sovereigns is not
In my estimation a very great lot
To pay for a church to sit two hundred people
You see we're content to be minus a steeple

I want you to help us to get in the rest
You'll surely say yes to my urgent request
A shilling is all that I ask you to send
Tho' a cheque for five pounds would in no way offend!!

The interior of the Barn Mass Centre
(from a painting by C.R. Sharp)

Thanks to such efforts, the new church was built – debt free – and the first Mass was said by Cardinal Bourne and Monsignor Jackman on 22nd June 1913.

The building of our Parish Church : 1912

Originally dedicated to Saint Joseph, the founding of this church marked the beginning of our Parish of Our Lady and St. Joseph. This year we are celebrating the centenary – the first centenary – of our parish.

And what of that first Mass? Cardinal Bourne took the opportunity to remind the Church of England of its roots.

Our Anglican friends would like, nowadays, to forget about Henry VIII. They try to make themselves believe sometimes that the lust and passion of Henry VIII had very little to do really with the change of religion in England. If Henry VIII had not been a man of lust and passions he would never have thought of separating himself from the unity of the Catholic Church.

The opening of Our Lady and St. Joseph's Church : 1913
(Nelly Sharpe is the little girl in the white dress, a member of the family who used to own the wet fish shop in the High Street where Brands office now stands.)

Interior of the new Church in 1915

What was our new church like? It was described as Byzantine, but it was really a concrete shell. On the outside it looked like an old cinema. It had a concrete floor, concrete walls and, disconcertingly, a flat concrete roof. There were simple wooden chairs for the congregation. In the wintertime it was very cold indeed. But it was ours.

If we had our own church, there was scarcely any money to run the parish. The collection from the little congregation at Corringham averaged just seven pence per week and even the big new church averaged just 63 pence per week from the offertory. Yet nothing went to waste. The financial returns of the parish show that the mown grass around the church was sold for a total of seventy five pence per year.

When Father Carless left the parish in 1919 he took his legendary zeal with him, on one occasion organising a parish tote, returning any winnings to the wives of the men who bet. Not surprisingly, Bishop Doubleday instructed him to close down the operation, as it did nothing for the Church's reputation.

Father Charles Snell

In 1920, Father Charles Snell arrived to become our Parish Priest. He was to remain here until his death in 1949, and some of our older parishioners still have memories of this dedicated and kind priest. Father Snell's first job was to persuade Bishop Doubleday not to close down this impoverished and barely viable parish. So a parish that now celebrates one hundred years, almost didn't make it past seven.

Yet if its finances hadn't improved, it had certainly got bigger. Apart from Stanford-le-Hope, it now covered Basildon, Bulphan, Corringham, Fobbing, Horndon on the Hill, Kynochtown (later Coryton), Laindon, Linford, Mucking, Nevedon, Pitsea, Shell Haven, Thames Haven and Vange. The area was 100 square miles.

This was a time of economic difficulty. At the end of the First World War, Lloyd George famously promised "a land fit for heroes", but by the early twenties the money simply ran out and we all had to accept the hardships that lay ahead.

One relic from the First World War became an icon for the new parish. A life-size crucifix was rescued from a wayside shrine close to the battlefront in Belgium, and subsequently restored by Father Snell and a parishioner, William McDade. This crucifix would remain in place until the old church was demolished in 1989, a local landmark for Catholics and non-Catholics alike.

By the nineteen thirties there were over 500 Catholics in the parish, and the average Sunday attendance was some 400, divided between the two Masses at Stanford, one at the little church at Vange and one at the little chapel at Horndon on the Hill. But while the parish was growing in numbers, times were hard for the working class congregation. There were three million people unemployed, benefits were subject to a savage and demeaning Means Test, and there was to be no improvement in the economy until the prospect of war began to stimulate a drive towards rearmament and wages began to improve. Conditions might not have matched the poverty experienced in Victorian times and life expectation was improving, but most working class people in our parish, as elsewhere in the country, had a poor diet, indifferent housing conditions, a low standard of education, and little help from the state in old age. When Father Snell was asked whether the tabernacle was proof against fire, he told Bishop Doubleday "Against fire, but scarcely against theft in these days".

The Bronze Statue of the Sacred Heart at Horndon on the Hill

With the start of the Second World War, it has to be admitted that the parish of Our Lady and St Joseph was comparatively unscathed. Grays and Tilbury were more obvious targets for German bombers, and just a few church windows were blown in by bomb blast. Some sandbags were placed on the roof of the little Catholic school to create a machine gun emplacement in the event of invasion, but that was it. A more obvious sign of the conflict was the presence of German POWs at Sunday Mass. They were brought in by lorry from their camp at Orsett. Parishioners remember that the Germans sat on one side of the church whilst the regulars sat on the other, although the Germans were very friendly, especially towards the children. Although they knew their way around the Latin Mass, the scripture readings in English were more problematic, and as a concession each English text was followed by the German text, read by one of the officers. The POWs were put to work building prefabs across the road from the church, and they took a special interest in painting the bronze statue of the Sacred Heart at the chapel at Horndon on the Hill.

Father John Watson

When Father Snell died at the presbytery in 1949, he was replaced by Father John Watson, who had himself been a POW with the Japanese. This experience affected him deeply and caused prolonged bouts of ill health. Apart from his more immediate responsibilities as our Parish Priest, Father Watson became closely involved in the planning of the new town of Basildon. He gave advice on the proposed siting of churches and the housing that would be needed for priests in the new town. The Minister of Town and Country Planning, Lewis Silkin, addressed a large gathering of people in Laindon in September 1948, talking about the establishment of the new town of Basildon:

> Basildon will become a city which people from all over the world will want to visit. It will be a place where all classes of community can meet freely together on equal terms and enjoy common cultural recreational facilities.

Father John Hibbert

Father Watson's successor as Parish Priest was Father John Hibbert, another priest who had been deeply affected by the war, serving as chaplain to the British Expeditionary Force and coming under heavy bombardment during the retreat to the coast in 1940. The shellshock he suffered made it impossible for him to play a full part in the religious life until after the war. He brought his mother with him as housekeeper, but she was a poor cook, and visiting priests lived in hope of a meal from the nuns at the nearby convent. When his mother died, the new housekeeper was an elderly Irish woman with a personality disorder, who would try to take over the entire parish if the priest were away. When she heard the children at their rote learning in the class room across the fence she thought the chanting children were defaming her character, and would hurry off to the local police station to complain.

If the war had left our parish comparatively untouched, big changes were now about to occur in peacetime. A surge in post-war house building was taking place, with the efforts of Thurrock Council more than matched by the London Boroughs of East Ham and West Ham, who began to build a great number of council houses on land they had purchased in Stanford and Corringham. Our little church was soon full to bursting, although it was now slightly more comfortable with a wooden floor and finally central heating. Which didn't work. Oh those winter months!

With the general rise in population in our area, there now being an estimated 1,650 Catholics amongst a population of over 30,000, the parish was now seeing its largest congregations, with average attendance at Sunday Mass of 630, a figure unequalled to this day.

One particular wedding took place in October 1968, when parishioner Sandra Williams married Declan Cluskey, of The Bachelors. And yes, the lady seated IS Vera Lynn. But it is our assistant priest, Father John Timmins, with the guitar.

Father John Taylor, the Parish Priest who arrived in 1974 was ably supported by an assistant priest, Father Bart Lynch. These two priests worked so well together and had such a rapport with their parishioners that many people still look back on these times as "the golden years".

A First Communion Breakfast in 1971 – how happy they all look!

Father Gerald Gostling

Father Gerald Gostling arrived in the parish in 1982. He too had a close and warm relationship with his parishioners. Whenever church maintenance was needed, volunteers were always on hand. Yet during his tenure, the parish suffered a major set-back. In 1989, a frayed flex on an electric heater used to warm up the Confessional caused a fire to break out in the empty church. Before it was discovered, it had caused real damage to the fabric of the building. Worse was to follow. Engineers inspecting the fire damage discovered that the concrete construction of the building was literally crumbling away. There was no alternative but to pull down the existing Parish Church and to build a new one.

Father Gostling speaks with a Very Important Person

Tricia Dollard and Marian Sharp 1983
painting – mostly themselves – before their Confirmation

Of course, the parish didn't have the money for such a costly venture, and it was obliged to close down and sell off its outlying church and chapel. The site occupied by St. Augustine's in Corringham was sold off for development and the little Chapel of the Sacred Heart in Horndon on the Hill was sold, to be converted into a private dwelling.

The Parish Priest with the responsibility to organise all this was Father Richard Ashton, or Father Dick, as he liked to be called. He came to us from Basildon where he had just helped to plan and build a new church, so the task ahead of him was not entirely unfamiliar. The style chosen for Stanford was Italianate, with a low square bell tower and buff bricks inside and out, a colour most would call yellow. The building is quite unlike its predecessor, and its design was the consequence of lengthy discussions between parishioners, their priest and members of the diocesan art and architecture committee. The contrast with the older church almost certainly ruffled a few feathers. The situation was summed up by our Parish Priest :

> Many of those who live in Stanford had been brought up with the old church. Their fathers had built it. They had been baptised and married in it and wanted nothing to do with a wooden hall or a modern monstrosity masquerading as a church. To them St. Joseph's was beautiful- and real beauty in churches has to be chiefly in the lives of those who make up the church community, united in Christ. However the three years wait turned out to be worth it. The new church of Our Lady and St Joseph is, according to parishioners, warm, homely and beautiful.

The new Parish Church was consecrated by Bishop Thomas McMahon on February 11th, 1993, so we have now been in our new church for twenty-five years. To mark the centenary, a new marble floor was placed around the altar, the interior of the church was repainted, a new carpet fitted, extensive cleaning took place and the bell from the original church was hung in the bell tower, from where its voice can be heard once again in the small community of Stanford-le-Hope.

Our current Parish Priest, Father Paul Dynan, arrived in the parish in October 2010. Unusually for a Catholic priest, he had earlier been married, and had a successful career in the National Health Service. When his wife died, he brought up his three young children and saw them grow to adulthood before talking with them about the possibility that he might now train to be a Catholic priest. Father Paul is also the Parish Priest for the neighbouring but entirely independent parish of Tilbury, so he spends half of his week in each parish, commuting regularly between the two. Father Paul considers this arrangement “a privilege”.

The history has so far concentrated on the Parish Church of Our Lady and Saint Joseph, but this has not been the whole story. Other churches, chapels and Mass Centres, even a Methodist church, are also part of the story. Let us begin with Corringham.

When the little Catholic Church of St. Francis de Sales was sold in 1921, the Catholics in Corringham were without a church of their own. For over thirty years the Corringham Catholics had to travel to either Stanford or Vange, making use of an uncertain bus service which was suspended entirely during the Second World War. In a world where few families owned a car, this made life difficult for the elderly or infirm. Anglican colleagues offered the use of a room in Corringham to say Mass, but this was rejected by the diocese as an unsuitable arrangement, although during the War a monthly Mass was said in a billiard hall in Corringham.

Corringham had three more goes at providing a suitable place for the community to say Mass. The first, in 1955, was a basic, Nissan style hut. The local people rallied round and made it look presentable and St. Teresa's, as it was called, served the community for over ten years, until it became so dilapidated that it had to be closed down. The second was in 1972, when St. Augustine's Church was built as part of the redevelopment of Corringham. St. Augustine is the patron saint of brewers. The wooden construction was formally opened by Bishop Casey in May 1977.

St. Augustine's Church : rebuilt where the furniture store now stands

Two years later a supermarket wanted to build on this land, and so St. Augustine's was moved down the road in Corringham. There it stood for another 13 years, coming into its own when it became the main parish centre for the saying of Mass, after the fire at Our Lady and St. Joseph's. But it was this very fire that created the need to sell St. Augustine's to raise money to build a new Parish Church in Stanford, so that once again the Corringham Catholics are without a Mass Centre of their own.

Another area to consider is Horndon on the Hill. In 1901, the evangelist Doctor John Stansfield bought 23 acres of land for the work of the Oxford Medical Mission, part of the Oxford Movement. It was designed as a camping ground for poor and sick London boys, complete with a mock castle and a swimming pool.

The Priory : September 1917

Among the helpers was Geoffrey Fisher, later to become the Archbishop of Canterbury. The land was later bought by Miss Alice Green who, with her associate Miss Woollard, created a sort of home for unfortunate children. A small chapel was built, and Miss Green wished the diocese to formally take responsibility for the chapel, something Bishop Doubleday did not want to do. When all of the ramshackle buildings around the little chapel were considered by the Council to be unsafe, they had to be demolished. More substantial dwellings were built, and Miss Green offered a better plot of land for the building of a new chapel. This eventually became the Sacred Heart Chapel and Bishop Doubleday arrived to say the inaugural Mass in May 1938. He didn't want the responsibility of having the chapel as an official, diocesan Mass Centre, and it wasn't until 1949 that the Chapel and its land were finally sold to the diocese for the sum of five shillings. Dave Arnold and his family looked after the chapel for many years, and Dave was known to us all as "the Bishop of Horndon".

The Sacred Heart Chapel at Horndon on the Hill

The Two Bishops : Bishop Thomas McMahon and 'The Bishop of Horndon', Dave Arnold

In another part of the parish, the Catholics in East Tilbury used the dining room of the Bata factory, still smelling of cabbage, for their weekly Mass, until this was sold off and converted into shops and flats. For a while, they made use of the East Tilbury Social Hall, and then bought land near to the railway line.

Unfortunately, the town planners did not consider the land to be suitable for development. When the Social Hall was closed for refurbishment in 1998, the area's Catholics were again without a home. And then a most unusual thing happened. The Linford Methodist Church offered shared use of its building, an arrangement that continued happily for many years.

The Catholics who lived in the area of Vange and Pitsea in the later part of the nineteenth century had a choice between Mass in Westcliff to the east, and Grays and Tilbury to the west. The train to Westcliff was more reliable, but those who attended the 11.00 a.m. Mass there had to wait for the return train, which was not until 2.15. Attending Mass took up the greater part of the day. When the Parish of Stanford-le-Hope was set up, there was the prospect of a shorter journey, although few enough owned a car.

When Father Snell realised that there were quite a few Catholics around Pitsea and Vange, in October 1923 he began to hold a monthly Mass in Pitsea, in the garage attached to the home of the aptly named Mr. and Mrs. Bishop. Confessions were heard in the ditch outside, where the kitchen smell of a cooking breakfast proved to be something of a distraction. The energetic community began to raise money in earnest for a chapel of their own. It was built in 1925 and was known as the Church of the Sacred Heart. It was a timber framed construction that required an annual licence as a temporary structure. Temporary or not, it served the community for 62 years, until it was closed as part of the reorganisation of the new Parish of St. Basil the Great in Basildon.

St. Joseph's School

Catholic communities have always liked to have a school for the children of their parish, and from the start of our parish a school has been there. Originally called The School of St. Mary, it was housed on the site of the little black barn where the first Masses were said. It originally had eight children. In 1914, two brick classrooms were built next to the new church. They could accommodate 100 children. The class teacher was a Mr. John, described as being of "Hindoo extraction". He was thought to be a good fellow but not good enough, although he unexpectedly claimed the ability to teach any language in the world. Father Snell was reluctant to dismiss him, not least because he was, himself, a lodger in Mr. John's house.

The school limped on in the nineteen twenties. The accommodation and equipment were barely adequate, but the Council was unwilling to provide additional funding when there were many unfilled places in its own schools. The teaching staff were untrained, and the future looked uncertain.

All this changed when in April 1930 Father Snell managed to persuade the Sisters of Mercy, based at Wanstead, to send some of the nuns to the school as teachers. These qualified teachers changed the status of the school entirely. It was officially recognised as a public elementary school. The sisters moved into a little convent, next to the school.

Bishop Thomas McMahon talks to the children of St. Joseph's School

The nuns were to remain at the school until the Head Teacher, Sister Philippa, left the school in 1992. The school, which was barely viable in 1930, grew to become the successful, popular and confident school it is today. And so much of this success is directly attributable to the Sisters of Mercy. Over the years there were many battles to be fought, most of them linked to the vexed question of suitable school buildings. Today, there is a purpose built and well equipped modern school, but it was not always so.

Temporary buildings, ancient outside toilets, freezing classrooms, a site divided by a busy street, absence of staffroom or office for the Head, lack of suitable playing fields, no school hall, leaking roofs, the list was seemingly endless, but somehow these adversities were met and overcome.

Chapter Eleven : The Apostleship of the Sea

There is another dimension to the work of the Parish of Our Lady Star of the Sea, because within the parish boundaries there is a major sea port. This means that our Tilbury Parish Priest must also concern himself with the spiritual and social welfare of seafarers who visit the port, and the seafarers themselves often build a relationship with a community whom they see from time to time. In the history of the Tilbury Parish this has certainly been the case with the Goanese sailors, usually devout Catholics, who have played a real part in the development of Tilbury Parish.

There will always have been a spiritual need felt by those who travel across the world. Away from families and homeland for long periods of time, the loneliness and isolation which many experience can be a major problem. Some sea travellers regard the land as a place to renew their faith or to give thanks for their very survival. If Chaucer's *gentil and parfait knight* joined the Canterbury pilgrims to give thanks for his safe arrival back home from the Crusades, no less would have been felt by those who undertook lengthy sea journeys at a time when navigation made every long sea voyage hazardous. Hostile enemy ships, pirates and harsh shipboard conditions must have made many early sailors long for landfall. There is no doubt that conscientious priests in the past would have recognised and responded to the needs of such men, but a national organisation to co-ordinate support arrived at a surprisingly late date.

At the end of the First World War, Britain had one of the largest merchant fleets in the world. There were also thousands of foreign registered ships docking regularly in British ports. In the days before containerisation, the sailors would be obliged to wait in port whilst their ships were first unloaded and then reloaded with fresh cargo, a process that would take the dock workers many days to complete. Yet nothing at all was done for the waiting seafarers. Left to their own devices and with no immediate contact with the people who lived in and around the port, the sailors could be as isolated as they often were at sea. In 1922, an organisation was set up, initially in Glasgow. Called The Apostleship of the Sea, it set up and ran a number of hostels for the sailors in every major port in Britain. A Catholic foundation, it became known internationally as Stella Maris, or Star of the Sea, a reference to the Virgin Mary who became effectively the patroness for this work to support seafarers. It is for this very reason that our own Parish Church has been given the name Our Lady Star of the Sea, a name it shares with many Catholic churches established in or near sea ports around the world.

When the Apostleship of the Sea was set up, the sailors were assured of good food, clean beds and a programme of events designed to keep them occupied whilst they waited to rejoin their ships. The local parishes took it upon themselves to organise socials and other activities so that the men no longer felt like outcasts. Much of this work was initiated by conscientious Parish Priests, but there was always a team of positive and caring parishioners who tried to make the seafarers feel at home, even though many were very far from the land of their birth. Access to regular Masses was organised on land, priests began to visit the sailors on board ship so that Mass could be said there and arrangements were made for many ships to carry the necessary equipment to enable Mass to be said whilst the ships were on the high seas, as long as a priest were also present.

During the course of the twentieth century, much was to change in the carrying of cargo across the world. With the arrival of container ships, vessels could be unloaded and restocked with new cargo in a matter of hours rather than days. New computerisation and on-board technology resulted in a marked decrease in the numbers of a ship's crew. Many large container ships now carry a crew of only twelve people, with each person working in a particular part of the gigantic ship, so loneliness and a sense of isolation can still be felt. Yet the Apostleship of the Sea continues its work to this day. Whilst sailors may no longer need accommodation and support lasting days, they are still able to use the facilities offered by the Apostleship of the Sea to contact loved ones at home, to stock up on personal items needed on their next voyage or to exchange information and conversation with people engaged in the same work as themselves. Of equal importance are the visits to the Chapel and the pastoral care offered by chaplaincy staff and vistors.

In 1922, the fledgling Apostleship of the Sea presented a copy of its Constitution to the Holy See, through the good offices of the Archbishop of Glasgow, the Most Rev. D. Mackintosh. It obviously made a good impression, because on April 17th 1922 the following Papal Message was sent to the Council.

> The work which your Reverence has just brought to the notice of His Holiness – work of deep spiritual charity which undertakes the religious assistance of seafarers, especially those of the mercantile marine – is such that it cannot be without the Blessing of the Vicar of Jesus Christ and also his August word of approval and encouragement.
>
> With the certain knowledge that so noble an enterprise, ably seconded by the zeal of priestly souls, both secular and regular, will spread more and more along the sea-coasts of the two hemispheres and will gather a most

abundant harvest of salutary fruits, The Holy Father is pleased to invoke on it the choicest grace of heaven and to bless with special paternal affection all those who by their prayers, their offerings or their individual service, contribute to its final success for the greater glory of God and the spread of his Holy Kingdom among souls.

At the time of this Papal Message there were only twelve Institutes for Catholic seafarers in the whole world, but its influence spread as its work became known in ports across the world. Within a short space of time, there were Apostleship of the Sea foundations in Belgium, France, Germany, Holland, Italy, Spain, Canada, South America and the United States. This remarkable growth was to continue in succeeding years.

By 1927, when the first Maritime Congress was held in France there were Sea Apostleships in over 50 ports in fifteen countries, mostly based upon ship visiting by laymen. The number of Catholic Institutes had been doubled. In 1931 Cardinal Bourne presided at a meeting in London of the sea-apostolate organisers of nine countries, where the Apostolatus Maris Internationale Concilium was inaugurated. There were now 150 ports in which the sea apostolate was operating.

When the AMIC Congress met in Hamburg in 1934, there were 54 Institutes and Hostels for Catholic seafarers, and they had a presence in over 300 ports. I6 full-time Chaplains had been employed and a further 200 priests had offered their services to the seafarers. Regular prayers were said for both the seafarers and the apostolate in over 5,000 convents, monasteries and schools. No fewer than 21 Cardinals had given their patronage and blessing to the work of the Apostleship of the Sea. By Christmas 1934 the people involved in the work of the Apostleship or directly affected by it as sailors numbered one hundred thousand. Its headquarters was in South West London, and it was chaired by Vice-Admiral R.A. Hornell D.S.O.

His Eminence Cardinal Fumasoni-Biondi wrote to the Apostleship of the Sea in August 1933:

Hearkening to the cry "Lord save us, lest we perish" which is on the lips of the lowly seafaring people on all the seacoasts, and which so long ago had sounded on the Lake of Genezareth, penetrating into the divine heart of the Master, thus have you, worthy guides of this grand association, inclined your souls to understanding and succouring the grave moral and material needs of the seafarers, ever protecting them by all the means which religion and charity suggest, against the surging waves of evil which overwhelm so many poor souls especially in the great ports. Whilst therefore I congratulate you and the International Council, I most gladly confirm the moral support previously accorded by the Sacred

Congregation …. so that Apostulatus Maris may flourish and may extend also into the missionary countries, under the shining and maternal guidance of Our Lady, Star of the Sea.

Meanwhile, in the Diocese of Brentwood the Apostleship of the Sea had already made its presence felt. In 1927, its representatives asked Bishop Doubleday if he would permit the appointment of a District Secretary of the organisation to co-ordinate the work of those who wished to help Catholic seafarers who visited the Brentwood Diocese, principally Tilbury. There was a conflict of interest here, because the care of Catholic sailors was already the responsibility of S.V.P. Brothers. Bishop Doubleday sought advice from the priest who was already making a name for himself as a conscientious guide and friend to visiting Catholic seafarers, the Tilbury Parish Priest, Father O'Donnell. Father O'Donnell considered the matter carefully before replying to the diocese in June 1927.

Dear Fr. Wilson,

In reference to your letter of 6th inst. and that from Miss Pearce, Southampton, I have carefully thought over the matter and am definitely of the opinion that at the moment it would be very unwise to grant the Apostleship of the Sea permission to appoint a District Secretary for the Brentwood Diocese.

At present, the work for seafarers along the riverside is in the capable hands of S.V.P. Brothers, and I do not think that the addition of another Society would result in greater efficiency; it would almost inevitably bring about friction. As a matter of fact a certain amount of friction already exists between the two Societies, as can be seen from the enclosed documents which you may keep for further reference.

Briefly, it arose out of the efforts of the Apostleship of the Sea to get the General Council S.V.P. at Paris to abandon what is known as the "short" scheme for linking up all the S.V.P. Seaport Conferences throughout the world. We in England were to undertake the linking up of all the British Empire Conferences, and the Paris General Council were to do likewise for all others in the rest of the world.

I might add that about 8 or 10 months ago the S.V.P. made an agreement with the A.S. to the effect that we would enrol at our ports seafaring members for the A.S., and distribute membership cards and badges, but we declined to enrol associate members.

I take it that the proposed appointment of the District Secretary is primarily to enrol associate members throughout the Diocese to gain financial support for the A.S. in Glasgow.

At the moment, it seems best that each Society should confine itself to the Ports where it is established, and that the unorganised Ports should be taken in hand by the first comer.

Yours sincerely,

Fr. P. O'Donnell

In the nicest possible way, it seems that a kind of turf war had opened up between the two organisations, both focused on the needs of Catholic seafarers and each hoping to consolidate the work under its own banner. This was scarcely surprising, given the all-encompassing objectives of the Apostleship of the Sea contained within their Memorandum of Association. These included

a) To co-ordinate all Catholic effort for the spiritual, moral and social welfare of the seafarers of Great Britain or using the Ports of Great Britain, and for those who are dependent on the sea for their livelihood, by all and every means either temporary or permanent.
b) To initiate, carry out, encourage, advertise or otherwise deal with schemes for the spiritual, moral, and social welfare of seafarers and their dependants.
c) To initiate, carry out, encourage, advertise or otherwise deal with schemes for the training of young Catholics who may be desirous of eventually following the sea as a profession.
d) To represent the Catholic seafarers of Great Britain at all Meetings and Conferences of the Apostolatus Maris International Concilium and or any National or International Seafarers Organisation and to apply for and obtain affiliation to the Apostolatus Maris International Concilium or any other International Catholic Seamen's organisation as the Council in General Session or the Executive Committee may think fit.

One of the responsibilities for those who cared for the spiritual needs of the Catholic sailors was the provision of ships' altars to enable Mass to be said by priests during a sea voyage. In 1930 the Apostleship of the Sea became concerned with the way in which these items were handled. There were numerous reports of non-Catholic clergy making use of the altars, and there were occasions when the altars were left in an unsatisfactory condition or had not been locked away securely. Some ship-owners who wished to provide their ships with altars had not liaised with religious authorities to ensure that suitable and safe outfits were provided. The Apostleship of the Sea recommended that all purchases of altars be supervised by a Bishop or Port Chaplain. A card was to be placed with the equipment so that a priest could report any damage or deficiency to the ship's Purser.

In Tilbury, the responsibility of such items was in the hands of the redoubtable Father O'Donnell. In December 1933, he wrote to Bishop Doubleday assuring him of the steps he took personally to ensure that the care of ship's altars in his area was most carefully monitored.

> In reference to your enquiries on my care of the Ships' Altars:
>
> 1. The wine is purchased from Firms approved by me.
> 2. The same applies to the P. & O. Candles. Both the Shipping Firms and the workers are aware of the standard required for Mass candles. If any of the ladies purchase candles at repositories which are not of the required standard they do so without my knowledge and I am making enquiries on this point.
> 3. I do not supply Holy Oil to any of the stocks.
> 4. The consecration of Chalices and Altar Stones is seen to by the Firm supplying them and I bless the other articles – in the case of renewals they are sometimes taken to a nearer Priest.
> 5. Breads are renewed every time the ships return to their home ports and the unused breads are burnt. I have a slip of paper placed in each box bearing the date on which the Breads were supplied, and further, I send Breads direct to certain Cruising Boats that set out on a new Cruise without returning to their "base".
> 6. I inspect the Altars periodically and have a notice in each case requesting priests to write to me if they do not find everything in order.
>
> Finally, my Lord, I humbly suggest that it would be a good thing if the Bishops of England and Wales invited the Port Chaplains of say Liverpool, Southampton and London to draw up a joint report on the provision and care of Ships' Altars and after due deliberation to issue instructions that would make for uniform action in dealing with the Shipping Companies and Firms supplying Altars.

There were two docks lying within the boundaries of the Brentwood Diocese, Tilbury and the Royal Docks. Father O'Donnell wrote to Bishop Doubleday in 1933.

> My Lord Bishop,
>
> I have at last been authorised by the P. & O. Marine Superintendent, whom I interviewed in London last week, to take over the care of the portable altars on their Boats. I am making local arrangements at Tilbury and George V Docks for the regular tending of the cases.

Father O'Donnell understood that the Goanese crewmen who visited the Tilbury Parish so frequently should be encouraged and one aspect of this was to find priests with whom these seafarers could more easily identify.

One such was Father Pinto from Ceylon. In December 1933, Fr. O'Donnell asked Bishop Doubleday to help with this young man's work.

> My Lord Bishop,
>
> Father Pinto has come and gone and left a good impression behind him. He is anxious to work amongst the Goanese seamen at the Port of London and further afield, if it can be arranged. There is plenty of scope for his activities and I am confident that he will do much good. He had three and a half hours Confessions of Goans in preparation for the Feast of St. Fr. Xavier and preached a nice simple sermon, partly in English, partly in Konkanim on Sunday evening.
>
> He speaks English better than his own dialect as he has spent most of his life in Ceylon. He is aged 24 and is destined to become a Professor at his Diocesan Seminary in Columbo after receiving his B.Sc. degree at London University. He expects to be over here for at least three years.
>
> I hope your Lordship can see your way to giving him permanent faculties at the Port of London. I propose establishing a fund from the regular contributions of the Seamen from which would come his expenses and say a stipend of ten shillings per visit.
>
> Yours respectfully

There was certainly a considerable need for Fr. Pinto's services. That same month three P. & O. ships docked in Tilbury and that meant that 400 Goan seafarers were in dock. Most of them would be looking for Confession and in their own language, a service that Fr. Pinto was uniquely able to provide.

By 1931 the Apostleship of the Sea wished to take charge of all matters relating to church services on board ship. One of the issues was the arrangement for priests to be able to supervise any Sisters who were making the same journey. Sometimes, as many as eight priests would be on a ship bound for America whilst another ship sailing from the same port on the same day to the same destination would have eight or ten Sisters and many young people but no priest at all. Priests crossing the Atlantic from Liverpool were asked to register details of their sailing with a representative of the Apostleship of the Sea so that Sisterhoods could be informed about which ships would have facilities for Holy Mass.

The pressing need was for a Port Chaplain, to take overall responsibility for the support offered to the seafarers who visited the Port of London.

This point was made by Arthur Gannon, the Organising Secretary of the AOS, in a letter to Bishop Doubleday in April 1936.

> Admiral Hornell has asked me to convey his thanks to Your Lordship for the appointments given us to meet you on Holy Saturday, and his regrets that circumstances prevented us from meeting you then, as explained in my communication with your Secretary. I have informed the Admiral of your further letter of April 8th and he has instructed me to outline the London Port Chaplain project in a letter to Your Lordship, and to inform you that we will be ready to keep any appointment which you may suggest, to discuss this project in greater detail.
>
> The need for a whole-time Port Chaplain is, we believe, generally recognised. London is the world's greatest port; every day, according to the latest returns, approx. 1,200 vessels enter and leave the port. Exact statistics are not available as to the proportion of Catholic seafarers on these ships, but it is certain that on any given day there are over 1,000 Catholic seamen in the port.
>
> A very small proportion of our seafarers who visit London are in effective contact with the Church. The Catholic Seamen's Home is the only fully-organised establishment we have (there are 30 Institutes, Homes etc. in London organised for seamen by non-Catholics) and the absence of a Port Chaplain lessens the value of that establishment and of the lay ship-visitors' work. There are at least ten Protestant clergymen who are devoting their ministry exclusively, in London. At Tilbury and Wapping the seamen have the most effective contacts of all, through the ministration of the Hon. Port Chaplains, Father O'Donnell and Father Bentley.
>
> Several ports, with smaller transient Catholic seafaring personnel than London, have whole-time Port Chaplains, e.g. Antwerp, Amsterdam, Bremerhaven, Le Havre, Marseilles, Liverpool, Gdynia, Rosario, Southampton and at other ports such as New York, Buenos Aires etc. Chaplains have been appointed who devote the greater part of their time to sailors. This latter development points to what we judge to be the vital factor in this matter.
>
> The Catholic Action programme of Apostolatus Maris cannot be carried out amongst the seafarers in London – a "key" port as regards that programme for the world – without the direction and help of a Port Chaplain. The lack of a Port Chaplain in the world's chief port militates against the efforts of Port Chaplains in other ports. The sailors themselves have asked us to try and get a Chaplain for them in London.
>
> The problem of organising the seafarers as Catholic Actionists ("The apostles of the seamen must be the seamen themselves" the Holy Father has recently said to our co-workers in France) is extremely difficult and can be solved, we believe, only by having Port Chaplains to direct the

sailors and their lay-helpers, at ports where seamen are found in the greatest numbers. London is vital in this respect.

This need is so great that we do not doubt but that the financial and other means of meeting it will be forthcoming. We have had a promise of a Port Chaplain's stipend in London, for two years, from Her Grace the Duchess of Norfolk. This offer was made some six years ago and Her Grace, when this matter was recalled recently, expressed willingness to proceed, when definite arrangement had been made.

Admiral Hornell has instructed me to inform Your Lordship that, if called upon, we will create organisation for covering the financial side of this project and do all that lies in our power otherwise, in support of this plan.

I have the honour to remain,

Your Lordship's devoted servant,

Arthur Gannon

Despite the best efforts of the Apostleship of the Sea, there were numerous reports in the nineteen thirties of Altar Breads so sour that the congregation onboard ship refused to come to Holy Communion. This led to a concerted effort from the Apostleship of the Sea to monitor the quality of the Mass requisites placed on board ships. The Brentwood Diocesan Branch of the Apostleship reported on their work in the nineteen thirties. Apart from the detail of what exactly comprises an Altar case, the report demonstrates the care that was taken at every stage to ensure that all contents were of the highest standard and the ways in which 'consumables' were readily refurbished.

<u>Brentwood Diocesan Branch</u>
<u>Altar Case Work</u>

This work is undertaken by members from Ilford, Stratford and Tilbury sections.

<u>DOCKS VISITED</u> Surrey Commercial, King George V and Tilbury

<u>LINES</u> Cunard, P. & O. and Orient

These companies send lists of sailings to the workers.

<u>P. & O. Ships with altars</u> S.S. Ballarat, Barradine, Balranald, Barrabool, Mooltan, Maloja, Narkunda, Strathnaver, Strathaird, Moldavia, Mongolia, Cathay.

Cunard liners with altars S.S. Samaria, Carinthia, Franconia, Alaunia, Ascania, Aurania, Ausania

There are two Altar cases on most steamers.

CONTENTS OF ALTAR CASES

2 sets of reversible vestments, Alb, girdle, five purificators, burse, stole, chalice veil, 4 amices, 1 corporal, 4 finger towels, 3 altar cloths, cruets and dish, 2 sconces, supply of candles, 1 pyx, 1 bell, 1 chalice and paten, 1 crucifix, 1 missal and stand, 1 altar stone, oil stock, Holy water bottle and altar breads. Supplied by the company.

ALTAR BREADS (Outward Journey)

These are supplied by the workers, who obtain them from Washburne's. They last about one month, as they are packed in air-tight tins.

ALTAR BREADS (Return Journey)

Nuns come on board on the other side (Sydney, New York etc.) or the cases are sent ashore to convents or repositories. Workers report that the Altar breads are always in excellent condition when ships arrive home. Tilbury workers take the surplus to Fr. O'Donnell. Some priests carry their own Altar breads.

WINE This is supplied by the company.

CANDLES The workers obtain these from their local repositories or from Farris. They buy 3 lbs at a time, and usually send out 6 or 8 large ones, as being steadier. The P. & O. Company supply their own candles.

Workers all report that the cases are perfectly tidy and in order when they open them. They visit the ships whenever one is in dock, usually about once a week. All the workers go aboard, except in the case of the Orient liners at Tilbury, where the cases are brought ashore to the Orient office in Tilbury and the workers go there.

Workers use special gloves when handling chalice and paten.

HOLY WATER Fresh water provided for each journey.

PURIFICATORS These are washed by the Franciscan Fathers at Stratford, by the assistant priests at Ilford, and by Fr. O'Donnell at Tilbury. Afterwards carefully washed again and ironed by the workers.

LINEN This is made, renewed and repaired by the workers. They usually wash it also, except the albs, which go to laundries.

BRASS This is cleaned by the workers.

Workers report that everything is quite satisfactory when cases are opened; they are kept locked, and the purser keeps the keys in his safe. The chalices are weighted, in order to be steadier.

Whilst the Apostleship of the Sea kept a careful eye on the Ships' Altars, Bishop Doubleday was keen to offer his own instructions and advice regarding onboard Mass services.

I should be obliged if you would publish this information.

I am constantly receiving enquiries from Priests in Great Britain and Eire about facilities for Mass on board ships sailing from the Port of London and I would like all interested to know that the following companies provide portable Altar outfits on their vessels: The Blue Star Line Ltd., Canadian Pacific Steamships Ltd. (cruises only), The Cunard White Star Ltd., Ellerman and Bucknall Steamship Co. Ltd., N.Y.K. Line (Nippon Yusen Kaisha), The Orient Line, The Peninsular and Oriental Steam Navigation Co. (P. & O.), The Union-Castle Mail Steamship Company Ltd.

In the matter of equipment, these Altars are not to be compared with those in our Churches, with their abundance and variety of sacred vessel and vestment, but they are reasonably adequate for their purpose. A goodly supply of wine, candles and fresh breads is available but it is not possible to gauge the needs of any voyage and so Priests are advised to replenish supplies at ports of call, whenever necessary and possible. Slips or soutanes are not included in the outfit.

Permission to say Mass on board should be sought from the Lord Bishop of Brentwood, through the Rev. Secretary, Bishop's House, Brentwood, Essex.

I am sometimes asked what the Laity could do on a Sunday morning, in the way of a public service, in the absence of a Priest. I suggest that they approach the ever courteous and helpful Purser who would usually be prepared to put a public room at their disposal, at an hour convenient to the general life aboard. He would publish the time on the notice board, when Catholics could meet and have, say, the Rosary, Litany, Hymn etc.

During the nineteen thirties, the Depression led to a marked decline in world trade. Merchant seamen were badly affected, as unemployment grew steadily. The Apostleship of the Sea found that it was doing ever more to support these men, yet economic conditions made it difficult for the organisation to raise money for their work. In the midst of this crisis, the AOS wrote to Bishop Doubleday in February 1935, to request help.

My Lord Bishop,

The late Cardinal Bourne informed me that the work and status of the Apostleship of the Sea would be considered at the forthcoming Low Week Meeting of the Hierarchy. Since his Eminence's lamented death I have been requested by the Vicar Capitular to postpone any public appeal until after that meeting. It therefore is my duty to give your Lordship, very briefly, certain facts which may possibly have escaped notice and are now assuming great importance in the sphere of Catholic Action.

1. This is the only Catholic Society of International status which has its headquarters in this country.
2. The mandate received from the Holy Father, and the approbation received from the Hierarchies in all maritime countries and British Dominions, conclusively indicate the necessity and importance of this work.
3. The Apostleship of the Sea entered into a new era of world-wide activity consequent upon the decision reached at the AMIC Congress at Hamburg, under the Presidency of the Archbishop of Edinburgh and His Excellency the Bishop of Osnabrueck, when it was determined to consolidate and expand the work throughout the world.

I have pleasure in forwarding copies of two documents to Your Lordship; that from Fr. Martindale will be, I think, of great interest to you because he touches upon several points which are of supreme importance. The first of them is the international character of the work. Secondly, Fr. Martindale is absolutely right when he stresses the importance of ship-visiting, and of getting the seamen, in no matter what condition, into a Catholic Institute or Hostel, thus keeping them out of the boarding-houses and brothels which are such a terrible menace to the sailor's life. Third and not least: there is the absolute necessity of a properly equipped Central Office whereby vital information as to ports of call and numbers of Catholics on board ships etc. may be sent in advance to the various Sea Apostolate Centres.

It is literally and absolutely true that though the organisation to do all this – and the many other AMIC tasks – exists and is daily being perfected, yet it is lamentably held up through lack of knowledge of the immense importance of our work. This lack of knowledge results in a loss of financial support.

Our President the Archbishop of Glasgow has taken steps to counteract these handicaps by arranging for an annual collection in all the churches in his Archdiocese, in aid of the AMIC.

Foreign countries are also straining every nerve to support the AMIC, but for political and other reasons it will be many years before they can send us any substantial help.

I hope that before the Low Week Meeting the AMIC "QUARTERLY BULLETIN" will be in Your Lordship's hands; that will give you the annual Statement of Accounts and other information.

In conclusion we cannot be content until there is an Honorary Chaplain and ship-visiting organisation in all the principal ports of the world. Our care is and must be chiefly for the visiting of seamen in whatever strange port they happen to find themselves.

Apostolatus Maris is a brotherhood for all who wish to work for seafarers, our chief concern being the seafarer who is away from home. Other anxieties exist – the unemployed seafarers – but these are, or should be, in touch with their own parish priests and come within the scope of charitable organisations whose primary obligation is the amelioration of the lot of the destitute. Such organisations, working for seafarers, should ipso facto be enrolled under the Sea Apostolate banner.

Respectfully asking for Your Lordship's blessing on this work,

I have the honour to remain

Your Lordship's devoted servant

Vice-Admiral R.A. Hornell, Chairman.

The reference to Father Martindale was the consequence of a report he issued on his visits to various ships travelling across the oceans of the world. It gives a detailed account of the experience both of a conscientious priest and the crews he served under the auspices of the Apostleship of the Sea and a part of the report is therefore included here.

Notes on recent voyages; Buenos Aires – Melbourne – London

S.S. "Highland Brigade", London – Buenos Aires. Not only were the officers very friendly and forthcoming, but the full equipment for Mass was provided. A room for Mass was spontaneously offered and hardly had the Purser addressed me as Father Martindale than a young man standing near asked the time and place of Mass. The presence of the Cardinal Patriarch of Lisbon on board proved most edifying; two non-Catholic seamen said in almost the same words : "If Jesus Christ was to come on this ship, He couldn't be no different from yon Cardinal". He (the Cardinal) and his friends could not talk English so they could not actively do anything. He said several times most emphatically that he knew of no one doing this work in Portugal and even asked me to come there and discuss it and any other such question. Cardinal Leme at Rio de Janeiro I could see for only a few minutes, but he was no less clear about the necessity. On this ship was a young 2nd Mate going to the Falkland Islands; he came to the Sacraments and was keen to know details of the AMIC. All the seamen – so far as I know – came to Mass twice at 4.30; some got up an hour or even two before they needed; all fasted, even after their engine-room watch – this held good throughout. They went to Confession on deck. Lest I seem even remotely to infringe upon the "secret", I will say that on one of the five ships I was on, every man except two, I think, was a "return" – 2 years often; 6, 13, 20. None made difficulties or very few. The interesting fact was that not only did the Commander make me explain at length what a Eucharistic Congress was, but I wrote out – clearly I hope – an account of the Catholic Eucharistic doctrine, of what a Congress was, and of the social and other good effects it might be likely to have. This was pinned up in the recreation rooms and they sent me a message of surprised thanks for the trouble taken.

S.S. "Rangitane": Panama to Wellington. Here I had good luck; several of the men – hardly any Catholics amongst them – had been on the "Rotorua" 6 years ago; great reunions, therefore, and the Chief Steward gave me a simply huge cabin on the strength of it. I should have said that on the "Highland Brigade", a Steward asked me to arrange for his instruction. On the "Rangitane" my bath-steward was a Catholic, and after finding all the Catholics he knew, kept finding further ones, amongst whom two were specially important. One was quite uninstructed, wishing to be taught and (I think) make his First Communion; the other had given up his Faith but was longing to get it back. He has written me 6 large pages, misspelt but really profound stuff, one sentence being that he thinks that he has not lost his Faith in God but in His followers … of course there is a lot too about miracles, evolution, the Bible and Church and ignorance – and above all, what they keep coming back to: that as from childhood they have received Religion in terms of <u>fear</u>. "God will punish you if you don't." I observe that it is terribly rare for them to have got their Religion in terms of <u>Christ</u>. "God forbids, is pleased, punishes" etc., "the Church says" … but their ignorance of Our Lord's life or meaning is as complete almost always, as that of any Protestant. But on the "Rangitane" too all the men I knew by the time we had Mass went to the Sacraments.

S.S. "Aorangi": Auckland to Sydney. Only 4 days but some very happy Confessions and one Steward told me that by an amazing chance he, alone of his family, had not made his First Communion. Meanwhile a deckboy (!) had given him so much information that I felt justified after 4 instructions in giving it to him, especially as it was his confession that was really sticking in his throat. He asked me to hunt up his mother in Port Melbourne – "It will make her happy" – I did – and found a brother who, well, had never 'been' since his First Communion. I shrove him and he went next Sunday and wrote that things were going better all round already.

S.S. "Cathay": Adelaide to Perth. Goan seamen. Mass for them early on St. Thomas' day and Sunday; night-prayers. To have a priest on board who did not assist at their night-prayers, heat or no heat, would almost shake their faith in him. I forget other details of this.

S.S. "Orama": Perth to Tilbury. Officers, as usual, excellent (all these ships were equipped with Mass furniture). Lay Catholic passengers not bad – especially a dozen Italians who came better to daily Mass than to Sunday – but still. Crew excellent in all departments. 4 sailors; several stewards and cooks; especially the oilers etc. when I first saw them in their peak they said reproachfully "We thought you was going to give us Mass last Sunday". I said "Next Sunday, last was for the stewards." (Stewards like 5.30, oilers etc. rather earlier). On the last night I went down to say goodbye, and they said "X left word that he wanted to see you." I said "He's asleep." " He said for us to wake him." In he came in singlet and shirt. "When can I go to Confession tomorrow?" "You can't. Port. Too much noise etc." So then and there he went, on the iron floor, round the corner of the L-shaped cabin. So did another. The rest talked loud so as not to hear.

Institutes: Buenos Aires, doubled in size: it includes a shooting gallery – a place where men who are drunk can sit and sleep it off; else they'd do so in some brothel. It is the greatest mistake to keep our Seamen's Institutes for the respectable … I went there constantly and met Germans, Italians, Belgians, French, Irish, English, Argentines and Poles. Half the "Highland Brigade" were there, partly in consequence of my explaining the Congress. (Fr. Martindale visited the new Institutes at Wellington and Melbourne; had a few moments only at Sydney and Adelaide Institutes).

Comments: I needn't dwell on the unique chance of getting at men, probably long away from the Sacraments, provided by their being on a ship and only too grateful for being visited. Nor on the special position of young boys aged 15-17: impossibility of the Sacraments or the Mass or instruction; total lack of privacy and association with older men of whom a large percentage take immorality for granted and talk much more than they do. But the boy can't judge that. Wrong to say "They can go to their duties on shore." Practically impossible in a foreign port unless good provision and visiting be ensured; they get about 6 weeks in the year at home. Sea Work ought to be nationally co-ordinated in the first place, as in Australia, one port in touch with every other port and with home parishes via the parish priest; he must be able to write to one address, not to a dozen ports. Societies doing Sea Work should be co-ordinated. Thus a local S.V.P., one of the Societies which does much Sea Work, may well be otherwise overworked and not contain the right men for this work, though another society might. Supreme necessity of Sea Work being internationally co-ordinated: most of the seamen on our shores are not English and of these, few are in their native ports …. who can be written to by a Warwickshire priest, save an HQ? - which can easily inform a national HQ of seamen due in S.S. ---.

> Finally, the majority of seamen are not English, and their national HQ must be in touch directly with International HQ; 90% of postage is saved in this way by not looking further. I could write on many other points but I add only this – no local port can afford to produce that essential – a polyglot Prayer Book and system for making and hearing Confessions in polyglot; what exists is not adequate, and as to confessional questions – far too long.

There is something elemental in this account. Here is a priest devoting his life to the spiritual needs of Catholics across the world. In all sorts of conditions, climates and environments, a priest is reaching out to support people who are often complete strangers but who share a need for the Sacraments. In all the talking and planning that surrounds the societies which organise the support of seafarers, here is the actual work.

Father Martindale's plea for some kind of co-ordination of Sea Work found a response in the appointment of a Chaplain to the London docks in 1937, Reverend William Ruhman. Although his health prevented him from playing as full a part as he would have wished, the precedent had been set for a Chaplain to supervise the support to seafarers in the docks on the River Thames, including Tilbury.

During the years of the Second World War, the Apostleship of the Sea continued its work as well as it could, but there is little written evidence of the support it gave. There can be little doubt, however, that the dangers to merchant shipping created by the U-boats would have increased the tensions felt by those who travelled to these shores.

After the War, a Sea Sunday was appointed every year by the Archbishops and Bishops, when a sermon about the precarious lives of seafarers would usually be preached and a collection made for the benefit of the Apostleship of the Sea. They now provided support for nearly one million Catholic seafarers, over half of all the seafarers in the world.

It was often the case that even when sailors made landfall they did not find it easy to attend local Masses. Father Byrne followed the excellent example of his predecessor, Canon O'Donnell, in ministering to seafarers. Here is a letter dated February 1955 in which Father Byrne sought permission to say Mass on board ship.

> Dear Rev. Father,
>
> When I visited S.S. Strathnaver today, the Goanese Chief Pantry Man asked if I could say Mass on the ship on Sunday evening, 6th Feb. for 164 Goanese on board, the majority of whom cannot come here on

Sunday morning for Mass. S.S. Himalayas comes in tomorrow with 180 Goanese on board. Many of these cannot come out on Sunday morning and so would welcome the opportunity of attending Mass on S.S. Strathnaver.

Would you please ask His Lordship to grant me or my curate permission to offer evening Mass on S.S. Strathnaver on Sunday evening, also for Goanese on other liners in like circumstances. I shall have two Masses as usual on Sunday morning.

With kind regards

In 1956 a diocesan report on the Port of London Chaplaincy illustrated the complexities of organising support for seafarers in London, where a single co-ordinating Chaplain was preferred but no fewer than three dioceses had part of the London docks within their boundaries. The report outlined the geographic details of the Port of London docks and the religious support for seafarers before giving a historical account of the Catholic Chaplaincy.

<u>The Port</u>

The Port of London includes the whole of the tidal basin of the River Thames extending from just below Teddington Lock to beyond Southend Pier, a distance of nearly 70 miles. It includes five large dock systems on the banks of the Thames which are named as follows:

1.
London and St. Katherine Docks (1 & 2 – 664 acres; 12.5 miles of quays; Westminster Diocese)
2.
East and West India Millwall Docks
3.
Surrey Commercial Docks (376 acres; 8.75 miles of quays; Southwark Diocese)
4.
Royal Group of Docks (4 & 5 – 1,777 acres; 16.75 miles of quays; Brentwood Diocese)
5.
Tilbury Docks

In addition to these dock systems, there are miles of wharves and reaches of the river used for moorings. (There is a plan to build a large dock in the Beckton area of East Ham, thus extending the Royal Group still further.)

The Religious provision for seamen

In the Port of London there are two Church of England organisations for seamen: The Missions to Seamen (Flying Angel), and the St. Andrew's Waterside Mission. There are also two non-Conformist bodies, the Seamen's Christian Friends Society and the Wesleyan Mission. There is a Catholic Seamen's Home in Custom House which provides sleeping space for about 40 men (if some sleep on the floor).

The Catholic Chaplaincy

In the last 36 years there have been several attempts to provide a Chaplain to the Catholic sailors who pass through the Port of London. This has always come to nothing because the Port of London is divided in three dioceses and the provision of a chaplain by one diocese cannot provide for the whole Port unless there is united action. It will be seen that about one half of the Port lies within the diocese of Brentwood.

Another difficulty which has arisen in this matter is the clash of Societies. In 1920 the S.V.P. was starting to visit the ships, but at the same time the newly-founded Apostleship of the Sea was starting the same work; eventually the S.V.P. agreed to leave this work entirely to the Apostleship of the Sea. The S.V.P. however continue to own and run the home that was built for the benefit of seamen who had nowhere to go between their voyages.

In 1927 the parish priest of Tilbury (Father O'Donnell – now Canon) was asked by Bishop Doubleday to be Port Chaplain, but this was only for part of the Port in Brentwood diocese, and moreover Father O'Donnell was not allowed to visit ships in other parishes without informing the parish priest of that place. His own duties as parish priest and the limitations imposed on the appointment made it impossible for him to devote the time necessary to the work.

In 1931 the Duchess of Norfolk offered to provide the stipend if a full-time Port Chaplain were appointed. This offer was not taken up. In April 1936 the Duchess of Norfolk again offered the money to the Apostleship of the Sea and the AOS wrote to Bishop Doubleday stating the need for a Chaplain and asking for his support. Bishop Doubleday agreed to support any scheme that had the approval of the Cardinal.

In January 1937 the Cardinal appointed Father William Ruhman, a Westminster priest, as Port Chaplain, and gave him faculties to hear confessions on board ship only. In 1937, premises for a Catholic Seamen's Institute were rented in Shadwell. In 1938 it is reported that Fr. Ruhman was sick and wished to be released. The Cardinal (Hinsley) asked Bishop Doubleday to release Father George Steadman (a Brentwood priest) for the work, but this apparently came to nothing because in 1939 Father Ruhman was still Port Chaplain. He wrote to Bishop Doubleday saying that he hoped to be able to spend more time at the Seamen's home in Custom House, which was dying out because of the wonderful new Flying Angel that had been built next door to it.

I do not know what happened to this Port Chaplaincy; it may have ceased to exist during the war.

In 1947 a Father John R. Fox passed through London on his way to India and Father More O'Ferrall proposed to Bishop Doubleday that he be appointed as Port Chaplain. However Father Fox went out to India and later to Singapore and nothing was done.

The Apostleship of the Sea had started as a diocesan organisation in Glasgow, in 1920; but by 1945 it was worldwide and the Hierarchy appointed a National Secretary and an office was opened in the West End of London. In 1949 there was an International Congress of the Apostleship of the Sea held in Rome, and it was decided that an International Catholic Organisation could not be based in Glasgow, but would have to be centred in Rome. Accordingly the Apostolatus Maris was established as an Opus Pontificium on the same terms as the work for exiles and for emigrants, and placed under the supervision of the Sacred Consistorial Congregation which established a special section for it. The organisation envisaged by the Holy See was that there should be a "Director" of the Apostolatus with a team of Chaplains under him; the Director should be proposed by the Hierarchy and the Chaplains by the Ordinaries of the various ports in the country. It seems that the National Secretary of the Apostolatus Maris in England (Father More O'Ferrall) is the "Director" for England, and he has under him as Chaplains the Chaplains at Newcastle, Liverpool, Middlesborough, Hull etc. The Chaplains at these ports are priests of the local diocese, but they get their special faculties from the Consistorial.

In April 1955 Father More O'Ferrall sent us two documents by which the parish priest of Custom House (Father Moore) and of Tilbury (Father Byrne) were given the special faculties of Port Chaplains, but of course they remained parish priests with their prime duty to their own parish, and with no authority outside those sections of the Port which lay within their parishes.

In May 1955 Father John R. Fox returned home from Singapore, ostensibly for a visit to his Abbey. However he offered himself to Bishop Beck for work as Port Chaplain to the Port of London. Bishop Beck was impressed by his capabilities and his enthusiasm and he wrote to the Cardinal asking for him to be approved as Chaplain to the Port of London. The correspondence will show that Bishop Beck and the Cardinal were talking at cross-purposes: that Bishop Beck thought that Father Fox was going to be Chaplain to the whole Port including those parts in Westminster and Southwark (which Father Fox also thought, as witness his articles in *The Tablet* and elsewhere), whereas the Cardinal thought he was to be Chaplain only for the section of the docks which lay in Brentwood diocese.

This uncertainty led to a flurry of letters in 1956, involving the Cardinal, Bishop Beck, Father More O'Ferrall and Father Fox. The position of which priest held responsibility as Port Chaplain for which part of the Port of London was not successfully clarified, and after some disagreements with colleagues and with the S.V.P. which ran the Seamen's Home where he was living, Father Fox was eventually recalled by his Abbey, the Abbey of St-Maurice The problem of having three dioceses each containing a section of the Port of London remained something of a problem.

The diocese continued to support the work of the Apostleship of the Sea over the years. An annual collection was held and the money sent to Anchor House in Canning Town, where activities were co-ordinated. Anchor House provided temporary accommodation for seafarers when in port and longer-term accommodation for about twenty sailors, a similar facility to that offered by our own Stella Maris hostel in Dock Road. As the need for this facility declined, Bishop McMahon was concerned about the viability of Anchor House. Rooms were already being offered to migrant workers during the week, with most of them returning home at weekends. This led Bishop McMahon to consider a widening of the charity's remit, to include some of the homeless and destitute whose presence was becoming ever more evident on London streets. The AOS would continue to provide short and longer term accommodation to seafarers, but those not connected to the sea might also find shelter.

Part of the problem, of course, was that times were changing, and the provision of accommodation for seafarers was no longer a pressing matter. The same was true in Tilbury Docks, where the Stella Maris Club had long been offering accommodation and spiritual, social and welfare support. The Port Chaplain for the London Docks and National Director for the Apostleship of the Sea, Father John Maguire, acknowledged the changing scene in a letter addressed to Bishop Thomas in April 1992.

> Dear Bishop McMahon,
>
> I am writing to you about the current situation and future plans regarding the work of the Apostleship of the Sea in the Port of Tilbury, which also embraces the oil terminals of Mobil and Shellhaven.
>
> Historically, the A.O.S. has focused its apostolate and channelled its resources on the establishment of Residential Centres. They provided a place of welcome for seafarers whilst in port and accommodation for those seafarers in transit, or in between trips. Also, they provided a home for British seafarers who did not have any family roots. However, the number

of British seafarers requiring this type of accommodation has declined steadily over the past few years. Nowadays, the British seafarer tends to come from a more stable family background and does not avail himself of the facilities offered by residential clubs in the same way.

With the advent of the Flag of Convenience the majority of shipowners have opted to employ crews from developing countries. These crews are employed at lower rates of pay and must sign contracts of at least 10 months. Many of these crews are victims of exploitation and turn to us for help. Thus our centre continues to be a place of welcome for seafarers visiting the Port of Tilbury. However, the need for accommodation is receding quickly.

Our ministry continues to be one that is deeply appreciated by seafarers. The Catholic seafarers are delighted to have access to the Sacraments. It is not uncommon for crews to go 6 / 7 months without the Eucharist. Without our presence in their midst, encouraging them to pray, to live out their Faith on board ship, their Faith would weaken to the extent that it would be very anonymous. Also, our presence is appreciated by other Christian denominations whom we also encourage to pray and live out their Faith. Ship-visiting also gives us the opportunity to dialogue with other religions such as Hinduism, Islam, Buddhism.

In order to maintain the Centre as a place of welcome for seafarers, Residential Clubs, such as Stella Maris Tilbury, have diversified, opening their doors to non-seafarers. In this way the facilities are maintained for seafarers visiting the port. However, there is a price to pay. It means that resources are used to run a hotel for people who have no connection with the sea. The Apostleship of the Sea was founded to care for the material and spiritual welfare of seafarers. This can not be done in an effective way if resources and manpower are being deployed to run a hotel for those who have nothing to do with the sea.

In the Port of Tilbury, the ever growing number of Shipping Movements warrants the presence of facilities that only the Apostleship of the Sea can provide. To ensure that the Spiritual and Material needs of seafarers are ministered to we propose, after much reflection, that a site near to the existing building be purchased and planning permission obtained to build a non-residential centre that will adequately cater for the needs of seafarers whilst in port. To proceed along these lines it will be necessary to sell the existing building. Monies raised from the sale would finance the proposed plans.

We could bury our heads in the sand, continue to operate at a loss and pretend that everything is and will continue to be all right. However, the present economic climate would soon drain away our resources and we would be faced with a closure within a very short time. To avoid such a situation developing I would ask you, as a trustee, to support our proposals so that our presence can continue to be very effective in this part of the River Thames. Also, I would ask you to support our sense of stewardship

> which is asking that we use our resources wisely so that the Spiritual and Material needs of seafarers can be met in the Port of Tilbury.

Bishop Thomas saw these proposals as 'very radical' and wished to consult with Bishop Kevin O'Connor, the Episcopal Adviser to the Apostleship of the Sea. Later that month a meeting was arranged with the Trustees of the Stella Maris Club, Cardinal Hume, Archbishop Bowen, Bishop Thomas Mcmahon and Bishop O'Connor to discuss the options for the future of the A.O.S. in Tilbury. The Stella Maris Club was to be closed down and it was agreed that the A.O.S. National Director should be allowed to look into the possibility of re-siting the Club in smaller premises, a process that could be implemented over a few years. All three dioceses covering the Port of London would be kept informed, as would the Trustees of the Stella Maris Club. Subsequently, a plot of land for the new building was purchased for £100,000. But this plan came to nothing. The changes that were already taking place in the world of merchant shipping were to have a bearing on all of these proposals. The advent of containerisation meant that sea cargoes could be unloaded and loaded in a matter of hours rather than days and the need for sailors to find clean and safe shore accommodation had been removed at a stroke.

No further building of shore-based accommodation for seafarers was carried out at Tilbury, and support services were set up port-side. These were to concentrate on communication channels, so that the sailors could contact their loved ones. Initially involving the provision of telephone lines, the support moved on to internet services and more modern technologies. Seafarers are still visited on board ship by our Parish Priest and some of the parishioners, although the volume of work is somewhat reduced. Many parishioners still contribute regularly with the knitting of hats, scarves and other warm clothing, and by placing items in a box left in the church specifically for the needs of the sailors. The annual Sea Sunday has a particular resonance in a parish which contains Tilbury Docks. Whilst Stella Maris no longer exists as a haven for seafarers, it is nevertheless part of the proud history of an area which owes its existence and prosperity to the merchant fleets of the world.

Wojciech Holub : Port Chaplain for Tilbury and Thames

The work of the Apostleship of the Sea continues today. In 2013, Wojciech Holub from Gdansk in Poland was appointed as the new Port Chaplain for Tilbury and Thames. In an article on the Apostleship of the Sea website he commented on his work.

> I usually get requests for crucifixes and Tagalog bibles by Filipino seafarers and other day-to day things like telephone cards as well as arranging for Mass to be celebrated. Ship visiting is a very important part of AOS' work. I find it a real joy meeting and listening to the experiences of the crew and try to spend as much time as I can onboard.
>
> It is sad that despite the age of technology, some crew still cannot get internet access on board their vessels. Also, no matter how large ships have become, seafarers are still subject to the perils of the sea and I can

> see how much respect they have for the sea and the forces of nature. Our work as port chaplains and ship visitors has become more important than ever as shipping becomes more globalised and automated. It can be hard work but I find it rewarding.

Over the years, the Apostleship of the Sea has played a major part in the life of the Parish of Our Lady Star of the Sea. Over forty years ago, the Stella Maris centre for seamen was transformed into a major centre for seafarers, with its own accommodation for the sailors, regular dances, a bar and cafe and a spacious living area. And, of course, its own chapel. In the place of the Stella Maris centre there is now a block of flats. This building occupies the same footprint as did Stella Maris, so an idea can be gained as to the size and significance of the original project by looking at the block of flats on Dock Road, just along from the Parish Church itself. Perhaps the best way to gain an understanding of the life of Stella Maris is to listen to a parishioner who lived across the road and who was just a young girl when the new building was constructed.

Teresa Beadle (nee Farr)

My dad, Bill Farr, was the Sacristan of Our Lady Star of the Sea for a very long time, and when he stood down his daughter, Dorothy, took over. He was a convert to Catholicism and he wrote to my mother during the war on behalf of 'a friend' who wanted to know about the Catholic faith. When he came back home he took instruction from Canon Byrne and didn't tell her until the course was completed. As well as carrying out the duties of Sacristan, my father used to visit parishioners in Orsett Hospital, often walking there and back in his retirement years. My mum, Dorothy, was a member of the Legion of Mary which she helped to start with the Sisters and also the Catholic Women's League. Our Legion of Mary has had 2,365 meetings to date. There is a meeting every week and I don't think we have ever missed a week since it was founded. My sister, another Dorothy, was a founder member of the Junior Legion of Mary about fifty years ago.

When I was a young girl I was so proud that Tilbury Docks was the biggest port in the UK and possibly the world. We used to live across the road from what was the old Seamen's Mission. One day, I saw a priest painting the old building. The priest was Father Heekin and he had come over from Anchor House in East London to start up a Catholic Seamen's Mission. It was a single storey building with just one room above, Father Heekin's flat. I got chatting to him and then introduced him to my family. My sister, Dorothy, would end up running the bar for him with my parents helping out in the evening. Father Heekin was an Irishman and was full of Irish jokes. I worked in the shop there and would often cook his lunches for him. Mum would also send meals from over the road to keep him going. Father Heekin would pick up the seafarers from the docks and arrange for some women to come over for a dance, local girls at first but then nurses from the hospitals. It was all very proper, with Father Heekin supervising everything most carefully. There was no canoodling, and Father would vet any young man who walked you home. The same was true of any non-seamen who came into Stella Maris. Father Heekin was most keen to ensure that those people who were allowed to enter the building were known either by him or by the volunteers who worked there.

I loved working in the shop and the snack bar. But there was soon to be a new Stella Maris round about 1970, a really big building of three or four storeys, with rooms the seafarers could sleep in overnight. There was a chapel, a television room, a games room, a bar, a lounge, a ballroom, a kitchen and restaurant, and it all looked very posh to us. There were even lifts installed. I remember how excited we all were when we saw the plans. Quite a few parishioners helped out in the new building, although all of the work was on a voluntary basis. Father Heekin eventually found a full-time assistant and she was paid, but she was the only one.

Most of the sailors would stay for about five days while their ships were unloaded and reloaded, but some stayed longer. There were seafarers who were sick and even retired seafarers who stayed at Stella Maris. I knew about the Goanese seamen who were part of the life of the parish many years ago, but that was before my time. These sailors came from all over the world, and Father trained me up to man the switchboard and arrange ship to shore calls and help the sailors to talk to their friends and family in many countries across the world. I think that some of their families even stayed at Stella Maris from time to time. Although I was just a youngster, I helped with the foreign exchange that was offered as a service. I also worked there as a waitress. I loved being at Stella Maris and still went over there to help out after I was married.

Over the years I had seven children, two boys and five girls. We lived with my husband's mother until we managed to get a council house in Tilbury, moving to Chadwell in 1990. Our children have been altar servers at Our Lady Star of the Sea and my oldest boy was eventually in charge of the altar servers. Now I have two grandsons who have served for ten years and my youngest daughter almost five years. Although my husband wasn't a Catholic he was very supportive of the Catholic Church and he helped to ensure that all of our children were brought up in the Catholic faith. He also cooked, alongside my brother Joseph, at many parish barbecues as well as doing several jobs in the church and school grounds.

For many years, the dances at Stella Maris, in both the old and new buildings, were every day. There was always Mass beforehand in the little chapel. There were also additional Masses at Stella Maris and some parishioners were able to make use of these, especially if they were working or had young children to look after. As the years went by and there weren't quite so many seamen, Father Heekin would hire out the ballroom to the local community. There were also well-attended bingo sessions in the evenings, so the people who enjoyed Stella Maris were not exclusively sailors. During the daytime many of the sailors would take walks around Tilbury and take a look at the sights such as Tilbury Fort. Father Heekin would often ferry them places in his minibus.

When we finally heard that Stella Maris was to close down we were all shocked and very, very sad. We felt like it had been there forever, and we were also sad that Father Heekin was to retire and move away. Later on, when he was dying, he asked to see Dorothy and I and we were able to go to see him. We felt so privileged to have the chance to see him before he died. We considered him to be a good friend. He was such a lovely man.

There was still to be the link with the seafarers, however. I remember that one of our parishioners, Bill Terry, went on board ship as a member of the Legion of Mary. He would often go with the Parish Priest and Mass would be said on the ship. In this way, the Apostleship of the Sea continued its support to the sailors who came to Tilbury.

These days, Father Paul helps to keep strong the links with Tilbury Docks. The weekly Church Bulletin often contains requests for parishioners to help with ship visiting and Sea Sunday is consciously made one of the big Masses of the year. There is a box kept permanently in the church where donations for the seamen are stored. Parishioners are asked to knit scarves, jumpers and gloves for the men, although now it is often easier to pick up these items in the pound shop.

My sister, Dorothy, used to do a lot of knitting for the sailors and nowadays she continues to place things in the seafarers' box. There is a steady flow of personal items like toothbrushes and toothpaste. Dorothy always seems able to keep them in mind, but with seven children and nine grandchildren I always seem to be shopping for the family.

Dorothy also used to be the gardener for the church grounds for about twenty years, using a hand-mower from home to cut all the grass. When they provided an electric mower for the work she didn't like it, and that was when I took over mowing the lawns. She continued her gardening work until a heart operation two years ago. A task she sorely misses.

Chapter Twelve : Parish Voices

The family of Gabriel and Grace Omorogbe-Amu

Gabriel: I began attending Our Lady Star of the Sea Catholic Church after moving to Tilbury in 2006, having spent some years living in various parts of London. The church has been a huge part of my Christian faith since.

My wife Grace and I were married in Nigeria in 2007 and we have been blessed with four lovely children – all of whom have been baptised in the church. Our eldest child had her First Holy Communion in the church in 2015 at a Mass celebrated by Fr. Paul Dynan and our second child will hopefully have had hers in 2017.

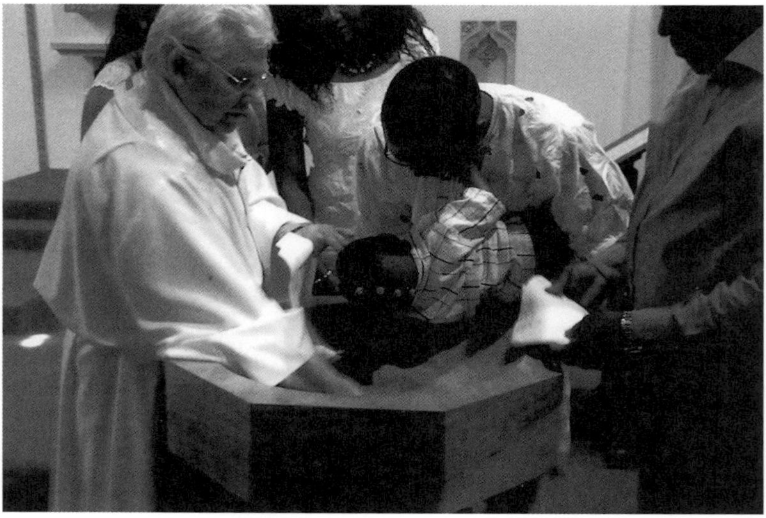

Baptism of Osaheni, 3rd June 2011

Grace: Our children attend St. Mary's Catholic Primary School. It is a good school with very dedicated teachers. One of our children's favourite teachers at the school was Mrs. Roberts. She was a gracious lady and was the nursery teacher for three of our older children. She has now moved on from the school. She was really lovely; she knew exactly what the children needed and involved the parents in the education of their children. The whole school does this, keeping the parents involved in the children's learning. Another good teacher was Mrs. Onyema (formerly Miss Vassel). She taught our oldest daughter. She was very kind and helped the children a lot. She was able to set the pupils real challenges, pushing them and moving them on the next level. Her effort was really appreciated. Our children really enjoy school and we are happy that the school's yearly result is consistently above the national average across all of the subjects.

Gabriel: I became a Minister of Holy Communion at Our Lady Star of the Sea in 2011 to assist with giving Holy Communion at Mass. I feel quite privileged and honoured to be serving in the house of God and, together with my family, supporting the church in any way possible.

In October 2013, I and my mum (Mrs Agnes Amu) and some other members of the parish went on a pilgrimage to the Holy Land (Israel), led by Fr. Paul. It was a brilliant trip. Visiting the Holy Land brought the bible to life for me. It gave me the opportunity to ask questions about the bible and the Christian faith and get answers from both our tour guide and Fr. Paul. The whole journey brought me closer to God and strengthened my Christian faith. I will relish the opportunity to go again.

A special surprise party was organised for my mother's seventy-fifth birthday in April 2016 by all her children. We began the celebration with a special Mass at Our Lady Star of the Sea. The Mass was officiated by Rev. Fr. Victor Darlington of Sacred Heart Catholic Church, Camberwell and Rev. Fr. Omoruyi Ereyi-Usoh, a relative of our family from Canada. We wanted to celebrate our mother's life as well as acknowledge the way she brought us up and cared for us so well, especially in the years after our father died when she devoted her life to us all – and still does. After the Mass, we all went on to a reception in Basildon, all of the family and many friends and well-wishers. It was a very special day for the mother of five children, three sons-in-law, a daughter-in-law, eleven grandchildren and two great grandchildren.

Being a part of this parish and our relationship with the school has also helped my family to be a part of this local community. We have enjoyed God's blessings and have grown to know him better. The message of love that comes from the altar has enabled us to appreciate both our fellow parishioners and our neighbours. It has also taught us to celebrate the presence of Christ in our lives daily. (Note: For a photograph of the 75th Birthday Celebration for Mrs. Agnes Agharese Amu, please see centre pages.)

George Cluer

I was born in Christchurch Road, Tilbury. My mother wasn't a Catholic but she took instruction and joined the Catholic Church. Sometimes I stayed with Nan and Grandad. He was a bookmaker. Over a period of time he had everybody in Tilbury in the house, putting on their bets. My nan would do the bets in the house and my grandad would take the bets in the Working Men's Club, every day. Of course betting off course wasn't legal then. My grandad was involved with everybody, so you never knew who was going to come in the house. On a Sunday I used to help him, carrying the bag with the clock which timed the bets, so that there couldn't be any fiddles. We would walk down to the Working Men's Club. The people would come up when we were walking around and say "Is it too late to put on a bet?" I would pick up my grandad later from the club and we would walk home for dinner. My nan had nine children who survived. I was never in the house without someone coming in to put their bets on. It was often six pence each way, but if it was a bigger bet my grandad used to lay it off with a man who lived across the back, he was a big bookie. People used to bet on anything. The *News of the World* used to do a fashion page, and each week one fashion from the previous week was voted as the best. People would even bet on that.

I went to St. Mary's School in Tilbury. When my mum's dad died we moved over to Grays and I went to St. Thomas's School for a while. When the war started I was evacuated. I must have been about nine. All I can remember is going down to the railway station with big labels on me. I went with my sister, Joyce. When we got to Devizes, I went to a woman called Mrs. Brown. She wasn't very nice. My friend from Tilbury, Billy, stayed in the same house with me. Mrs. Brown didn't like me. We went to St. Joseph's School in Devizes and we had to catch a bus to get there.

One day I fell over at school and hurt my leg. I walked home from school and when I got there she gave me a box round the earhole and sent me to bed. She wouldn't take me to the doctors. In the end my sister told my mum and she came and took me back home. When my mum took me to the doctors he said "You should have come before." You know, I've always had trouble with that left leg, because Mrs. Brown wouldn't take me to the doctors. My sister stayed on in Devizes for a while. The family she stayed with were quite posh, and when she came back to Tilbury she spoke nicely. She called dad "Pa" but that didn't last long.

In the war Tilbury was bombed and there were lots of air raid sirens. Sometimes at school we would be in the shelters three or four times in the one day. Most of the teachers were nuns. I remember Sister Francis, she was nice. And there was also Sister Margaret Mary. The school was all right. It was a bit strict. Sister Theresa used to take round those little bottles of milk and I used to help her. I remember one day I was taking milk to Sister Margaret Mary in the Junior school. She shouted at someone and I dropped a crate of milk bottles. I ran out crying and Sister Theresa said "What's up?" and I told her I'd broken a couple of bottles of milk. She checked that I hadn't hurt myself. She told me to clean up and take two more bottles to the classroom, but I wouldn't go back. Sister Margaret Mary had frightened the life out of me. Sister Theresa said "She doesn't mean it really" but I still wouldn't go back.

There were so many air raid warnings that some days we used to wonder whether it was worth going down the shelter again. We had big concrete shelters at school and a small metal one at home. One day I was queuing at the fish and chips shop for our tea and there was yet another air raid warning. No-one wanted to lose their place in the queue, so we stayed put. Some bombs fell quite close and plaster fell down from the ceiling of the shop. That night we had fish, chips and plaster for our tea.

After the air raids the boys would run out to gather up the shrapnel. When you had a lot of it you took it down to the fire station where they would give you a couple of pennies for it. I think it was used to make more planes and armaments. We would sometimes see German prisoners of war. They mostly worked on the local farms. They seemed nice enough. After the war some of them stayed on and made a home here.

Towards the end of the war there were French Canadians camped out in the fields near us. They even used the grass verges. They were waiting for the D-Day invasion. There were even tanks and Bren gun carriers there. My mother felt sorry for the soldiers and she began to organise hot baths in our house for some of them. My dad asked "Who's paying for all that hot water?" and she showed him a cupboard full of bottles of coffee and tinned goods that the soldiers gave her in return.

I delivered newspapers to a lot of the soldiers each day, and they were very friendly and had a big Alsatian dog. But one morning I went over the fields and they were all gone. The place was completely empty, men, vehicles, everything. All they left was the Alsatian dog. It was scrabbling with its paws in the ground. We helped and found blankets and big tins of corned beef. We went and told our parents and they all came over with spades and began to dig up all the things the soldiers had buried. But the police finally turned up and that was the end of that. We heard later that the French Canadians had a really tough time in the D-day landings. They were right in the thick of it and it made us all very sad when we heard the news.

The education in those days wasn't as good as what it is now. I don't know whether all of the teachers were qualified. The classrooms were all crowded. We sat in those desks built for two, always the same desk. They were strict, the nuns, but fair.

We played football. My cousin, Reggie Webb, was a very good goalkeeper. His father was a goalkeeper too. At the football matches there were often scouts from the big clubs, some of them trying to get schoolboys signed up. Reggie's father would tell him they weren't good enough, and Reggie got fed up with it. He had trials for Tottenham and West Ham. He ended up playing for West Ham in one of the Junior teams and then played for Batas and Tilbury.

We would see dear old Father O'Donnell, he must have been there thirty years. He was made a Canon in the end. He used to dig all his garden and grow his own vegetables. If anyone had troubles and went to speak to him he would say "While we're speaking, grab a shovel and dig a few rows with me." His housekeeper, Mrs. Mcguire, used to make home-made toffee and give it to you in a little white bag. Every week we went round the church after school for Benediction. We were marched round and some of us would try to bunk off through the back gate, but the nuns always caught you.

My dad was in the Home Guard. He had a 303 rifle but no bullets. Nobody had any bullets. When he went to work we would get it out and play with it. If he found out we were in trouble. My dad worked for Esso in West Thurrock, near Thames Board Mills. It was the Anglo American Oil Company first, and the man who owned it worked alongside the men. Then he sold the company to Esso, but he checked first that the men would be all right with the new company. My dad worked there all his life. The company is still there now.

My mother did lots of jobs. She worked for the council as a home help. She also used to help the midwife, who must still have been doing that job when she was eighty. The midwife would come round on her bike. My mother helped the undertaker when things got busy. Of course everyone had a big family then. I have two sisters, Julie and Joyce, and a brother, Tommy. They are all still alive.

We had a cycling club that my sister Joyce started up with a friend, Les Hodgetts. It was called St. Christopher's. We took the newcomers out on rides during the week, somewhere local, perhaps over to Maldon. On the Friday we used to meet in St. Mary's School in some buildings next to the school. We had a place to put the bikes and we had table tennis. Quite a few people joined. Then someone came up with the idea that we would go to Walsingham, and perhaps go on round the Norfolk Broads. We left on a Friday evening in August 1950 and cycled to Walsingham overnight. We arrived early Saturday morning, pitched our tents, had a kip and then went to join the procession. In those days there were just two little chapels. The procession was from the village to the two chapels, the same route that they do now.

The Procession at Walsingham : August 1950

Once when we were there they were expecting some lads, student priests, who were carrying a Cross all the way from Harlow to Walsingham. We were at Walsingham with Father Brian. The lads arrived a bit early because they had been stopped by the police. They had got about three quarters of the way there and the police had told them "You can't go any further". They had asked permission from the Essex police in Harlow, because some people get upset when they see a big Cross being carried.

The lads told the police in Harlow where they were going and they thought that they would contact the Suffolk police, but no such luck. They had to leave the Cross in someone's garden and go back for it later.

I still go to Walsingham, a couple of times a year. I used to go with the Grays parish, it was four days in May. We got to know the Bishop, Alan Williams, because he was there in charge, although he wasn't the Bishop then of course. When he got made Bishop I spoke to him about it and he said that when he first heard the news he was very surprised. I made Bishop Alan a keepsake of his time in Walsingham, from some wood and flint that I had been given there. It had the name *Walsingham* on it and the dates he had been there. Bishop Alan says that it is the first thing he sees when he goes into his office in the morning. I also made one for Father Paul, Sister Monica, Father Francis and Father Brian.

I left school at fourteen. I wanted to be a carpenter, but they said I wasn't clever enough so I went to work for Bata, the shoe people. I never really had a good education. I lost some time at school because I had to go to hospital with a nevis on my head. Doctor Dunlop referred me to the London Hospital and I was moved over to Berkhamstead. They had to build me up there so that I would be strong enough for the operation. I didn't really catch up at school afterwards. In those days there was nothing like special needs to help you catch up.

St. Christopher's Cycling Club : George and Ron

Tilbury had a gym run by Jim Jackson. He had a brother, Bob Jackson, who was a very good boxer. He fought for the English Lightweight Championship. I trained at the gym to be a boxer and I boxed for the army in 1952, when I was stationed in Hong Kong. They were good old days.

I liked my job at Bata. I ended up on the staff as a checker. My ambition was to earn twenty pounds a week, which I did when I became a checker. It's not much of an ambition, is it, twenty pounds a week. But it didn't work out and I gave my notice in and went to work for Thames Board Mills. My wife wasn't very happy because I had to work nights, and she would stay at my sister's, Julie. Then I got a job at West Thurrock Power Station. I should have gone there at the beginning. I liked that job. I became a Local Advisory Committee rep. and had to go all over the country to meetings. The Power Station shut down eighteen months after I took early retirement. I enjoyed every moment of it. There were two shifts, six to two and two till nine, and you worked weekends once a month.

When I got married I was twenty-six. I was the last one to get married. I met my future wife, Brenda, at a dance in the hall at Torell's School. In those days everybody went, ballroom dancing. She worked in a shop. We didn't get married in a Catholic Church, we married in the church at Chadwell St. Mary. We moved over to Corringham to live. Years later, when a friend of mine died in a road accident, I was very upset. I asked Brenda whether we could get married in a Catholic Church and she agreed. We spoke to Father Timmins, the curate over in Stanford-le-Hope. He agreed to give Brenda the necessary instruction. One day I was washing the car outside our place in Corringham when Father Timmins drove up. He said "I've come to give instruction to your wife. When you've finished that, chuck a bucket of water over mine." When he came out, Father Timmins told me that we should make the arrangements for the wedding. The next week we went over to the old Church of Our Lady and St. Joseph in Stanford, together with my sister and husband as witnesses, and we were married. We went across the road for a few drinks in the pub, the family and Father Timmins, and then I said I would have to leave as I was on the night shift at Thames Board Mills.

My sister and her husband, Joyce and Ken Clarke, helped to raise money in the nineteen fifties to buy land for a little church in East Tilbury. Bata offered a plot of land next to the Bata Hotel for a knock-down price. I remember that there were a lot of Poles and Czechs living in the area.

Unfortunately, the diocese didn't give the go-ahead as they said that they wouldn't be able to find a priest. Everybody was very disappointed. I think that the money raised went to the parish of Our Lady and St. Joseph in Stanford-le-Hope. Joyce was very much involved in the life of the Catholic community in the area. I remember that Joyce and Ken helped organise the transport for four or five annual pilgrimages to Lourdes. When Joyce first met Ken he wasn't a Catholic. He quietly took instruction in the Catholic faith with Fr. Byrne and then told Joyce afterwards, so that they were able to marry in a Catholic Church with a full Nuptial Mass.

Father Paul asked me to have a go at the garden at our Lady and St. Joseph in Stanford. When they took down the conifers it was all a bit of a mess. I talked about it with Father Paul and he agreed that I should have a try at making the garden look better. Grazianno Palagi, who lives across the road, joins me each Thursday. We always check with Father Paul when we are going to do something new. It took us two years to kill off all the weeds and get the first shrubs started. Brenda gave me advice on which shrubs to buy because she's a keen gardener. She sat down and did a design for me and helped me to buy the right plants. Sometimes people give me plants for the garden. I get some help in the garden from Will, May and Kay.

<u>Pauline Lacey</u>

I was born in Grays parish and moved to Chadwell St. Mary when I was married. I worked in London for an accountants as a secretary before I was married and then in Tilbury Docks for thirty-two years. The company was known as TCS (Tilbury Container Services, part of P. & O.) and they were brilliant to our parish. They allowed me to photocopy all the newsletters when I became responsible for compiling them. They also let me use minibuses when we needed them and it was always said that TCS stood for Tilbury Catholic Services!

I married Tony Lacey in 1970 and lived in Chadwell St. Mary. As a youngster Tony was an altar server, riding on his bike to Tilbury from Chadwell for early morning Mass (6.00 a.m.) and then back to Chadwell to serve there. Fr. Byrne took the family under his wing when Tony's father, a famous Irish boxer, was tragically killed whilst on flood duties. Tony served his apprenticeship as an engraver but the job moved to London and as he didn't like the travelling managed to get a job in the docks as a docker, which he loved. When he retired from the docks he was a taxi driver and then a school driver for children with learning difficulties, which he enjoyed. We have two sons and we also brought up my niece. All the children went to St. Mary's School. One son went to St. Cedd's and the other to De La Salle. My niece went on to Grays Convent.

I assisted with the netball team at St. Mary's, as I have played netball all my life and helped with the training and also umpiring matches. I got to know Sister Carmel at St. Mary's and Mr. and Mrs. Fitzgerald and Mrs. Edmunds. Mr. Fitzgerald was Deputy Head and ran the football team and his wife was the school secretary. My husband remembered Mr. Bolger when he attended the senior school. All of the school buildings, primary and secondary were crammed into that little space which meant that class sizes were usually big. I helped with the Youth Club in St. Joseph's with Frank Thompson, whom I met in Chadwell, and later on worked there with Sr. Carmel and Mary Pollard.

When the Parish of Chadwell St. Mary was closed down and merged with Tilbury, the money from the parish was transferred to Tilbury Parish, where it was used to refurbish the presbytery, which was in a dreadful state. It needed doing, but it was a bone of contention for many living in Chadwell who had not expected the money they had raised to be used in this way.

Eileen Edmunds used to type the weekly newsletter for Father Donal Donegan, but the job passed on to Lynn Davey and then to me. We worked on the Parish Magazine together with Jean Nuttall and Bernadette Terry. One evening the parish Gestetner machine did not work and we ended up in Tilbury Docks until midnight at - you guessed it – Tilbury Container Services.

When Father John Duckett came to the parish he would write down everything he wanted to go in the newsletter and I would type it so it made the job very easy to do. Subsequent priests would concentrate on the front page of the newsletter and I would put in the things that I knew had to be mentioned each week.

Fr. John asked me to be the authorised person to act as registrar for marriages in the church completing two registers, a certificate of marriage and place an entry in the church records. All of this has to be completed during the wedding. You had to be present when the priest asked the question "Do you take ….?" The additional work I did depended on the priest. For example, some priests did all the management of the church offertory, counting the money and paying it into the bank. Others didn't and I might step in to help. Of course there have been times when we haven't had a priest at all and we have had to rely entirely on supply priests. When this happens there is a lot more work to do as supply priests don't become involved in financial matters like the paying of bills and the writing of cheques.

Father John Duckett started a group called Faith Friends, where parishioners made weekly visits to new mothers and supported them through to baptism. He also started the Care Group with Diane Connelly, Barbara Sturgess, Kath Buckle, Lynn Davey, Maureen Fletcher, Ginny Rooney, Nance Watt, Lily Bolger and Sister Carmel, among others. The Care Group had many helpers, including Win Pollard, Maureen Sullivan, Pauline Forshew, Eileen Jepson and Lesley Ferguson. From this group a new SVP was set up, which used to meet in the convent. Lily Bolger was the Chairperson, with Maureen Fletcher, Gladys Bianchi, Barbara Sturgess, Nance Watt, Sister Carmel and me, although others joined later.

In the early days the Care Group arranged Healing Masses with lunch afterwards and then we organised a Christmas lunch for the housebound and elderly parishioners, where everyone was given a small Christmas present. We also took on lunches once a month, but during Easter and Advent every Monday! These activities were possible as we still had the church hall in Chadwell St. Mary. The Group arranged a day out each year to Aylesford, and also trips to Leeds Castle, Hever Castle and Walton-on-the-Naze. There was also a trip into London to see the Christmas lights and a fish and chip supper. We took tables and chairs on the coach and prepared a meal for everyone.

Afternoon Tea with the Care Group at Aylesford

We would arrange for a room with a kitchen at Aylesford to prepare lunch and then afternoon tea before the return journey. A coach with a lift for those in wheelchairs was used and we hired a bus from Thurrock Council's TransVol. Many parishioners offered their help with transport for functions in the hall and we simply could not have managed without them. We raised funds for all of this by holding raffles and we received many donations. Everything was paid for by donations and often fund raising by St. Mary's School. When Fr. David Clemens came to the parish he decided we would have Quiz Nights with the help of Terry Gilby and his famous music section. They weren't just ordinary nights but cheese and wine in the cost of the ticket (another lot of hard work but great fun), and very successful.

An Advent Lunch at St. Joseph's Hall, Chadwell St. Mary

When Father Bob (Hamill) became Parish Priest he used to write a book every week for the newsletter! Fr. Bob upgraded the kitchen in St. Joseph's and was even more adventurous escalating to more activities as he started a Senior Citizens Club with Vi Morgan as Vice President. We were exhausted, of course, but loved every minute of it. Diane Connelly and I would be in the hall at 5.00 a.m. on Sunday and Monday mornings, preparing the meal, with help from parishioners attending the 9.00 a.m. Mass on Sunday, and then I would nip back from work during Monday lunchtime to serve or wait on tables before rushing back to work. The helpers were magnificent and worked so hard. Diane and I would give them a treat every 6th January (Little Women's Christmas – although

Father Bob also came along) and each year there was a theme. The first was just a German waitress, Helga with blacked out teeth, and later on a Bunny Girl! Suffice to say that there was no way that Diane was dressing up! We ventured into bigger themes, and had an Hawaiian Night, Halloween, a Bedouin Tent with plenty of sand but, sadly, no sea, and themed food. The girls and Father Bob were thoroughly spoilt. The theme was always a closely guarded secret so that the helpers had a big surprise each time they came along.

Every year the SVP would organise Christmas hampers which would be given to families in need. There was one family living in Orsett, who always donated a really fine hamper and would deliver it with Lily Bolger to a needy family and take along their own children so that they could see how lucky they were.

When the beef mountain and butter mountain were stockpiled in Europe, the Care Group/SVP were given some of the produce to distribute to the poor/housebound. By law we had to cook the beef as it wasn't legal to hand it out raw and we were able to use the school kitchen on a Saturday to cook the beef, and Keith Fletcher would deliver it on his motorbike. Later on we were given meat in cans and of course butter, which all parishes in the U.K. could collect and distribute.

When I retired from the Docks, Fr. Paul suggested that I might like to work at the presbytery as secretary, although I had been doing similar work previously in the evenings and at weekends. Since 2014, I have been working in the office Monday to Friday from 9.00 until 12 noon.

I have lived in Chadwell for over forty years now and during that time many priests have come and gone. I've liked all of the Parish Priests, but one particular favourite was Fr. John Duckett who I still see from time to time. He is an old fashioned priest and visited everyone in the parish, not just the sick. I am always trying to bring him into the twenty-first century but he has a traditional view of marriage, divorce and separation. Father John reordered the Parish Church and the beautiful old altar was removed. Many people thought that it was marble but it was actually made from something else, possibly alabaster, and painted over. There were some massive cracks in it and it could have fallen down, so it had to be removed. The remains of the old altar are underneath the Sanctuary together with some of the old statues.

There have been many priests in my time in the parish besides those mentioned: Frs. David Clemens, James McShane, Paul Bhanji, Peter

Connor, John Meehan and now Fr. Paul. Fr. Francis van Son supplied for us on many occasions and whilst Fr. Paul had major surgery. They are all special in one way or another.

A Tribute to Parishioner Vi Morgan (Prepared by Pauline Lacey)

Vi always seemed to be there – she met you at the door for Saturday evening Mass and depending how she felt was how she met you. She loved to order people about – it was her way.

Her life concerning the parish was hectic when she was able. She always wanted to help the Care Group and one huge way to help was to raise funds. Vi always held an Easter Raffle and if you didn't buy the tickets this week then she made sure you bought them the next and the next and the next! She didn't just sell them in the parish but also visited the local shops and asked people there to buy them and also in one of the Tilbury Clubs.

Receiving Cheque for Care Group : Money Raised by Vi Morgan and St. Mary's School
(From left: Lynn Davey, Vi Morgan, Diane Connelly)

Vi loved to go to Aylesford and also all the events that the Care Group held but always wanted to help, and yet she was invited to just enjoy. The Care Group certainly missed her and have always been extremely grateful for the help she gave them over the years, as fund-raising is a thankless task. There has been a gap for many years at the Christmas Bazaar as her 'baby' was the Christmas Hamper Raffle.

Vi had been a member of the Senior Citizens Club for many years. There were about 80 members in the beginning but when there were only a few, with funds so low it was not possible to invite people to come along and give talks etc. and go for trips out. In the last few years of Vi's life she arranged the raffles, bingo and refreshments every week to raise funds. She was the Vice President for many years and it was difficult with so few members to arrange a Committee.

Vi was amazing; she fought her illness and in no way was it going to stop her from helping others.

Diane Connelly

Mass used to be held at the Cross Keys in Chadwell St. Mary. At the time I moved from Corringham to Chadwell, we had Mass in Chadwell St. Mary Working Men's Club. A couple of people used to go in there beforehand to make sure it was clean, but it always smelt of beer, but at least we had somewhere to have Mass, that was the main thing. It was a trudge in the winter with the pram, as I lived in the back end of Chadwell, in a road backing onto the farm.

We held coffee mornings in Chadwell to try and get money towards building a Mass Centre. We would organise bring and buy events but all we had was a community of people, no buildings at all. We turned out to be quite good at raising money. Of course when the Hall opened it was brilliant. At the official opening *The Universe* came down and I think the Bishop was there. That was the only building we had on the site, although there was talk in our Parish Council of having a presbytery built in the time of Father Mills. But he went to live in a house in Cedar Road and the presbytery was never built.

The money we raised went to Tilbury Parish when we were amalgamated and it was used to renovate the presbytery there. Father Donegan was given a couple of rooms at Stella Maris whilst the presbytery was being refurbished. It needed to be done, but the parishioners in Chadwell were not very happy, especially as they were going to lose their priest. Some people felt rather peeved about it.

On a Sunday, Father Mills would come round to a parishioner's house for his dinner. There was a rota of people and we all took turns to do it, Jean and Terry Nuttall, Stan and Win Pollard, among others. Of course it was fine for the adults, but the children didn't always appreciate it when it was their turn to eat Sunday dinner with Father Mills. We also tried to keep the house in Cedar Road looking neat and tidy, as Father Mills didn't want to spend money on cleaners and we went round there in pairs. I was paired with Marie Pettit, and there was Win Pollard and Ellen Campbell.

I remember when Jane McLoughlin, the District Nurse, and her friend Marie were looking for volunteers to go round visiting sick people in their homes. The volunteers included Lily Bolger, Nancy Watt, my sister Barbara and of course the nuns. It was to give the partners of the sick people a break, a sort of respite care. I was lucky because my first visit was just around the corner to me, as I didn't drive a car. The scheme didn't last that long but we did it while we were needed.

I came into the area as a young woman with my aunt and uncle, Chris and Christopher Scanlan, after living in Wales for a time. They moved into the area and I came with them and got a job in the buffet at the Riverside Centre in Tilbury. One of my friends there, Eunice, was getting married just before me, round about 1960, and asked me to be her bridesmaid. My aunt and uncle told me that I wouldn't be able to do that, because Eunice was not a Catholic and I would not be able to go into a non-Catholic church. Eunice had only a mother, father and brother in her family, nobody else and so I visited Father Byrne to explain the situation but he wasn't at all sympathetic. So I told Father Byrne "I'm going to do it, as Eunice doesn't have anyone else. But when I'm in that church, I won't pray."

My uncle, Christopher Scanlan and George Gill always tended the gardens and did odd jobs around the church in Tilbury, even devising ways to fix the stained glass

Father Byrne used to say Mass at East Tilbury, Chadwell St. Mary and then Tilbury. It was a lot for him to have to do, especially when he was older. When he came to us at Chadwell, we would provide him with a breakfast in our homes so that he didn't have to go back to Tilbury to eat. Again, a few of us took turns to look after him.

One parishioner, Stan Pollard, Mary's father, used to visit the three big blocks of flats every week, giving out and collecting the envelopes for donations to the church funds. He would leave his bike at our house while he did his rounds. Jean Nuttall and I would deliver the church bulletins every week to the Catholics we knew in the flats. It wasn't that easy because I can't travel in lifts. Jean would take the lift right to the top and I would start at the bottom and then we would meet in the middle.

When St. Joseph's Hall opened there was a Ladies Guild, which was brilliant. We got quite a lot of ladies who weren't going out to work, as they had young children of their own. Once a year we would go up to London on a night out as a treat. We also had a Social Committee and organised socials for the parishioners in our new Hall. So with that and the Parish Council there was a lot going on in our community. We managed to get a licence to run a bar at our dances in the Hall and we had live bands. The Hall became something of a centre for the whole community, Catholics and non-Catholics alike. Our dances were confined to 200 people and we always sold out of tickets. As soon as people heard there was a dance they would rush to buy the tickets.

At the New Year Dance people would dress up as the Old Year and the New Year. Arthur Matthews used to be the Old Year and one year I had to race home to get our 8 year old daughter, Sharon, out of bed and dress her up to be the New Year and take her up to the Hall. I don't think she was very impressed! But it was only a bit of fun. We were all having a lot of fun in those days.

Mass at the Side Altar, St. Joseph's Hall
Father Bob Hamill and Father David Clemens

Father Bob (Hamill) was really great. He really took the Care Group on when he came after Father John Duckett. He was a great support when the meals were prepared in Lent and Advent. He would come shopping with us for the food and he put a lot of his own money into the kitchen in the Hall. The kitchen had to be updated and Father Bob took responsibility for the modernisation. There were new cupboards needed and steel topped work surfaces.

Father Heekin at Stella Maris was a great help and we were always in communication with him. As a result he arranged many volunteers from the parish to help at Stella Maris. We would help in the shop and the little snack bar. The place was always packed in those days when the big ships came in, and the sailors would be in Tilbury for quite a while when the ships were being unloaded, not like the container ships today when the seamen are here for no time at all. There was also a restaurant in the daytime to provide meals for the seamen. We helped in there and served in the bar.

Gerry Butcher, an assistant priest, tried to organise some discos in St. Joseph's Hall for the youngsters but Father Byrne was opposed to this. When the first disco was to take place, Father Byrne stood at the door to the Hall and wouldn't let any of the children go in. So that was the end of that idea. In those days, there were children down the far side of Tilbury near the World's End pub and there were no buses to bring the children to school. Father Gerry Butcher used to borrow Father Heekin's coach in the morning, drive over there and pick up the children and take them to school, before returning the coach to Father Heekin. After school each day he would drive them all back home again. There was always this great link between the parish and Stella Maris. When Father Heekin was actually leaving Stella Maris we had a do for him at St. Joseph's and made a presentation to him from the parish.

For us, the centre of our community was St. Joseph's Hall. When we rejoined Tilbury Parish we still had our Hall and there were so many events, Masses, socials and dances that brought us all together. When the Hall closed, that was it. Father Peter Connor was our Parish Priest then. He really fought hard to keep the Hall open, and as a result the closure of the Hall was delayed for quite a while. A priest from Grays, who thought that the area of Chadwell St. Mary might be transferred to Grays, joined up with Father Peter to keep the Hall open, but in the end it just went. Now, saying that, the Hall needed a lot of refurbishment. All the parish money was spent on the Church of Our Lady Star of the Sea, which was fair enough, and the Hall became really neglected. Apart from that there simply weren't enough priests to go round, so you can understand to some extent the reasons to close the Hall.

One of many Care Group Christmas Meals being prepared at St. Joseph's Hall

At the time that St. Joseph's was to be closed and the land was to be sold off, I reminded the Parish Council that we didn't own the land but it had been leased to us by the Council for a peppercorn rent. We owned the land the Hall was built on as long as there was a church there. Father Peter informed Bishop Thomas a few days later when he came for his Visitation to the parish, and it was a surprise to him. Eventually everything was closed down in Chadwell St. Mary, despite the best efforts of Father Peter and Father John Meehan. At the end of the day these things happen and you can't keep going back to them.

Councillor Pat Rice was one of our parishioners in Chadwell St. Mary and he became Mayor of Thurrock. Then his son, Gerard Rice, also became a Thurrock Councillor and we were invited to the big celebration at The Civic Hall in Blackshots when Pat Rice became Mayor. We realised that the do was on a Friday, when we were not allowed to eat meat. We asked Father Byrne for a special dispensation, but that was a definite no. The food that night was gorgeous but we didn't cheat. We just had to eat the veg and spuds and that and it was all right.

I remember Malcolm Rogers, a teacher who used to play the organ. We set up a choir under his leadership, and we used to practise in the Hall once a week even though we couldn't sing for peanuts. Malcolm made home-made wine and in those days I didn't really drink, but after a little drop of Malcolm's wine we all went home quite merry. That was all part of the fun we all had in those days.

I recall that Arthur Matthews and possibly Con Parker built the altar in St. Joseph's Hall. Michael Maloney made some Stations of the Cross. Father Bob arranged for new wood for the Stations of the Cross at a cost of £50 pounds for each one. Father asked us if we would be prepared to either buy the wood for one of them outright, or share with others to buy the wood for one of the Stations and that's how we paid for the Stations of the Cross.

There was a curate here, I think his name was Father Collingwood. He had a motorbike and he would bike round the parish visiting the parishioners. One time I was at home after giving birth to my daughter, Sharon. My mother was with me and she heard a motorbike pull up outside. She said, "Oh, there's a man coming up to the front door with a motorbike helmet on." I said "That'll be Father Collingwood, coming on a visit." My mother said, "Father? A priest? Riding a motorbike?" I said to her, "Well, they do do things like that. They haven't all got cars."
(Readers may know that the printing of the centenary book at Our Lady and St. Joseph's, Stanford-le-Hope, was financed by the sale of Father Paul Dynan's much loved Harley Davidson.)

The sad thing is that the community spirit which was so much in evidence in those days, with the dances, social events, meals for the elderly, all of them centred on St. Joseph's Hall, is now reduced. There is no hall for the parish and there is just one garden party a year. I miss the work we did in the old days and the taking part.

<u>Joyanna Shaw</u>

I was born in the West Indies, on the island of Barbados. I came to the United Kingdom when I was twenty-four and I lived first of all in Newport, in South Wales. When I was promoted in my job I came to Tilbury, and I have now been here for twenty years. I am an office manager for a shipping company. These days, their cargoes are all containerised, and we handle shipping back and forth from here to the Continent.

My mum brought me up as a Catholic in Barbados, although my father was a Methodist. My mum insisted that we were all brought up as Catholics. I went to a Convent School, St. Ursula's, an all girls school. It was lovely and I had a good education. When I left school, I went to work for an estate agent and still went to church every Sunday. My sister was more involved in the Church and she was in the Catechists. She was sent to Italy for two years training to pursue her work in the Church.

We have always been a very close family. There are six girls and one boy. I was the youngest girl, and I had a brother after me. The island of Barbados is the size of the Isle of Wight and it has six Catholic Churches. Religion is a very important part of the life of the island. In my early years we went to a church in the north of the island, and when we later moved closer to the south of the island we went to the Cathedral, St. Patrick's, in Bridgetown. It has great pillars supporting the roof, but what is different is that every door, every window is wide open as it can be so very hot. As the years have gone by, fans have been put in. With all those windows open you could always hear a service taking place if you were walking near to any of the churches.

When I first came to Britain it wasn't at all what I expected. To begin with, I got rid of all my swimsuits as I was told it was just too cold to even think about swimming in the U.K. I came over in the August of 1983 and it was quite a warm August so I had to go and buy a swimsuit. That was not the only surprise: in the winter the snow was fantastic. I had never seen snow so it was absolutely amazing.

My family knew that I already had a sister over here, someone I could turn to when I was settling in. It was a wrench to leave most of my family behind in Barbados. I still say that if I could move my family over here I would be 100% happy.

When I joined the congregation at our Lady Star of the Sea, Father David Clemens was just coming to the end of his time in Tilbury, but then Father James arrived. I didn't know anyone in the parish. I came to church on a Sunday, sometimes at St. Joseph's in Chadwell and sometimes at the church here in Tilbury. I would walk in, have Mass and walk back out. People would be polite and smile at you, but no-one asked about you, whether you were here on holiday or had just arrived to live here. It didn't seem as though there was much atmosphere, not much in the way of welcoming, as far as I was concerned. And then I saw an advert in the newsletter for someone to arrange the flowers in the church. I was doing a flower-arranging course at that time and I volunteered to do the flowers here. It has really been brilliant, as I have got to know so many people, and I feel part of the family. I have been arranging the flowers now for about ten or fifteen years. I don't usually get help with the flowers, although we have to try to find someone when I go back to Barbados to see my family there.

A Flower Arrangement for Palm Sunday

The church pays for all the flowers, which I collect each week from the supermarkets. I supplement the flowers with greenery from my garden. I come here to the church each Saturday morning and it usually takes me about two hours to prepare five different arrangements for the church. There is one arrangement for the altar, one for the candle, one for the Sacred Heart, one for Mary and one for Joseph. My favourite colour is orange, but I keep a brake on that as it will not be everyone's favourite. I create a wreath for Remembrance Sunday, which is later placed on the cenotaph outside. I try to do something appropriate at the time of the Harvest festival. Some of the priests would offer advice. I remember that Father John was always very theatrical in his ideas and he taught me a lot. It was his idea to create the cave motif which we still use in the church every Easter. Two parishioners, Brenda and Mick, who have now left the parish, would offer a lot of support and help me to decorate the Christmas tree.

I remember that the crib which we used at Christmas was beginning to look a bit the worse for wear. It was a lovely nativity scene, but the heads were starting to fall off. Our parishioner, Mick, did his best to repair it, and would repaint it all, but eventually we realised that we needed a new set. We decided on a cake sale once a month as the way to raise money for a new crib set. That was another very good way of meeting new people. I would make cakes on a Saturday morning and we would all bring our cakes in to the Saturday evening Mass and again to the Sunday Mass. We managed to raise about a thousand pounds, the church gave the rest and the new nativity set was purchased. The whole scheme demonstrated just how generous this community is.

The Nativity Set at Our Lady Star of the Sea, Tilbury

When Father James was our Parish Priest, he organised a series of meetings in the presbytery to discuss various areas in the life of the church. There would be a lot of discussion and even some lively arguments. There was such a variety of topics. I remember that on one evening he took us over to the church and showed us all the priestly garments. I believe he was encouraging us to think about the church as well as bringing us together. This coming together as a community is so difficult in a parish that doesn't have a Parish Hall. Since the closure of St. Joseph's Hall in Chadwell, there simply isn't a place where we can all get together and socialise.

The Christmas Tree : Another Example of Teamwork

I have seen a few changes in the parish in the twenty years I have been here. In the last four or five years we have seen a new community developing with the arrival of Nigerian Catholics. They are very friendly and are always willing to help. With their support we have now organised a Prayer Group that meets together the second and fourth Friday of each month. We usually meet in the convent with two of the Sisters, although there are plans to expand the group and to use the church for some of the meetings. We have a Bible reading, we discuss the reading together, there are prayers related to what has been happening to us in the past fortnight and we talk about our lives. We also have singing. It is lovely. It's supposed to last an hour but it is usually an hour and a half because nobody looks at a watch and the time goes quickly.

I am very happy living in Tilbury. Sometimes you hear people saying negative things about the area, but I like where I live and I like the people I meet. Family and friends in Barbados often come over to visit me.

I am a governor of St. Mary's Primary School. In March 2017 I shall have done four years so I will have to put myself up for re-election. I am really glad to be part of that. We meet once a term for the actual Governors' Meeting, and then we have sub-committees, which might meet once a term, depending on which sub-committee you are on. The work is interesting and it's nice to see the children blossoming. The kids are so happy. We have lots of training courses organised by the Diocese of Brentwood. Much of it is delivered by Mgr. George Stokes. The courses include what being a Governor is all about, and helping and supporting the Headteacher. You do get very involved in the work. There is a lot of emphasis on the Governors these days, so the work is much more than a once a term meeting. We've had one Inspection whilst I've been a Governor, but it was not a real Inspection, it was more to guide us on where we were at present, where we were getting things right, and where we were going wrong. The Inspection report helped the Governors to prioritise their work, and what we needed to help to change. Fortunately, the school has been making some real improvements, and the Headteacher has been a major participant in this improvement.

These days, although we have our nuns at the convent, they don't do any of the teaching any more. This is a pity because I think that the nuns have a presence, an influence above and beyond their teaching, when they are on the teaching staff of a school And of course it is appropriate to have nuns teaching the religious aspects of the curriculum. The

Sisters of Mercy are still very involved with the parish community and they do very good work.

It is good that our church is involved with the welfare of the seafarers who come into Tilbury. We have parishioners who go to visit the ships when they are in dock, as part of the Apostleship of the Sea. A lot of the sailors are Filipinos, and the majority of them are Catholic. When the ships arrive in port they have just twelve hours to turn the ships around. Some of the seamen ask at the docks for information about which churches are open. The Seafarers' Association has an office actually in the dock and someone will go on board every ship to answer questions like that.

In recent times, when Father Paul was unwell, we have had a number of priests coming to the parish for short periods of time. We have been very lucky with the priests who have helped out, including Father Francis, Father David from Uganda and, of course, Father Anthony. They each have their own style, but they have all made a real contribution to the life of our parish. A particular favourite was Father Frank who has now moved on to Frinton. He is such a lovely person. He came down to the level of the children so naturally and his sermons always left you thinking. Father Francis has a lovely singing voice. You knew if you were late for Mass because you could hear his singing from outside the church.

One memorable event for me in recent years was the pilgrimage to the Holy Land in October 2013. That was another thing that brought the community together, both here and in Stanford-le-Hope. Every time I go to the church in Stanford I keep bumping into people who were on that trip. We went to so many places and Father Paul was always there, referring to the Biblical aspects of what we were seeing. Our tour guide, Amnon, was just wonderful. His favourite phrase was "Chop! Chop!" as he guided us from one place to another. We had so many Masses and the weather was lovely and warm. At the end of our pilgrimage we went on the Sea of Galilee. This was a surprise organised by Father Paul, and we had a special Mass on board our boat. Other highlights were the River Jordan and the Garden of Gethsemane. I took my sister with me on the pilgrimage, the one who lives in Portsmouth. We all spent ten days in the area, and I actually had my birthday when we were there. Evenings were spent socialising with others in the group or shopping for souvenirs. Father Paul was amazing, with all that he was going through at the time. Nothing held him back. He has indicated that there might be another pilgrimage to the Holy Land, perhaps in 2018. I think all of us will want to go again.

<u>Gwen Perkins</u>

I moved into Tilbury in 1954. I was living in Limehouse before that and I wasn't very happy there, although it was a lovely new flat. I was originally from Catford, south east London, and when I moved to Limehouse I heard more bad language there than I knew existed. We were only in Limehouse for two years and then we got a part-exchange for Tilbury, in one of the prefabs. We had three children by then, aged one, two and three, and I didn't want them to grow up on the estate in Limehouse. After another two years we got another part exchange to this house. An elderly lady wanted a home all on one level, which the prefab was, and we wanted more space for our growing family. I remember we had a wonderful time with the children running up and down the stairs and hiding in cupboards. We moved to this house in 1956, and I've been here ever since. We had six children altogether, five boys and a girl.

All the children went to Manor Way Junior School. I was baptised a Catholic, but wasn't brought up in the Catholic faith. The children loved that school; it was more like a country school. There was a main building and a lot of little prefab buildings next to it. Our children all did wonderfully well, both at school and later on in life.

When we arrived in Tilbury in 1954 it wasn't at all like it is now. It was a lovely little country village, with cows and horses in the fields. You've got to remember that I came from London, where you didn't see such things. There was lots of space in Tilbury and parks for children to play. There was a very friendly community. Although there have been lots of new neighbours in the houses around, my immediate neighbours have been there for a long time. I know that I could always bang on the wall if I needed help. The only thing is, we used to have low fences in the back gardens and we would often talk to each other. But now the fences are higher and we can't do that any more.

When my daughter Jane met her future husband Joe, he was a member of a very faithful Catholic family, the Farrs, who are still heavily involved in the Tilbury Church community in many ways. Jane became interested in the Catholic family way of life, including Mass, prayers and the Rosary, as this was something she had never experienced before. Jane took instruction and was received into the Catholic Church. This prompted me to consider my own situation. All of our children had been brought up as Christians, but Jane was the only one to become a Catholic. When Jane went to church with her little ones I would go along as well to help out. It was suggested that I might join the Catholic faith and I thought it would be a good idea. I was given instruction by Sister Margaret Mary, and I was sponsored by Jane's mother-in-law, so that was really nice. Attendance at Mass became part of my life until recently, when illness stopped me from going. I am still brought Communion regularly.

My husband worked for Crosse and Blackwell and then Fords. When we came to Tilbury he got a job in the Docks. They were looking for skilled men and he was a Maintenance Engineer. Our two oldest boys got apprenticeships at Fords, in electrical work and electronics. They did very well, although they're retired now. All of my boys are retired.

I was very upset when they closed St. Joseph's Church Hall in Chadwell. I used to join my daughter and her family for Mass on a Sunday and go back for Sunday dinner. I was driving in those days. But it was more than a church, it was the centre of the community. Everything you needed was there, including a nice kitchen. We had so many parties and socials there, and Christmas meals for the Seniors and now we don't have a hall in the parish where everyone can gather.

Of all the Parish Priests, I remember particularly Father Bob, a lovely man. Some priests weren't that approachable, but with Father Bob you could always have a laugh and a joke. I was also very fond of Sister Veronica who used to come to my sewing class in Tilbury, almost from the beginning. She did some lovely wall hangings, of the church and the school and one was a panorama of the Docks. We still keep in contact at Christmas, which is rather nice. The Sewing Class meets in the Band Hall, almost opposite the church. We meet twice a week, and we do knitting, crochet, embroidery, cross stitch, hardanger embroidery, crouting, alterations, dressmaking, anything creative really. I teach but when I'm not there the people support each other. There is always someone with sufficient knowledge of one area or another to be able to help.

We began meeting about 1997/1998. The Fire Station was empty and they decided to make it into a kind of activity centre for the community. I saw an advert in the *Thurrock Gazette* asking for people who had skills they could pass on to others and I applied. I then had to sell the idea to other people, and I manned a table at the Methodist Church with some of the things I had made, and did the same on a couple of mornings when they had an Open Day at the Methodist Church. In this way I got sufficient people interested to be able to start a class at the old Fire Station. We were there for about four or five years and paid only a peppercorn rent but then there was more competition for the rooms. We were often moved at short notice to give way to organisations that were able to pay more money than we could. That caused us to look for another venue and we found the Band Hall.

We meet every Monday afternoon, 1.00 until 4.00 and every Friday morning, 9.30 until 12.30. The sessions now cost £4 for the three hours and we provide two cups of tea or coffee for a total of 50 pence. The money we raise goes to pay the rent on the room each month, to keep our heads above water. We managed to get a couple of grants to help us to buy three good sewing machines, and other equipment like decent scissors and pins.

We make a lot of quilts for two hospices, Little Haven and Fair Haven. We try to make quilts for members of the family not in the hospices, because the focus is often on the one who is really ill and the other members of the family might feel themselves overlooked. Over the years we have probably made about three hundred quilts for families at the hospices. They are stored in a big blanket box at the hospice and a child coming to the hospice can pick one and then take it home with them after two or three weeks of respite care. We make sure that the siblings also have a quilt as well, so that they don't feel left out. We often get a card saying, "Thank you for my quilt. It's beautiful." We make knitted blankets and quilts for the adults in Fair Haven Hospice, and we make memory quilts, with lots of little pictures included in the design, which can help conversation with people suffering from dementia. We make alphabet quilts for the children with all of the letters and pictures of things beginning with that letter.

All the members of our club provide the materials for the quilts they make, so that there is no charge either for the hospice or the people there. Sometimes we receive gifts of wool and materials and we turn these into gifts for the hospices. From time to time one or other of the ladies at our Class suffers a bereavement, and then their families want to talk a lot about the person who has died. When they come to the Class, although everyone is supportive, there is still the opportunity for a laugh and a joke, which can be a comfort at a difficult time. Sometimes we make quilts to be raffled for different charities, including diabetes charities as we have members of our family with type one diabetes.

When Father James organised a parish trip to Aylesford I saw a painting representing Stella Maris in the church there. I asked Father James if it would be all right to do something creative based on the painting for our church in Tilbury. We took some really good photographs of the painting and got permission from the artist to make something based on it. One photograph was divided into six pieces and enlarged, so that each section was the same size as the work I would do. It was put up against a wall, and I was able to work out what the background would be and then it was like putting a jigsaw together. The picture is built up a bit at a time, starting with the background and placing other materials on top. The main work is sourcing the materials. Everywhere you go you are always looking for resources. I kept a little picture of the painting in my purse, and would take it out whenever I was in a fabric shop, trying to get a suitable match for areas of the painting.

Altogether, it took about two years to get all of the materials and about eight months to construct the picture. I didn't start the creative work until all the materials for it had been collected. Father James often popped in to see the progress I was making. When it was finished my son in Norfolk put a frame round the work, and it was placed in the church on Mother's Day. Sometimes I sit in the church and look at it and think "How did I do that?" I put an envelope on the back of the picture explaining how it was made, so people can see that in years to come.

Some of the Early Stages in the Creation of the Icon

(Note: For a picture of the completed icon, please refer to the cover of this book.)

Raymond Scott

I was born in Tilbury and at one time we lived in Sydney Road. One of my earliest memories was of the Great Flood in 1953. I remember being woken up and dressed by my mum about 5.00 o'clock in the morning. I was led from the bedroom to the top of the stairs and when I looked down I could see black water which reached half way up the stairs. The army came out to rescue us. Great big trucks pulled up outside and I was carried from the stairs by a huge man. I thought my dad was big but all of these men looked so much bigger. They all looked well fed, which was unusual at that time. It turned out that they were Canadian. They were very jolly and made a big fuss of my brother and me. We were put into the back of a ten ton truck and taken over to Orsett army camp. We were given baked beans and I watched the first colour film I had ever seen. Our family was there for about a week, whilst the Tilbury houses dried out a bit, although our house never dried out completely. It was always damp after that.

Mum was on the lookout for another house quickly, and they were just building some new houses in Malta Road. We learned that a large bomb had dropped in the area and so there was space to build a row of houses.

Mum went to the Council and they offered her the keys to one of the houses and we moved in. Right away, the big thing in the neighbourhood was the convent across the road. It was a secret place. As children we were quite wary of it. In those days there was a high wall all around it, about six feet, and a little green door. The door had no handle and you needed a key to get in as it was always locked. We never saw the nuns from one day to the next. We knew that there were about twenty nuns in the convent and quite a few were teenagers, probably Novices, wearing white. Older nuns wore black and they all wore the wimple. It was all very strange to us. At that time the nuns kept themselves to themselves. But then the wall came down and the nuns began to come out. Of course they would have come out before then, because I think some of them taught in the school, but now the nuns were seen more in the community.

I started school in Lansdowne Road, Tilbury and the Catholic children would come over to our school at lunchtime to use the canteen. They used to tramp across our playground in a long line and I can remember the animosity from the boys in our school shouting abuse at the Catholic children, who never responded. To begin with I thought it was all part of the competition between schools but then it seemed deeper than that and my father explained it to me. My own grandfather had once lived in Glasgow and he had had to move away from the city after he married an Irish Catholic. I don't suppose the boys at school knew really knew why they were so hostile to the Catholic children; it was just something they had learned from the neighbourhood.

We certainly didn't learn things like that from our own parents, but we were aware of the distance between ourselves and the Catholic families. It turned out that my father had been brought up as a Catholic. Every Sunday he would walk us round to the Anglican Church, St. John's, and go in with us. He would not sing, however, and when we young children looked up at him and saw that he didn't sing we followed his example. Later on I became friends at secondary school with a family of Polish Catholics, and seeing the very structured life the boys followed helped me to understand more about my father when he was growing up in the Catholic faith.

Sometimes I would find myself in the presbytery, after Father Byrne caught me taking short cuts through the church grounds. He would give me a very serious face and a ticking off, but he was a gentleman. He carried himself well and you couldn't have anything but respect for him.

I passed the eleven plus although we took so many exams in those days I didn't even realise it was the eleven plus until it was over. As it turned out, most of the teachers in Lansdowne Road were Welsh. I remember just before I left primary school my teacher, Mr. Williams, asked the children in the class how many of them went to church. Some of the boys, perhaps out of bravado, said they didn't go or didn't believe in that sort of thing. Some of the girls went to church. Mr. Williams listened to everyone, accepted their answers quietly and then told us a story. It was about a group of men in a fast launch during the last war. He said that none of them believed in God. One day they were out in the North Sea and the engine failed; they were sitting ducks. They saw enemy ships approaching and the guns began to fire. All of the men gathered on the far side of the launch whilst the shells found their range. Shells began to hit the launch and the boat began to settle into the oily, grey sea. Suddenly the men began to say "Our Father, which art in Heaven..." and Mr. Williams then left the room. It was only later that I realised that this had probably happened to him.

I didn't want to go the grammar school and opted for Aveley County Technical School instead. With hindsight, I should have chosen Palmer's Grammar School, but at the time it seemed to be a school for more gentrified people. Technical School wasn't really for me. I got good passes in all of my subjects but there was a strong bias towards the dextrous and the technical. All employment discussions were channelled towards becoming fitters in factories and I remember thinking 'I'm not a fitter'. Only one teacher saw my potential and advised me to concentrate on the written courses, French, German, History, the Humanities.

I began work as a draughtsman at a small engineering place in Thurrock. I did the normal thing, night school, HNC, but then the engineering company folded. That was a pity as it was a lovely office and nice people, but I found myself commuting to London for quite a few years working in a drawing office. I finally decided on a change, bought myself a motorbike, took a three month sabbatical and went off to tour the Continent. I met up with a couple of Dutch fellows and we toured Europe, including the whole of Italy and the Alps. It was glorious, the sort of thing you can do when you're young.

I ended up on my own in West Berlin, travelling on a visa through East Germany. It was very cold, too cold to be on a motorbike really. I parked under a bridge out of the rain and was drying myself off when I saw a building across the road, with drawing boards on the top two floors.

On a whim, I walked over to see if they would give me a job. To my surprise, the receptionist spoke perfect English and she introduced me to the manager, who agreed to take me on. Within three weeks, I had relocated to Berlin. My mother was horrified, as there was a lot of anti-German feeling after the war. I spent five happy years there and am now even able to draw a German pension. The German people are so courteous with a great attention to detail. Every increase in my German pension, even though it is only for one or two euros, is accompanied by a careful explanation in both German and English. During my time in Germany I was promoted in the office and took charge of a section of the work on a new airport at Riyadh, out in the desert of Saudi Arabia.

Family responsibilities finally brought me home. Back in Malta Road, my father had become seriously ill and my mother needed help to cope with the situation. My German employers were very understanding and held a job open for me should I choose to return. When my father died, my mother just didn't know what to do. My younger sister was married with children, so I looked after mum. I didn't go back to working in a drawing office as I had never really liked it. I got a job delivering new cars for a motor company. My last job was working for Toyota in Romford. I was happy there. I'd always wanted a job where I could think my own thoughts - a job I didn't have to take home with me.

When I returned from Germany, I noticed that there were fewer nuns at the convent, about twelve, and there were no youngsters any more. There were no replacements coming in. I remember one priest at that time, Fr. Bob Hamill. He had three dogs but one of them died. He was a gentleman. When my mother died he offered to do the funeral, even though she wasn't a Catholic. "I'll make the service as Anglican as I'm allowed", he said and that is what he did, including the longer version of the Lord's Prayer, both in the church and at her graveside. You couldn't help but admire the man. He was a strong and confident man and could easily manage the drunks who sometimes interrupted his services. He served the entire community. We would go to him to have our passport photos signed and he was happy to do it. In his eyes we were all his flock, Catholic and non-Catholic alike. The contrast between those two

Parish Priests, Father Byrne and Father Hamill, and the other priests who came to the church was quite marked. The latter kept their distance and didn't become part of the neighbourhood.

The nuns at the convent were not confident drivers and I began to take them to the airport when they asked. I was ready at a moment's notice to drive someone to the airport or to meet a nun who was arriving at Heathrow. I enjoyed taking them the direct route through London and pointing out the landmarks that I knew. I thought that some of the nuns were not all that worldly and didn't know their way around the city, and I was happy to point out the landmarks. In the old days I would eat my lunch in Tothill Street and go into Westminster Abbey for the shade it provided in the summer. There was always something to see in there.

At the convent, one of the nuns, Sister Agnes, was particularly keen on gardening. There was a greenhouse and a large garden to tend. When the Sister left, I was asked if I could help out with the garden. I could only do the grass. I eventually bought a narrower motor mower, because it was a struggle getting through the gate into the convent garden. I would do the back lawns, keep the garden looking trim and maybe cut back the hedges. I was eventually asked if I would take on the presbytery garden and the grounds around the church, so I was soon mowing a very big area every week. I believe that these days someone is paid to keep the gardens in trim, which seems a shame. It really should be part of the work of the church community.

I suppose having the church and convent so close to my house has encouraged me to think about religious matters. I'm Anglican, and I really couldn't be anything else. I loved the morning assemblies conducted by the headmaster of Aveley Technical School and I love the various services of the Anglican Church. The eulogies of Thomas Cranmer speak directly to me as a fellow Englishman.

I remember the Easter Parades, very grand traditional affairs with Father Byrne leading the procession with the Cross. To me it seemed like a foreign thing; I'd never seen anything like it. I didn't understand why it was being done because our church didn't do that. It was certainly very impressive. I recall that there was a statue at the top of the convent which was damaged by a bomb blast, and it was not replaced for many years. In fact it has only recently been reinstalled. I remember that the trees around the church were poplars when I was a young boy, and we used to creep into the grounds to climb the trees and collect the shrapnel that was still lodged there after the war.

Of course the world has changed as the years have slipped by. These days I know hardly anybody in Tilbury. The town has got a lot bigger, and there is no longer a sense of a neighbourhood which existed when my mother was alive. Behind our school in Lansdowne Road there used to be fields of waving corn and butterflies. We would help the farmers catch their horses running loose in the fields. After Easter every year, Farmer King would mow a field behind the primary school and let the children play in it all the summer. It was all to do with being part of a community.

Later on in life, I got to know something of the lives of some of the nuns in the convent. It helped me to see them in the round and to understand them better. One told me that she spent her childhood in rural Ireland taking the long daily walk to school in the company of a boy of her age, who would carry her books. It was always understood by the families that when they grew up they would be married, although nothing was ever said. When she had left school she discovered that her friend had gone to Liverpool to start work on an ocean steamer, and she never heard from him again. It left me thinking what might have been, although she did choose to follow her vocation as a nun.

Evelyn Gormley

My association with Our Lady Star of the Sea Church and St. Mary's School began with my mother and her six siblings, who all attended the school and church and all married in the church. My parents were married in Our Lady Star of the Sea in 1939 and went on to have 7 children, myself being the second. We also all attended the school and the church. My two brothers were altar servers. I married my late husband Patrick (who also attended the school) in 1964. We actually met in the late 1950s when there were dances in the school on Sunday nights, when Canon Byrne was Parish Priest.

Patrick and I also had seven children who all attended the school and church. My four sons were altar servers too.

I have three grandchildren attending the school and, at present, two great grandchildren.

I was a mid-day assistant and School Governor in St. Mary's for a number of years.

I have very fond memories of my time at school when Sister Bernadette was Head Mistress. Many times she called me to her office to try on an item of clothing that was donated. One particular time she had a lovely pair of black shiny shoes; they had to fit me!!! Then later in senior school, which was also in the same grounds as the junior school, I was regularly called to go to the convent (the big house) to escort a Sister, usually Reverent Mother, to Tilbury Station and carry her suitcase. On the way she would ask what lesson I was missing and would question me on that lesson (usually French verbs). Then I would go to the back door of the convent and get a cake or some fruit. I kept in contact with Sister Bernadette over the years and would often get a telephone call from her asking me about certain people from school days. She had a better memory than me!!!

In 1953, the year of the floods, I was one of four children from St. Mary's Senior School to go with a party of children from other flooded areas to have a three weeks holiday in Belgium. What a time we had, especially never having been away from home before. The late Pat Bolger was the teacher to accompany us, with a teacher from each of the other schools.

Sister Bernadette on her 90th Birthday together with Evelyn Gormley

The big day we would all look forward to was our May Procession. Tilbury Band would lead playing all our lovely hymns and the streets were lined with so many people. Benediction followed.

Ray Gnanapragasam

I was born into a large family in Jaffna, in the north of Sri Lanka. There are nine boys and seven girls. We are Tamils. My father was a Government agent, working for the British Commonwealth Office. Eventually he rose to the rank of Provincial Governor. He was posted to a lot of different places in Sri Lanka in the north and south of the island, including Colombo and Kandy. Wherever he went he bought land and had a house built there. Later on these houses were given as dowries when my sisters got married. I went to school in St. Benedict's College in Colombo and was taught by the Christian brothers.

Members of Ray's Family

The north east of Sri Lanka is where the Tamils live. It is quite dry and there is only one harvest a year. In the south, where the Sinhalese live, there is a lot of rain and you can get four or five crops a year. The people in the north have plenty of time for reading and writing, whilst those in the south spend more time in bringing in the harvests. When the British set up their administration in Ceylon they relied heavily on the Tamils who had a reputation for high levels of literacy. Many were moved to the south of the island where they became bookkeepers and shopkeepers.

As a member of a Catholic family, some of my early years had a religious aspect. When I was a teenager in Sri Lanka, I was part of a team organised by the Legion of Mary. We would go every Saturday into the slums in the company of priests. We would take medicines and first aid, and cut people's hair. We would help the people to clean up the places where they lived. We made paths and even roads to make life easier for the people living there.

When I left college I worked for a while on one of the family estates and then applied for a career in nursing. Most of my brothers and sisters eventually left Sri Lanka and moved to other places across the world, including Canada, Singapore and the United Kingdom. One of my brothers became a Jesuit priest and a sister became a Carmelite nun. As for me, I came to the UK in the nineteen sixties and went into psychiatric nursing, doing my training in Nottingham. One of our family friends was a doctor in the hospital where I was trained and that helped to settle me. I made friends with a couple of students from Mauritius and I did rather well in my training, winning prizes for my studies. Unfortunately, some of the white students didn't like me and I was attacked a few times until the police became involved. We all had to shake hands as a sign that we would put it all behind us.

After my course had finished in Nottingham I moved to Whitechapel in London to start my career. I did my post-graduate training in Whitechapel and I was much happier there. I had worked in the area during my holidays in Nottingham so I knew Whitechapel quite well. My sister was in London, working as a nurse in Wanstead Hospital, so I would see her as often as possible, but I soon made friends of my own. My sister became a midwife.

When I came to England I joined the East-West Club which introduced me to a lot of families living in the UK. These people realised that we were far from home and a bit lost and they tried to make us feel part of their world. I had meals with many of them and went to stay with families in Wales and the Midlands. The Club had links with the Rotary Club and the Lions Club so there were plenty of people to meet and lots of meals. From time to time I had to make a speech about what it was like growing up in Sri Lanka. The patron of the East-West Club was Princess Margaret and I was introduced to her at Kensington Palace. She shook hands with me and asked me what I did and then commented that it must be difficult to be a male nurse in a mainly female world.

Right from the start of my career, I came into contact with a lot of people with acute psychiatric conditions, and was eventually given the responsibility of developing a new way of responding to psychiatric patients, working closely with people living in a special centre and supporting them. My main focus was on trying to get them back into the community, which worked so well that the numbers in the centre declined steadily as the patients began to become independent. I was able to introduce psychotherapy, art therapy, and occupational therapy on the ward itself. This was an entirely new system. When the patients were ready to live independently, a community worker would accompany them to their home, evaluate their ability to manage their lives and teach them the skills they needed to develop. They would then organise liaison with local Day Centres so that the people would not need to rely so heavily on the hospital. The support workers also found employment for many of their charges in local supermarkets.

It became apparent that much of this work was merging with the world of social work and so I joined the Social Services team. Social Services owned a number of houses in Manor Park but they didn't really know how to manage those places. They asked me if I could run the homes. Eventually I was the head of three of these homes with a staff of forty five. I preferred to employ middle-aged people, men and women, people with some experience of life or who had raised a family. They were to be the role models for the patients we were helping to become independent. Our new system didn't just work better than the old system, it was also cheaper. Newham Council began to save a lot of money as the system was rolled out across the borough. Our patients were taking on regular work and attending Day Centres successfully. When our patients became more independent, we would organise regular visits to them to check that they were managing all right. We would check that the fridge was properly stocked and that the people were taking good care of themselves.

This Social Work programme ran very successfully from the nineteen seventies through to the nineteen nineties, but then the Director of Social Services changed and things became less harmonious. In the new system I was asked to employ people on the recommendation of my superiors, but I would not do so unless they went through the same application and interview procedures that I had set up over the years. I was not prepared to cut corners, because the quality of the staff was vital to the work we were all doing. This caused a lot of friction and unpleasantness for me, so I finally decided to take early retirement in 1995.

After I retired they began to employ people without going through the procedures I had established, and soon there were problems in the homes. Within three years they were closed down.

When I was working in the hospital I met a young woman from Poplar called Iris, who was also working in the hospital. We married in the nineteen seventies and went on to have three children, two girls and a boy. Iris had started work at the age of fourteen, on the railway. She became a signalwoman, possibly the first woman to do this on the railway. We lived first of all in Forest Gate, moved to Dagenham for a couple of years and then to our home here in Tilbury. I wanted a place with a garden, big enough to have a pond in it. We were married for over thirty years, but Iris died in 2009. Our children have all moved out now, with one in Wales, one in Witham and one just round the corner in Brentwood. She comes over to see me most weekends.

I came to the parish in the early nineteen eighties. Father Bob Hamill was the Parish Priest then. When Father David Clemens came to the parish, he asked me if I would become a Minister of Holy Communion, but I wasn't at all sure if I was suitable. I was asked again when Father Peter Connor became the Parish Priest and I underwent some training to teach me what to do. The reason I agreed to do this was that some parishioners were ill and it was necessary for someone to visit them and take them Communion. My first visits were to what we call the Three Sisters, the tower blocks on the edge of the parish. One person I visited there lived on the twenty-fifth floor.

I remember in the early days of my time in the parish I was asked by Father James if I could stand in for a Eucharistic Service that used to be said in St. Joseph's Hall. At first it was on a Wednesday and a Saturday, but eventually it was each Saturday morning at 9.00 a.m. I wrote my own prayers and organised the service for sick people. I did that until the Hall itself closed down. Becoming a Minister of Holy Communion is an important thing for me, and I believe that once you become a Minister of Holy Communion you should not attend other churches regularly but stay with your own Parish Church.

From time to time I like to organise a meal in my home for some of the people in our parish. Two or three priests are invited and some of the Sisters. It is an Indian buffet, and it allows people to relax and chat together informally.

I do a range of things in the parish, helping Father Paul out whenever I can. Now that I am getting older, I am trying to find people to train up so that they can take over from me, but it is difficult these days to find volunteers. From time to time I am asked to assist at a funeral, and these duties need to be learned by some people from the younger generation, as I shall not always be able to help. It is a privilege to be able to help in the church but I will be not be able to carry on for ever. It is even difficult to find someone to do the gardening.

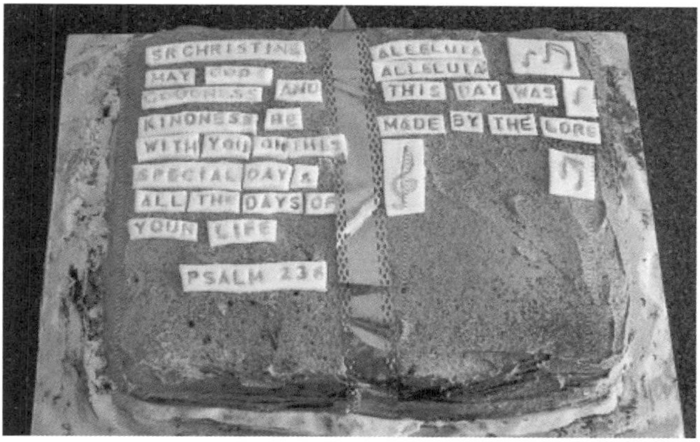

A Cake for Sister Christine

A Cake for Father Paul

I have now been in the parish for over thirty years. When I first came here there was Mass every day. In those days, when someone became a Minister of Holy Communion there was quite a lot of training involved.

Of course there have been many Parish Priests here over the years. I get on particularly well with Father Paul. Another favourite was Father David; he was very friendly with me. He knew my brother's family in Ilford where he had been a priest. He has stayed with my sister in Singapore for a holiday. When Father Paul fell sick, I wrote prayers for him which we said in our church.

When I helped in St. Joseph's Hall, Chadwell with the service for the healing of the sick, I remember that Pauline Lacey and her friends used to prepare a meal for everyone. Now that we no longer have that church hall there isn't really any place where people can gather together socially and I am sorry that that is missing now. People have spoken to me about it. When the first rumours began about the closure of St. Joseph's Church Hall and even possibly the presbytery in Dock Road we held a big meeting about it in Stella Maris to protest about it. I remember that Bill Terry was involved. It was no secret that Bishop Thomas wanted the church hall and the presbytery in Dock Road closed, but at the end of the meeting our Parish Priest, Father Peter, assured us that nothing would happen whilst he was in Tilbury. There were plans for the parish to be merged with the parish over at Grays, and many of our parishioners feared that this would result in the Tilbury Parish becoming somewhat neglected. Eventually, St. Joseph's Hall was deconsecrated but the Dock Road presbytery survived. Even now, so many years later, parishioners have requested a hall for the parish, but I understand that the Bishop is not keen.

Note : This is one example of the prayers that Ray wrote. He has given permission for it to be placed in the book.

> St. John Paul II, please intercede and help Fr. Paul, our Parish Priest, to heal. We are very worried about him and his physical problems. We, the people of our Parish, want to see him progress in health. Please allow him to heal so that he may fulfil God's will. We know you are very close to God. Without his paschal ministry we are like lost sheep.
>
> Almighty ever living God who has given your faithful servant Fr. Paul grace to maintain his priestly ministry, graciously bestow upon him, we pray, the consolation of your Holy Spirit and your healing Grace.
>
> Mary our Mother, Queen of peace and health of the sick, pray for us.

Margaret Crowley

I have been in the parish for over seventy-five years. I was born in Ireland, Co. Cork, in a small town called Youghal. My mother, sister, brother and myself came to England in 1942, in the middle of the war. My father was a seaman and his ship had been torpedoed. He was in the water for a long time and he lost the use of some of his fingers and some of his toes, so he could not go back to sea. His ship sank near Greenland, which is pretty cold. The Seamen's Association found him an alternative job ashore, which was just as well because there was no work back in Ireland. He had been a boilerman on ship, and they found him a job at Thames Board Mills as a boilerman. When D-Day arrived, they were desperate for seamen and my father went to sea again. He stayed on in the Merchant Navy after the war until he retired.

When we first came to Tilbury, my father got us into a bed and breakfast. Not long after we arrived, we were walking along on the pavement when we heard this funny noise, but we didn't take any notice of it. My mother said to us "Isn't this a quiet town? You'd expect more people to be walking about, wouldn't you?" When we got back, the lady in the house said "Oh, you're all right then? Did you hear the sirens?" My mother said "We heard a funny noise." The lady said "You're supposed to hide when that happens!"

I went to St. Mary's School from the age of nine until I was fifteen. We had four brick built air raid shelters in the playground, with nothing in them but benches. When the air raid siren went off, we had to line up and walk to the shelters. There were four classrooms in the junior school and two classrooms in the senior school. When we were in the shelter we had to stand up and our teacher, one of the nuns, would ask us spellings or mental arithmetic questions. If we got the answer right we could sit down, so you made sure to get the answer right. Even now, I can add up in my head just like that. I work in the retail trade and often add things up in my head, which surprises people.

I remember that my teacher was Sister Bernadette. She was a teacher but she was also the Headmistress. The other Sister was Sister Margaret Mary. They were the junior school teachers. There were two lay teachers in the senior school, Miss Clare and Miss O'Keyne, who just happened to be sisters. I remember Sister Borgia and Sister Angela, who were also sisters to each other, and there was a Sister Francis. After the war, other teachers came to the school, but now they were always lay teachers.

The air raids tended to come in the evenings and at night, so that most days we were free from them at school. One bomb landed in Malta Road and badly damaged two rows of back to back terraces. As for Our Lady Star of the Sea, there was just a small crack in the church bell. After a while we just accepted the air raids and I don't think we were especially afraid. Our Parish Priest, Father O'Donnell, a big Kerry man, used to walk about the parish during the air raids, visiting his partishioners. After about a month in Tilbury, my father managed to get a house for us in Chad's Road. It had been bombed and there were no windows in it, but we moved in. There were two flats in the house and my mother rented both of them as there were quite a few of us.

I had a wonderful time in school. All the nuns in the school were Irish, and I had spent three years speaking Gaelic in an Irish school before coming to England. I could do my arithmetic only in Gaelic, and I think that the nuns felt sorry for me. Sister Bernadette in particular took me under her wing. The classrooms were pretty basic. We had books to write in and to read, and Sister had the blackboard. The nuns were quite strict but they were really well regarded. I remember after the war that when the nuns walked from the convent across the school playground the boys would stop their football game immediately and stand back as a mark of respect. The nearest boys would step forward to carry the nuns' cases. We had been brought up to automatically show respect to the Parish Priest if we saw him out and about and we knew not to talk to him unless he talked to us first, because he would have important things on his mind or might be carrying the Blessed Sacrament. Of course, in those days the priests would walk everywhere, so we would often see them. The same kind of respect was shown to the lay teachers, although in their case we did have a bit of a laugh behind their backs.

We would say morning prayers in our own classroom at the start of the day in school and at the end of the day before we went home. Grace was said before we had our school dinner and at the end of the meal.

At lunchtime, we had to queue up in the playground and we were walked over to Lansdowne Road School where we had our dinner in a dining hall next to the school. It was always a cooked meal, always hot. We didn't mix with the children from Lansdowne Road School. They would have their dinner and then the room was cleared up and cleaned before we all came in.

Quite often, I would take a shopping list from the convent down to the local shop at the start of the day and bring the shopping back to the convent at the end of the school day. That was when I would meet Sister Patrick, who was the cook. In the wintertime she would invite me in for a hot drink, perhaps a cup of cocoa. In the summer, it would be a cold drink. My mother was a cleaner in the school and she had many an argument with Sister Theresa about Irish politics. They would end up laughing with each other. Most of the teachers in the school were Sisters, but that changed after the war.

I left school at the age of fifteen. The older people in the class above us were allowed to leave at the age of fourteen, but we had to wait until we were fifteen. I didn't really have a clue what I wanted to do when I left school. I worked first in a shop and then moved on to an office job at the Bata Shoe factory. I was there for three years. When I was eighteen I got a job in a pub and I stayed in that work for many years, in different pubs. I always fancied that work, the social life. The pub manager said I was too young to even be in a pub, but I told him that it was my eighteenth birthday. He gave me the job for my cheek. I was trained up properly by the governor, and he tried to find a drink that I would like to have when I began my work in the pub. But I didn't like any of them, and although I spent many years in pubs I never drank any alcohol at all.

I got married at nineteen. I met my husband, Fred, when I was working as a barmaid in the pub. He wasn't a Catholic, so that didn't go down very well with my mother. When I went to see Canon O'Donnell about the arrangements, he told me that he was being moved to Canning Town, and that a young priest, Father Byrne, was coming in his place. I was quite shocked, because Canon O'Donnell had seen me through my school years and supervised my Confirmation and so I had assumed that he would marry us. We were married on the nearest Saturday to St. Patrick's Day in 1953, and my husband became a good friend of Father

Byrne. As far as I am aware, we were the first couple that Father Byrne married when he came to Tilbury. He was here in the parish for over thirty years. Our children were all christened in Our Lady Star of the Sea, they had their First Communion there and were all Confirmed there. Both of my sons were altar boys with Father Byrne. Occasionally they would help out at a funeral service and sometimes were given a couple of bob by the family.

Pictures of the May Procession at Our Lady Star of the Sea, Tilbury

Apart from Father Byrne and Father O'Donnell, I particularly remember Father Butcher. He was good with the boys and would take them camping. My sons still remember him kindly, particularly the younger one.

When I was a child at St. Mary's School, we always had the Latin Mass. I was in the school choir and we had to memorise the Latin words. Even now I can hear those words in my head when the congregation is singing a hymn in English. I was sorry when the Mass began to be said in English. Many years ago, Fred and I were on holiday in Malta. I went to Mass at the beautiful cathedral in Valetta, St. John's, and Fred came with me. He was amazed that the whole service was in Latin, and even more amazed that I understood it. There was a lovely choir in the cathedral, and Fred said it was like going to the opera.

First Communions at St. Mary's School in the early sixties, with Father Byrne, Sister Bernadette, Sister Francis, Mr. Fitzgerald and Mr Hart

(Note: The following extract from the Thurrock Gazette was provided by Margaret Crowley.)

Parish mourns priest's death

HUNDREDS of mourners are expected at the funeral of Canon John Byrne being held at Our Lady Star of the Sea Church in Tilbury this morning (Friday).

Father Byrne, who was parish priest at the Dock Road church for 30 years, died last week after a short illness. He was 80 years old.

He celebrated his last mass at the church on Boxing Day despite not feeling well and was taken to Orsett Hospital on Thursday where he died later that evening.

His body was received into the church on Wednesday evening which was followed by a mass. There was also a special mass yesterday (Thursday) afternoon.

The funeral service will be held at Father Byrne's church at 11 am after which Father Byrne will be buried at Chadwell St Mary cemetery.

Unwell

The Bishop of Brentwood, the Rev Thomas McMahon, will be a co-celebrant and 70 priests from all over the diocese are hoping to attend the service, including the former Bishop, the Rev Patrick Casey.

Port chaplain at the Stella Maris in Tilbury Father Gerard Greatrex said: "He hadn't been well recently and was advised by his doctor not to go out.

But he kept working right up to the end. He took midnight mass and conducted mass last Monday. It was a great shock. He was loved by everyone. He was a father figure in Tilbury." Father Byrne was ordained as a priest in Ireland 55 years ago and was at Witham before coming to Tilbury. He celebrated his 80th birthday two months ago and to mark his birthday and 30 years at Tilbury there was a huge party at the Stella Maris.

As a student, Father Byrne achieved fame at the Gaelic Games and played at Croke Park, Dublin, in the all-Ireland final.

He was a well-known and much-loved man in the borough and was involved with schools, clubs and organisations

Parishioner Mrs Margaret Greenan knew Father Byrne from when he first came to the parish. She said: "He was a very wonderful man. Everybody loved him because he was such a marvellous priest.

"We thought the world of him and he will be missed by so many people."

Father Brian O'Shea, press officer for the Brentwood diocese, said: "He was very much an elder statesman of the diocese and was much loved and respected.

"He was a devoted priest, and had a quiet and very gentle manner. In 1977 he was mane an honorary canon of the cathedral at Brentwood.

THURROCK GAZETTE Friday, January 7, 1983

I remember that when the changes came about in the Church and the beautiful old altar was to be broken up, Father Byrne would not agree to it. It fell to the English priest, Father Duckett, to manage the changes. The parishioners were not happy about it at all. The old altar was a lovely part of the church. One or two of the congregation kept a piece of the altar as a memento.

When Canon Byrne died, there was a huge funeral here in Tilbury. Father Greatorex, from Stella Maris, conducted the funeral Mass. I arrived an hour before the service and Our Lady Star of the Sea was already packed to the doors. They put up a loudspeaker system for the crowds outside and they had to close the roads because there were so many people who were standing out in the street. Canon Byrne was buried in Chadwell St. Mary.

Damien Ngugi

I moved into the area about ten years ago and I've been in the parish about seven years. My work schedule makes it difficult for me to attend church every weekend, as I am often working on Saturdays and Sundays, but I attend when I can.

I was born in Kenya, and lived in Nairobi. I studied Graphic Design at college, and eventually I was able to set up my own printing company. Unfortunately, the Kenyan economy was having difficulties and it was difficult to grow the company. It was necessary for me to head in a different direction. I came to the UK when I was about twenty eight. I moved here by myself and it was all a bit of a culture shock at first. Everything seemed to move so much faster.

The African continent is very religious, including Catholics and Protestants, Moslems, and many forms of traditional religion and the places of worship are full. When I first came to the UK I was really shocked at how empty the churches were.

I came here to study Computer Science and so I soon got to know people at the university and some Kenyans within the community. I was supported by friends and family back home in Kenya, but I was unable to finish my university course because eventually the money ran out and I had to take employment here where I could find it.

I worked for a networking company at first but the pay was very poor. I was earning less than the security guards who protected the premises. I carried on studying and eventually managed to get a job in a company that supplied and fitted carpets. You had to start on the shop floor and I was a driver, but I was eventually able to work my way up to a more senior position. The people are very good there, although the pay could be better, like most places I suppose.

When I first came to the UK I lived in Ilford. My landlord was a fireman, and he was very supportive. He wanted to help me because he saw me as a really good tenant. He recommended that I got a mortgage to buy a house, rather than paying out rent. He suggested I looked for a property outside the M25, and offered to drive me around to see what was available. I looked at properties in Grays, West Thurrock, Chadwell and Tilbury. Eventually I found a house in Tilbury, solidly built but needing a bit of work doing on it. It had a front and back garden. There were just the two of us then and the house was just what we wanted. We moved into the area about the time that Father Paul became the Parish Priest, though I did meet the previous Parish Priest, Father John Meehan.

Now we have two daughters, aged eleven and six. They go to St. Mary's School. They particularly liked one of the nursery school teachers, who took a special interest in her pupils. I remember that there were tears all round when they moved on to the next stage of their school life. Our older daughter is about to move on to Grays Convent School in September 2017. She has already had an introductory week at the Convent School. Fortunately, one or two other friends are also going to the Convent School, so she'll have some company. Our two girls like going to school and take pride in their achievements.

The family go to Mass at Our Lady Star of the Sea each week, even though my wife was brought up as a Protestant. At the time of our marriage in Kenya, the Catholic Church was beginning to relax its attitude towards Catholics and non-Catholics getting married. Our daughters were baptised in the Parish Church and each has had their First Communion there.

At the moment, I don't do any particular jobs in the church, apart from small tasks like bringing up the offertory, but perhaps I will help out in the future on the days when I am not working. The Catholic Church is still quite traditional in its outlook and its services, although sometimes we do have a musician who plays as part of the Mass, and that makes things feel a bit more modern. In Kenya, they have tried to modernise church services, installing big screens and encouraging people to bring their musical instruments into the Mass, helping the services to become more family friendly. Having said that, church attendance here in Tilbury is very good, and has increased steadily since I joined the Parish. There has been a big influx of people of different races, including African and Polish people, and this accounts for much of the recent growth in the numbers attending church.

One time of the year that I particularly like is Easter. I often have to work at Easter time, because everyone likes to have time off then. I finally decided to have a word with my boss, and I explained that I would like some time off at that time of year because Easter is really important to me. To my surprise, he was very understanding and supportive. It turned out that he was a Catholic and many years before he had been in training to become a Catholic priest.

Bernadette Terry

My mother was born in Wales, and during the time of the Depression my grandfather came to Essex, looking for a job. So my mother, aged six, with her Welsh accent, arrived in Tilbury and went straight to St Mary's School. This was around 1928. She grew up in Tilbury and lived in Brennan Rd. My father came from St. Helens in Lancashire. He worked for British Rail and as a young man was transferred to Tilbury Riverside to work in the booking office. He found digs in a house across the road from the church and introduced himself to the Parish Priest, Father O'Donnell. Dad also became an Altar Server at the Church of Our Lady Star of the Sea. Fr. O' Donnell introduced him to one of the men in the parish to look after him, and my father eventually married the man's daughter, my mother. But not before the enforced separation of the Second World War.

During the war my mother's family had moved to Grays. But because they had met in Tilbury, my parents got married in Our Lady Star of the Sea Church in November 1945. My grandmother particularly liked the Tilbury church and she sang in the choir. I was very fond of her, and we would travel, by bus, from Grays to Tilbury on Sunday afternoons for Benediction. I remember there were always sweets in the shop on the way back. There are still some hymns which make me remember her singing upstairs in the church choir. She had a lovely voice.

I went to St Thomas's School in Grays. The school was situated in rooms beneath the church and when there was a funeral everyone had to be quiet. Some of the classes had fifty children in them. Most of the teachers there were La Sainte Union Sisters, with only three or four lay teachers. I moved on to Grays Convent School, where again many of the teachers were La Sainte Union Sisters. I believe there are no longer any Sisters teaching in the school these days. I remember that the May Procession always took place in Tilbury and the Corpus Christi Procession in Grays so that the two parishes joined together for these festivals. I remember that the Tilbury Band used to play in the May Procession, but I didn't know then that my future husband was playing in the band.

When I left school I went to La Sainte Union College of Education, Southampton, to train to be a teacher. My first teaching post was in Grays Park School but then I found a job at St. Chad's School in Tilbury, as Head of Modern Languages. I had various different posts in that school and I eventually became the Deputy Headteacher when the school amalgamated with Torells School to become The Gateway Community College.

My husband and I rented a house in Tilbury, when we got married. The day after we moved into the house, Canon Byrne was knocking at the door. The Catholic grapevine was alive and well. My grandmother was delighted with our move to Tilbury, because she was still coming to Mass down here. In my eyes we were only going to be in that house for six months, but we are still there.

We have two children, a boy first and then a girl. They both went to St. Mary's School. My son went on to Campion School in Hornchurch and my daughter went to Grays Convent. My son went to University in Manchester and my daughter to Liverpool University. Eventually, my daughter became a teacher, but now with four young sons to look after she isn't teaching at present. They live in Wiltshire. My son works for an accounting firm in Warrington. He and his wife have one son, with another baby on the way – a boy again! On reflection, many of the children who attended St. Mary's School have been very successful. The school gave them a good start in life.

There were many special teachers, over the years, at the school. We particularly remember Sister Patricia, who was Headteacher while our children were at school. Also, there was Sister Emmanuel, who had such a lovely, calm manner with the pupils. My daughter was very fond of Miss Hunt. Sadly, Miss Hunt died in a car crash a short time after leaving the school for a new post. My husband was very involved with

St. Mary's School. He was Chairman of a thriving PTA and became a School Governor and then Chair of Governors. Much later on, when I retired, I was Chair of Governors. Our family has had a long association with the school as my mother and two aunties attended both the primary and secondary schools.

Father O'Donnell

I remember several priests who have served here in Tilbury. Father Donal Donegan made some real changes in the parish. He had the presbytery completely refurbished because his predecessor, Canon Byrne, had been reluctant to spend money on his own comfort and as a result the house had become rather dilapidated and old fashioned. Fr. Donal set up the Parish Council and oversaw the remerging of the Chadwell Parish with Tilbury. I know that many parishioners in Chadwell were understandably sad that they no longer had their own Parish Priest. We did have a parish magazine at that time. It was produced by a group of women in the parish and we named it "Unitas" to celebrate the new unity of the two formerly independent parishes.

Jeanne Burdon, Fr. O'Donnell's Belgian Housekeeper

Father Bob Hamill is another memorable priest. He had a very big influence on the parish. Fr. Bob was very keen on encouraging the development of the social life of the parish and St Joseph's Hall was ideal for that. There were so many activities, meals for the elderly, social events and Lenten lunches each year. Fr. Bob had the kitchens at St. Joseph's Hall refurbished to a really high standard. We used to have a special Passover Meal each Easter at the beginning of Holy Week. My husband used to go with Fr. Bob to buy the proper kosher food and wine and there would be an authentic service before we sat down to eat. My husband would even dress as a Rabbi for the occasion and all the men wore skullcaps. They were most particular in respecting the traditions and rules of the Passover meal. Apart from the social aspect, I think Fr. Bob was trying to show us something of the roots of early Christianity. It was quite an ecumenical activity.

There seemed to be more emphasis on ecumenism back in the nineteen eighties. There were prayer meetings and regular discussion groups in the area where we would meet with people of other denominations and talk and pray together and gain a better understanding of each other's customs and beliefs. Fr. Bob had many good qualities; you could speak your mind to him and he was a good listener.

At the time the parish was as lively as I can remember. Apart from the frequent use of St. Joseph's Hall, there was Stella Maris, just down the road. The PTA made use of the facilities there to organise socials, dances and fancy dress parties for the children. It is all closed down now and there are flats where Stella Maris used to be. We also used the Methodist Church Hall for some activities but, sadly, that church has closed down and has been replaced by a "Tesco Express" .

I also remember when we had two Christmas Bazaars each year. One was held in Chadwell and one in Tilbury. These were significant social events as well as being good fund raising opportunities. One year, my husband organised a leafleting of the local area in Tilbury, informing residents about the bazaar. On the day, crowds were queuing around the block, much to the consternation of the nuns. Sister Patricia was in her element and as usual turned a young child into an elf with just some crepe paper and a few pins. People loved those events and looked forward to them. I think that we have changed our expectations nowadays and have many more opportunities for Christmas shopping. Times have moved on.

Our parish now doesn't have any central meeting place for social events and there seems to be a diocesan moratorium on the construction of new buildings. Even something as localised as a cake sale has its own complications, as we have to conduct the event in the porch of our Parish Church, not the biggest space in the world. It's a pity because people go to a lot of trouble preparing items for sale and there is just insufficient room for people to see what's on offer. It is also difficult when we wish to welcome new people to the parish. We can't involve them in any social events or even give them a cup of tea because we simply don't have a venue. We even have to use the hall of our local Anglican Church, St John's, to hold First Communion classes.

In addition, I am a big fan of succession planning, encouraging younger parishioners to become involved and to start taking on some of the responsibilities that are currently being carried out by mainly older people. You don't get much chance to talk with people as there is nowhere to just have a chat. It would be so helpful if there was a place where we could meet up, after Mass, even once a month, for a cup of coffee and a chat.

There are a number of African based churches which have been set up in Tilbury. Some of them have services in local schools and one is based in a building that used to be a public house. This has all happened in the last six or seven years, as a good number of African families have moved into the area. Many of these families are devout Catholics and they are the future of our parish. It is difficult to reach out to newcomers in the absence of a thriving social life. Of course, it can be done in small ways to begin with, by encouraging new people to take part in organising the offertory at Mass or becoming Readers, Catechists or Ministers of Holy Communion.

This sort of change has already started in the composition of the School Governing body. Once this was the domain of comparatively older, white people but in recent years the younger new School Governors have begun to reflect more accurately the cultural background of the pupils themselves, and they are a more appropriate representation of the community.

As to the future, we have a growing congregation which should ensure the continuation of our Parish of Our Lady Star of the Sea. I certainly hope and pray that this will be the case.

<u>Anne Ofeke</u>

I moved into Tilbury in 2003. I have always been a Catholic, even if I have lapsed from time to time. When I moved here, my daughter Precious was barely two years old. We came from Beckton in East London. When Precious was very young it was difficult to concentrate in Mass, so I wasn't that regular in attendance. I remember that the Parish Priest at that time was Father James. One of my first memories was going to a few meetings about a pilgrimage to Lourdes, but then I realised that the pilgrimage was not very practical for me with a little girl to look after.

For a while I went to a Pentecostal Church in Chadwell, but my daughter didn't like the noisy atmosphere. In 2008, my mother came from Nigeria to stay with me. She is a strong Catholic, and it was her influence that brought me back to the Catholic Church. My daughter was really pleased.

She went to St. Mary's School, and did her First Communion at Our Lady Star of the Sea. She must have been about eight. All the preparations were done by Brenda, and the priest was then Father John. As we walked out of the church on her First Communion day, Precious said to me "Mum, I want to be an altar server." This is what Precious did, and she was joined by her cousin, Lawrence.

With my daughter now an altar server, I wanted to find some way to contribute something of myself to the church, but with a busy life-style it was difficult to find the right thing. I became a Reader in the church and then began to help Joyanna with the church flowers. She showed me what to do, and now it is a regular thing for us to arrange the flowers on a Saturday morning. I sometimes sit in Mass and look at the flowers we have prepared and it feels good.

My daughter went to St. Mary's School and really likes it there. She particularly liked Miss Vassal, Mrs. Bridget and Mr. Shields, who was the Headmaster. Although he lived in Kent, I think, he sometimes came to Our Lady Star of the Sea on a Sunday. We all like the school secretary, Mrs. Alison Bishop, who has been at the school a long time.

Last year I went to London with the Sisters to an event, but I wasn't able to go this year. Gradually I am becoming involved in activities in the church, not just attending Mass on Sundays. I also try to involve friends in the life of the church. Some of them hesitate, but I say "Come on, because the church belongs to us."

We have a prayer group that meets twice a month, on the second and fourth Friday. It starts at 7.00 and we aim to finish by 8.30, although we sometimes run over. We used to meet in the convent, but then Father Paul allowed us to use part of the church for the meetings. At the meetings, nobody takes the lead. Somebody picks up a Bible passage that they like and they read it, explaining what they understand about the extract. Everyone else contributes to the discussion. The prayers we say together are good, but for me the best part is the Bible readings.

My daughter is now almost 16, and she goes to the Ursuline School in Brentwood. A school bus picks her up at Blackshots each day. This year is an important one for her as it is the GCSE year.

Of course, with friends and family attending church regularly, we soon notice if someone is missing. Not that we are checking up on people, but we are likely to phone or text anyone who is not there, to make sure that they are all right. We always let each other know if we are going to be away on holiday so that people don't worry. It's funny, I never thought that the church community would be so close, and I would be so much part of it.

Although I lived in a few places in East London before I came to Tilbury, I was born into a Catholic family in Nigeria. When I came to the UK at about the age of 26, I came here for a better life. Having worked in a bank in Nigeria, I started doing Care Work in the UK. I occasionally went to a Catholic Church in Hackney, but my attendance was certainly not every week. I worked at the London Hospital for about ten years. I studied Health Management at what is now the London Metropolitan University and gradually worked my way up. I eventually did a masters degree course in Business Administration.

When I moved to Tilbury I found employment in the Probation Office, Ministry of Justice, in Grays. I thought I would do the work for a month or two, and ended up working there for almost twelve years. I did a range of jobs there, but I eventually became the Business Manager. I enjoyed the work there, although it could be quite stressful at times. There were long hours, and it was often necessary to work there in my own time at weekends just to catch up with the workload. When I left that employment I did some freelance work, trying to set up my own business, but I am now working as a Business Manager, again in the Probation Service, this time over in Maidstone, which is quite a journey each day.

I am now the Safeguarding Representative in the church. When a new person takes on a role that involves contact with young people or vulnerable adults in the parish, I organise the background checks to ensure the appointments are appropriate. When I was asked if I would like to be a School Governor I was delighted. I am now in my third year as a Governor and I am really enjoying it. The Governors work together as a group and the school is doing well. We like to support the Head and the teaching staff, and we are encouraged to come up with ideas to make the school better.

I've noticed over the years that people in Tilbury tend to remain in their homes; there are not many people who move house. It is a settled community and that is one of the things that makes the area unique. I am aware that some outsiders regard Tilbury as a difficult place to live in, but that reputation is not accurate. Some of my work colleagues expressed surprise that I had chosen to live in Tilbury, but right from the start I knew I had made the right choice. My work for the Probation Service gives me first-hand experience of real criminal activity, but Tilbury is not affected by major crime. I think that this is due to the strong community feeling around here, and it one of the reasons that I enjoy living in the area.

My brother and his family also live in Tilbury. Fortunately we are a close family and we often see each other. My mother lives with me and my daughter. We all look after each other. I still have family back in Nigeria, a sister and a brother. We see them from time to time, but when you have family of your own you tend to rely on texting and Facebook to keep in touch.

Apart from the Parish Priests I have known in Tilbury, Father James, Father John and now Father Paul, I have also met the priests who helped out in the parish during Father Paul's illness. We were lucky with these priests, including Father Anthony, Father Francis and Father Frank. I particularly liked Father Frank and his wife Anne. He was so good with the congregation and we all warmed to him.

The one thing we don't have in the parish is a place where we can all gather together socially. Of course there used to be St. Joseph's in Chadwell, but now there isn't anywhere. Sometimes you see another parishioner whom you would like to encourage to help out in the parish in some way, and what you need to do is to sit down with them and have a chat. You can't really do that if the only chance you get is when they are leaving church after Mass. There is a real instinct among many Nigerians to participate, to become involved, and this potential is stifled if we don't have the chance to sit down and chat together.

When I first became a Reader in church, someone asked me if I was a teacher. Apparently, I sounded confident. I explained to the lady that actually I was anything but confident, but it gave me the opportunity to encourage her to take a more active role in the Mass. I keep telling people "This is our church". I try to encourage my daughter, my nephew and other young people to help out preparing the church for Mass. It is important for the future of the Catholic Church to involve young people as much as possible. When I first came to the UK all those years ago, it seemed to me that in the Catholic Church the people were quite old, whereas in the Pentecostal Church there was a younger congregation. We have to learn to encourage our younger people to take an active part in the parish. After all, they are its future.

It is so easy to overlook the complexity of our parish. When Father Anthony was here, he recognised that there was a large group of Polish people living in the parish. He organised a special Polish thanksgiving service, a kind of harvest festival, and the church was packed. There was such a display of food and produce and the church looked especially beautiful. I am glad that Father Paul has continued with this festival, for it is another way of celebrating who we are. In a similar way, Father Paul celebrates the very youngest parishioners, involving them in the Mass as they report back on the activities they have being doing in the Children's Eucharist. They are are always given a big round of applause.

Sister Paula Cleary

I came to Tilbury in January 2000 at a kind of crossroads in my life as a Sister of Mercy. Having just finished my six year term as local superior at our Wanstead Convent, followed by three months at St. Joseph's Hospice, Hackney on a 'Care of the Dying' course, I needed also to complete the mandatory 'Return to Practice' course before returning to employment as a nurse, because of my six-year break from practice. Having been accepted for the Summer term cohort at what was then the Anglia Polytechnic University in Chelmsford, I had time to settle in Tilbury, and also continue to honour my ongoing commitments in the London area. While in Wanstead, I had gradually become involved in assisting assylum-seekers, and others in need of support, to access the various agencies they had to deal with for legal status issues, employment, housing, and social/health problems.

When I came here, Stella Maris (the Hostel for Seafarers) was still in operation on Dock Road and many members of the parish were, or had been, involved in assisting the Chaplains and Manager (Veronica Hughes) to provide spiritual and practical support for the Catholic seafaring workers who passed through the Port. However, when working practices changed at the Docks (due, I understand, to greater mechanisation) cargo ships had a much faster turn-around schedule and so the quite extensive provision for residential accommodation at Stella Maris was scarcely being used by seafarers. Consequently, the AOS (Apostleship of the Sea) found it necessary to close it down. Because the replacement provision (an Ecumenical drop-in Centre) is on the Port side there is now only minimal parish involvement. Traditional support activities, such as the knitting of hats and scarves, have continued however and memories of 'good old days' still live on among those who remember.

Having had a long-standing interest in the Hospice movement I was hoping to work at St. Luke's, Basildon, but when I applied there was no vacancy so my application was put on file. In the meantime, I happened to meet the late Sr. Philomena O'Driscoll at a Spirituality Day in Brentwood Cathedral. She invited me to come and see the Marillac saying that they needed another staff nurse – and the rest is history as the saying goes! I continued to work there until my retirement in 2015. By then I could almost drive along the A128 blindfolded!

The residents are young people (under 65) who are disabled, to varying degrees, by neurological trauma or disease. Many are unable to speak and very few recover enough to be cared for at home. I was prepared for an atmosphere of sad hopelessness, but soon found that the bond which develops between staff, residents and relatives somehow creates a soothing layer of serene acceptance. This was especially true during Sr. Philomena's time as Director of Nursing. As a Daughter of Charity she radiated a very unique brand of caring which inspired all who worked under her direction. Long after her sudden death, one resident, Jackie, who had been there many years, insisted on always having a photo of Sister Philomena, whom she called her 'Mum', on her bedside table.

Another resident, Sally, who regularly patrolled the corridors in her wheelchair, happened to be at reception one day when Bishop Thomas paid an informal visit. She confidently assured him and the receptionist that she would take him on his tour and launched off ahead of the Bishop, pausing outside each bedroom as she introduced the occupant by name. When the designated escort hurriedly arrived on the scene, Sally bowed out graciously! Jackie and Sally (both now deceased) reflected for me the Marillac ethos of feeling valued and at home. Staff also experience that homely feeling and I enjoyed working there so much that I continued for five more years after the official retirement age.

Now at another crossroads, it's probably time for me to look back rather than forward. On October 4th 1962, a school friend and I travelled from Ireland to Leeds-Bradford Airport and arrived at the Mercy Novitiate in Clifford with the advice of our parents, to come back home if we weren't happy, still ringing in our ears. At the time, it was not unusual for girls to take such a step at the end of secondary school. My friend, who came from a much more religious family than mine, had a younger brother who became a priest a few years later. After the sad death of my own youngest brother from a brain tumour in 1960, I began to think seriously about life. From reading '*The Far East*' and other missionary magazines I gradually developed an admiration for what missionaries did with their lives. Although inspired to follow in their footsteps, I didn't think I could tolerate the very hot climates where they worked, which I suppose led me to consider England instead. About half-way through our final (Leaving Certificate) year my friend decided to apply to a Mercy Convent in Leeds, where I had a great-aunt, and asked me for the address.

We and our two sisters were among forty or so boarders at a convent school in Claremorris, because our homes were too far away for daily travel to any secondary school. Due to the fact that secondary education was still optional in Ireland at the time there was no school bus service. Despite our dormitories being under the same roof, there was little social interaction with the Sisters who taught us, because of their quite strict regime back then. However, depending on personality, some were a bit more approachable than others. One evening at the end of Study, Sister Joseph, the elderly nun supervising us, called me aside, gently reprimanded me for reading a book instead of doing my homework, and then to my complete surprise asked if I had ever thought of becoming a nun! She admitted, rather awkwardly, that a friend of hers in another part of Ireland was recruiting for vocations. Because she was so open, I felt encouraged to be frank with her. She responded to my questions about her own experience of convent life very honestly and then finished our conversation by saying "Whatever you do, you will be a good girl". Strangely, that little bit of affirmation gave me confidence to believe that it might be for me and to finally decide that I should give it a try.

My home parish of Ballycroy had very few vocations, to either the priesthood or religious life, compared to some other places, and so when my father knew that three of my age group were joining convents and a seminary he declared it: "a wave of insanity sweeping the countryside". Nevertheless, he dutifully supported me and when the time came to say goodbye to relatives and neighbours, he took me round as a passenger on his motorbike. It was only when he turned away to hide his face at his cousin's remark: "You'll miss her now", that I realised how much he was affected by my leaving. My mother wasn't unduly anxious about my decision. She had spent some years in Leeds during the War, including a few weeks at the convent where her aunt was, and had herself considered "joining the nuns", as she put it.

The bedtime stories we had as children were often about her experiences of trying to find her way through Leeds city "in the pitch dark", without any street lights, in buses and trams without lights, and of her night-time fire-watching duties (for German incendiary attacks) on the roof-top of

St. James's Hospital during her training. Half-way through the course they were given a holiday and she went home to Ireland. However, while there she was persuaded by her family not to return because of the War, which she sometimes seemed to regret. Her attitude was that each of us should have a chance to do whatever we wanted in life. She even encouraged my eldest brother, who traditionally should have remained at home, to find construction work with her cousin in Warwickshire, which is where he eventually settled.

Life moved on quickly during the first few years after I left home. Communication was by post only because, like most people then, my family didn't have a house-phone. My mother and sister were very faithful letter writers, which kept me in touch quite well.

Even though we had spent five years at a Mercy school we knew virtually nothing about the Foundress, Catherine McAuley, or the history of the Order. During our two years of Novitiate training, we had a thorough education about her charism and spirituality. I was deeply impressed by her courageous spirit and selfless generosity towards the most needy people of 1830s Dublin, especially women and children. She experienced opposition and criticism, even from within the Church, because she was challenging the status quo, but was not deterred.

In 1965 we made out temporary Profession of Vows (for three years). Our parents were invited to attend and my mother came. We completed our professional training during the following three years and then in 1968 had our first visit home. My only sister, also newly qualified as a teacher by then, was at home for the summer holidays and drove me round to visit everyone. My parents were still working hard at running their two small farms, but my three brothers had already moved away for study and work. After two lovely weeks of being back home again, my sense of vocation was reassured. On returning to the convent, I renewed my temporary Profession of Vows for a further two years, then settled down to Community life and my first teaching post.

My teacher training was for Secondary level but when I began work at the all-through Convent Collegiate School, attached to the convent building in Doncaster, the newly appointed PE teacher and I were 'commandeered' to share Grade 1 class (7 year olds) for a couple of months to cover for their class teacher who had become ill over the summer. I had to take a 'crash course' from the Infants Teacher in what is now called 'phonics', in order to help those who hadn't yet fully mastered the art of reading. How I wished I had attended the

Infant/Junior Lectures at College! A memory which has stayed with me from the senior school is of going to see 'Dr. Zhivago' at the local cinema with the Sixth-Formers. I don't remember how that decision got past our very strict Headmistress, or how I happened to be chosen to accompany them, but it was certainly an 'education' at the time! I still find the theme music haunting, in part because I associate it with the tragic death of one of the girls in a car accident soon afterwards, which cast a cloud of grief over the class for the rest of the year.

Five of my family were able to attend my Final Profession in July 1970 and stay on for a couple of days. My mother and sister were quite familiar with convent environments but I think the men-folk felt a bit like 'fish out of water'. There was no visitor accommodation at that convent so they had to book into the local B&B. On arriving from the Liverpool Ferry late into the night they discovered that, due to some 'hiccup' in the booking, the landlady did not expect them until the next night. As the guest rooms were mostly occupied, they had to wait in a lounge while the lady and some of her family vacated their own beds! Despite the upheaval, they quickly saw the funny side and of course their story gained in the telling! Having met the Community and seen how settled I was among them, my parents returned home fully satisfied that I was happy there.

My next teaching appointment was to a large diocesan secondary school which served the local deanery and had about 1,500 on roll. It had been more or less Comprehensive until just before, when a new building (partly funded by the Sisters of Mercy to replace the Convent Collegiate School) opened nearby and began to attract away the more academic pupils, much to the annoyance of my new Headteacher and many of his staff. Although there were two other Sisters teaching there already, I felt distinctly 'alien' at first but the atmosphere of grievance gradually faded into the background. In time, I was appointed Head of Religious Education and also Year Tutor (pastoral/disciplinary role) for First Year girls, while continuing to teach English as well. Because of having to cover for absent colleagues during our free (marking) lessons, the more 'nodding acquaintance' one had with other subjects the easier it was to set work on such occasions. Supply teachers were usually provided only for planned absences in those days. Needless to say, the members of staff who 'enjoyed bad health' regularly were not very popular!

As the years went by, I watched the classes move up through the school and eventually knew most of them by name, especially the 'naughty' ones! Somewhere along the way, we Sisters went through another Habit (dress) change which this time involved showing our hair! On my first day in the new outfit, I explained to the classes as they came along for lessons but somehow felt more nervous about venturing into the Senior Dining Room at lunchtime. The only vacant place was at a table of Fourth Year boys. There was a kind of stunned silence as I sat down among them, until the jovial character beside me quietly asked: "Has yer other stuff gone to the wash then …?" triggering a laugh all around – me included!

After twelve years of working there, a decision to merge the two secondary schools was reached and all staff were notified that we would have to re-apply for our jobs. Having always felt drawn to nursing more than teaching, I saw this as an ideal opportunity to change direction. Luckily, the Superior of the time was herself a nurse and gave me permission to explore the possibility. Being just within the age limit to apply and having recently completed an Open University BA degree in Humanities, I was easily accepted for training at the South Manchester Hospitals Group (Withington/Wythenshawe/Christie). My three and a half years of living in a Nurses Home in Withington was an enlightening experience. The majority of my fellow students were straight from school, although there were a few other 'mature students' besides me. By the end of the course our 'November 82' set had formed quite a strong bond of friendship and some of us still exchange 'round robins' at Christmas!

My convent-base while training was attached to the convalescent home in Leeds, where my great-aunt had been Matron until her retirement. By the end of the course, when I was appointed to work there, it already felt like home because I had gone regularly on my off-duty days. There was a constant succession of patients coming from the Leeds Hospitals. Very often, the patients who qualified for the two weeks of convalescence, men especially, had various social problems as well, including even homelessness in some cases. The concept of 'total patient care' took on a new dimension for me there, which sometimes involved discreetly supplying new clothes or even negotiating urgently for a place to live at the Little Sisters of the Poor or the Salvation Army Hostel after discharge. There was never a dull moment and inevitably some very sad episodes too.

After a year of feeling settled and increasingly involved there, I was gently but firmly persuaded by the Provincial Superior to replace a Sister in our Sheffield Hospital, who was going to have major surgery. The main work there was insurance-funded elective surgery. The NHS periodically contracted work to us to reduce waiting lists. Also, our hospital funded a Respite Charity scheme for disabled patients to give them and their home care-givers a break. That appointment, which was intended to be temporary, lasted for six years until the same gentle, persuasive Provincial steered me towards Wanstead, a large 'Convent with Care', adapted to provide special assistance for elderly members of the Community.

About two weeks after my arrival in Wanstead Convent in 1993, I opened the door to a couple of bedraggled young men who couldn't speak enough English to explain their situation. Accompanying them through the Home Office procedure in Croydon and onwards was for me the beginning of a whole new chapter of involvement in the plight of migrants/asylum seekers. To keep the balance between my routine commitments as Superior/Care Manager and such unexpected but crucial demands on my time and attention was not always easy but, with the help of many human and divine 'guardian angels', things somehow fell into place in support of what I was trying to achieve. It always strikes me that the little fragments of our lives can evolve into an amazing kind of jigsaw picture, when viewed backwards. All the experiences and skills of my previous life became valuable assets for this sometimes very challenging and rather 'unorthodox' apostolate. I was not easily intimidated by officialdom of any kind!

The signposts which have guided me through the journey of life are very significant and sometimes 'awesome' – to borrow an overworked American expression! On Final Profession Day as Sisters of Mercy we traditionally receive a silver ring on which are inscribed two mottoes of our choice, based on the Bible. Just before my Final Profession, I had read the very moving account of an Australian missionary priest's experience as a Missionary during the Korean War (1950s). The title of his work, 'Thy People My People', had echoes of the Book of Ruth (1:16-18) and I chose that for my outer motto. My inner motto: 'Behold Thy Mother', appealed to me because I have always been touched by how Jesus, when gasping for breath and in such pain at His Crucifixion, thought of arranging for His Mother Mary and John, probably the youngest of his disciples, to take care of each other (John 19: 26-27). I know that there is a much more 'theological' interpretation, but that was how I responded then and basically still do. Another spiritual 'signpost' for me has been John Henry Newman's Meditation: 'God has created me to do Him some definite service.....'

Sometimes my 'definite service' has taken me into very strange territory where I needed the courage of my convictions and a skin thick enough to face whatever critical reactions were provoked! One such occasion was in 1995 while waiting in Whipps Cross A&E for the lengthy admission procedure of a sick, elderly Sister to be completed. I became involved in helping two young Vietnamese brothers to contact Social Services when their father who had heart disease was to be admitted and the younger (11 year old) approached me for coins to use in the Payphone. By 11 p.m. my patient was already settled on a Ward and there was still no response from the Duty Social Worker. Feeling I couldn't just abandon them, I asked the Nursing Team Manager whether it would be in order to take them to the convent until something could be arranged She got the Dad's consent through the interpreter and agreed to notify Social Services as soon as she could get through. Luckily, the Korean priest who was due to occupy the visitor's flat (attached to the convent) while attending a language school in London, had delayed his arrival due to illness, so they had somewhere to sleep.

By morning, however, the older brother was very unwell with a high temperature. While I tried to get through to the surgery for an urgent visit from our GP, the younger brother was at my elbow trying to persuade me not to ring the Social Worker! They had been down that road several times already and dreaded the temporary fostering experience. Needless to say, I had a very fraught situation on my hands but, thanks to a lot of Divine intervention, things worked out well in the end. The GP who came was a lovely lady (past student of Brentwood Ursuline High School) who not only prescribed antibiotics but also returned later from the surgery with a nebuliser so that the medicine for his breathing could be administered urgently. The Community, although quite bewildered by what they woke up to, rallied round and were mostly supportive. When a social worker finally got in touch, it was accepted that as the boys were safe and happy at the convent they could remain until the Dad was home again. The Sister's health problem turned out a lot less serious than initially diagnosed and both patients were discharged after a short time in hospital.

Situations like these have arisen time and again during my lifetime and have resulted in a rich tapestry of experience and relationships in which I can see the good outcomes of being guided by God's signposts. Inevitably, there were times of failure too where selfishness, lack of empathy or just my characteristic judgmental response overruled my spiritual ideals and, sadly, one cannot usually turn the clock back. One memory in particular haunts me. I was in the Tesco car park in Leyton late one evening before Christmas when approached by a young woman who asked me for money for her electric meter. I dared not produce my purse because it contained the Community debit card and I suspected that she might snatch it as there was no-one else around at the time. I will never know whether that instinctive reaction was right, but it affected me so much that since then I find it hard to refuse such a request even from those whom I know to be exploiting our goodwill!

Whilst a sense of vocation has always stayed at the core of my being, life has not always been plain sailing. There were times of personal struggle, especially in my younger days in religious life, when I felt seriously tempted to turn back or choose another path in life. In the late 1960s I came across a kind of mantra, when the Nobel Peace Prize winner Dag Hammarskjold quoted some lines from Robert Frost's poem 'Stopping by Woods on a Snowy Evening' :The woods are lovely dark and deep,/ But I have promises to keep,/ And miles to walk before I sleep, / And miles to walk before I sleep.' Because it resonated with the conflicting feelings I sometimes experienced, I adopted it for the stormy times of my life and it has never failed to steer me forward!

Certain sad and joyful events float to the surface of my memory whenever I look back on my life. I have a photo of Pope John Paul's UK visit in May/June 1982, taken at York. Our great excitement was tinged with sadness because we had brought our Parish Priest, Father Matt Malone, who was undergoing radiotherapy for throat cancer but determined to be there to 'meet' the Pope. I recall how he feebly waved farewell towards the Papal helicopter as it took off and that by the end of August he had died. Another poignant memory, from 2008, is of standing with the two (grown-up) Vietnamese brothers by the bedside of their father in the Intensive Care Unit of Bart's Hospital, to support them, when his life-support was being switched off following failed cardiac surgery.

Happiness and sadness are somehow part of the fabric of our human existence and we are lucky if nothing too catastrophic crashes into our lives. My photo albums contain many reminders of happy family occasions, like my parents' Golden Wedding, my Silver Jubilee, Dad's 80th Birthday and his 100th Birthday, when he used the President's cheque to throw a big hotel party for all and sundry! When Mum's Alzheimer's disease took over, they both spent their last years together in a lovely Nursing Home close to Ballycroy where friends and neighbours could drop in to visit them. Dad reached 102 but Mum, who was 11 years younger, went downhill more quickly and died at 89. They were understandably very proud of what they had achieved through careful management and very hard work. Having a good elementary education themselves, they very much valued education and were prepared to sacrifice whatever it took to give each of us the chances they never had. My two younger brothers, who in due course became professors in the USA, were their pride and joy but they also rejoiced in whatever the rest of us achieved.

Sister Paula celebrates her Silver Jubilee with family

Having been in Tilbury for 17 years, almost as a 'lodger' because so much of my work has been outside the parish boundaries, I have come to believe that the more passive role of just being here is hopefully an important contribution. Since arriving here at the beginning of the new century, I have seen very many changes apart from the end of Stella Maris. A lot of the people who were very active in parish life then have gone to their reward or are no longer able to participate as before. A new generation, many of whom have migrated from places as far away as Africa, Poland, Romania, Slovakia, the Philippines, India, Sri Lanka and South America, is gradually following in their footsteps. Maybe because of its history of involvement with seafaring, the people of Tilbury, and our parishioners in particular, seem very willing to welcome strangers and help them feel part of the local community. Not so many months ago, I noticed during Mass a young African mother struggling to divide her attention between her restless twin toddlers. The two ladies next to her, long-standing members of the parish, very spontaneously took turns at giving attention to one of the twins while the mother focused on the other. To me, it was a touching gesture of helpfulness and solidarity.

Praying with Vietnamese Family after the Death of Mr. Ninh

I am concluding this rambling contribution on 4th October 2017 (Feast of St. Francis of Assisi) fifty-five years to the day since my friend, Sister Bridget, and I were picked up at Leeds Airport by Sister Winefride, our Novice Mistress, and Mr. Kraker, the village plumber in Clifford who doubled as convent 'chauffeur' whenever the need arose. Because he had picked up a fairly regular sequence of would-be novices like us, it seems that he had developed a tendency to make predictions on whether they would stay! We never heard his predictions for us two but hope that he and Sr. Winefride are rejoicing in heaven that we did manage to stay the course! Sister Bridget and I have remained friends through life but have not spent much time under the same roof because of our different apostolates. She continued to work at St. Joseph's Convalescent Home, Leeds, as Matron until her retirement and is now Superior/Care Manager of the convent in Doncaster where I lived while teaching and where Sr. Monica went to live on 8th June 2017.

<u>Anne (Nancy) Cantwell</u>

I was born in the countryside near Church Clara, County Kilkenny. There were just a few houses. I was one of fourteen children, but my mother lost five so there were nine of us, six girls and three boys. I was the sixth child born into the family. My mother lived to the age of 101, and died in 2016.

The children all went to the national school in Clara and we walked the two miles there and back each day. We walked it in all weathers, but we never saw it as a hardship. The pupils at the school had to bring money for the turf to put on the fire. Not that we felt the benefit of any warmth, as it was right next to where the teacher sat. In the cold weather, we never wanted to go outside and play, and sometimes the teacher let us stay indoors.

There were only two classrooms in the school and there were about forty pupils. A master took the fifth and sixth pupils, and the mistress took the infants up to class four. We went to school about the age of four, and we left at fourteen. After national school there was a technical college and a Presentation Convent, where you had to pay. We couldn't afford to pay. I went to the technical college, which was about six miles away and I cycled there and back. I learnt shorthand and typewriting. When I had an appendix operation I lost quite a bit of time and I never really caught up.

I went to work in a little shop and met Tom, the man who was to become my husband, at a house dance. His sister, Peggy, was a nurse over in Orsett Hospital, and she said we should come over and train to be nurses. I was seventeen years of age. Tom started the nursing course but couldn't put up with the nurse's uniform he had to wear. He eventually went into the building trade, where he became a master carpenter. I was married at nineteen; we went back to Ireland for the wedding.

I followed the nursing course but I failed the examination and went to work in Woolworths. Fresh out of Ireland and knowing almost nobody, I wouldn't even go to Grays by myself. We had a room in Chadwell, but we managed to get rooms in Tilbury in November 1962. By the age of 25, I had three children, two boys and a girl, and we had moved into our own house in Elgar Gardens, a little cul-de-sac. I am still there, 51 years later. When my daughter was about 5, Sister Bernadette contacted me and offered me some work at St. Mary's School, supervising the playground and then working as a dinner lady for about eight years. By 1980 I was back working in a hospital, at Thurrock Hospital in Long Lane. I was to continue working there for nearly thirty years.

A First Communion Picture of Joe Cantwell and his friend Thomas Crowley with Sister Annunciata

My three children went to St. Mary's School, the boys moving on to St. Cedds and my daughter to the Convent School in Grays. Father Byrne bought her a violin to learn to play, but she didn't like carrying it around as some of the children made fun of her. She never did learn to play it. She went on to Palmer's College but couldn't afford all the fashionable clothes that many of the youngster wore and she eventually left. She works now in the Retail Park in Thurrock.

My two sons are both married, each with four children. Joe lives in Basildon and Larry went back to Ireland in 2000, where he built his own house, in a little village in County Kilkenny. My daughter has two children.

We all went to Our Lady Star of the Sea every week, and over time we saw a lot of different priests. I particularly remember Canon Byrne. He would often come and visit you in your home. He would sit down without any fuss and chat. I used to bake him soda bread and he liked that. Every week I would send a cake down to him. He loved his honey, which he would take straight from the comb. I think he had a sweet tooth. His favourite cakes were those little coconut macaroons. When Canon Byrne went home to Ireland for a holiday, he would go and visit Tom's mother and father. Canon Byrne was so down to earth. He was a lovely man. He had a miniature collie dog, Doxie.

There were, of course, many priests over the years and we respected all of them, but we didn't really get to know them that well because they didn't come to visit us. When we saw them in church we could sometimes talk with them, but often they wouldn't have time. Some of the Sisters occasionally came round to the parishioners' homes.

The highlight of the year was the May Procession. We would take a route through Tilbury, beginning and ending at Our Lady Star of the Sea. The big statue of the Virgin Mary, crowned with lilies, was carried on a platform by the men and we all said the rosary as we walked. Everything has changed now, they don't do the procession any more. But we still have the parish bazaar. In the past I couldn't always get to it because it is on a Saturday and I might be working nights at the hospital. But I am able to come now that I am a free agent.

Sister Mary Barry

In 1952, Sister Mary Barry, as a young girl, entered the Convent of Mercy at Tilbury. In order to continue her education, she travelled daily on the ferry to the Sisters of Mercy High School in Gravesend. In her early years at Tilbury, she was called Sr. Assumpta. These are a few of her memories from the past:

> The people of Our Lady Star of the Sea Parish were big-hearted, kind and respected the Sisters. They were poor and dads who worked were either in the Docks or at Fords Motor Works at Dagenham. Parents, especially mothers, always asked for prayers that Fords would not go or strike – if they did, there was no money. The Sisters did a lot of visitation and worked hard. Life was quite strict but we had lots of fun too. (Sr. Mary).

Later on, in life, Sr. Mary, when living in Wanstead Mercy Convent, was Head of Religious Education at Our Lady of Lourdes Primary School and was the liaison person between the school and the parish.

When she moved to the convent on Canvey Island, she was Head Teacher of the Holy Family Primary School at Benfleet, Essex. On retirement, she moved to Bridge Gate Mercy Convent in Derby. Here, her main ministry is being a team member of the Chaplaincy Team to the Royal Derby Infirmary.

Back Row : Sisters Anne Marie, Rosario and Kathleen Staunton
Front : Sisters Brendan Mary and Mary Barry

Sister Rosario Staunton

Memories of Tilbury Convent

I remember that Saturday night so well. It was February 2nd about 11 p.m. when I rang the doorbell of the Convent of Mercy in Malta Road for the very first time. I expected the door to open wide, instead a small panel flew open and I got my first glance of the Rev. Mother, Mother Borgia, R.I.P. My sister Mary (she only came for the ride and returned to Ireland the next day) and I were hugged and treated to what I now know as "a comfortable cup of tea" and a lot of food.

Things were easy and relaxed for the first couple of weeks as I eased into a different mode of living and joined others in the noviciate. We were a group of seven Junior Professed, Novices and Postulants. I was overjoyed when a friend, Mary, from my home town joined us a couple of months later. The day to day rhythm of convent life, prayer, work and study, made time fly between the good and bad days. Our Novice Mistress, Sr. Bernadette, was kind and guided us gently but firmly. One thing I definitely developed during my noviciate days was a love of reading. We would finish our "charges" (cleaning, cooking) as quickly as possible and get lost in a good book. On Sundays our walk generally took us up Feenan Highway and down St. Chads. Occasionally one of us would accompany a Professed Sister visiting a family in their home.

One of the highlights was when Mary and I were to receive the Religious Habit on the 28th of October, the feast of Saints Simon and Jude. However, the excitement was dampened by the thought that we might be given those names. We prayed, wondered and waited. What a relief when we were told we got two titles of Our Lady, Dolores and Rosario. What a day! The icing on the cake was the election of John the XXIII as Pope. My hero.

The Community had a branch house in Thorpe Bay which was a holiday guest house with a few resident guests. Part of our time was spent there mostly as a working holiday. On my first holiday there I got half-a-crown to spend! We enjoyed long walks along the sea front and occasionally into the town. However, that house was eventually closed. Lack of vocations and change meant Tilbury was also likely to be closed, some of us transferred to different convents. It was an anxious time but the Wanstead Community with faith and generosity stepped in and continued to serve the Parish.

I was fortunate to move to Brentwood Convent, a much bigger Community, with a number of young lively sisters involved in teaching in the Parish Schools. I had three guardians, Mothers Gerard (Superior) Thecla (Assistant) and Louis (Novice Mistress) three great women who left a lasting impression on me. I was sent to teacher training college – La Sainte Union in Southampton. My first teaching job in St. Teresa's, Lexden gave me a love of teaching which I still have and practise now in South Sudan.

I often think of those early days in Tilbury. I learned many life skills and am truly grateful to the sisters for their example and for lasting friendships formed in those early days. I have fond memories of the hardworking, lonely seamen visiting the church, often sharing family worries with the Sisters. The Docks in those days had regular passenger ships docking for a couple of days. The seamen had a true friend in the late Parish Priest, Canon Byrne, who was indeed a saintly priest – one in a million.

Sisters Mary Dolores Horan and Rosario Staunton

Sr. Kathleen (Patricia) Staunton

Sr. Kathleen (Patricia) Staunton was the first of three sisters to enter Tilbury Mercy Convent. She was followed by Sr. Anne Marie and Sr. Rosario. Sr. Kathleen became Headteacher of St. Edwards Primary School, Upton Park, next to West Ham's Football ground (1975 – 1981). Later she was Headteacher of St. Mary's Primary School Tilbury (1981 – 1994). Here, she was known as Sr. Patricia. She was also the organist in Our Lady Star of the Sea Parish.

On retirement, after a sabbatical at Berkeley, U.S.A., she worked for some years with the Catholic Missionary Society and at one stage was the only female member among all the priests. Following on from there she spent a year or so at Buckton Towers with the Claretians. She then moved to the Mercy Convent at Worthing where she died on 5th June 2016 R.I.P.

Sister M. Brendan Finnane

My name is Sr. M. Brendan Finnane. I entered the Convent of Mercy at Tilbury in 1948 – 16 years old! In due course, I attended the Mercy Sisters' High School at Gravesend for further studies. Then, I followed a two years teacher training course at Southampton Teacher Training

College, which led to a teaching post at St. Mary's Primary School in Calcutta Road, Tilbury.

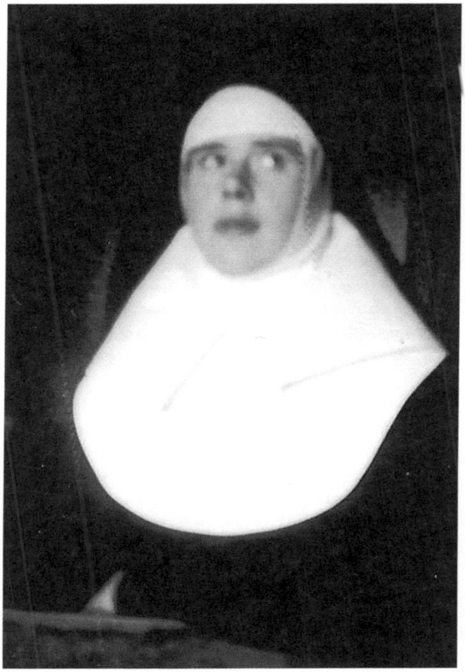

I continued in St. Mary's till 1964 when I transferred to St. Helen's Primary School at Brentwood – also run by the Sisters of Mercy. From there, in 1984, I progressed to our South American Mercy Mission in Lima, Peru – where I spent seventeen very happy years. The Mission was tough but very rewarding.

On retirement from Peru I was sent to Doncaster as Community Leader for a few years. I'm still here thank God and my work now is pastoral in St. Paul's Parish, Cantley, Doncaster. I'm now in my 85th year and hope to continue for another while in the very noble, mercy work in the vineyard of the Lord. I can still remember well my early years in Tilbury. I remember with gratitude and affection the good Sisters who were there at that time. I hope and pray that they are all enjoying their reward in Heaven. They all did tremendous work in school and parish – may the good Lord rest them.

Sister Veronica Walker

Sr. Veronica Walker came to Tilbury at the beginning of year 2000 as Leader of the small Community of Sisters Concepta Guidera, Stanislaus Cullen, Dominic Gollogley and Teresa Croston, who was helping at a house of prayer in Ireland. Later that year Sr. Paula Cleary, who was a nurse, joined the community. The other Sisters were actively engaged in visitation of the housebound and the local hospital.

I used to help by taking the Sisters by car to parishioners living a distance away. I gradually got to know parishioners through meeting them in church and when I chauffeured the Sisters. Being interested in music, I offered my services in Saint Mary's School as a recorder teacher as I was very interested in recorder playing in schools, and was able to form some good groups who played at school concerts and sometimes in church.

With being regularly in school I had good contact with the Headteachers and members of the staff. I was also on the Board of Governors. When Ruth Diprose had to give up playing the organ I took over as organist in church which gave me contact with parishioners and families through weekly Sunday Mass, weddings and funerals. I was sorry to leave Tilbury in September 2006 but pleased to be further north in the country nearer my family.

Sisters Veronica Walker and Camillus Walsh

Sister Camillus Walsh

When I finished my Teacher Training Course in 1954, I came to teach Home Science in Tilbury Secondary School, later called St. Mary's. Mr Harty was the Headmaster and he was very supportive. The subject had not been taught for some time, so the large classroom allocated for the subject needed decorating. Eventually, I began teaching Home Science and Needlework to the girls. They were enthusiastic and some became exceptionally skilled in both subjects. Towards the end of my first year, an Inspector of Secondary Schools paid a visit and she seemed pleased with what she saw. Shortly after her visit, she had the classroom equipped with specially made furniture and new equipment was also provided. I made gingham curtains for the windows and these made the large classroom look more homely. Parents of the girls were grateful for what was being done.

At that time, I was living in the convent at Stanford-le-Hope and I commuted each day by train to Tilbury. When a new Superior was elected in Wanstead Convent (the Mother House Convent), she decided that all this travelling was too much for me. So, I was asked to move to Canvey Island Convent, which was another Branch House of Wanstead, to teach the children in the Junior School there. Once I understood the different needs of the younger pupils, I soon settled in and was happy with the new experience, minus the travelling. A Home Science Teacher took over where I had left off in Tilbury. Unfortunately, she did not stay there very long, as she, too, travelled a long distance.

However, in 1964, Tilbury Convent became a Branch House of Wanstead Convent and some Sisters moved from Wanstead to Tilbury. I was then asked to return to teach in Tilbury and to live there. So I was able to resume my teaching as a Home Science Tutor. Mr. Harty had retired and was replaced by Mr. Bolger, who asked me to be his Deputy Headteacher.

This post I held until moving to Wanstead in 1966. Some years later the staff and pupils of the secondary school moved to another area in Essex which left more playground space and other facilities for the primary school pupils.

In 1973, I began to train as a Registered General Nurse and Midwife to re-open a Health Centre in Kenya, East Africa. This was a challenge but the need was there. When I went out to Kenya, to the Centre, I was helped by a qualified nurse and other staff. It was rewarding work for me to be with the poor and sick.

However, I saw the urgent need for schools for girls only, as they were seldom sent to school, but if they did so, they were bullied by the male pupils. A friend of mine came to Kenya to take over the Health Centre and her nursing skills were also greatly appreciated. That left me free to open a Junior School for Girls (6 – 14 years). This was followed by another one in a different area.

One of the girls schools was at Kakuma in Turkana, which took about five hours to reach from Kitali, the nearest town, in a double cab 4 wheel drive vehicle. The road was composed of stones, large and small and plenty of red soil. Naturally, I did not often go to Kitali. The school terms were 14 weeks long and in the break I went to Kitali for whatever I might need for the next term. Some years later, travelling became easier when a beautiful tarmac road was built.

Turkana is a desert area in North West Kenya where there is very little rainfall. Midday temperatures could reach 120 degrees Fahrenheit. The USA was very generous in supplying beans, the main staple food for the children. The camels from which our milk was supplied lived and grazed up on the mountain tops where there was very little grass and only thorny shrubs with a few green leaves. Sometimes when I was down country in Kenya, I would purchase sacks of dried milk. School life was very different to that in Tilbury!

Schools for "Girls" <u>only</u> are now popular and I am grateful for the opportunity I had to promote the education of the female population, especially in the remote (bush) areas. It is all taken for granted now. Actually, parents are fined if they do not send their children of both sexes to school.

(For some years now, Sister Camillus lives in the Mercy Convent at Wanstead. She is retired but carried out an active ministry of visiting the sick and housebound in the Parish).

Sister Mary Dolores

I joined the Sisters of Mercy in Tilbury in 1957 and spent five of the most formative years of my life there. Sister Bernadette Roche was my Novice Mistress, the person who gave me a life-long love for Catherine McAuley and her vision for the service of people in need.

I have fond memories of the Sisters who formed the Community and of the Parish and local area, especially our weekly walk up Feenan Highway and down St. Chads! Also our trips across the river to Gravesend, when we were given sixpence to buy treats.

I have wonderful memories too of the Goanese seamen praying for hours and lighting candles before the statue of St. Francis Xavier.

I helped Sister Mary Kelly in the Sacristy and spent hours every Saturday morning cleaning the silver and arranging flowers, which had come from every garden in the parish.

Sister Mary Dolores

After Tilbury I lived in many and diverse places and faced all the ups and downs of life, like everyone else. Tilbury prepared me for some real challenges, like teaching in an inner city Comprehensive School in Sheffield, working in an Interfaith Community in Bradford and in a school for special needs children in Kings Lynn and in various projects for homeless people. All this as well as spending a short time in a Carmelite Monastery.

But wherever and in whatever circumstances, I have always carried in my heart "Mercy unto Thousands" and Sr. Bernadette's words "Be Mercy in action, not just words."

Sister Christine Mather

In September 1969, I was moved to Tilbury Convent, as a teacher with musical ability was needed in St. Mary's School. Here I taught 9-11 year olds. A highlight on the pupils' curriculum was swimming. A number of them, especially boys, could swim quite a few lengths and had certificates for life-saving skills. One of the classes I had were excellent at gymnastics and a local Education Inspector used them for demonstration to other teachers. Academically, there were some very gifted children and on the other hand some who needed a lot of help.

In 1970, Sr. Bernadette, Sr. Margaret Mary, Mr. and Mrs. Fitzgerald and I took pupils from the top two classes to Ostend for about six days. We travelled by plane from Southend Airport, which was a new experience for most of them. It was a short journey and the plane did not fly at a very high altitude so it was possible to see the sea most of the time.

The weather was good and so we were able to go on the beach. There was just one morning when it was raining, and we had been told that there was a ship with a museum, so we took the party there. It was museum about Father Damien who gave his life to look after lepers. The memorabilia were most interesting and the children were fascinated with them and with the various parts of the ship.

On Board the Museum Ship in Ostend

A coach took us on some excursions. We visited Valkenburg in Holland. There we took a trip on a cable car from the Queen Wilhemina Tower high across the land below. I could feel my sandals beginning to slip off and as our legs were dangling I could not do anything about it except hope that they would stay on, which they did. We also visited Cologne where souvenirs were purchased for the children's families and we went into the magnificent Cathedral. Another place was in Belgium, where there were beehives in glass cases and honey was being produced.

From reports back it was one of the best school trips and this was due to the excellent behaviour at all times and to the enthusiasm of the children!

In 1970, the two older classes were invited to the celebration of the centenary of the 1870 Education Act It was held at the Civic Hall at Blackshots, Stifford Clays. St. Mary's Staff also received invitations to shows at Palmers and Gray's Convent Schools.

On one occasion, I and three other Sisters were going by car to a course. Sr. Bernadette was driving and the car suddenly stopped on the hill at The Cross Keys, Chadwell. Despite all our efforts it would not restart. The traffic was piling up behind us. A kind gentleman came to the rescue. He discovered that the fan belt had broken and suggested if a pair of tights or stockings were available a temporary repair could be carried out!

My classroom was detached from the rest of the school buildings, next to the presbytery wall. Later on, it became the nursery. There was a piano in it and when the class were singing Canon Byrne would love to pop in.

On Sundays, about twenty-six children would come up into the church gallery to help with the singing at Mass. I played the organ which needed the bellows to be blown up! On weekdays, the Sisters were in the church very early for their personal prayer before Mass, which was celebrated at 7.00 a.m. if I remember rightly.

In May, a procession in honour of Our Lady was held around the streets of Tilbury. Many parishioners made an altar with a statue surrounded by flowers at the end of their path to the road. On occasions, seafarers from Goa and other places would come along Dock Road to the church for Mass. Sometimes there would be 200 of them. At times, well attended and very enjoyable socials took place in the Hall at Chadwell or Stella Maris.

In the first month that I was in Tilbury, I went back to Wanstead for two days, in order to make my Final Profession at St. Bede's Church, Chadwell Heath on the 27th of September. This was during a Parish Mission given by Priests of The Catholic Missionary Society. The church was packed and after the Mass there was a social.

In October 1970 I had the privilege, together with some other Sisters, of being sent to Rome for the Canonisation of the Forty Martyrs. I had always said that I would never go up in a plane even if you gave me a thousand pounds. However, once the plane was up above the clouds, I was in my element marvelling at the cloud formations, which in my imagination resembled the icy landscapes of the North and South Poles.

We were there for nearly a week and everything was wonderful, especially the Canonisation Ceremony in St. Peter's and the celebrations in the other Basilicas. I and Sr. Philippa carried the special banner for the Brentwood Diocese. We visited all the famous sites and had a trip to the Palazzola monastery, and Mass was celebrated in the Catacombs and other churches.

One of the afternoons, I met up with Fr. Cardoso, who had been in Tilbury Parish for some months previously. Later in life, he was Chaplain to the Portuguese Embassy in Rome for many years until he retired back to Portugal not so long ago.

At that time, Wanstead was the "Mother House" of Branch Houses at Canvey Island, Tilbury and Stanford-le-Hope and the Superior of Wanstead was in overall charge, but each convent had a local Superior. In April 1971, a new Superior was appointed to Tilbury from Canvey Convent. She had been teaching in St. Joseph's School there. I was transferred to Canvey Convent for the summer term. She took over my upper Junior Class at St. Mary's and I replaced her as teacher of the Reception Class, of which twenty-one remained (the others had moved up) and there was an intake of twenty new children. It was quite a challenge. I would take the class daily for some kind of movement to music in the Hall and the line of forty-one children walking in single file into the Hall seemed never ending!

At that time, I was three years into studying for the Westminster Diploma in Theology (which included also Scripture, Liturgy and Church History) set up by Cardinal Heenan and the Hierarchy. It was a correspondence course which involved submitting frequent essays and annual exams. I was late to bed and up very early but that summer the weather was lovely and Canvey air was very refreshing. Morning Prayer and Mass were in the Chapel on weekdays and on Sundays we walked along Long Road to the church. In the evenings at sunset, crowds of starlings would gather chattering away as they wheeled together before settling in the numerous trees in the grounds before the night.

When my mother became very ill, I was allowed to spend some time with her each week, supporting and comforting her just as I had done during my father's last years. After my mother died I was back at the Tilbury Convent full time. A friend of mine, Sister Annunciata, was very involved in the Apostleship of the Sea. When the chaplain there moved over to the Parish of St. Peter the Apostle in Woolwich, he got in touch with Sister Annunciata and offered her a position as a Parish Sister in Woolwich. I was allowed to transfer over to Woolwich in 1999 and to work alongside Sister Annunciata in a wonderful parish.

In 2006, the Provincial was looking for personnel to make up the Community in Tilbury, as three Sisters were moving elsewhere, and she approached me. At that time, I had been seven years in Woolwich and the ministries in which I had been involved had reached the stage when they could be handed over and I felt that God wanted me in Tilbury. Sister Deborah had also been asked. She moved in at the beginning of September, and I moved in on 23rd of September, the eve of the feast of Our Lady of Mercy.

Fr. James McShane requested me to take responsibility for playing the organ for Mass and funerals. As time went on I formed a small group of singers to help to lead the liturgy. Now, I play only for the Sunday Mass. I was also asked to run the Baptism Programme for the parents of the children to be baptised and to prepare, separately, children over the age of seven in a course which could last for a few months.

For some years, I attended Assemblies in St. Mary's School and helped out in Year 2.

Weekly, a class would come to the convent chapel, on rota, for half an hour, and Fr. James used to take them. Not long afterwards, he handed it over to me and I continued this for eight years. I spent a short time on an R.E. topic, then we prayed, sang hymns and finished with adoration before the exposed Blessed Sacrament.

Sometimes, when I passed by the younger children's playground and it was their playtime, a horde of them would come rushing over to the wire netting. They loved to ask me questions such as "How old are you?" and to tell me about what they had been doing.

On Wednesdays, I used to lead the Liturgy of the Word in the Church. At present, I am still on the evening Saturday Mass rota for reading.

Over the years I have become friends with some local residential "traveller" families, who come to me for prayer. Their deep faith, love of God and kindness are a great inspiration to me.

People ring the convent door, for information about nursery and school enrolment, baptism, becoming a Catholic, for example, and so, having explained the procedure, I tell them to get in touch with Fr. Paul, the presbytery and school. Other persons come in distress and need a listening ear and practical help.

Within the Community, I do office work and also deal with the maintenance of the convent building in some areas. I have learned a lot and still am doing so, especially in connection with electrics, water, gas central heating, asbestos, roofing, the fire system, risk assessment, employment regulations, Health and Safety issues and emergencies.

Each Sister is involved in their individual ministries. The Blessed Sacrament is reserved in our chapel, which is always available for prayer. We meet together regularly for the daily "Evening Prayer of the Church".

There is a Holy Hour on a Thursday to pray for Priests and Vocations. On the last Tuesday of the month, others join us for the Divine Mercy Devotions. We also gather together at the midday and evening meal sessions.

I celebrated my Golden Jubilee on 24th July 2014, the Feast Day of Saint Christine. From dawn until dusk, the sun shone brilliantly. The guests who arrived early were able to sit out in the convent garden and enjoy a chat and a welcome cuppa provided by my companion Sisters at Tilbury, namely Sr. Paula, Sr. Monica, Sr. Teresa and Sr. Deborah. My brother James arrived with his son, wife and their two children – a toddler and a baby just a few weeks old. Later, a cousin and her husband arrived. The Thanksgiving Mass was at 11.30 a.m. in the Church of Our Lady Star of the Sea.

The Parish Priest, Fr. Paul Dynan, had not been sure that he would be able to be present for the event, as he was recovering from an operation, but to our delight he was able to come and to concelebrate with six other priests, five of whom had travelled from a distance. He invited the priests into the presbytery to meet each other and to vest there. The chief concelebrant was Fr. Philip Newbold who was joined by Fr. Paul, Fr. Brian Boyle SCJ, Fr. Bill Keogh, Fr. Geoffrey Smith, Fr. Paul Gunter OSB and Fr. Kevin Hale. Among the guests were ten Sisters of Mercy from different convents, including the Mercy Institute Leader – Sr. Colette and two members of her team. Then, there were a few friends from various parts of England. Sr. Philippa was the organist, who had been in College with me and at one time was in Stanford-le-Hope. Members of the Sunday Mass Choir led the singing. I did the layout of the Jubilee Booklet for the Mass and had chosen the liturgy, hymns and illustrations. Sr. Deborah typed out the pages and Michael Akinyemi photocopied them to form the booklet. A number of parishioners attended the Mass.

A reception for the guests was held in St. Mary's School Hall, through the kindness of the Head Teacher and Chair of Governors. Mrs. Pauline Darke, the Caretaker, saw to the opening of the school doors and car park. Mrs. Alison Bishop, the School Secretary, helped with the planning and setting up and decorating the tables. Sr. Paula had provided wine and soft drinks and the delicious buffet meal was provided by Quin's Caterers led by Mrs. Shirley Baker. Near the end of the meal Sr. Joan Breen gave a speech. The Jubilee Cake, given by a Nigerian friend – Mrs. S. Akintayo – was cut by Sr. Colette and myself, then sent to the caterers to slice and distribute.

Later in the day, when the guests had departed, Fr. Paul, Fr. Philip, the Tilbury Sisters and my relations returned to the convent and enjoyed a cup of tea with a slice of chocolate cake that Ray Gnanapragasam had baked. I am very grateful to all mentioned and others behind the scenes who contributed to make my Jubilee Day a very happy and joyful occasion. (Note: For a photograph of Sister Christine on the day of her Golden Jubilee, please see the centre pages of this book.)

I have had a wonderful life and I thank God for all the graces and blessings and support that I have received.

Chapter Thirteen : A Brief Look Around our Parish Church

High above the gable end of the church she stands, Our Lady Star of the Sea, gazing towards the port where so many seafarers have landed, looking for her comfort and protection. We are just outside our Parish Church where, on the right, there is a Statue of Calvary beneath which are inscribed the names of the parishioners who gave up their lives in the Second World War. It is late November 2017, and the memorial is bedecked with new poppies.

To the left of the entrance to the church there is an older memorial, The Sacred Heart, erected by Goanese seafarers in memory of their comrades who died in the First World War. There was a time when these Goanese sailors were a regular and significant part of the life of the parish. There is a reference to Matthew 14, verse 25: *And in the fourth watch of the night Jesus went unto them, walking on the sea.*

Just outside the church entrance there is a large block of stone in the wall of the church. The words on the stone, once sharply in focus, inform the reader that this is the foundation stone of the church, marking a date in June 1906 when the story of the Church of Our Lady Star of the Sea first began.

As we enter the church, in the narthex there is a beautiful statue of St. Francis, a saint so venerated by the Goanese seafarers that they brought their own statue of him as a gift to the parish.

Through the doors into the nave, we see two plaques on the wall below the choir loft. On the right is a plaque in memory of Canon Keens, described here as the founder of the Mission which he set up in 1887. He was to become the first Parish Priest in Tilbury.

A matching plaque is found on the left of the wall, dedicated to Ada Mary Auguste Stephenson, otherwise known as 'Sister Mary', whose generosity to the parish in its early days helped to put it on its feet.

One of the first things to catch the eye is a series of magnificent Stations of the Cross. In their ornamentation and complexity they serve as a fine contrast with the restrained Early English architecture which is a hallmark of the church. (Note: For a photograph of some of these Stations of the Cross, please see the centre pages of this book.)

On the right-hand side of the church there hangs a particularly fine representation of Our Lady Star of the Sea, created by parishioner Gwen Perkins, and installed on Mother's Day 2007. Gwen was inspired by a painting of Stella Maris she saw at Aylesford, and was give permission by the artist to create her own version. An account of the creation of this work is contained in the chapter entitled Parish Voices, under the heading Gwen Perkins, together with some photographs. For a picture of the completed icon, please refer to the cover of this book.

Towards the front of the church, on the left of the Sanctuary, there is a beautiful wall plaque donated by John L'Estrange, the former editor of the Diocesan Directory. Created at Prinknash Abbey in Gloucestershire, it depicts Our Lady Star of the Sea and carries the inscription *Hail Thou Star of the Ocean.* Prinknash Abbey houses a Catholic community of monks who live in the spirit of the Rule of St. Benedict. Father Paul Dynan accepted the gift on behalf of the Tilbury Parish. A photograph of this wall plaque is to be found in the centre pages of this book.

On the other side of the Lady Chapel we see a copy of the painting by Holman Hunt, *The Light of the World,* in which the figure of Jesus is shown about to knock on an old door that is overgrown with weeds. The painting illustrates a passage from Revelation 3: 20, *Behold, I stand at the door and knock: if any man hear my voice, and open the door, I will come into him and sup with him, and he with me.* The painting commemorates the visit of Pope Benedict to the U.K. in 2010. Underneath the painting there is a candle blessed by Pope Benedict, again to mark his visit to the U.K. in 2010.

Holman Hunt : The Light of the World

The Lady Chapel is decorated with flowers. The pale blue background was chosen by Father Paul during the recent refurbishment of the church, the colour being closely associated with Our Lady. For the past thousand years, she has been depicted clothed in blue, a symbol of her obedience to God. Similarly, the background to the statue of St. Joseph is painted in purple, a colour associated with mourning, as he is the patron saint of a happy death. Although there is no scriptural reference, it is believed that St. Joseph died in the company of Jesus and Mary. He is carrying a spray of lilies, symbolising Peace, Chastity and Purity. The Chapel of the Sacred Heart, to the right of the Sanctuary, is painted in red, to represent the blood of Christ.

The Lectern, Altar and Font are made from a matching polished stone. Each is inscribed with a symbol. On the front of the Lectern there is the sign for Alpha and Omega (the beginning and the end), a reference often associated with God the Father. The Altar carries the sign of the Cross, representing Christ. The Font depicts a dove flying down from Heaven at the time of Christ's Baptism in the River Jordan. It is the traditional symbol for the Holy Spirit, recalling St. Mark's Gospel 1:9-11 : *And it came to pass in those days that Jesus came from Nazareth of Galilee, and was baptized by John in the Jordan. And straightway coming up out of the water, he saw the heavens opened, and the Spirit like a dove descending upon him. And there came a voice from heaven, saying Thou art my beloved Son, in whom I am well pleased.* In this way, the Trinity of Father, Son and Holy Spirit is represented in the three symbols.

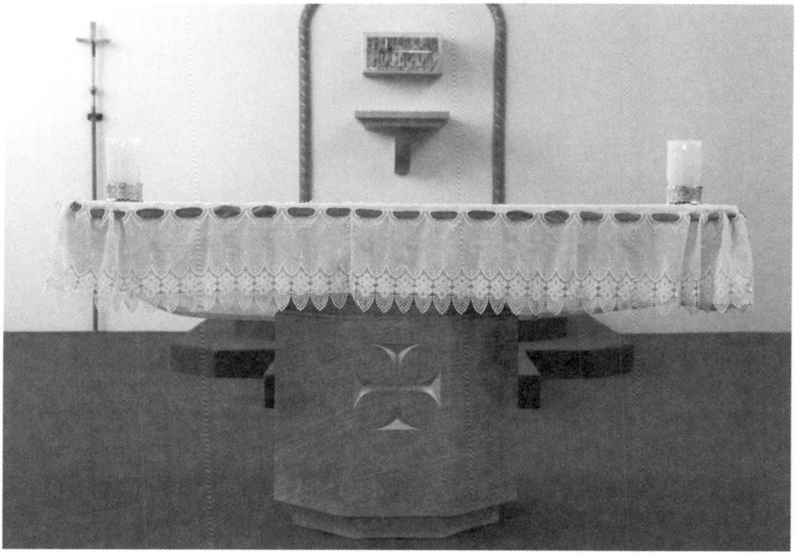

High above the Sanctuary is the wooden ceiling which is directly beneath the Bell Tower. In the recent renovations to the church, carried out under Father Paul's direction, the wooden supports of the tower were found to be in a state of advanced decay. Had these supports failed, the huge church bell would have come crashing down onto the Sanctuary. Fortunately, all is now well and we should be safe for another hundred years or so.

On the east wall of the church, at the rear of the Sanctuary, there are two small niches built into the wall itself, presumably part of the original building. The one on the left would earlier have served as a credence table whilst the one on the right contains a drain which once led directly to the earth outside, allowing for the washing of holy vessels after Mass.

Opposite the Chapel of the Sacred Heart is a small room which serves both as the church's Reconciliation Room and the venue for the Children's Liturgy during Mass on Sunday morning. In the Children's Liturgy, up to twenty children are ably instructed and supervised by 'Trish' before they report back on what they have learned, under the rapt gaze of the congregation.

You may have noticed a series of red crosses on the walls of the church, each cross linked with a candle. These crosses mark the points where Bishop Andrew Beck anointed the walls with holy chrism oil during the church's Consecration in June 1954.

Appendix (i) : Priests of the Parish of Tilbury

Archdiocese of Westminster

1901 – 1904	Father Joseph Upton
1904 – 1907	Father Jules Van Meenan
1907 – 1911	Father John Mulcahy
1911 – 1917	Father Jerome Deady

Diocese of Brentwood

1917	Father Jerome Deady
1917 – 1921	Father Michael Hannan (first Parish Priest, 1918)
1921 – 1952	Father Patrick O'Donnell
1952 – 1982	Father John Byrne
1983 – 1985	Father Donal Donegan
1985 – 1987	Father John Duckett
1987 – 1994	Father Bob Hamill
1994 – 1995	Father Paul Bhanji
1995 – 2000	Father David Clemens
2000 – 2004	Father Peter Connor
2004 – 2009	Father James McShane
2009 – 2010	Father John Meehan
2010 – present	Father Paul Dynan

Assistant Priests of the Parish of Tilbury

1932 – 1937	Father Francis Brennan (Kilmore)
1937 – 1940	Father Hugh McGrail (Kilmore)
1944 – 1950	Father Denis Petry
1950	Father Kevin Vincent Connolly (Armagh)
1950 – 1951	Father Martin Kirwan (Killaloe)
1951 – 1953	Father Philip Finnegan S.S.C.
1953 – 1954	Father William Caffrey (Melbourne)
1954 – 1957	Father William Luby
1957	Father John Ryder (Derry)
1957 – 1961	Father Christopher Nigel Collingwood
1961 – 1962	Father Gordon Godfrey
1962 – 1969	Father Donald Mills

1969 – 1970	Father Gerard Butcher
1970 – 1972	Father Joseph Tuohey S.D.S. (Incardinated 1971)
1972 – 1973	Father Albert Fitzgerald

Priests of the Parish of Chadwell St. Mary

1975 – 1983	Father Donald Mills

(*With thanks to Mary Pollard)*

Appendix (ii) : The Sisters of Mercy in the first hundred years in Tilbury

Secular Name	Religious Name	Convent of Entry	Date in Tilbury
	Sr. Joseph	Macklin Street	1909
Barry, Mary	Sr. Assumpta	Tilbury	1952
Boyden, Mary	Sr. Francis	Tilbury	1930
Brady, Margaret	Sr. Anthony	Macklin Street	1923
Breen, Johanna	Sr. Peter/Joan	Wanstead	1968
Casey, Bridget	Sr. Assumpta	Wanstead	1962
Clarke, Josephine	Sr. Vianney	Wanstead	1970
Cleary, Mary	Sr. Paula	Clifford/Doncaster	2000
Colahan, Agnes	Sr. Angela	Macklin Street	1905
Colahan, Jane Frances	Sr. Borgia	Macklin Street	1923
Connolly, Catherine	Sr. Theresa	Tilbury	1925
Croston, Teresa	Sr. Teresa	Derby	1997
Crowe, Maureen	Sr. Augustine	Wanstead	1962
Culligan, Eileen	Sr. Stanislaus	Clifford/Doncaster	1999
Doyle, Mary	Sr. Josephine	Wanstead	1982
Dwyer, Mary	Sr. Ethelburga	Macklin Street	1905
Finnane, Marie	Sr. Brendan Mary	Tilbury	1948
Flanagan, Marion	Sr.Joseph	Tilbury	1922
Furness, Helen	Sr. Helen	Wanstead	1977
Gollogley, Bridie	Sr. Dominic	Brentwood	1988
Gosbee, Carol	Sr. Carol	Bermondsey	1985
Grogan, Mary	Sr. Rita	Wanstead	1966
Guidera, Margaret	Sr. Concepta	Hunslet	1994
Gunning, Anne	Sr. Bernard	Wanstead	1969
Horan, Mary	Sr. Dolores	Tilbury	1957
Horrigan, Mary	Sr. Gertrude	Wanstead	1966
Keena, Brigid	Sr. Imelda	Clifford/Doncaster	1988
Keena, Catherine	Sr. Columba	Clifford/Doncaster	1987
Kelly, Kathleen	Sr. Margaret Mary	Tilbury	1927
Kennedy, Mary	Sr. Dominic	Wanstead	1970
Keogh, Mary	Sr. Mary	Wanstead	1990
Lehane, Bina	Sr. Benignus	Wanstead	1965
Leonard, Marion	Sr. Aloysius	Macklin Street	1923
Lynch, Elizabeth	St. Patrick	Tilbury	1922
Lynch, Julia	Sr. Rita	Derby	1994
Lynch, Margaret	Sr. Perpetua	Wanstead	1970
Maher, Mary Christine	Sr. De Paul	Tilbury	1949
Maloney, Marion	Sr. Gerard	Macklin Street	1919
Mather, Christine	Sr. Magdalen	Wanstead	1969

McCarthy, Joan	Sr. Gerard	Wanstead	1964
McEnery, Bridget	Sr. Carmel	Wanstead	1974 & 1982
McGrath, Ellen	Sr. Annunciata	Wanstead	1969 & 1997
McLoughlin, Marie	Sr. De Lourdes	Tilbury/St. John's Wood	1956
O'Connor, Bridget	Sr. Teresa	Macklin Street	1905
O'Connor, Helen	Sr. Borgia	Wanstead	
O'Connor, Helena	Sr. Aquinas	Wanstead	1974
O'Doherty, Ann Teresa	Sr. Michael	Wanstead	1972
O'Farrell, Elizabeth	Sr. Joseph	Macklin Street	1909
O'Gorman,Helena	Sr. Stanislaus	Macklin Street	1909
O'Grady, Mary	Sr. Therese	Wanstead	1967
Orton, Mary Elizabeth	Sr. Bernadette	Wanstead	1966
Phelan, Bridget	Sr. Clare Joseph	Macklin Street	1905
Powell, Eleanor	Sr. Catherine	Wanstead	1964
Roche, Ellen	Sr. Bernadette	Tilbury	1926
Ryan, Josephine	Sr. Anthony	Wanstead	1964
Ryan, Mary Agnes	Sr. Camillus	Macklin Street	1905
Smith, Jane Mary	Sr. Dunstan	St. John's Wood	1963
Smyth, Harriet	Sr. Alphonsus	Macklin Street	1923
Staunton, Bridget	Sr. Anne Marie	Tilbury	1952
Staunton, Kathleen	Sr. Kathleen	Tilbury	1948
Staunton, Teresa	Sr. Rosario	Tilbury	1957
Stuart, Ellen	Sr. Vincent	Macklin Street	1909
Sullivan, Mary	Sr. Maria Goretti	Wanstead	1971
Walker, Maria	Sr. Veronica	Sheffield	1999
Walsh, Helen	Sr. Emmanuel	Wanstead	1977
Walsh, Mary Ann	Sr. Camillus	Wanstead	1965
Waugh, Anne	Sr. Anne	Wigton	1989
Williams, Ellen	Sr. Agnes	Wanstead	1972

(Taken from the centenary booklet marking one hundred years of the Sisters of Mercy in Tilbury – 1905/2005)

Appendix (iii) : St. Mary's Youth Club

St. Mary's Youth Club was first envisaged by Sr. Carmel in 1980. She was very aware of the need for the young people of the parish to be actively involved in the church in some way and decided that her parish, the Parish of Our Lady Star of the Sea, Tilbury, must really have somewhere that these young people could meet. St. Mary's Youth Club was primarily for the young people of this parish.

There was already a very active youth club at St. Joseph's Church Hall in Chadwell. At this time, however, Chadwell St. Mary and Tilbury were two separate parishes. The Parish of St. Joseph, Chadwell St. Mary had been formed in 1975. However, the club in Chadwell closed in 1981 as Pauline Lacey remained the only leader.

A meeting was held in October 1980 with a view to establishing a youth club in Tilbury and Mary Pollard was asked to attend. It was hoped that she would liaise with the girls at Grays Convent. In December 1980, at a second meeting, a committee was elected and St. Mary's Youth Club was chosen as the title for the club. It was decided to limit membership to past pupils of St. Mary's School, Tilbury who were aged 14 years or older. The first event of the new youth club was to be a free disco held on Friday, 23rd January 1981.

The club was beginning to take shape and several people made offers of financial help to see the club through the early stages of its life.

There was now something to offer the young people of the parish, but was it what they wanted? At the disco they were asked this question and the basic reply was that they needed somewhere to meet their friends. They seemed to want a club.

Getting the parish hall cleaned up and ready was the next task. The hall was sited in the grounds of St. Mary's School and was part of the old St. Mary's Secondary School. The club was opened on Friday, 13th February by Mr. Bolger and was to meet fortnightly. Twenty-five members enrolled, some from Chadwell and some from Tilbury. The first trip took place eleven days later to a Diocesan Disco at Tiffany's, Ilford. By now, news of the Diocesan Junior Sports Committee had reached St. Mary's and the Club entered their first (the first of many!) Sports Day at Canon Palmer School, Seven Kings. This was also to be the first year we entered the *Sunday Times* Fun Run in Hyde Park and the final ‘first’ was when St. Mary’s Youth Club ran the bottle stall at the Parish Bazaar.

By now, Mary had become Treasurer of St. Mary’s Youth Club, as the person who first took the job had to resign.

As a result of the Sports Day at Canon Palmer we now had some younger people wanting to join the youth club. (The Diocesan Junior Sports Committee runs events for junior youth clubs throughout the diocese. Children from 9 – 13 years of age are encouraged to take part in various events which have included discos, quizzes, swimming galas, athletics, pool and fun nights as well as a sports day. To take part in any of these events all that is needed is to send a representative from the club to the meetings where the events are organised. At this time, Mrs. Edmunds represented St. Mary’s, but later Mary took over.) The younger people from our parish who were not yet old enough to join St. Mary’s Youth Club were encouraged to take part in these events.

The first major drawback, but which in retrospect was probably a huge step forward for the Youth Club, was when Essex County Council decided to cut off the electricity and gas in the hall where the club met. This happened towards the end of 1981, but fortunately Father Mills, the Parish Priest of St. Joseph’s, Chadwell St. Mary, offered the use of St. Joseph’s Hall to the youth club and so the fortnightly meetings continued there.

St. Mary's Youth Club also began to take an active part in the Sunday Liturgy. Once each month its members joined the choir and played instruments at the 10.30 a.m. Mass. Later, the youth club was to be responsible for the readings, bidding prayers and offertory too.

The club sent a representative to the Mersea Island Youth Conference and also began to participate in liturgical functions organised by the deanery. A group went to St. Clares, Clacton for the weekend and some of our club went to Ninian Park, Cardiff for the Youth Mass concelebrated by Pope John Paul II.

All went well for the next two years and then the problems began. The original group of 14 – 15 year olds were now two years older and many of them had started work. They no longer came to the youth nights and more youngsters were leaving as opposed to those joining. Some of the original leaders had also left and there were now only three adults actively involved.

It was decided that we needed to organise a junior youth club so that hopefully our younger members, some of whom we already worked with, would naturally progress from the junior club to the senior. Mary, Pauline, Sr. Emmanuel and Cath Sage got together and decided that this club would meet from 6.00 – 7.30 p.m. on Friday evenings just before the senior club from 7.30 - 9.30 p.m. It would be open to 3rd and 4th year juniors from St. Mary's Primary School and those in their 1st – 3rd years at secondary school. Soon we had about 30 members.

Having hoped our problems were solved, things soon got worse! It wasn't long before the senior club was down to just two leaders, and next there were days when the 'junior leaders' found that no 'senior leaders' arrived to take over on club nights. The junior club changed evenings and began to open on Thursday evening instead. Eventually the senior club closed. This left us with a new problem. What happened to our children when they became what we considered the youth of our parish? We couldn't just ignore their needs but we didn't have the necessary expertise or wish to cater for both age groups. Appeal after appeal was made for new leaders but nobody was forthcoming.

In 1984 the Parishes of Our Lady Star of the Sea, Tilbury and St. Joseph's, Chadwell St. Mary were re-amalgamated with slight changes to the parish boundaries. This had little effect on our youth club as we really operated as one group anyway. Both parishes were comparatively small.

We decided that we had to revert to our original plan: hold our junior club from 6.00 – 7.30 p.m. and remain open till 9.00 p.m. for those who were 13 years or older. We also produced a newsletter which we sent out to all those over 13 who at any time had belonged to St. Mary's Youth Club. It worked well. We continued to have 30 or so junior members and probably averaged ten older ones. Sean (Parsons) then joined with us, but unfortunately Sister Emmanuel was about to be moved and Cath was now working in London and was often unable to come to club nights.

In 1987 / 88 we had quite a large youth group. They didn't actually 'join' St. Mary's Youth Club but just came along most Thursday evenings and often came on trips with the junior club members. Alton Towers was certainly the most popular. (In fact we took only those at secondary school to Alton Towers.) On some evenings up to 20 youngsters came. Some nights we were beginning to worry as to whether we could safely cater for them all. Our hall, St. Joseph's, is situated at the edge of a local shopping parade, where many youngsters 'hung around' at night. We didn't want trouble from those we didn't cater for – we only admitted members of our parish and their friends.

Our worries, however, were short-lived. When the new school year began in September 1988, we suddenly found that the 16 – 17 year olds who had been coming no longer did. At the same time our regular junior members were now 13 – 14 years and most decided not to come to club nights any more. We had to begin again with a group of about fifteen 10 to 11 year old boys. Where were the girls? (At one time in the past we had mainly girls and only one or two boys! The roles had been reversed.) By the end of the year we had 21 members with an age span from 9 – 16 years. Normally only those between 9 and 13 came to club nights, so late evenings were dropped.

As the new club year begins (1989/1990) our members' age range is more concentrated, ranging from 9 to 13 years, with mainly 11 – 12 year old boys. We need to plan for the future and see what we can do to continue to care for these as they grow into adolescence and young adults.

\- - - -

It would be interesting to see what the members of St. Mary's Youth Club could expect during the course of one year. In 1989, there were outings on club nights to Ice Skating, Swimming, a Nature Ramble, a visit to use athletics facilities and a tour of Tilbury Power Station. Club competitions organised by the Diocese of Brentwood Junior Sports Committee included a Swimming Gala, Fun Night, Pool Competition, Sports Day and a Gala. Weekend visits included Chessington, Youth Day at Aylesford, Sports Day, Hyde Park Fun Run and Parish Bazaars.

The club had a number of facilities for the young people to enjoy – a pool table, table tennis, a snooker table, a football machine, Atari and television, a twin deck cassette radio, a Hohner keyboard, bar billiards, table squash, a dartboard, indoor football, rounders' bats, foam balls, tennis racquets, Beetle Drive set, balls, cones, skittles, skipping ropes, disco lights, and a wide range of table games.

In addition, club members assisted in the church choir, and in Masses at Our Lady Star of The Sea often played musical instruments and provided Readers.

The Youth Club members were asked what they thought of their club, and here are three of their replies.

<u>Paul Terry</u>

I have just joined St. Mary's Youth Club. The first night I went we played football and other games. The Church meetings are held every Thursday night in term-time. The Youth Club starts at six o'clock and ends at about seven-thirty. I waited through the summer holidays for the first meeting of the new term. This was held last week. I played computer games on the Atari computer. The games were: Pac-man, a race game, Golf, Carnival and the Wizard of Oz. I also played table tennis and also some football.

On Sunday I went to the Sunday Times National Fun Race held in Hyde Park in London. The race I was in was two and a half kilometres long. There were thousands and thousands of people who were running or spectating. I went faster when I saw the Youth Club cheering me on. So far I have really enjoyed the Youth Club.

We are going to do lots more activities like a Quiz Night, a pool competition and a darts competition.

<u>Robert Lacey</u>

Our Youth Club is very good really even though there aren't a lot of members. There is always something going on and we often have trips out during the year, not just on youth club evenings but also at the weekend. There are many trips out which I enjoy except for the annual Fun Run. I do enjoy the day out but find it an effort to do the run.

We have Masses and take part in many Diocesan events. It is nice to meet other people and then meet up with them again at the next competition.

Maybe we will be able to have a senior club again and then go away. We could also have a video evening if everyone was interested.

Luke Davey

I think the youth club is utter brill. Though I think it should be called Chadwell St. Joseph's Youth Club.

I like all the trips the club goes on, and I like old mini buses that break down a lot!

Though there should be more going on at night, different things to do.

But I still think that our Youth Club is the BEST! ! !

BIBLIOGRAPHY

- Peter F. Anson : The Sea Apostolate in the Port of London : John S. Burns & Sons : 1991 : ISBN 0 946356 12 2
- Peter Benson (presenter): Tilbury : The Story Behind The Roads: Tilbury Riverside Project : 2013 : DVD
- R. Bingley: Country Life in West Tilbury, Essex 1700 -1850 Witley Press : 2009 : ISBN 0 9506141 8 1
- Richard Burrell : Victorian Freemasonry and the Building of Tilbury Docks : Thurrock Local History Society : 2015 : ISBN 978 0 9558352 9 2
- Terry Carney : Thurrock in the Thirties : Thurrock Museum Publications : 1995 : ISBN 0 9506141 8 1
- Dr. Edwin Course : Tilbury Loop : Middleton Press . 2002 : ISBN 1 901706 86 9
- A.C. Edwards : A History of Essex : 1985 : Phillimore and Company Limited : ISBN 0 85033 280 4
- Father Stewart Foster : The Deceased Clergy of the Diocese of Brentwood : Brentwood Diocesan Archives : 2013
- P. R. Gifford (ed.) : Resist The Invader : The Story of Essex Forts and Castles : Essex Libraries : 1982 : ISBN 0 903630 176
- Campbell McCutcheon : Port of Tilbury in the 60s and 70s : Amberley Publishing : 2013 : ISBN 978 1 4456 2279 8
- Ministry of Works : Tilbury Fort : Ministry of Works Official Guide Book : 1960 : HMSO
- Glynn H. Morgan : Forgotten Thameside : 1969 : Essex Countryside : ASIN B000JVLMPC
- John Ormston : The Five Minute Crossing : The Tilbury-Gravesend Ferries : Thurrock Local History Society : 1992
- Kevin Redmond : The Parish of Our Lady and St. Joseph : 2012 : ISBN 978 0 9573479 0 8
- Patricia Rennoldson Smith : The 1953 Essex Flood Disaster : The History Press : 2012 : ISBN 978 0 7524 6541 8
- M.A. Rumsey : The Origin and Development of the Bata Factory and Estate and Social Examination of the Community : Thurrock Thames Gateway Development Corporation
- V.T.C. Smith : Defending London's River : 1985 : North Kent Books : ISBN 0 948305 00 2
- I.G. Sparkes : Tilbury Town and Docks : 1964